**Plains Histories**

*John R. Wunder, Series Editor*

*Editorial Board*

*Also in Plains Histories*

*America's 100th Meridian: A Plains Journey,* by Monte Hartman

*American Outback: The Oklahoma Panhandle in the Twentieth Century,*
by Richard Lowitt

*As a Farm Woman Thinks: Life and Land on the Texas High Plains, 1890–1960,*
by Nellie Witt Spikes; edited by Geoff Cunfer

*Children of the Dust: An Okie Family Story,* by Betty Grant Henshaw;
edited by Sandra Scofield

*The Death of Raymond Yellow Thunder: And Other True Stories from the
Nebraska–Pine Ridge Border Towns,* by Stew Magnuson

*Free Radical: Ernest Chambers, Black Power, and the Politics of Race,*
by Tekla Agbala Ali Johnson

*From Syria to Seminole: Memoir of a High Plains Merchant,*
by Ed Aryain; edited by J'Nell Pate

*"I Do Not Apologize for the Length of This Letter": The Mari Sandoz Letters
on Native American Rights, 1940–1965,* edited by Kimberli A. Lee

*Indigenous Albuquerque,* by Myla Vicenti Carpio

*Nikkei Farmer on the Nebraska Plains: A Memoir,*
by The Reverend Hisanori Kano; edited by Tai Kreidler

*The Notorious Dr. Flippin: Abortion and Consequence in the
Early Twentieth Century,* by Jamie Q. Tallman

*Oysters, Macaroni, and Beer: Thurber, Texas, and the Company Store,*
by Gene Rhea Tucker

*Railwayman's Son: A Plains Family Memoir,* by Hugh Hawkins

*Rights in the Balance: Free Press, Fair Trial, and Nebraska Press
Association v. Stuart,* by Mark R. Scherer

*Route 66: A Road to America's Landscape, History, and Culture,* by Markku Henriksson

*Ruling Pine Ridge: Oglala Lakota Politics from the IRA to
Wounded Knee,* by Akim D. Reinhardt

*Trail Sisters: Freedwomen in Indian Territory, 1850–1890,* by Linda Williams Reese

*Where the West Begins: Debating Texas Identity,* by Glen Sample Ely

*Women on the North American Plains,* edited by Renee M. Laegreid
and Sandra K. Mathews

# Urban Villages and Local Identities

# Urban Villages and Local Identities

*Germans from Russia,*

*Omaha Indians, and*

*Vietnamese in*

*Lincoln, Nebraska*

**Kurt E. Kinbacher**

Plainsword by Timothy R. Mahoney

Texas Tech University Press

This book is typeset in Minion Pro. The paper used in this book meets the minimum requirements of ANSI/NISO Z39.48-1992 (R1997). ∞

Cover designed by Barbara Werden
Cover photograph Courtesy of Nebraska State Historical Society, Amercan Folklife Center - Library of Congress, and Gabrielle Elliott.

Library of Congress Cataloging-in-Publication Data
Kinbacher, Kurt E.
    Urban villages and local identities : Germans from Russia, Omaha Indians, and Vietnamese in Lincoln, Nebraska / Kurt E. Kinbacher ; plainsword by Timothy R. Mahoney.
        pages cm. — (Plains histories)
    Includes bibliographical references and index.
    ISBN 978-0-89672-893-6 (hardcover : alkaline paper) — ISBN 978-0-89672-894-3 (paperback : alkaline paper) — ISBN 978-0-89672-895-0 (e-book) 1. Lincoln (Neb.)—Ethnic relations. 2. Russian Germans—Nebraska—Lincoln—Social conditions. 3. Omaha Indians—Nebraska—Lincoln—Social conditions. 4. Vietnamese—Nebraska—Lincoln—Social conditions. 5. Immigrants—Nebraska—Lincoln—Social conditions. 6. Ethnicity—Nebraska—Lincoln. 7. Ethnic neighborhoods—Nebraska—Lincoln. 8. Community life—Nebraska—Lincoln. 9. City and town life—Nebraska—Lincoln. 10. Lincoln (Neb.)—Emigration and immigration—Social aspects. I. Peck, Gunther. Reinventing free labor. II. Title.
        F674.L7K47 2015
        305.8009782'293—dc23
                                                                    2014047397

15 16 17 18 19 20 21 22 23 / 9 8 7 6 5 4 3 2 1

Texas Tech University Press
Box 41037 | Lubbock, Texas 79409-1037 USA
800.832.4042 | ttup@ttu.edu | www.ttupress.org

# Contents

| | |
|---|---|
| *Illustrations* | *ix* |
| *Plainsword* | *xi* |

| | |
|---|---|
| Introduction | 3 |
| Ethnicity and Identity in Lincoln | 5 |
| Performed Culture | 7 |
| Ethnic Saliency | 11 |
| Urban Villages | 13 |
| Frameworks of this Study | 14 |

**Chapter 1**

| | |
|---|---|
| Local Knowledge and National Perspectives: | |
| Ethnicities and the Mainstream in Lincoln | 19 |
| Omaha Confinement and Disfranchisement | 21 |
| Volga German Immigration | 25 |
| Omahas Return to the Salt Basin | 32 |
| Vietnamese Immigration | 38 |
| Multiculturalism in the Modern Mainstream | 40 |

**Chapter 2**

| | |
|---|---|
| Life in the Russian Bottoms: Community Building and | |
| Identity Transformation among Germans from Russia | 44 |
| The Founding Generation | 47 |
| "We Became Americanized": The Second Fifty Years | 67 |
| Survivals, Revivals, and a New German-from-Russia Identity | 82 |
| Conclusion | 89 |

**Chapter 3**

| | |
|---|---|
| From the Big Village to the Urban Village: Omahas in Lincoln | 91 |
| Community | 93 |
| Particularism: The Omaha Way | 99 |
| Cosmopolitanism | 113 |
| Transnationalism | 120 |
| Conclusion | 125 |

**Chapter 4**
Vietnamese Urban Villagers in Lincoln:
Clustered Communities and Flexible Identities                          129
    Immigrant Communities                            131
    Particularism                                    139
    Cosmopolitanism                                  152
    Transnationalism                                 164
    Conclusion                                       171

**Chapter 5**
Comparisons: Identities and Communities during
the Long Twentieth Century                                            173
    Pluralistic Communities                          174
    Ethnicity and Race                               178
    Transnationalism, Internationalism, and Nationalism   181
    Performed Culture                                186
    Conclusion                                       189

*Notes*                                                               *191*
*Index*                                                               *257*

# Illustrations

**Maps**

2-1: Map of North and South Russian Bottoms in 1925.                46

2-2: Map of Volga Colonies.                48

3-1: Map of Core Omaha Urban Village in Lincoln, Nebraska.                96

3-2: Map of Omaha Nation and Surrounding Areas.                102

4-1: Map of Vietnamese Urban Villages and Institutions.                136

4-2: Map of Vietnam, 1975.                140


**Photographs, following p. 127**

Henry Amen, Sr., and Family, 1915

Exterior of the H. J. Amen Store, 1947

Aerial view of Lincoln, Nebraska, ca. 1920

German-Russian mothers and children, Lincoln, Nebraska, ca. 1910

Citizenship class with Germans from Russia, ca. 1916

American Historical Society of Germans from Russia Headquarters

First German Congregational Church, South Bottoms

Friedens Lutheran Church, South Bottoms

Children at the Grand Entry of the 1983 Omaha Nation Pow-Wow
    in Macy, Nebraska

Adults at the Grand Entry of the 1983 Omaha Nation Pow-Wow
    in Macy, Nebraska

Dancing to wax cylinder records at the 1983 Omaha Nation Pow-Wow
    in Macy, Nebraska

Lincoln Indian Center, present location

Lincoln Indian Center Pow-Wow Grounds

Interior of *Linh Quang* Buddhist Temple

Performers practicing at the *Linh Quang* Buddhist Temple

*Linh Quang* Buddhist Temple, location since 2011

Vietnamese Roman Catholic Church

Sacred Heart Roman Catholic Church

Sacred Heart School

Immaculate Heart of Mary Roman Catholic Church, present location

Vietnamese Missionary and Alliance Church, present location

Vung-Tau Restaurant, Twenty-Seventh and Y Streets

Pho Nguyenn Restaurant, Twenty-Seventh and Vine Streets

Vina Market, Twenty-Seventh and Vine Streets

Saigon Plaza, Twenty-Seventh and Apple Streets

## Tables

1-1. City and State Population and Population Growth, 1860–2005.   28

1-2. Total Indian Population in Nebraska and Lincoln, 1950–2000.   34

2-1. German-Russian Congregations in Lincoln, Nebraska: Point of Origin and Confirmed Membership, 1891–1928.   51

2-2. Population Growth in Six Volga Colonies, 1772–1912.   54

3-1. Estimated American Indian Populations in Lincoln, Nebraska, and the United States, 1930–2000.   94

4-1. Foreign-Born Vietnamese in Lincoln, Nebraska, 1970–2003.   131

4-2. Vietnamese Refugee and Immigrant Arrivals into the United States, 1952–2000.   133

4-3. Estimated Population of Vietnam, 1890–2005.   168

# Plainsword

Across the eastern Great Plains lie a number of small cities that serve as regional business centers, the state capital, or home to a state university. They are known for a low cost of living, low crime rates, and high quality of life, and have populations between 100,000 and 250,000. They also have among the highest percentages of white residents in the United States, ranging from over 75 to 90 percent. This demography is the result, as historians have noted, of a combination of national and international migration patterns; economic, social, and institutional developments; and political tradition and culture. Their demography reflects that of the Great Plains in general, one of the nation's most homogeneous regions.

Because of this homogeneity, relatively few studies exist of race and ethnicity in the cities of the Great Plains. The histories of Native Americans, African Americans, Latinos, and Asian Americans who moved to cities across the Great Plains are generally ignored, remaining hidden in plain sight. Happily, Kurt Kinbacher's fascinating book *Urban Villages and Local Identities: Germans from Russia, Omaha Indians, and Vietnamese in Lincoln, Nebraska*, the latest addition to the Plains History series, uncovers the histories of three very different understudied groups in Lincoln, Nebraska. He provides us with stories of how Germans from Russia, Omaha Indians, and Vietnamese Americans interacted at different times with the mostly white host mainstream community.

In general, Kinbacher relates how Germans from Russia formed distinctive urban villages apart from mainstream society. Gaining sufficient capital from jobs downtown, in nearby small industries, and in the sugar beet industry, Germans from Russia gradually built their own churches; established a Main Street of stores, restaurants, and halls; and constructed a neighborhood of small houses that they, for the most part, owned outright. As they established themselves, more community members—and especially their children—received more education, acquired better jobs, and eventually began to move out across the city from their ethnic enclaves. In time, their ethnicity, like that of many European Americans, was forgotten, remaining a private cultural trait occasionally performed but not lived.

In contrast, a smaller number of members of the Omaha tribe, rooted in their homeland in northeastern Nebraska, lived more transient lives in Lincoln. Only able to rent their residences and forced to take some of the least desirable jobs in town, Omaha Indians struggled to gain a foothold. Not until the 1960s were they able to establish an Indian center—a facility that was moved to the edge of the old Germans-from-Russia North Bottoms neighborhood in 1980. There Omahas would self-consciously cultivate their deep connections to their homeland and their spirituality, maintain a vital tribal identity, and develop connections with the Pan-Indian movement.

Finally, Vietnamese residents, arriving in three waves—evacuees after the Vietnam War, refugees, and later émigrés, who were more distant from mainstream life by reason of race, language, culture, history, as well as geography—gradually formed a cultural outpost in Lincoln. In contrast to the Germans from Russia, however, they were never able to establish a spatial beachhead in any neighborhood. Religion also divided them. Catholics, the majority, as well as smaller numbers of Protestants and Buddhists, each formed their own churches and temples at different locations in the city. Hence, the institutional framework of Vietnamese life in Lincoln in the 1970s and 1980s spread across the city; in terms of restaurants and stores, though they gradually focused on North Twenty-Seventh Street, Lincoln's most diverse business area. There, generations of Vietnamese residents navigated the complexities of assimilation, interaction with American life, erosion of language skills, and wavering contacts with their homeland.

In the end, each of these three groups had different trajectories, living in two worlds and maintaining a performed culture, while worrying about becoming indistinct from the mass commercial and Euro-American ethos of the United States.

Contemplating the different experiences of these three groups unexpectedly focuses one's attention on the similarity of their struggles as they confronted the challenges of dealing with a mostly white host or mainstream society. Viewed close up, one notes the particular dynamics, pressures, and burdens of being a small minority in a mostly white city. Lacking sufficient population to develop their own enclaves fully, groups must interact more with the mainstream and thus risk assimilation—or even rebuffing. Again and again, one encounters not so much overt acts of violence, racism, or discrimination—though each group met plenty—but mainstream indifference, detachment, and an unwillingness to engage with others as part of city life.

Minority groups find it hard just to be noticed, much less accepted, because the mainstream is never challenged enough to step out of its complacency and routine. Suddenly, three separate groups that seemingly have little to do with each other have everything to do with each other. In studying their various responses, one gains insight into the complex nature of ethnicity and interactions with a dominant mainstream society, and how, in different ways, ethnicity is maintained, is held together piecemeal in performed culture, or gradually fades. Ironically, this intriguing study illuminates why the history of minorities in Great Plains cities has still not been incorporated into that larger story, remaining hidden or forgotten.

Lincoln, Nebraska, was founded in the later nineteenth century by white settlers from towns and cities across Illinois and Iowa who simply re-created the predominantly Republican booster culture: an institutional structure that cultivated a set of public and private mainstream middle-class behaviors and practices. Located away from the main currents of urban and industrial development, town leaders were unchallenged by dramatic social and hence political change that large minority-group immigration caused. From the 1880s through the 1970s and beyond, the leading families of the old elite were able to rule these cities with little interference or input from other either residents or newcomers. Their domination generally became inward-looking, localist, cautious, and above all, conservative. As a result, the Great Plains cities have maintained reputations as orderly places where life and culture are dominated by a white, mostly Protestant, conservative mainstream that willingly embraces the generic, homogenizing, mass-consumer culture of modern life. They took pride that Lincoln, with its low unemployment and slow steady growth, was routinely described as homogeneous, quiet, a good place to raise children, conservative, and even a bit dull.

Even though many Lincoln residents will tell you that the low percentage of minority groups in the local population obscures a rich and vibrant diversity in its people, most residents remain untouched by that very diversity. Of course, most European American groups, once a vibrant part of the city's cultural heterogeneity, have been assimilated within the white majority. In addition, most immigrants into the city initially moved to and lived in the older core areas of the city. In moving out to newer suburban neighborhoods, more and more white residents have left behind the diversity; the mass-produced, depersonalized, built environment of urban sprawl dominates. Most white residents would never consider living in the Near South area—not only because it is considered dangerous, but also because its more diverse schools have lower test scores. Conformity, economics, and social anxiety compel one to live on the new edges of the city, where mainstream residents practice a benign, live-and-let-live, laid-back conservatism that some Nebraskans call "nice."

So, most Great Plains city dwellers are content to acknowledge diversity but not embrace it. Lincolnites are generally proud that the city has been a National Refugee Center for a generation. It reflects how reasonably low-cost, stress-free, and safe city life is. Too, the Lincoln Public Schools take pride in having a student body drawn from sixty-four different countries—speaking fifty-six different languages—with over two thousand students enrolled in English as a Second Language programs. Parents of white schoolchildren generally note their children's stories of diverse classmates and find comfort that their children will learn to understand, even in Lincoln, Nebraska, how diverse U.S. society is.

And yet, through the "nice" veneer and the accompanying supportive rhetoric, residents, employers, and public officials routinely distance and disassociate themselves from others, concerned that embracing them might break the code of a polite status quo. As Kinbacher notes, the police seem unable or unwilling to speak much about or address Vietnamese youth gang issues. The schools and churches struggle to navigate diversity and integrate it within everyday activities. At the schools, white students rarely play or interact with minority students. Most parents admit that play dates or parties where white and immigrant students mingle are infrequent, prevented not only by language or cultural or socioeconomic class barriers that separate parents, but also because their children rarely make friends with minority students. Diversity is a goal that many parents seek; many more view it indifferently. But true diversity is rarely lived or rarely becomes part of city life, which constitutes the core conundrum in small, mostly white cities. In this compelling book, Kurt Kinbacher unravels this intriguing puzzle—and much more about how ethnicity and race are shaped in particular ways in a small Great Plains city.

Timothy R. Mahoney
University of Nebraska–Lincoln

# Urban Villages and Local Identities

# Introduction

Jacob Giebelhaus, Charles Stabler, and Tran Bai Si were all drawn to Lincoln, Nebraska, by opportunities to "materially or spiritually" improve themselves and their families.[1] Giebelhaus departed Norka, Russia—an ethnically German settlement—at the turn of the twentieth century; Stabler moved from Omaha Nation—an Indian Reservation within the United States—during World War II; and Tran fled the Republic of Vietnam—a conquered country—in the late 1970s. Although they came from dramatically different worlds in different eras, all three took employment with the Burlington Northern Railroad and helped build urban villages as a means to surround themselves with other members of their own ethnic groups.[2] These enclaves served as comfortable centers for group adaptation to a mainstream community that did not always welcome or accept heterogeneity. From these havens, Germans from Russia, Omaha Indians (hereinafter "Omahas"), and Vietnamese all negotiated flexible and changing identities that responded to multiple forces from both old and new milieus.

While these urban villages and their residents were not always acknowledged, Lincoln has long hosted multicultural communities. Successive waves of immigrants and migrants have arrived since the city's founding. The three groups included in this volume share their experiences with other peoples, but they are considered here together because all contributed significant populations to the greater community, and because their combined movements span the entire history of the Capital City. Volga German immigrants accounted for about 25 percent of the city's population by 1920. Their scions remained in Lincoln and largely merged into the mainstream following World War II. Omahas took part in a worldwide indigenous movement toward urban areas that began in the mid-twentieth century. They have long been the largest Indian group in Lincoln, and about one-third of Omaha Nation's enrollment now lives within the city's boundaries. Finally, in a series of movements that spanned the course of three decades, five thousand Vietnamese immigrants and their families made Lincoln their home. In the process, a regional ethnic population center for Southeast Asians was established.

New arrivals—whether immigrants or migrants—may have come to escape the dire situations they faced in their home nations, but they generally had no intentions of abandoning their imported cultural identities. Indeed, ethnic identities remained important components in an adaptation process that was ongoing throughout the long twentieth century (1876–2005).[3] These urban villagers were influenced simultaneously by particular, cosmopolitan, and transnational forces that allowed them to negotiate "unique and often exceptional ethnic cultures" within their new settings.[4]

*Particularism* refers largely to the beliefs, behaviors, organizational patterns, and material objects that urban villagers import from their sending cultures. Not necessarily nostalgic survivals, these cultural components were maintained in Lincoln as long as they were useful for day-to-day living. Some items thrived into the twenty-first century while others did not. The saliency of ethnic identity often was defined by the retention and survival of these cultural artifacts.

*Cosmopolitanism* added outside factors to the urban villagers' experiences.[5] Generally defined as worldly influences, for this narrative's purposes, these were forces dictated from beyond the urban villages largely, but not exclusively, by the mainstream. Work, school, and Lincoln's social and political structures were all controlled and responsive to mainstream norms. Interactions with other ethnic groups and even kinspeople who migrated to other locales sometimes constituted cosmopolitan influences as well.

*Transnationalism* is best defined as persistent, intense contact across international boundaries. Transnational behaviors among Lincoln's urban villagers included sending remittances, networking to ease additional immigration or return migration, humanitarian aid, business aid, frequent correspondence or communication, regular travel to the homeland, and notable consumption of art or popular culture from the sending society. These activities and influences were important as they allowed dispersed peoples to remain connected to "imagined communities of race and nation."[6] Connections between "homeland and hostland," however, vary remarkably not only among communities but also among individuals. Some severed all ties immediately, others maintained casual contacts, and in many instances, old-world loyalties remained intense in the new milieu.[7] In some cases these influences and contacts persisted for generations. Truly a category full of nuances, the sending culture often remained a central component of local cultural identity.

### Ethnicity and Identity in Lincoln

While people living in Lincoln, Nebraska, certainly label themselves as Omahas, Germans from Russia, and Vietnamese, they necessarily interacted with and participated in a mainstream culture largely created and directed by "Anglo" Americans. This larger community was established by a lateral migration from Illinois, Ohio, Iowa, and Pennsylvania that began in the 1850s and 1860s.[8] It was erected around educational and state governmental institutions. Lincoln was also a transportation hub and a regional center for agribusiness, and much of the labor that built both corporate wealth and modern infrastructure was provided by ethnic workers who entered the economy at the bottom.[9]

Shared space and economic exchange forced a number of interactions among the new arrivals and the "white" mainstream. Still, residential separation was generally the norm. Once in urban villages, ethnic practices, especially the retention of performed culture and the preference to remain in distinct neighborhoods, reinforced desires to maintain connections with the sending cultures' traditions.

Unique patterns of interaction and separation required immigrant and migrant groups to negotiate identities—best defined as sets of core communal values augmented by shared social behaviors—that interwove components of several cultures, including the mainstream.[10] Although none of their sending societies existed in stasis, immigrants in Lincoln often imported cultures that existed for hundreds of years. Once transplanted, the newcomers' identities continued to evolve when they encountered novel social and political situations.[11] In many instances, the modern urban environment accelerated identity changes even among the most conservative individuals.[12]

Because of the great flexibility in identity formation, ethnic groups in America need to be viewed as evolving entities.[13] Like identity, ethnicity changed constantly as local immigrant groups responded to the demands of

the host society.[14] Germans from Russia, Omahas, and Vietnamese all modified their ethnic attachments while living in Lincoln—sometimes subtly
and other times overtly. Once settled in their new locations, they necessarily
displayed different outlooks from their counterparts who remained in the
sending communities.

Although ethnicity "can feel very primal," it is a social construction rather
than a biological imperative.[15] Despite individual differences and subgroup
formation, members of each distinct ethnic population shared a sense of
peoplehood. A common history, shared social structures, and familiar institutions constructed for distinct populations helped to solidify this concept.
In its most complete form, exclusion of other group loyalties—save American nationalism—was one of the hallmarks of ethnic identity.[16]

This study focuses on discrete identities that developed in Lincoln.[17] Because "place-specific" studies yield important place-specific results, identity construction among similar populations in Topeka, Wichita, Oklahoma
City, Sioux City, or Omaha would be at least slightly different.[18] Kathleen
Neils Conzen attributes this to the process of "localization." Immigrant cultures were influenced both by their experiences within the urban village
and their wide-ranging experiences within the host society.[19] Consequently,
sweeping generalizations often hide amazingly diverse place-bound experiences.[20] National social, political, economic, and cultural constraints "set
outer limits on the range of local variance, but within these limits, place-to-
place variation" was certainly significant.[21]

Ethnic groups and their subsocieties in Lincoln served three main purposes. First, they provided a source of self-identification for individuals
within the groups. This allowed individuals to declare "*Umónhón bthín*" (I
am Omaha), "*Ich bin Daitsch*" (vernacular—I am German), or "*Tôi là người
Việt Nam*" (I am Vietnamese), for instance. Second, they provided support
networks and institutions that allowed individuals to associate with a single
ethnic group from cradle to grave. Finally, they molded American cultural
patterns into new shapes and forms in order to include them into their own
cultures.[22]

In short, ethnic identity and community formation in Lincoln attempted
to create safe havens that allowed their residents to interact with mainstream
society without having to become full-fledged members. While internal and
external pressures were omnipresent, within these spaces ethnic popula-

tions both resisted change and accommodated favorable components of the receiving society. As a result, they became something new: "ethnic Americans." These unique cultures have proven so dynamic that they are often easily identified for three or four generations.[23]

**Performed Culture**

Those who maintained the core values of an ethnic group often worked very hard to publicly proclaim their identities.[24] In Lincoln, Volga Germans, Omahas, and Vietnamese employed "idiosyncratic" behaviors in order to reinforce group identities. These distinct manners and activities served as blueprints to convey acceptable social behavior.[25] Ultimately, performed cultures provided defensive weapons that allowed immigrants to fight off mainstream efforts to assimilate individuals into what was sometimes perceived as a homogeneous American society.[26]

Best defined as sets of "cultural assumptions" and remembered "physical features," performed cultures were imported from sending societies and transformed to meet the needs of immigrants in their new communities. They were derived from each group's heritage.[27] Social gatherings, worship services, funerals, and a variety of celebrations served as platforms for communal expressions of old values. Language, oral and written histories, religion, and folkways—especially food, dance, and music—were among the most powerful components of performed culture.

Language, even in a bilingual household, was an artifact of great importance, and conversing in German, Omaha, or Vietnamese was a proactive expression of identity. For Native Americans who remained physically and psychologically close to their original countries, indigenous language retention preserved deep and intimate connections to their cultural hearths. Additionally, unique words and linguistic logic preserved many ideas that would be nearly impossible to express clearly in another tongue.[28]

Similarly, language preservation fostered by foreign-language presses eased the transition of moving from *Vaterland*—an ideological fatherland—to *Heimat*—a local homeland. These outlets for public expression and communication were vital because learning social English takes anywhere from one to three years of fairly concentrated effort.[29] Consequently, weekly, monthly, and a few daily newspapers addressed scattered peoples and connected them to kinfolk in many corners of the world. Often leaving the local news to word of mouth, many of these organs were national, and they reported news from the sending society along with major developments of interest in the larger receiving society. Additionally, substantial space was devoted to the noble but sometimes mythical history of the place left behind.[30]

Group history also served to strengthen ethnic identity. Oral and written narratives provided collective biographies that included facts, traditions, and mysteries that fostered cohesion within the community.[31] Even when they focused more on myth than reality, the cultural memories found in these histories preserved ancient stories and served as tools of empowerment.[32]

Creation stories are where many of these narratives began, especially among Native American peoples, who lay claim to almost as many creation beliefs as there are Indian nations. Passed down from generation to generation, these stories root identities deep in the past and often give a group permission to occupy a specific place.[33] Stories of origin may be a more salient marker of identity for peoples who share their versions of creation with only a select group. Omahas, for instance, share their creation only with their cognates—Quapaws, Poncas, Kansas, and Osages. Similarly, traditional Vietnamese creation stories are common only to peoples of the Indochinese peninsula. Germans from Russia, on the other hand, have the same story as all of Christendom; consequently, this portion of their narrative was a less useful tool in constructing social distinctions.

Houses of worship—whether a Christian church, Indian ceremonial grounds, or Buddhist temple—were often vital to the maintenance of ethnic identities and to the preservation of distinct communities.[34] Religion, however, united as well as separated groups, as most urban villages hosted multiple venues for religious ceremonies. In Lincoln, most Germans from Russia subscribed to Protestant Christianity, but they separated themselves into several denominations. Vietnamese divided into a large Roman Catholic parish, a sizable Buddhist congregation, and a smaller Protestant community. Most Omahas belonged to the Native American Church (NAC), but smaller groups preferred other Christian denominations.

Omahas' religious preferences mirrored regional trends on the Great Plains. The destruction of indigenous economies, occupation of Indian lands, and confinement on reservations often made ancient practices impossible. Those who persisted were frequently forced to abbreviate their ceremonies as ritualistic elements were lost or made meaningless.[35] While some Native Americans managed to continue practicing their traditional religions, others converted to mainstream Christianity; still others joined the Pan-Indian NAC. Filling a spiritual void, the NAC was incorporated in the early twentieth century as a multitribal organization that connected traditional Indian religions with mainstream Christianity.[36] Omahas and many other Native nations established their own rituals in accordance with their own cultures.

Similarly, many Asian immigrants practiced Buddhism. Founded on the Indian subcontinent, the religion began to spread across Asia in the third century BCE. In the late twentieth century, a number of forms of Buddhism were imported to United States, and by 1995, there were an estimated three to four million practicing Buddhists in the country. In many respects, Buddhism is a nationalistic enterprise, as Indian, Tibetan, Japanese, and Vietnamese branches of the religion all incorporate cultural traditions that make ceremonies and meanings unique. Consequently, the 160 Vietnamese Buddhist centers in the United States support the continuation of a Vietnamese, rather than a Pan-Buddhist, identity.[37]

Having ministered to immigrant practitioners for hundreds of years, the American Catholic Church incorporated Vietnamese parishioners into a time-honored system. They constructed "national parishes," assigned them priests from within their ethnic community, and performed Masses in the language of the people.[38] While the use of German, Czech, and Polish have long since subsided in Nebraska, services in Spanish and Vietnamese remain a vital part of the Catholic Church's mission. Immigrants who imported Protestant traditions also founded congregations serviced by ethnic clergy who conducted services in familiar tongues.

The persistence of folkways—particularly family and gender structures, music and dance, and food—reinforced an ethnic group's otherness and demonstrated that many markers of ethnic culture were retained among acculturated individuals as well as those preferring cultural separation.[39] Folkways are maintained in four distinct ways. "Ethnic survivals" existed as retained sets of folklore that were practiced with little concern for ethnic identity. "Retentions," on the other hand, celebrated ethnicity, sometimes by preserving practices no longer used in the sending culture. "Ethnic revivals" are cultural forms that have returned to a community after a period of ethnic fade. While these forms venerated ethnic identity, they often incorporated practices from outside the culture. Finally, "ethnic reintensification" occurred when American-born ethnics learned folkways directly from immigrant generations and continued performance without lapses. This form may be the most powerful for identity construction.[40]

For most immigrants, family—both nuclear and extended—constituted the single most important institution imported from the sending culture.[41] Older constructions of family almost universally favored community over individuality, and fierce loyalty to insiders and corresponding wariness of outsiders often developed. As such, families were sustaining and constraining simultaneously, especially in cultures where traditional roles were well defined.[42] Traditionalists preferred to marry within the community, a habit that reinforced strong identities.

Despite conservative inclinations, family construction and preservation rarely remained static in immigrant societies. Among groups with small populations, marital exogamy was common as early as the second generation.[43] Intermarriage, more often than not, led to identities favoring the mainstream as two ethnicities were hard to preserve. Even among households with a single ethnicity, traditional hierarchies and practices often remained strong at home and in the urban villages but were weakened when individuals interacted with the greater community.[44] While some immigrants were able to live comfortably with such a dichotomy, other groups experienced remarkable friction as a result.

Food, as a general rule, was more a source of comfort than friction, and many scholars agree that the maintenance of ethnic eating patterns contributed directly to cultural perseverance.[45] Kitchens were often the social centers of immigrant households.[46] Gender roles were learned there, and recipes for dishes that reinforced identities were passed on from one generation to another. Food and food preparation were also important in the larger community as feasting on religious holidays was common among many ethnic groups. For Indians, food connected sacred and secular practices.[47] The ritualized feeding of participants at an Omaha handgame, for instance, was consistent with the core values of indigenous societies and an expected service to the community. Finally, entrepreneurship and food sometimes intersected as ethnic grocery stores and restaurants were often the social focal points of urban villages.[48]

Some forms of music also connected urban villagers to their ethnicities. As a case in point, singing, drumming, and dancing remain sacred to Native peoples precisely because they reinforced Indian identities.[49] In addition to culturally specific forms, pow-wows—famous venues of "ceremonial song and dance"—aid in the construction of Pan-Indian identities.[50] While there is still national variation, many "contest" pow-wows incorporate a certain amount of homogeneity.

While Indians are not alone in their love of traditional music, the modern consumer culture has eroded many once important traditions. Indeed, many second- and third-generation urban villagers abandoned older forms of music and dance in favor of popular entertainments.[51] Still, in some communities, modernized music and dance forms loosely based on old practices were expressed as tradition, especially if those varieties were dormant for a time. Created traditions, however, often carry as much weight as those carefully handed down.

In total, many immigrants employed aspects of performed culture in order to hold on to the best components of their old cultures. Such practices, however, did not preclude efforts toward adding the best elements of the new milieu to their traditions.[52] Rather, these remembered behaviors were part of the complex dialogue that accompanied identity transformation. The construction of ethnicity in Lincoln depended as much on conditions in the host community as it did on the nuances of culture brought in from the sending society.[53]

## Ethnic Saliency

As this investigation is comparative in nature, it is important to consider the issue of "*salience* of identity," as the intensity of assigned or volunteered ethnic connections depended on any number of variables.[54] Race, class, gender, family, generation, the number of years spent in the community, age, the era of immigration, education, and employment possibilities all affected identification with any specific group. Not surprisingly, those closest to arrival maintained more cultural practices and felt a stronger sense of ethnic identity. Subsequent generations rehashed the ethnic and mainstream discussion and redefined, reinvented, or rediscovered identities that served them best. Consequently, identities ranged from divisive to symbolic as some individuals refused to include any cultural information from the mainstream and others only used ethnic customs during holidays.[55] More commonly, when "an identity" stopped being one and started "being another" was not always clear.[56]

Apart from place and performed culture, economic considerations frequently influenced ethnic identities.[57] Most urban villagers in Lincoln, despite dramatically different worldviews, shared a common economic starting point; they generally "arrived with preindustrial cultural values and confronted a complex urban-industrial economy."[58] Peoples who entered the modern economy tended to bend their identities to fit into a mainstream that valued individualism. Those who maintained communal practices often favored sending-culture conservatism. Both approaches offered unique material advantages, and immigrants frequently made rational economic choices when they considered moving toward the mainstream or remaining firmly in urban villages.[59]

While communal economies supported many urban villagers, those entering the market without reaping its rewards also favored close ties to their enclaves. Cohesive ethnic groups often maintained ways for peoples to deal with shared poverty.[60] Conversely, some urban villagers used their relative economic successes to improve their social standing within their enclaves. As distinct class structures that mimicked the host community's economic norms emerged in the urban villages, "Ethclass" became a vital component of individual identities.[61] Immigrants with a high socioeconomic status tended to be more acculturated than those of lesser means.[62]

Despite individual success stories, urban villagers were often unable to enter the prevailing economic system and, consequently, struggled to gain wealth and even to access American political institutions.[63] At times, these factors only strengthened ethnic identity. Other times, isolation took heavy tolls, and those able to appear "American" did so. The political advantage of life in the mainstream often caused identity shifts. Most immigrants moved into this direction after a generation or two. Those who did not were largely impoverished, and as a result, "reactive ethnicity" developed; individuals intentionally continued their isolation.[64]

In any event, changes in identity and shifts in community were multidirectional. Clearly, human movements increased the cultural diversity within Lincoln.[65] For members of the receiving society open to cultural enrichment, newcomers brought intriguing customs, exotic foods, and important values. They offered their hosts equal opportunity to transform their own identities into something more cosmopolitan.

## Urban Villages

The most important units of space for Lincoln's new arrivals were the urban villages they constructed or organized. Indeed, Germans from Russia, Omahas, and Vietnamese in Lincoln tended to live in geographic proximity to their cultural kinspeople. Intimately familiar places, urban villages are regularly envisioned by city planners and architects in the twenty-first century. Responding to the depersonalized sprawl of suburban America, they emphasize polynucleated communities with a mixture of residential, commercial, and open spaces that provide residents with a "sense of place." Ideally, the urban village would also provide affordable housing and access to transportation.[66] While not benefiting from central planning, an older form of urban village grew organically in most American cities. Allowing residents to avoid complete disaffection in a strange society, they became the homes for cultural expression in a world where "*environment* was surely altered, but *community*" persisted.[67]

Although rarely homogeneous communities, urban villages were well-defined ethnic enclaves that offered their residents a variety of important services. Within regions and within cities, ethnic communities formed through a process that proceeded in three general stages. The "preparatory state" began when a collective of immigrants clustered in an amorphous pattern in close vicinity to one another. After several years of almost haphazard settlement, "community formation" started. During this stage, ethnic populations acquired greater permanence and increased stability. Finally, the urban village formed during the "supralocal stage." At this point, religious and secular institutions matured to the point where they offered the community a more defined structure.[68] Depending on the immigrant group, these structures may have included houses of worship, centers for congregation, and local business designed specifically to serve an ethnic population. Development, however, was never uniform, and not all organizations and services were present in every enclave.

Within these urban villages, ethnicity was created or reinforced and propagated. They allowed large concentrations of ethnic individuals—some quite Americanized, others not—to engage with each other on a regular basis.[69] Ethnic individuals within the enclave, however, were often just as mobile as the average mainstream American. While population turnover was a fact of life in urban villages, "institutional continuity" in the form of churches and businesses often fostered community stability and the continuation of specific identities.[70] Clearly, ethnic neighborhoods served as homes to specific cultures and, consequently, magnets for all institutions that could serve or profit from their presence.[71]

Over time, older urban villages appear to have been forgotten. Like residents across the Great Plains, mainstream Lincolnites confronted new Latino/a and Asian communities in their midst in the late-twentieth and early-twenty-first centuries. By the mid-1990s, Guatemalans and Mexicans constructed large enclaves in Lincoln and in nearby Crete. Iraqi expatriates and other individuals from the Mideast made Lincoln their home as well. For many citizens and scholars alike, these new arrivals were seen as part of something unique: an infusion of culturally distinct, nonwhite peoples engaging with a nearly homogeneous population. Even observers who valued cultural diversity suggested that in Nebraska the mainstream "identity the last 150 years has mainly been European."[72] This view, however, has a very short historical memory.

### Frameworks of This Study

Viewing the population as an undifferentiated mass of white people is problematic, especially when examining Nebraska over a long period of time. In reality, ethnic diversity was and remains commonplace. Still, as historian Frederick Luebke noted, "European immigrants are the forgotten people" of the Great Plains and of the American West.[73] Luebke's career focused on bringing stories of the diverse peoples living in the region in the nineteenth century to light. Much work is still to be done, and as Elliott Barkan suggests, works "not focused on a specific group have been limited" and "one-dimensional."[74]

Indeed, new comparative studies, such as Barkan's *From All Points*, offer dynamic lenses to understand the immigrant experience from multiple perspectives. He argues that a regional "preoccupation with whiteness" created "hierarchies of power and control" throughout the West.[75] While social rankings were place-specific, racial or cultural profiling was a central part of most immigrant and migrant experiences. Native Americans, African Americans, and Asian Americans were clearly not white and could expect to be treated as second-class citizens as result. European immigrants ranked above these groups, but parity with native-born Americans was not necessarily assured by skin color alone. In the end, inclusion required gaining, accepting, and exhibiting traits with which mainstream America was comfortable. Such efforts often took several generations to complete.[76]

Gunther Peck concentrated on three not-quite white transient ethnic communities that moved across the entire trans-Missouri West. Focusing on Canada and the United States as receiving cultures and Italy, Greece, and Mexico as sending cultures, he deviated from the pattern of many immigration histories that tied ethnicity to specific cities and discreet neighborhoods.[77] A groundbreaking monograph, *Reinventing Free Labor* also diverged from the prevailing emphasis on the transition from old-milieu artisan work to new-milieu wage labor. Consequently, the familiar construction of work found in most labor histories is reformed to include spatial considerations.[78]

While expanding notions of place and broadening intellectual horizons, Peck's temporal scope was confined to a well-studied era of late-nineteenth and early-twentieth-century immigration that brought eighteen million individuals into the United States before nativist restrictions redefined international movement in the 1920s. Barkan's broader study covered an eighty-year period beginning in 1870 and ending in 1952. The long twentieth century, however, has been distinguished by another era of immigration that since 1965 has added even more people to the American body politic.[79] Additionally, a smaller but no less significant movement of peoples from indigenous nations—long isolated from the mainstream by the same forces that excluded foreign-born peoples between 1921 and 1965—began immediately after World War II.

In narrowing space and broadening time, a different view of multicultural human migration emerges. Comparing three divergent populations over the course of 130 years yields insights into the complexity, flexibility, and durability of cultural identities. These ascriptions were undoubtedly influenced by mainstream attitudes that were also continuously evolving. These particular urban villages—all three underrepresented in current scholarship—are ideal laboratories for exploring the interaction of ethnic groups and the urban mainstream on the Great Plains and in a capital city. They also serve as a platform to bring the ideas and methods employed in immigration history, American Indian history, Southeast Asian Studies, and Western History together in a single study.

*Urban Villages and Local Identities* is a narrative with two inherent biases.

First, it suggests that ethnic diversity is generally a positive state of affairs as it allows multiple cultures to contribute to the intellectual health and economic vitality of the greater community. As the mainstream increasingly recognizes that great strength can be garnered from all its human components, urban villagers must strive to keep the best of the sending culture and enrich it with the best of the host society.[80]

Second, cultural identities are rarely surrendered to the mainstream. Despite the vaunted "American melting pot" ideal, suggesting that immigrant communities dissolved and urban villagers simply assimilated into the mainstream is the wrong approach.[81] Indeed, complete group amalgamation into a state of mainstream conformity is rare.[82] Over the course of generations, ethnic fade occurs when younger urban villagers abandon aspects of performed culture and meld in the larger community; once behaviors and traditions are lost, they are rarely revived.[83] Still, culturally specific behaviors and beliefs, no matter how faded they become, often outlast the enclaves that sheltered them.

The presence of long-term cultural persistence and the need to avoid semantic pitfalls is best served by suggesting that immigrants and migrants do not actually "assimilate" into the mainstream, but rather "adapt" themselves to the receiving culture.[84] Certainly some individuals abandon ethnicity in favor of mainstream identities. Variations in backgrounds, age, era of arrival, and myriad other forces make immigration a very personal experience. Still, many members of all three subject groups maintain deep connections to the sending societies despite ethnic fade and generational shifts.

This volume is organized to reflect the dichotomy between ethnic and mainstream cultures. Chapter 1 discusses mainstream attitudes and regulations surrounding immigration, addresses federal and state Native American policies, and constructs a historical picture of Lincoln, Nebraska. The next three chapters examine individual constructions of community and identity formation for German-from-Russia, Omaha, and Vietnamese urban villagers. Finally, chapter 5 makes comparisons and draws conclusions about the entire project.

This narrative focuses on three ethnic groups that revered extended families and patriarchal hierarchies. Indeed, Jacob and Anna Giebelhaus, Charles and Elizabeth Stabler, and Tran Bai Si and Tran My Loc all centered their lives around raising their many children and interacting with their many relatives.[85] Consequently, stable communities were economically desirable and culturally necessary as all these urban villagers fully intended on passing down their ethnic identities to future generations.

# Chapter 1
# Local Knowledge and National Perspectives

Ethnicities and the Mainstream in Lincoln

The city of Lincoln sits amid the drift hills of southeastern Nebraska just on the wet side of the ninety-eighth parallel.[1] Today, it hosts 258,000 residents of Indigenous, Asian, African, Pacific Island, and European descents. Its general character, however, has always been "American." Like many communities on the Great Plains, Lincoln maintained its dominant frontier-era ethnic composition for over one hundred years. Early census records revealed a distinctly native-born population that migrated from Ohio, New York, Pennsylvania, Illinois, Iowa, Indiana, and Missouri.[2] These pioneers—as they were later celebrated—built small empires in their images and made Lincoln comfortable for other people of their ilk. All other ethnic identities necessarily confronted this mainstream.

Still, Lincoln was a magnet for ethnic newcomers for most of its history. While they rarely accumulated great wealth during their first generation of residence, they were generally able to find work and affordable housing. The urban villages they constructed or organized were simultaneously part of the greater community and separate worlds all to themselves.

Immigration into any community is at once a national and a local issue. As such, Lincoln combined American "systemic forces" and discrete community factors in order to construct "a particular local reality."[3] This public culture formed the mainstream backdrop that all contributing ethnic groups confronted as they defined and then redefined their cultural identities.[4] Existing in a state of symbiosis, the mainstream chose its course, in part, in response to the demands of its immigrants. Two hundred years of national policies and 130 years of local interpretations of these official guidelines affected Lincoln's Volga German, Omaha, and Vietnamese urban villagers.

As ethnicity involves a dialogue between mainstream and contributing cultures, ethnic identities are at least partly ascribed by a rather dominant

American culture. Even in the twenty-first century, as the United States is accepting its greatest wave of non-European immigration ever, few would contest that white Anglo-Saxon Protestant values define America's "core society."[5] While not inherently racist in sentiment, males who dominated this mainstream frequently promoted Anglo-conformity as vital to national interests. Consequently, ethnic groups were widely marginalized.[6] Additionally because the non-European world was long constructed as "backward, un-Christian, and semi-barbaric,"[7] Native Americans, African Americans, and Asian Americans consistently faced prejudice and discrimination.[8] As a result, the mainstream often actively discouraged integration into American society, and competing constructions of race and ethnicity had dynamic consequences for many immigrant peoples.[9] As a general rule, most European groups, at least by 1940, were ethnic minorities, but racially mainstream. Omahas and Vietnamese in Lincoln, on the other hand, were ethnic, but they often faced an additional racial assignation.

While still of great social importance, the concept of "race" has no basis in modern biology; moreover, since the isolation of the human genome, it is more accurately defined as human geography. This modern explanation of physical differences among peoples insists that the global pallet of skin colors exists because pigmentation evolved in response to environmental circumstances.[10] Human intermingling, however, led earlier generations of Western scholars to produce arbitrary classification systems based on "biological descent."[11] By the late eighteenth century, racial rankings that ignored the great differences that existed among Asians, Caucasians, and Native Americans emerged. They encompassed essentialist ideas about social and intellectual capabilities. A century later, social Darwinists refined these categories by focusing on technological progress.[12] While "racism" in the early twentieth century was a word that was not yet in use, most Americans assumed that white supremacy was good for the entire body politic.[13] Racialism—a concept employed only after rankings fell out of favor—chronicled the practice of placing specific groups into caste systems.[14] Ethnicity is much more specific than race and depends on the "salience of group consciousness."[15] Often a source of pride among new arrivals, ethnicity may or may not be constructed by the mainstream in conjunction with race.

These nuances created extra layers of division that often caused racialized groups to be physically separated from mainstream populations. For

Indians this pattern existed both on the reservation and even more intensely off it.[16] Additionally, the mainstream depicted itself as both individualistic and exceptional, and most Americans accepted that independence and entrepreneurship were universal virtues.[17] Groups that did not share these values were viewed with suspicion.

Communal orientations among Indians, however, survived American colonization, and after centuries of population decline, they began a steady increase by 1910. Concurrently, between 1891 and 1920 eighteen million immigrants, including many Germans from Russia, disembarked on American shores. Between 1965 and 1996, sixteen million more—including over one million Vietnamese—arrived.[18] Most flocked to U.S. cities in search of better lives. Although not of the mainstream, these new arrivals were generally welcomed because they provided human capital to forward the prevailing economic system.

Still, tensions between mainstream society and the other persisted throughout American history, and attitudes toward non-Western European immigrants and Native Americans have been rather callous. Consequently, retention of an ethnic identity has often been encouraged from the inside and the outside. New arrivals in Lincoln, for example, sought to preserve many of their imported traditions. Desires to hold onto these cultural artifacts were augmented by a need for community acceptance not found in the mainstream. The urban village and performed culture were the most powerful ways to achieve cultural retention and construct an identity that celebrated separateness.

### Omaha Confinement and Disfranchisement

Political and intellectual developments in mainstream culture often deeply influenced identity construction among ethnic groups. As such, America is a land of paradoxes. Its motto—e pluribus unum (out of many, one)—and its insistence that "all men are created equal" seemed to reinforce pluralism, as did its needs for land and labor to construct a prosperous continental empire.[19] Equality under the law, however, was widely ignored in the construction of the nation-state. From its colonial beginnings, people outside the mainstream were denied full participation in American political and economic life. The intellectual currents behind these actions were both racist and xenophobic.[20]

Omahas—like all Great Plains peoples—were viewed as "part of nature itself" and detriments to progress.[21] Their resource use patterns seemed pre-modern to American settlers. Salt Creek, Lincoln's most significant water-shed, for instance, was a vital part of their gathering economy.[22] Its waters are 28.8 percent salt by weight, and regional Indians knew places in its basin where the vital mineral was naturally deposited on the banks. Omaha wom-en gathered salt by brushing it into piles with feathers and then transferring it to bladder bags.[23] Any surplus salt was traded for other desirable objects, but the quest for profit was not part of the equation. Consequently, most Americans had few qualms about conquering the "wilderness," removing Indians, and constructing communities that employed the region's natural abundance for the benefit of "civilization."[24]

Issues about resource use were similar all around the United States, and the nation's policy toward Native Americans was confrontational from the very beginning.[25] The Constitution mentions Indians only twice, and fails to include them in the body politic in both cases.[26] As a result, the Bill of Rights did not apply to indigenes, which left Indians—past and present—with little redress for grievances involving the federal government.[27]

The U.S. Supreme Court furthered prejudicial tendencies by defining Indians as "fierce savages" who were impossible to govern.[28] In *Cherokee Nation v. State of Georgia* (1831), the court determined that Indians "occu-pying our territory" were both "aliens," and, as Chief Justice John Marshall opined, "domestic dependent nations." As such, they were neither fully in-dependent nor subject to state jurisdiction; rather they existed "in a state of pupilage." This declaration set precedent for the long-lasting federal attitude that supposed Indians were "gradually sinking beneath our superior policy, our arts and our arms."[29]

Against this backdrop, Omaha Nation's move away from the Salt Creek basin began in 1830 with its first land cession; along with their Oto and Mis-souria allies, they agreed to "for ever cede relinquish and quit claim to the United States" their lands east of the Missouri River.[30] Despite the Supreme Court's decision in *Worcester v. Georgia* (1832) that proclaimed Indian na-tions were distinct communities that occupied their own territories, land se-cessions were never abated.[31] Pressure to open lands west of the river finally caused the creation of the Nebraska Territory on May 30, 1854, and Indian confinement was a legal prerequisite to American settlement. Ultimately,

Omahas removed to northeastern Nebraska after skillfully negotiating a reservation to their liking.[32]

In subsequent decades, Native Americans were conveyed no additional rights, and Omahas remained in legal limbo. Meanwhile, the Indian Appropriations Act of 1871 was forced through Congress in an effort to solve the "Indian problem."[33] Promoted by humanitarians as reform, this law ended the practice of treaty making, and its passage marked a serious legal challenge to federally recognized Indian sovereignty. The new policies forwarded an even more "virulent strain" of colonialism that attacked all aspects of indigenous culture.[34]

As a result, Indians continued to be denied citizenship by the U.S. Supreme Court despite claims that the Fourteenth Amendment applied to all peoples born within the boundaries of the United States. In *Elk v. Wilkins* (1884)—a case originating in Omaha, Nebraska, and involving an Omaha Indian—the court reiterated Indian exclusion, restating their "alien and dependent condition." It also determined that Native Americans, because they were born outside the pale of American citizenship, needed to be naturalized in the same manner as immigrants before exercising voting rights or other responsibilities.[35] In a dissenting opinion, Justice William Allen Woods suggested that Indians could merge with the "mass of our people," but only by separating themselves from their tribes and adopting mainstream religious and social values.[36]

The rise of American imperialism, scientific racialism, theories of civilization, Anglo-Saxonism, and social Darwinism all contributed to a hardening outlook toward many ethnic and racial groups.[37] These movements facilitated the advancement of allotment schemes promoted by reformers as well as the federal government. Under allotment, Indians, in theory, abandoned communal landownership in favor of rugged individualism offered by American-style farming. Included in most treaties negotiated between 1854 and 1871, its wide-scale practice was delayed until 1887 when the General Allotment (Dawes Severalty) Act was passed.

Once indigenous children were severed from communal lands, the American education system was charged with teaching them mainstream middle-class values.[38] This process was later applied to immigrants and lower-class youngsters as a means to limit national diversity.[39] In 1892 Indian commissioner Thomas J. Morgan justified the $2.25 million annual cost of

Indian education as necessary "for the proper discharge of their duties and for the enjoyment of their privileges as citizens."[40] Largely recruited from allotted families, Indian students were required to cut their hair, speak English, and accept American names assigned by their teachers. Ultimately, this education system worked to eradicate Native American cultures and languages.[41]

Allotment and education shared a common goal. Once the old ways were abandoned, Indians could be granted U.S. citizenship and theoretically could become productive American taxpayers. The programs were implemented despite resistance, and they became the bulwark of the new Indian Service until the 1930s.

Ironically, once displaced, Native peoples were celebrated on the Great Plains. The name "Nebraska," for instance, translates from its Siouan language roots (similar in both Oto and Omaha) as "water that is flat" and describes one of the area's most notable geographic feature—the Platte River. While the mainstream kept the title, they generally ignored both the sublimeness of aboriginal description and the people behind it.

Native iconography also appeared on public projects, but these images generally lacked reference to specific Indian nations. Frequently, such endeavors juxtaposed Native American and pioneer visual references. Relief sculptures on the north entrance of the Nebraska State capitol, for instance, celebrated "civilization" replacing indigenous economies. Large bison—the base of Plains Indians' economies—adorn the stairways. Over the door, a wagon and a family of pioneers led by an American eagle are moving west. Embossed nearby are the words "Honor the Pioneers who broke the sods that men to come might live." Coyotes and other creatures of the wild are portrayed moving out of the way.[42]

Similarly, just outside the city limits, Pioneers Park—a six-hundred-acre park donated to Lincoln in 1928—celebrated both the settlers for which it was named and Native Americans.[43] Today, elk and bison statues grace its two entrances, and small herds of both animals are enclosed in large natural habitats. On a hill just above the park's main picnic ground and athletic field, *Smoke Signal*, a large sculpture that pays tribute to Indians, is on prominent display. In 1935, Omahas, Winnebagos, Poncas, and "Sioux" camped en masse in the park to help dedicate the monument. While none of these peoples were welcomed eighty years before, this gathering suggests that, in Lincoln, ethnic groups of the past were easy to admire.[44]

## Volga German Immigration

The Volga German workers who provided much of the labor to build the capitol and landscape the park may or may not have considered the plight of Native Americans in Nebraska. The city was no longer Native space when the first small group of immigrants arrived in 1876. Despite a difficult social climate, tens of thousands of Volga Germans came into the United States between 1874 and 1914. Of these, sixty-five hundred individuals settled in Lincoln. They were pushed by economic uncertainty, linguistic and social retrenchment, and political disfranchisement. They were pulled by promises of reestablishing prosperity and freedom.[45]

Rather than a salt repository, first and foremost for the new arrivals, Lincoln served as "the railroad heart of as rich an agricultural country as exists in the world."[46] As railroads employed virtual armies of people, Lincoln was an ideal location for landless, hardworking men. Indeed, business, population, and labor market growth all paralleled the development of this infrastructure. Five major rail systems were established along the natural corridors formed by Salt, Rock, Oak, Stevens, and Middle Creeks over the course of two decades.[47] The Burlington line arrived in 1870 and was immediately vital to local development because "every pound of merchandise that passes into all this vast territory from eastern points of supply, and every pound of grain, and every hog and steer that goes out of the State" went through the Lincoln yards.[48] Additionally, the Union Pacific entered the market in 1879, the Missouri and Pacific in 1880, the Chicago and Northwestern in 1886, and the Rock Island in 1892.[49] In total, the yards hosted "forty-two miles of side track, on which 800 men handle from 1,000 to 2,000 cars a day."[50]

Volga German labor may have helped build a city, but the immigrant presence in Nebraska, as in the greater United States, was often a contentious issue. Mainstream Lincoln was of two minds on the subject of immigration; while hungry for labor, long-standing social tendencies favored exclusion. Still, the Constitution dispatched Congress to "establish an uniform Rule of Naturalization."[51] For over one hundred years, immigrants needed only to live in the country for two years (later extended to five), establish their good character, swear an oath to support the Constitution, and renounce foreign citizenship in order to gain American citizenship.[52]

Social pressures common by the mid-nineteenth century played against these plans. Americans often painted immigrants as problematic, whatever their backgrounds. While there were virtually no restrictions on immigration prior to 1882, Catholics, who were sometimes indistinguishable from the mainstream population, and Irish people, who were discernible, were the targets of prejudice. Nativists and Know-Nothings presented a united front to maintain the "proper" social makeup of the young nation in the years immediately before the Civil War.

Bucking these trends, federal policy in the 1860s and 1870s favored immigration. Anticipating a post–Civil War labor shortage, northern and western Europeans were actively encouraged to come the United States by the short-lived National Immigration Board. This agency mostly recruited white Protestants whom they defined as "desirable" aliens.[53] Still, proponents of social Darwinism and related theories questioned the wisdom of allowing any ethnic populations into America. Favoring assimilation and amalgamation for those who had arrived, they argued that Anglo-Saxon manners were the true foundation of an American identity.[54] Peoples not exhibiting these traits or refusing to adopt them with all deliberate speed should be barred entry into the country. These dialogues were reinforced by economic arguments suggesting that immigrants provided unnecessary competition for American workers.

Fin de siècle currents only intensified desires to either exclude or assimilate "others." The formation of the Bureau of Immigration in 1890 made federal regulations for all immigrants a reality. In 1891 a processing center was constructed on Ellis Island in New York harbor, and federal involvement in the immigration process became permanent. This project was all the more significant as an estimated 40 percent of the modern population of the United States—including most of Lincoln's Volga Germans—traces its heritage through Ellis Island.[55]

Federal immigration oversight was favored by Progressives of the era as the movement was dominated by middle-class moralists who believed that the presence of ethnic populations harmed American's social and political fabric. While moralists' efforts to further restrict entry into the United States failed, immigrant children confronted the full brunt of their expectations. They saw their names Americanized in schools and were directed by mainstream teachers to take on new modes of behavior. Although educators claimed to offer their pupils opportunity for future progress, new intellectual skills were acquired in a way that slighted old-country traditions.[56] Clearly, universal education in America weakened ethnicity, and classrooms inadvertently taught students more about "racism" and the "socioeconomic" divide than they did about the nation's political institutions.[57]

Against this background, Volga German movement into Lincoln proceeded fitfully. Uncertain about abandoning home and family, only about thirty immigrants a year arrived between 1872 and 1885. Opportunity in the new milieu, however, was bright between 1886 and 1892, just at a time when the storm clouds of famine rolled across the Russian Steppes. Consequently, the number of annual arrivals multiplied three to five times during this period. The Depression of 1893 briefly quieted the flow, and few arrived again until 1898. Then the floodgates opened. Over the next fifteen years, 100 to 576 individuals arrived each year, with over 3,000 coming between 1909 and 1913.[58]

Lincoln in the 1890s braced itself for a deluge of foreign-born residents. Their arrival sat poorly with a mainstream population that was still reeling from the effects of a significant depression. While *Reichs Deutsch*—ethnics born within the German nation-state—were generally tolerated in frontier Nebraska, these *Volks Deutsch*—ethnic Germans from outside national boundaries—were viewed with caution and suspicion. For the next fifty years, Volga Germans immigrants were either ignored or treated as an inferior Slavic population.

Separation of *Volks Deutsch* from other German speakers was predicated, in part, by developments within ethnic Nebraska. *Reichs Deutsch* were a conglomeration of peoples of "German stock" who had roots within the German empire but were in the process of creating a new identity in Nebraska.[59] Many were the products of "step migration," a process whereby culturally German peoples moved from eastern states to western ones over the course of decades, if not generations.[60] They moved to Nebraska from successful farms in the East to assure that their children had access to land, or they left Minnesota, Wisconsin, and Illinois because those places "curse immigrants," enacted nativist laws, or were home to a press that habitually made "false and unbalanced" reports.[61] Conversely, Volga German immigrants throughout the United States hoped to "retain their life-in-isolation" much in the way it developed while they lived in the Romanov realm.[62]

Prior to settling in Lincoln, there were few Russian-born residents in Lancaster County's rural areas. Instead, Volga German farmers chose to congregate in colonies seventy miles west of the Capital City. Inclusion among other German speakers was unusual, and mainstream Nebraskans had no reason to question such exclusion, especially in light of the growing ethnic intolerance during the Gilded Age and the Progressive Era.

Table 1-1. City and State Population and Population Growth, 1860–2005.

|      | Lincoln | Percent Change | Nebraska | Percent Change |
|------|---------|----------------|----------|----------------|
| 1860 | 800     |                | 29,000   |                |
| 1870 | 2,500   | 213%           | 123,000  | 324%           |
| 1880 | 13,000  | 420%           | 452,000  | 267%           |
| 1890 | 55,000  | 323%           | 1,000,000 | 121%          |
| 1900 | 37,000  | −33%           | 1,059,000 | 6%            |
| 1910 | 44,000  | 19%            | 1,066,000 | 1%            |
| 1920 | 55,000  | 25%            | 1,300,000 | 22%           |
| 1930 | 66,000  | 20%            | 1,370,000 | 5%            |
| 1940 | 82,000  | 24%            | 1,313,000 | −4%           |
| 1950 | 100,000 | 22%            | 1,325,000 | 1%            |
| 1960 | 129,000 | 29%            | 1,411,000 | 6%            |
| 1970 | 150,000 | 16%            | 1,483,000 | 5%            |
| 1980 | 172,000 | 15%            | 1,539,000 | 4%            |
| 1990 | 200,000 | 22%            | 1,584,000 | 3%            |
| 2000 | 225,000 | 13%            | 1,710,000 | 8%            |
| 2005 | 232,000 | 3%             | 1,759,000 | 5%            |

Sources: Nebraska Bluebook (Lincoln: Nebraska Legislative Council); U.S. Census Bureau.

In the greater demographic sense, Volga German immigration—almost entirely comprising large, young family units—was a blessing to Lincoln. Although the city and the entire state of Nebraska saw populations swell in the 1880s, this growth was not sustainable. The town-building bust began on the Great Plains after the severe winter of 1886–87 and was exacerbated by the Depression of 1893.[63] Populations contracted rapidly, and Lincoln was no longer a "First Class City" as its population was only forty-four thousand in 1910. Recovery to 1890s levels took thirty years to complete, and Lincoln grew in numbers partly because the city annexed surrounding suburban centers. Additionally, the final burst of immigration of Volga Germans helped the population recover to 55,000—its 1890 level—by 1920. (See Table 1-1.) Real growth did not occur again until the depressed 1930s, and a large portion of this growth can be attributed to high birthrates in the Volga German urban villages.

Rather than encouraging immigration and population recovery in the 1890s and 1900s, the tendency for racialization and segregation of individuals outside the Anglo-American mainstream prevailed. The brunt of these prejudices was aimed at the city's small African American and Jewish populations.[64] Volga Germans—culturally rather than physically distinct—were noted for maintaining "their own customs" and for being a distinct "racial element of the city" through the Great Depression of the 1930s.[65] Inclined to stay among kith and kin, they settled in the Salt Creek flood plains.

Their presence was clearly known but rarely acknowledged in official circles, even during the frequent floods that inundated their urban villages.[66] On August 12, 1889, for instance, the numerous "little cottages" in the flats were "partly submerged, though generally the water only covered the first floor but a few inches."[67] The plight of these householders was noted, but they were not officially identified as Volga Germans. Again during the record flood of 1908, families were "rescued from their homes," but remained anonymous otherwise.[68] In 1914 the flooding of a thinly populated neighborhood at Twentieth and K Streets along Antelope Creek was given a great deal of attention while newspapers generally ignored the troubles of those by Salt Creek.[69] This pattern held true through the 1930s. People scavenging the town dump—then just west of the North Bottoms—were celebrated because "their meager earnings out there enable them to keep off relief." The dump divers included William Keller of "West Lincoln," H. Jurgens, and Victor Gablehouse of 1062 Y Street. Although ethnicities were not mentioned, these were likely Volga Germans from the Bottoms.[70]

Indeed, ethnicity was increasingly problematic for the nation. The years between 1915 and 1920 were marked by U.S. involvement in World War I and the subsequent Red Scare. In an era of intense patriotism, notable public figures such as Theodore Roosevelt and Woodrow Wilson demanded an "unhyphenated America."[71] As U.S. involvement in the war became imminent, Germans and German Americans were persecuted for their ethnicity. Similarly, after the Bolshevik Revolution of 1917, Russians and other Eastern Europeans were suspected of being left-wing radicals. In total, the war era produced an all-out assault on heterogeneity that was not sorted out by the U.S. Supreme Court until the mid-1920s.[72]

Still, European immigrants—unlike Indians—rarely experienced official steps to end cultural expressions imported from sending societies.[73] German American culture, however, was targeted for extermination as the result of World War I. A 1920 amendment to Nebraska's constitution emphatically stated the point: "The English language is hereby declared to be the official language of this state, and all official proceedings, records and publications shall be in such language, and the common school branches shall be taught in said language in public, private, denominational and parochial schools."[74] Although a blanket decree covering all tongues, German was the true target. The state went on to ban foreign-language instruction in the classroom but the U.S. Supreme Court forced a retreat on the issue.[75] Still, the efforts of assimilationists had far-reaching influences, and many ethnic Germans abandoned *Deutsch*. Similarly, the use of Italian and the promotion of Italian culture in the United States were greatly curtailed during World War II. These experiences demonstrated that throughout much of the twentieth century, the use of English, whether it was the official language or not, was often required for acceptance and advancement.[76]

Against this backdrop, an almost "tribal" sense of Americanism quieted debate on the diversity issue. Initially, the federal government restricted immigration by passing the Emergency Quota Act of 1921. This law limited the number of foreign nationals admitted to the country to 357,800 individuals for one year. This number represented 3 percent of the foreign-born population as of the 1910 census. Further restrictions were legislated by the Immigration Act of 1924 (Johnson-Reed Act), which initially reduced the number of immigrants annually to 164,666—a figure that represented 2 percent of foreign-born residents as of the 1890 census. Ultimately, it established the National Origins System that went into effect in 1929 and remained in place until 1965. This system was based on the white population of the 1920 census and allowed for annual admittance of 153,714 immigrants.[77] Quota allocations favored northern and western Europeans who were the predominant and favored immigrant populations. The late arrival of most Germans from Russia—along with exceptional social changes in the young Soviet

Union—made a new influx of movement from the Volga River to Lincoln increasingly unlikely.

The agitation of the era had an interesting effect on European ethnic populations. Additionally, by World War II, the large second and third generations of Volga Germans had become increasingly Americanized. Their acculturation was hastened by assimilative efforts and partially accepted as their economic conditions improved. While these Germans from Russia were locally among the last groups to move into the mainstream, they began leaving their urban villages in large numbers after 1945.

This new mainstream identity was challenged in the 1960s and 1970s as national political crisis and racial dissent "set off" an ethnic revival. In Nebraska 93 percent of the population listed an ethnic identity in 1977. "German Russians"—a designation that included both Volga and Black Sea Germans—represented the fourth-largest group in the state.[78] *Reichs Deutsch*, Czech, and Swede identities were also proudly proclaimed. This national revival synthesized family traditions, memories from within shrinking urban villages, and new ideas about ethnicity.[79] Some scholars downplay the revival's significance. They suggest most groups involved were already acculturated and no longer confronted with economic, political, or geographic separation from the mainstream.[80] Still, the ethnic revival created a modern appreciation of a world that had nearly disappeared. The new manifestations of ethnicity, however, were both "synthetic" and "selective" as the third and fourth generations essentially chose aspects of their historical cultures they wanted to celebrate.[81]

Volga Germans in Lincoln were a case in point. Their neighborhoods— much like the original villages in Russia—were already "experience-distant" in the 1970s.[82] Vibrant in the 1920s, subsequent generations moved into the larger community, and the old enclaves became "remembered places."[83] By the time of the ethnic revival, the old neighborhoods were largely "symbolic" rather than vital.[84]

The South Bottoms—an old urban village—was even included in a historic preservation project. Ironically, the mechanisms that protected such places were part of mainstream federal policy. The National Park Service began preserving archaeological and historical sites in 1935, and their work expanded with the creation of the National Trust for Historic Preservation in 1949. The Historic Preservation Act of 1966 established the National Register that allowed buildings and sometimes entire neighborhoods to receive a certain amount of preservation. Finally, in 1976, federal tax incentives were approved to encourage conservation. The efforts promoted by these initiatives often gentrified the neighborhoods they were preserving, giving history a whitewashed look. Such projects generally showed a marked nostalgia for a simpler, almost rustic urban world.[85] As such, they celebrated a mainstream national identity while often marginalizing immigrants and the working classes. Indeed, little of the vigor or the clamor of the crowded Volga German enclave remains in the new neighborhood.

The mainstream often recognized the contributions that urban villagers made to the greater community only after their enclaves became memories. When the neighborhoods were actually vibrant, the preferred historical narrative concentrated on the heroic actions of long-term U.S. citizens. Although they tended to be less interested in the national myth, the largely integrated grandchildren of immigrants focused their histories on original sending communities in Russia rather than the urban villages. Consequently, the true role of ethnic enclaves in Lincoln's development was often a story left untold.

## Omahas Return to the Salt Basin

Omaha oral history still discusses trips to Salt Creek to gather commodities, but the place they migrated to after World War II would have been unrecognizable to their nineteenth-century relatives. Still, twentieth-century tribal members in Lincoln responded to distinct push and pull factors; they came to escape poverty on the reservation and to find economic and educational opportunities. Although Indians occupied the lowest rung on Lincoln's social and economic ladder, two world wars improved their legal status. Citizenship and a degree of respect came directly from martial contributions to the war efforts. Unfortunately, federal efforts to aid Native peoples in the wars' wakes had lingering negative consequences.

Omahas and all indigenous groups served the United States valiantly during World War I, and their sacrifices ended a long debate about Indian citizenship. An estimated eighty-five hundred Indians enlisted in the armed forces, and another fifteen hundred were drafted. As a result, those in uniform were granted citizenship in 1919, and in 1924 all remaining Indians were naturalized.[86] The Indian Citizenship Act was a concise piece of legislation, insisting that all non-citizen Indians born within the territorial limits of the United States be, and they are hereby, declared to be citizens of the United States: *Provided*, that the granting of such Citizenship shall not in any manner impair or otherwise affect the right of any Indian to tribal or other property.[87]

This blanket proclamation ended piecemeal attempts to issue Indians citizenship along with allotments, and the liberal naturalization policies formerly reserved for European immigrants were now applied to Native peoples.[88]

In many respects, Indian citizenship was a hollow designation. Some states—Arizona, Maine, New Mexico, and Utah, in particular—took decades to recognize its provisions.[89] More generally, the act was touted by its mainstream proponents as the final solution for creating responsible and respectable Indians. Still, these new citizens lacked full constitutional protections, and their favored social systems continued to face enormous assimilative pressures. By the 1930s, Indian rights were under full-scale assault, and the federal government habitually intervened in every aspect of Native life.[90]

Even the Indian New Deal was unable to rectify this dismal situation. In 1934 John Collier—commissioner of Indian Affairs for Franklin Roosevelt—spearheaded the Indian Reorganization Act (IRA). Changing almost a century of practice, Collier applied First Amendment protections to Indians through administrative action. He called for local self-government, the promotion of Indian civilization, the conservation of tribal land, the abolishment of the allotment system, and the creation of Courts of Indian Affairs. This act became the blueprint of federal policy until 1946.[91] Tribes were also encouraged to draft constitutions that gave them the tools to create economic growth and gain political stability.

Unfortunately, Collier's emphasis on self-determination created paternalistic programs that Indians were expected to accept without contestation.[92] Unexpectedly, seventy-seven tribes rejected the IRA outright. Even those that drafted and adopted constitutions—including Omahas—found that their full sovereignty rights were not restored. Instead, they created governments by permission that had "a powerful 'Big Brother' looking over their shoulders."[93] When the Indian New Deal was curtailed at the eve of World War II, Indian cultures were still not accepted by most Americans.

Still, twenty-five thousand Native Americans—fully one-third of all eligible Indians—served in uniform by war's end, and they represented the largest portion of an ethnic population in the armed forces. Despite the best efforts of indigenous peoples and a friendly press that heralded their achievements, the overwhelming image of Indians remained typecast in the movie Westerns. They were portrayed as peoples trapped in time; the American public saw Crazy Horse and Geronimo at best and cigar store Indians and "savages" at the worst.[94] For those individuals in the services, stereotypes of Indian warriors often placed them in the most dangerous combat assignments.[95] Still, as they were not segregated into all-Indian units, many Native Americans found a degree of acceptance in the military, and their efforts as Code Talkers were even celebrated. However, the significant number of Indian men and women who left the reservation for work in war industries largely remained unheralded.

By this time, demographic growth was on the upswing. After a century and a half of struggling to survive, Native peoples in Nebraska experienced a population boom in the post–World War II era. Table 1-2 demonstrates this impressive expansion. Job growth in cities, general unemployment in Indian Country, and federal policies encouraged many of these Indians to move away from the only homes their ancestors had known since the 1850s.

Table 1-2. Total Indian Population in Lincoln and Nebraska, 1950–2000.

| Year | Lincoln Population | State Population |
|------|-------------------|-----------------|
| 1950 | 75 | 4,000 |
| 1960 | 360 | 5,500 |
| 1970 | 530 | 6,600 |
| 1980 | 920 | 9,100 |
| 1990 | 1,300 | 12,400 |
| 2000 | 1,600 | 14,900 |

Sources: Kevin Allen Leonard, "Migrants, Immigrants, and Refugees: The Cold War and Population Growth in the American West," in Kevin J. Fernlund, ed., *The Cold War American West, 1945–1989* (Albuquerque: University of New Mexico Press, 1998), 39; U.S. Census Bureau, "Table 2. American Indian and Alaska Native Population for the United States, Regions, and States, and for Puerto Rico: 1900 and 2000," *The American Indian and Alaska Native Population: 2000* (Washington, DC: Government Printing Office, 2002), 5.

In order to reward Indians for their war service and to end the hopeless poverty of reservation life, the Bureau of Indian Affairs (BIA) and Congress promoted three new policies—Termination, Public Law 280 (PL 280), and Voluntary Relocation—as means of "emancipating" Indians from their status as federal wards and giving them the same protection of laws as other American citizens.[96] In concert, the new policies encouraged mass urban emigration. While these plans were eventually abandoned, they adversely affected most Native peoples, including Omahas.

Termination began with a congressional resolution stating that the BIA should be abolished as a detriment to Native progress. Nationally, eleven tribes and sixty-one bands were liquidated as corporate entities between 1947 and 1967, and all Indians were slated to be amalgamated into the greater American culture by 1976. Although only 3 percent of the Native American population was actually terminated when the policy was eliminated in 1973, a lingering breach of trust with policy makers ensued.[97]

While Omaha Nation was never liquidated, it was removed from the federal trust in 1953. PL 280 transferred jurisdiction of Indian lands to the states of Nebraska, California, Minnesota, Oregon, and Wisconsin.[98] This change created lawless conditions on the Omaha reservation as Nebraska never allocated funds or staffing to successfully administer their additional charge. The untenable situation created by PL 280 was undone in 1969 through a bill of retrocession. Never fully in control, the state of Nebraska removed itself from the affairs of Omaha Nation and federal control was reinstated.

Although never formalized by legislation, Voluntary Relocation was still quite effective at separating Native Americans from their reservations and cultures. Military service convinced policy makers that Indians could compete in a modern economy, and the best course of action was to recruit individuals to leave Indian nations for cities. Ideally, new homes would be so far away from sending cultures that commuting back and forth would be impossible.[99] Beginning on the overcrowded Navajo Nation in 1948, the program expanded to Oklahoma, New Mexico, California, Arizona, Utah, and Colorado by 1951. Between 1952 and 1970, one hundred thousand Indians were relocated to thirteen urban centers around the United States at a cost of over $15 million. While precise relocation records were not kept, cities in Nebraska were not official destinations, and recruitment on Omaha Nation was not widespread.[100] This program also was abandoned in 1973.

Termination, Public Law 280, and the Voluntary Relocation Program helped put Native Americans in motion. Many Indians were placed or pushed into urban areas only to face chronic underemployment in unfamiliar environments. Additionally, Indians' Fifth Amendment rights of liberty, property, and due process were severely limited.[101]

Amid these failing policies, Omaha migration into Lincoln started as a mere trickle. A few Native Americans lived among other ethnics in the Russian Bottoms as early as the 1930s, although most returned to Omaha Nation after brief stays. By 1960 the combined total of Native Americans in Lincoln and the city of Omaha had increased to almost 500 and then blossomed to over 3,000 twenty years later.[102] Probably underreported, the U.S. Census listed 1,196 Indians in Lincoln in 1990 and 1,599 in 2000.[103] Lincoln's urban Indians, then, were a sizable fraction of the statewide population (see Table 1-2).

Urban and reservation populations alike saw Indian policies continue to change throughout the late twentieth century. Indians were included in Lyndon Johnson's "Great Society" through the Indian Bill of Rights, passed in 1968. While this act increased their rights, it still failed to apply full constitutional protection for Native Americans.[104] Indians still relied on congressional action. Meanwhile, inter- and intratribal politics became increasingly contentious as conflicts regarding corporate versus individual rights and issues of self-determination reemerged. Additionally, a generation of Indians raised in cities—including a cohort from Lincoln's urban village—came of age during this time. Recognizing the successes of the African American Civil Rights Movement, they took direct action to affirm Indian rights. While not welcomed by all traditionalists, the American Indian Movement (AIM) was formed in 1968 and began fighting for social parity with previously unused tactics.[105]

For Omahas, this included reclaiming Blackbird Bend. In 1973, tribal members and AIM activists occupied part of the nation's original reservation, which was lost when the Missouri River changed course sometime in the late nineteenth century. Demanding Blackbird Bend's return, the Omaha tribal government filed three lawsuits in 1975. After case consolidation and years in the courts, twenty-nine hundred acres were restored to the tribe in 1987. Although their original suits asked for a great deal more land, these actions were points of pride among many Omahas.[106]

During this tumultuous era, President Richard Nixon lobbied for a more respectful Indian policy. As part of his legacy, the Indian Self-Determination and Education Act was passed in 1975, and a period of modern tribalism emerged. This act revitalized treaty rights, returned and protected sacred and traditional lands, and restored federal recognition of many terminated tribes by placing them back under federal trust. In short, Indians entered into a "new era of partnership based on mutual respect."[107] During this era, Omaha children from the reservation were able to attend high school at home rather than at a BIA boarding school.

Respectful treatment was not long-lived, and retrenchment and racism became apparent in U.S. Indian policy beginning in the 1980s. During this decade, basic treaty provisions came under attack, boarding schools and other acculturation programs were strengthened, and Indian communal traditions remained unprotected. Seemingly, Indian sovereignty and constitutional protection remained incompatible. As one legal scholar noted, only the historically fickle federal government can "prevent full-scale denials to Native Americans of those basic human rights" enumerated in the federal Bill of Rights.[108]

Long-standing Native efforts for sovereignty and stable financial opportunities also came to a head during this decade. In 1988 the Indian Gaming Regulatory Act—a twenty-five-page federal document—became law. By 1997, 142 tribes in twenty-four states had Las Vegas–style casinos.[109] Omahas—despite the state of Nebraska's efforts—opened their casino in 1994 on its Blackbird Bend lands.[110]

Gaming came to Omaha Nation as federal policy was shifting again. Indian sovereignty was newly promoted during Bill Clinton's tenure in the White House. In 1994 Clinton directed all agencies within the federal government to operate in a "sensitive manner respectful of tribal sovereignty." As a result, the Department of Justice confirmed that it was committed to "Indian self-governance," Indian "civil rights," and the protection of Indian "religious liberty."[111] Conversely, President George W. Bush was virtually silent about Native Americans during his eight years in the White House.

Lincoln residents in the twenty-first century recognize the Indians in their midst. Significantly, many also understand that Omahas and a number of other nations were "local tribes."[112] A few even attend annual pow-wows either at the Lincoln Indian Center or the University of Nebraska. Many others either ignore Native presence, or they still suspect Indians are unable to live in the modern mainstream world.

**Vietnamese Immigration**

In addition to being home to many Omahas, Lincoln was following a trend where "First World cities are being filled with Third World populations."[113] In the late twentieth century, the community hosted peoples from a new wave of immigration; in fact, Lincoln was one of the top twenty cities for refugees from Asia, Africa, and Europe. Peoples were pulled in to take advantage of low unemployment rates and a very reasonable cost of living. These factors encouraged the U.S. Office of Refugee Resettlement to select Lincoln as "preferred community" for new arrivals.[114] Consequently, fifty-two hundred recent immigrants lived in the Capital City in 1990, and thirteen thousand had relocated to the community by 2000. In total, they constituted almost 6 percent of its population.[115]

Asian immigration onto the Great Plains prior to the 1970s, however, was limited both by geography and by prejudicial federal policies, although Asian and Asian American experiences varied according to their respective nationalities. The Chinese Exclusion Act of 1882 was the first of many efforts to control eastern arrivals. It was passed because Chinese workers were perceived as a bane to the western economy. As other Asian groups also competed for wage work, Section 3 of the Immigration Act of 1917 created geographic restrictions that virtually eliminated all immigration from Indochina, the Indian subcontinent, and Indonesia as well.[116]

The U.S. Supreme Court further racialized naturalization through two important rulings. In *Ozawa v. United States* (1922) the Japanese-born plaintiff averred that he was "white" when compared to Chinese or African Americans and therefore a prime candidate for citizenship.[117] The court rejected his argument and insisted that only "Caucasians" or Africans were eligible for inclusion. The following year, "Caucasian" status was narrowed to exclude South Asians. In *United States v. Thind* (1923), the court opined that although Punjabis might technically be "Aryans," the majority of Americans would not recognize them as whites.[118]

During World War II, the federal government softened its stance to its Asian allies but hardened its outlook to people affiliated with its enemies. Most Japanese immigrants and their children—whether citizens or not— were detained and then relocated to isolated camps where two-thirds of them remained until the war was over. The Chinese Exclusion Act, however, was repealed in 1943, a decision that can be seen as the beginning of twenty-two years of congressional efforts to remove race and ethnicity from the immigration code.[119] Although no longer barred from entry, only 105 Chinese were admitted to the United States annually due to a quota established in 1924. The total Asian American population stood at 370,000 in 1952.[120]

International calamity, however, soon eased restrictive impulses, and Americans became interested in Southeast Asia. After China fell to Mao Zedong's forces in 1949, a free Indochina became central to containing communism in Asia. As a result, U.S. monetary and military aid propped up French colonial efforts to control Vietnam. After a decisive Viet Minh victory in 1954, the United States supported the "temporary" partition of the nation at the seventeenth parallel. Additionally, American forces ferried 311,000 of the 1 million boat people who fled Ho Chi Minh's regime in the North for the relative safety of the South.[121] Vietnamese immigration to the United States began at this time, although only 30,000 individuals made the journey prior to 1975.[122] None had yet arrived in Lincoln.

Following precedents set during the Eisenhower administration, Presidents Kennedy and Johnson promoted liberal immigration policies, and the Immigration and Nationality Act of 1965 finally abandoned the old quota system of the 1920s. Under the new arrangements, 74 percent of total immigrant slots were available for family reunification, 20 percent for occupational preference, and 6 percent for refugees. Although not anticipated by the authors of this legislation, immigrants from East Asian nations benefited most from this legislation as the 20,000-person annual cap represented a great increase from previous eras.[123]

In many respects, Indochinese refugees—mostly supporters of a nation that lost a long war—were the advance guard of this greater movement.[124] About 130,000 displaced Vietnamese entered the country immediately after the fall of Saigon in 1975. In 1978 the attorney general authorized admission of 240,000 boat people through the "Indochinese Parole Programs."[125] Alarmed by the high number of arrivals, however, Congress passed the Refugee Act of 1980, requiring that the president consult with Congress before admitting refugees and that the aliens apply for political asylum.[126] Still, under this act, 475,000 Vietnamese took up lawful residence in the United States; by 1990, between 24,000 and 72,000 entered the country annually.[127] Normalization of relations with the Socialist Republic of Vietnam in 1996 allowed the influx of more people opting to move to the United States to reunite with family.[128] Since then, immigration continued in a more tradition-al fashion as many newcomers came seeking economic opportunity. In 1990 the Vietnamese population in the United States was around 700,000—half of them in California. In 2000 the total was about 1.2 million.[129]

Hosting the thirty-fifth-largest urban community of Vietnamese in America, Lincoln is presently home to about 4,000 foreign-born individ-uals.[130] Like the Volga Germans a century earlier, many Vietnamese took employment in the lower end of the labor market.[131] Like Omahas, they con-structed urban villages and a community center to help them acclimate to their new milieu.

## Multiculturalism in the Modern Mainstream

In terms of political agency, "the people" as referenced in the Constitution slowly has become a much more inclusive concept.[132] For most of the twen-tieth century, mainstream Americans expected populations to acculturate themselves to prevailing American behavioral patterns. At the beginning of the twenty-first century, on the other hand, ethnicity was sometimes cele-brated or at least tolerated by many Americans.[133] Still, conservative, main-stream expectations have not disappeared altogether.

President George W. Bush's 2004 attempts to replace an immigration sys-tem he labeled "outdated—unsuited to the needs of our economy and to the values of our country" were largely rejected by Congress.[134] It appears his desires to foster a "reasonable increase in the annual limit of legal im-migrants" was out of step with national opinion.[135] Many Americans were responding to the huge Latino/a migration that emerged in the late 1970s. President Ronald Reagan's solution—the Immigration Reform and Control Act of 1986—legalized many undocumented aliens.[136] This action and the sheer force of these numbers caused a return to nativism.[137]

While Asians are not excluded from the new racialism, the major chal-lenge to the "American way" was generally perceived to be Latin American in origin. In Nebraska the concern tends to focus on illegal immigrants. Communities with large meatpacking plants near Lincoln, for instance, have passed laws making renting to undocumented workers illegal. State politicians over the last three decades averred that they welcome legal im-migrants, but they wanted to exclude an estimated forty-five thousand to fifty thousand undocumented Hispanics because they take local jobs and pay no taxes.[138] Nationally, organizations such as the American Immigration Control Foundation—a "non-partisan, non-profit public policy research organization"—spoke out against the "affirmative ethnicity" promoted by the latest immigrants.[139] Believing that the newcomers "threaten the very political integrity of the nation itself," the organization promoted the establishment of English as a national language in an effort to diffuse immigrant bloc politics.[140] Proposed legislation, including the English Language Unity Act of 2003, demanded that all educational services be conducted in English.[141] Although these efforts failed to become law, English-only proponents clearly agree that language is the key to both assimilation and the retention of ethnic identity.[142]

U.S. policy on language and education has never been particularly well defined, as the school systems are the responsibility of local governments.[143] Additionally, many positions exist on bilingualism. Studies by educators hailed it as a method to promote cognitive flexibility.[144] Other experts and citizens believed that being fluent in English was the only true measure of full integration into the American body politic, and that, although no languages need be banned, making English the official language of the United States was necessary. Still others insisted that the emphasis on English amounted to a statement of power.[145]

While all these positions have merit, they may overstate the dormancy of non-English languages. It may be true that language abandonment was often forced on immigrant populations through local discrimination and economic marginalization.[146] Still, not all people discarded language under duress. As a general rule, mother tongues remain vibrant only when they are used to express social intimacy or to conduct commerce.[147] For many immigrants, language and other cultural practices showed marked decline among members of the second generation who interacted regularly with the mainstream. Some suggest that assimilatory pressure leveled ethnic difference, and others assume identity was merely transformed by American culture and the composite result was a unique and separate identity.[148] Additionally, language denotes belonging to a group, but this function was often replaced by other aspects of performed culture.[149] While descriptive richness may be compromised, religious institutions, traditional economic practices, and other long-running traditions make excellent repositories of core cultural values. These values clearly survived language loss.[150]

In twenty-first-century Lincoln, language and identity run the gamut of possibilities. Germans from Russia lost virtually all of their imported language skills through a long process of ethnic fade, and their modern ethnicity is the result of revival. Omahas maintained their ethnic identity, but their language is rapidly disappearing.[151] Vietnamese—most of whom are foreign born—use the language of the sending culture on a daily basis. Some of these most recent immigrants, including Hoa Tran, believe that they will "have chance to choose" to maintain their language or slowly abandon it.[152]

Lincoln has grown more inclusive over the course of its 130-year history. Citizens and city leaders worked hard to diffuse racial and ethnic prejudices during most of the post–World War II era. During this era, Latvians, Iranis, Sudanese, and Iraqis made the Capital City their home. Social service organizations such as the Lincoln Interfaith Council have aided their ability to arrive and thrive. An association comprising sixty-two religious congregations, the council worked, and continues to work, for tolerance in the community. Originally the Lincoln Council of Churches, large numbers of Buddhists, Muslims, and Baha'is in the community prompted a name change in 1989. Over the years, the council has been involved in programming at the Lincoln Indian Center, the Asian Community and Cultural Center, the National Association for the Advancement of Colored People, and the Lincoln/Lancaster County Refugee Resettlement Task Force. The council and its supporters have long held that "Lincoln is fast becoming a global village," and, as a result, tolerance is vital.[153]

In a similar vein, an Equal Opportunity title was added to the Lincoln City Charter in 1973. The continually updated Title 11 boldly states, "It is the policy of the City of Lincoln to foster equal opportunity" and to "protect, preserve, and perpetuate all constitutional rights."[154] In law, at least, all people are protected from violations of their human rights as well as housing and employment discrimination. One significant result of Title 11 is that emergency signage and instructions for city services are printed in many languages, including Vietnamese.

These efforts may have put Lincoln ahead of the national curve, as Indians and immigrants have a growing presence in twenty-first-century America. Native American populations have increased remarkably over the last several decades. On the Great Plains, even the counties losing Euro-American populations are gaining indigenous residents. Portions of these growing populations will undoubtedly migrate to cities, including Lincoln. Similarly, immigration shows no signs of slowing. The United States presently hosts over thirty million foreign-born residents; 863,000 of these are Vietnamese and 650,000 are German.[155] Since 1990, these numbers have increased predictably, with about 10,000 Germans arriving annually and 24,000 to 30,000 Vietnamese coming to the United States each year. This makes Vietnam the seventh-largest contributing nation to U.S. immigration totals.[156]

Diversity in Lincoln is now often celebrated. In many cases, however, historical ethnicity is easier to recognize than present constructions. Neighborhoods, Inc., for instance, is a local nonprofit organization working to encourage home ownership in Lincoln's core. As part of its mission, the nonprofit produces and disseminates information describing the histories and amenities of various neighborhoods. The North and South Bottoms are noted for their distinct heritage, and Volga Germans are highlighted as major contributors to early Lincoln. Conversely, the description of the Malone neighborhood, the longtime home of many African Americans, mentions neither ethnicity nor group contribution.[157] Similarly, information regarding the Hartley and Clinton neighborhoods highlights the existence of "specialty shops along 27th Street" without mentioning the Vietnamese proprietors who run these establishments or their largely Vietnamese clientele.[158] Although Neighborhoods Inc. is likely barred from discussing the ethnic and racial composition of these areas, diversity is not yet valued enough to be discussed without trepidation.

Ultimately, distinct ethnic populations have always shared Lincoln's cityscape with the American mainstream. When compared, Omaha, German-from-Russia, and Vietnamese presences help illustrate the processes of identity construction in a specific local space. That space, however, was necessarily influenced by national and international developments.

## Chapter 2
# Life in the Russian Bottoms

Community Building and Identity Transformation
among Germans from Russia

Henry J. Amen was born in 1876 in Frank, Russia, an ethnically German agricultural colony on the Volga River. He immigrated to Lincoln, Nebraska, in 1888, where he apprenticed with an uncle before opening his "main street" grocery in the heart of the South Russian Bottoms in 1902. At this "hustling and bustling store," German-speaking customers were "treated right," and their money bought "the full value of the best wares."[1] Amen also served his community as a steamship ticket agent, a mortgage and personal banker, a home insurance agent, a landlord who provided reasonable rents, and the bookkeeper for the Ebenezer Congregational Church. He lived several doors up the street from his business until he built his dream house eight blocks away in 1918, where he and Barbara Amen raised their seven children.[2]

Like the first small group of 150 to 200 Volga Germans who settled on the southwest edge of Lincoln, Amen and his family experienced near-constant discrimination. The five thousand distinctly native-born "Americans" already inhabiting this small western city considered the squatters of 1876 an impediment to local development. Negative stereotypes were only strengthened as the immigrants sponsored their friends and families to join them in increasing numbers until 1913. In the interim, a near-continuous flow of "peasants" arrived in sheepskin coats, felt boots, wide-brimmed hats, and black shawls—garb they donned even in the scorching heat of summers on the Great Plains.[3] Because mainstream Lincolnites were uncomfortable with the immigrants' collective appearance, language, and social habits, they derisively called them "Rooshians," "dirty Rooshians," or "dumb" Russians.[4]

Aware but rarely fearful of these prejudices, Lincoln's Volga Germans built two urban villages along the floodplains of Salt Creek and began adapting to the local culture.[5] The South Bottoms emerged in the late 1870s as the first arrivals erected permanent structures. Responding to demographic trends, construction of the North Russian Bottoms began in 1888 as railroad maintenance personnel moved closer to the Burlington roundhouse then located two miles from the first settlement. (See Map 2-1.) Combined, the two enclaves housed sixty-five hundred people by 1915, and while migration slowed to a trickle as the result of war, revolution, and American immigration restrictions, natural increases rapidly built an even more impressive population.[6] An estimated eight thousand individuals lived in the Bottoms in 1920, as many as twelve thousand in 1925, and perhaps one-third of Lincoln's population lived in the urban villages by 1940.[7]

As the two communities grew, their residents negotiated new identities that combined aspects of their old and new milieus. As identity formation never relies solely on self-ascription,[8] the cultural designations the immigrants invented necessarily responded to the laws, norms, and economic structures they encountered in their new homes.[9] Wage labor and urbanization, for instance, often moved urban villagers closer to mainstream standards. Stimulus from within the enclaves, however, frequently mitigated such changes.[10] Ultimately, identity shifts were unavoidable, variable, and never absolute.

During the first fifty years of German Russian settlement in Lincoln, particular, cosmopolitan, and transnational factors combined to create complex and overlapping ascriptions.[11] Enhancing their connection to the past, the immigrants imported aspects of performed culture from their old environments.[12] Specifically, language, physical ordering of space, work rhythms, and nostalgia for the places they left behind were all retained by significant portions of the population. These habits and artifacts were altered by the urban villagers' associations with the Burlington Railroad, the sugar beet fields of the Great Plains, U.S. constitutional law, and *Die Welt-Post*—a German-language newspaper. Additionally, reactions to new events in the old Volga colonies, including World War I, the Russian Revolution, and the years of famine that followed these upheavals, drew great concern and occasionally led to cooperative action. Over the course of five decades, the immigrants affiliated themselves with their villages of origin, their two communities in Lincoln, ethnic Germans from Russia, ethnic Germans from all over Europe and the Americas, European immigrants battling for rights guaranteed by the U.S. Constitution, and Volga German nationals.

The second fifty years, 1926 to 1976, brought increased prosperity to Lin-

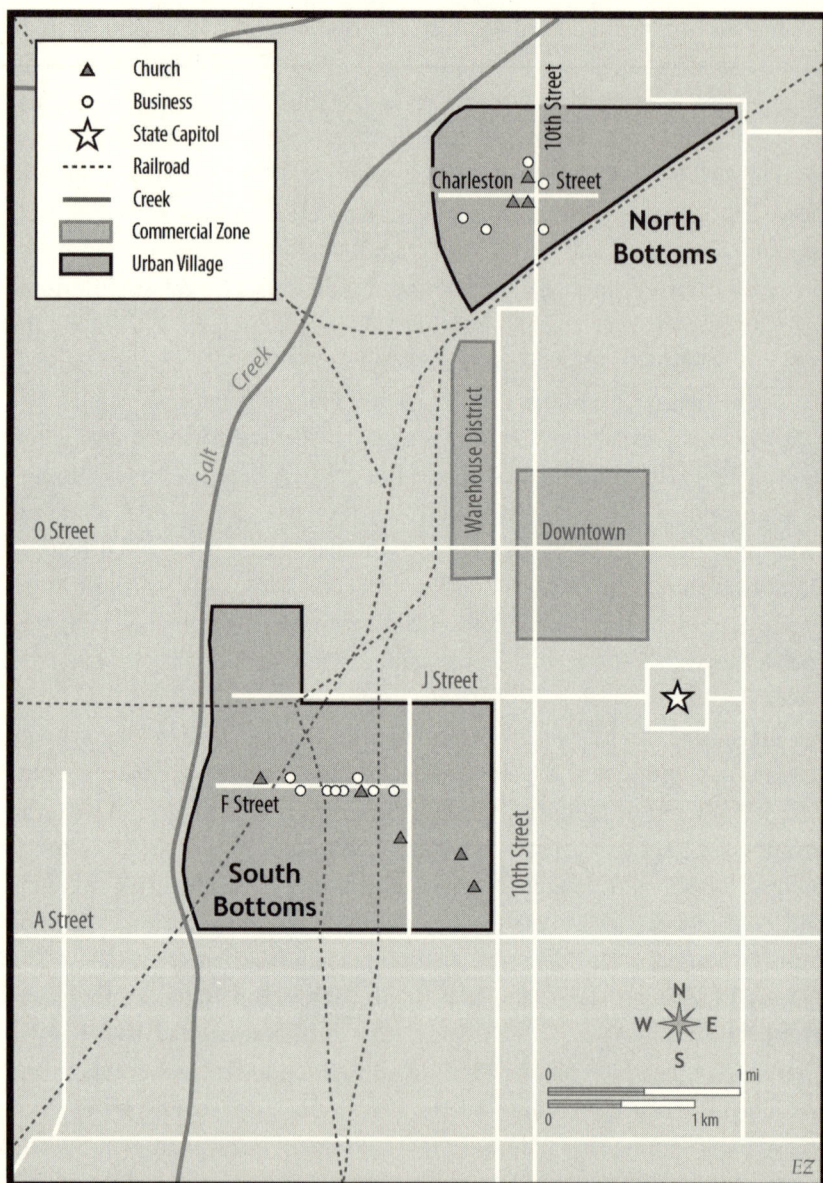

**Legend:**
- ▲ Church
- ○ Business
- ☆ State Capitol
- - - - Railroad
- —— Creek
- Commercial Zone
- Urban Village

Charleston Street

10th Street

**North Bottoms**

Salt Creek

Warehouse District

Downtown

O Street

J Street

F Street

10th Street

**South Bottoms**

A Street

N
W ✦ E
S

0 ———— 1 mi
0 ———— 1 km

EZ

Map 2-1: Map of North and South Russian Bottoms in 1925. Permission granted by Ezra Zeitler.

coln's ethnic neighborhoods and the greater population's gradual acceptance of the urban villagers. As both enclaves experienced mass exodus during the 1960s and 1970s, many second- and third-generation Volga Germans allowed their ethnic identities to fade.[13] In their new homes scattered across the city, they largely adapted to prevailing mainstream identities. The generation that came of age in the 1960s and 1970s, however, reexamined the heritage of their aging relatives. As the nation experienced an ethnic revival, the scions of Lincoln's Volga population helped construct a synthetic but international German from Russia identity.

### The Founding Generation

The Amens and their neighbors were the advance guard in Lincoln of an ethnic-German diaspora from the Volga basin that began in 1874 with an orderly emigration to the Great Plains and the Pampas of South America. These people's very presence in Russia recalled an earlier migration into the "ragged, semiarid southeastern frontier" of the Romanov domain.[14] Responding to Czarina Catherine II's promises of religious freedom and self-rule, twenty-three thousand to thirty thousand Teutons left war-torn western Germany between 1763 and 1767 and took up residence in the central Volga River valley.[15] Here the colonists provided the Russian Crown a "buffer" against bandits and "raiding" Tartar tribes of the region until conditions became untenable.[16] Although they built large, prosperous communities, the impetus to leave their homes was provided by Czar Alexander II, whose Russification projects included the gradual revocation of privileges granted to foreign colonists.[17] Familiar with grasslands environments, many disgruntled Volga Germans saw the young city of Lincoln, Nebraska, as a new field of opportunity, and the North and South Bottoms as safe havens for a beleaguered population. These communities spawned new identities.

### Particularism

Two ascriptions—villager and *Volger*—coexisted in the ethnic enclaves as nostalgia for specific Russian colonies, and a shared heritage born in Saratov and Samara provinces emerged as central components of identity construction in Lincoln. While the urban villagers hailed from all 104 of the original Volga colonies, 60 percent of them migrated from Norka, Frank, Balzer, Huck, Beideck, and Kukkus. (See Map 2-2.)

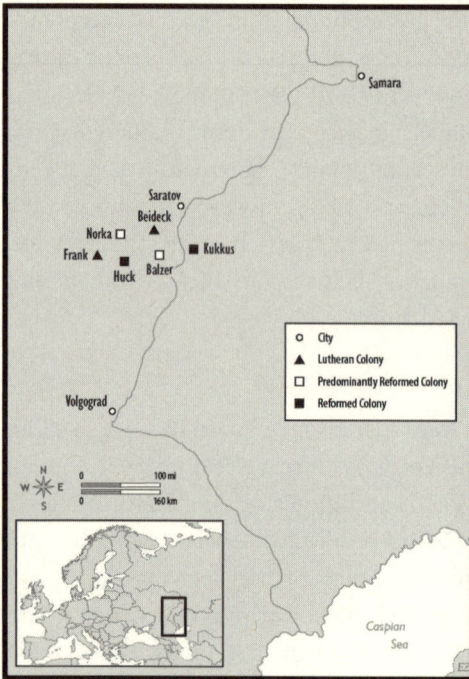

Map 2-2: Map of Volga Colonies.
Permission granted by Ezra Zeitler.

Favoring the largest of these places, the immigrants named the South Bottoms the *Franker Boden* and the North Bottoms the *Norkaer Boden*.[18] Identities were further subdivided as residents from the other colonies preferred to live as close to each other as possible. *Balzerers*, for instance, lived among *Balzerers*, and *Huckers* lived amid *Huckers*. Because populations were often small and the ethnic enclaves were surrounded by mainstream neighborhoods, a more inclusive *Volger* identity also developed as numerous villages combined into a greater community.[19]

The *Volger* identity was largely an expression of continued German solidarity in North America. In Russia, cultural unity was prevalent because the colonies were "islands of Germandom surrounded by a sea of Slavs."[20] Jealousy of Teutonic privileges was intense among Russian populations. Consequently, the colonists who arrived from Hesse, Rhineland, the Palatinate, Saxony, Würtemburg, and Switzerland learned to support each other.[21]

Still, particular religious, economic, and linguistic practices encouraged the colonists to identify with the "closed corporate communities" in which they lived.[22] Village loyalties were further strengthened by the underdeveloped infrastructure of the Russian provinces that made travel and communication arduous. Consequently, most colonists viewed their German-speaking villages as the center of their worlds, and few ventured beyond home and fields.

This curious development was partly the result of Catherine's directives regarding settlement patterns. To encourage unity, the enlightened despot assigned Catholics, Mennonites, and Protestants to separate communities; she further divided the Evangelicals by denomination. Thus, Lutherans and Reformed Christians, in theory, lived apart. Their only common thread was a royal "Instruction" that made church attendance mandatory.[23] In practice, Frank and Beideck were Lutheran colonies, Kukkus and Huck were almost exclusively Reformed, and Balzer and Norka were predominately Reformed. Seven percent of Norka's original citizenry was Lutheran, but this population gradually merged with the Reformed majority. Conversely, one-third of Balzer's founders were Lutherans, and they remained so over the years.[24]

Even in Balzer, however, the economic and political effects of the "mir" system supported village unity as well as community isolation. This organizational scheme evolved in Russia during the seventeenth century as the Romanov Crown—which maintained ultimate title to all farm lands—sought a way to anchor its formerly mobile peasantry. Over the course of seventy years, most Russian farmers were assigned to self-governing agrarian communes as serfs, a move that created a stable tax base and a pool for military conscription. Local autonomy allowed German colonists to avoid both service and servitude, but they chose to adopt the "mir" system from their Slavic neighbors around 1800. Originally, land was distributed to families in plots of uniform size regardless of household numbers. As populations expanded dramatically in the late eighteenth century, colonists charged their elected officials with the task of redistributing land in shares according to periodic censuses of adult males.[25] Once this system was in place, family patriarchs encouraged marital endogamy and high birthrates as methods to protect and increase their allotments. As a result, centripetal forces soon dominated the Volga German villages.[26]

The seclusion of the Volga colonies was so complete that linguists describe them as "speech islands." Residents of these communities fused divergent, archaic German dialects and a handful of Russian nouns into distinct vernaculars not spoken beyond community borders.[27] Speech patterns in

Balzer, for instance, betrayed origins from the Palatinate region. Only eighteen miles away, Norka residents produced and preserved a dialect dominated by Hessian structures. While mutually understandable, all *Volgers* recognized villages of origin through word usages and accents.[28]

Village separatism was reinforced by the limitations of the Volga infrastructure, which deterred both inter- and intraprovincial contact. The mighty Volga River divided two distinct German-speaking populations. Seventy-six percent of Lincoln immigrants came from Saratov Province, which was on the hilly west side of the river. Because the land was not particularly fertile, industry developed in the region during the mid-nineteenth century. Industrial units, however, tended to be confined to households, and a great deal of production and income merely supplemented agricultural pursuits. Still, Saratov immigrants in Lincoln thought of their peers from the less-developed "Meadow Side" as country cousins.[29] Enjoying flatter and more fertile environments, colonists in Samara Province lived in smaller communities and were unfamiliar with industry. Cross-river contact was surprisingly minimal, and even interprovincial communication was barely more frequent, partly because of road conditions. As late as 1906, it took two days by wagon to travel the forty miles from Norka to the provincial capital.[30] While distances between villages were often half that, at least as the crow flies, railroads did not serve the hinterland, and the muddy highways were rarely direct. Under such conditions, the village "protected the Volga German from the outside world and the colonist reciprocated by remaining loyal to its values and traditions."[31]

This faithfulness to tradition was best observed in Lincoln's German Protestant churches that were jammed to the rafters as often as three days a week. Never questioning Catherine's attendance mandates while in Russia, Lincoln residents continued to use churches as community anchors and social focal points. From these institutions, the German language was maintained in Lincoln through 1926 and beyond, as schoolchildren generally attended German school on Friday evenings, Confirmation school on Saturday morning, and Sunday school. While instruction was Bible-based, students also learned "how to read, write, and speak German."[32] Even in Russia, however, standard German—the language of Luther's Bible—was a central part of religious instruction and worship. Its usage was reinforced by ministers who were rarely native sons of the Volga colonies. Even though the language of the clergy was a cosmopolitan influence, the culturally conservative *Volgers* preferred to use the *Wolga Gesangbuch* (the *Volga Hymnbook*) for both worship and social singing. This hymnal became so familiar that a new edition was printed and marketed by the Wolga Book Company in Chicago in 1916.[33]

Ironically, while religion and language could sometimes unite *Volgers*, particularism remained apparent in church-based settlement patterns. The relatively late growth of the North Bottoms in the 1910s allowed for an orderly distribution of worshippers along village lines. (See Table 2-1.) Perhaps vital to these divisions, virtually all the Kukkus people—the only sizable village in Samara to send emigrants—settled in the newer urban village and worshipped exclusively at Salem Congregational and St. John's Evangelical Churches. True to the religion of their sending culture, most *Norkaers* remained at Immanuel Reformed Church, the North Bottom's oldest house of worship. All three congregations expanded in regular intervals that corresponded to the growth of the community. The available baptismal records demonstrate the general fecundity of the *Volgers*, who enjoyed birthrates of sixty per one thousand. In the greater community, twenty-five births per thousand was the norm.[34] While not wealthy people, they supported the church generously and erected substantial structures. The old frame Salem Church, for example, was razed by the community in 1916 and replaced by a larger "sturdy" structure with a "brick veneer" and a "dignified" stone foundation.[35]

Residents in the South Bottoms were equally church conscious. Rudy Amen (Henry and Barbara's son) noted that "our people dug down deep" to support the construction and maintenance of five congregations.[36] Splits according to village of origin and Protestant sect were equally apparent in this neighborhood. The two Lutheran organizations in the South Bottoms maintained a liturgy full of ceremony—a practice that Reformed practitioners disdained.[37] Emmanuel Evangelical Lutheran—whose records are not available—had a thriving congregation and hosted an important Saturday German school; breaking the general pattern of particularism, it welcomed students from other local congregations, especially Friedens Evangelical Lutheran Church. More in line with developments in most other parishes, Friedens was dominated by *Frankers* who hailed from the largest Lutheran Volga colony. Perhaps designed to attract minority-faith *Balzerers*, the structure itself is an architectural clone of the Third Evangelical Reformed Church in Balzer, Russia.[38] Although the presence of *Huckers* is not readily explainable, *Beideckers* were a logical addition to the parish.

Table 2-1. German-Russian Congregations in Lincoln, Nebraska: Point of Origin and Confirmed Membership, 1891–1928.

| Church | Nation | First Village | Other Villages | Members 1913 | Members 1925 |
|---|---|---|---|---|---|
| | | | South Bottoms | | |
| Immanuel | Russia | Norka | Huck | 220 | 634 |
| Salem | Russia | Kukkus | Norka, Huck | NA | 325 |
| St. John's | Russia | Kukkus | Norka, Balzer | 260 | 400 |
| | | | North Bottoms | | |
| First German | Russia | Norka | Frank | 130 | 365 |
| Zion | Russia | Frank | Beideck | 350 | 575 |
| Ebenezer | Russia | Balzer | Frank, Beideck | NA | 75 |
| Friedens | Russia | Frank | Balzer, Huck | 400 | 525 |
| Emmanuel | NA | NA | NA | 70 | 500 |

Sources: *Immanuel Church Official Record,* "Konfirmation Register, 1895–1924," and "Trau Register, 1892–1920"; *Gemeinde-Buch—Salem der Deutschen Ev. Kong. Gemeinde, 1901–67; Kirchenbuch der Evangelischen Johannes Gemeinde, 1907–67; Ersten Deutschen, Kongregationalen Gemeinde, 1899–1919; Ebenezer United Church of Christ Minute Book, 1915–1928;* "Records," German Evangelical Congregational Zion Church, 1900–1966, Series 2. For membership censuses, see *Hoye's City Directory of Lincoln* (Lincoln, NE: State Journal Co., 1891–1922); *Lincoln City Directory* (Lincoln, NE: Lincoln Directory Company, 1909–1910); *Polk's Lincoln City Directory* (Kansas City, MO: Polk, 1911–1925).

The other three institutions in the neighborhood were German Congregational churches, which were simply not present in the Volga colonies. Almost exclusively a German Russian organization in the western United States, the denomination comfortably housed Lutheran, Reformed, Evangelical, and Presbyterian Christians.[39] The leap from the doctrines of the Reformed Church and the Presbyterian Church—which began in South Germany and Scotland, respectively—to English Congregationalism was not a great one; all three were Calvinist faiths that celebrated the "revelation of Christ" and focused on biblical text rather than ritual.[40] Despite this connection, the real draw of Congregationalism in Lincoln appears to have been local autonomy. The urban villagers simply wanted to worship in their own fashion without direction from a synod run by *Reichs* Germans (immigrants from within the borders of the united German empire) or Americans.

Although they all belonged to a single denomination, the South Bottoms' division into multiple Congregational churches was remarkably contentious. Finally able to locate a minister in 1889, First German Congregational was the only church in the neighborhood for over a decade. Consequently, all *Volgers* attended. Zion Congregational appears to have taken the *Frankers*— at least those not affiliated with Friedens—and the *Balzerers* away from First German in 1900 and left mostly *Norkaers*. Similarly, Ebenezer Congregational was dominated by *Balzerers* who broke away from Zion in 1915. (See Table 2-1.) Interestingly, Rudy Amen—the son of a *Franker*—belonged to Ebenezer, where "they served Communion both Lutheran and Reform" rather than in a manner dictated by any synod.[41] While true to the inclusive nature of German Congregationalism, developments within these three institutions indicated that church members were more concerned about village and neighborhood affiliations than theology when choosing a parish.

Avoiding the tensions in the churches, the general ordering of space and construction of houses in the Bottoms relied primarily on shared old-world patterns. Because the Volga colonies were planned communities, residents were comfortable with symmetrical urbanscapes that focused economic activities around a town center built on a main street.[42] Consequently, the grid in Lincoln was a familiar template, and construction of linear business districts on F and North Tenth Streets seemed almost organic. Additionally, immigrants imported a vernacular architecture that synthesized central European and Russian components. In Lincoln, two basic types of one-story, rectangular houses were built. *Semelanka* were small structures that were one room wide and two or three rooms deep; *Kolinistenhausen*, also narrow and deep, generally had six rooms. Summer kitchens, gardens, and chickens and cows were all fixtures on the lots.[43] In Lincoln as in Russia, "Order, system, and economy of arrangement characterized the homes" of the urban villagers.[44]

Compact settlement patterns developed to meet economic needs in the Bottoms. Existing lots—standard size was 50 feet by 142 feet in both enclaves—were frequently subdivided, and many houses were built on parcels that were only 25 or 35 feet wide. While narrow, these properties accommodated the profiles of the preferred structures. Similarly, high neighborhood population density reminded residents of life along the Volga; indeed, it was one of the reasons people emigrated. Throughout the nineteenth century, many of the Russian colonies experienced exponential demographic growth while village plats rarely changed.[45] (See Table 2-2.)

Table 2-2. Population Growth in Six Volga Colonies, 1772–1912.

| Village | 1772 Population | 1912 Population |
|---------|-----------------|-----------------|
| Norka   | 957             | 14,236          |
| Frank   | 525             | 11,577          |
| Balzer  | 479             | 11,110          |
| Huck    | 380             | 9,600           |
| Beideck | 360             | 7,054           |
| Kukkus  | 181             | 3,796           |

Source: Karl Stumpp, *The Immigration from Germany to Russia in the Years 1763 to 1862*, trans. Joseph S. Height (Lincoln, NE: American Historical Society of Germans from Russia, 1978), 67–73.

While the urban villages seemed crowded to visitors from mainstream Lincoln, this condition did not cause undue concern among *Volgers*, who valued extended family unity more than personal space. In the most traditional families, sons remained part of a patriarchal family economy until they were at least twenty-one, and daughters stayed home until age eighteen or until they married. Even after matrimony, the oldest son sometimes continued living in the household and eventually took over ownership of a business and the home from his parents. Consequently, an average of six persons lived in each of these dwellings, and many four-room homes in the Bottoms housed a dozen residents.[46]

This intimate use of space created opportunities rather than squalor as multiple incomes facilitated home ownership. This practice, too, was imported from the Volga region, where "the colonists' concept of freedom was psychologically associated with the ownership of land." In Lincoln (where farming was an uncommon occupation) as in Russia (where the individual only owned "the land upon which his house" stood), this relationship was expressed through the purchase of city lots. By the mid-1920s, about 90 percent of the enclaves' adult population held titles to their own homes, and the few renters were generally young couples just starting out.[47] In the South Bottoms, Henry Amen often aided the home-buying process by writing multiple five-hundred-dollar mortgages and allowing borrowers to repay him at about thirty dollars a month. Mortgages tended to be paid in full within seven to thirty-six months.[48]

As homes were established and business thrived in the urban villages, "Residents didn't have to go to town for anything." In the *Franker Boden*, for instance, the Amens shared the commercial strip with at least six other merchants, all of whom served the local residents exclusively. (See Map 2-1.) This arrangement was convenient as most of the "people couldn't speak the English language very well."[49] Even those who could were poorly treated by most Lincolnites when they ventured into the mainstream, and consequently the immigrants preferred to shop and socialize within the confines of their neighborhoods. Insularity remained a common feature of life in the Bottoms, and divisions even existed between the two enclaves as residents in the *Norkaer* and *Franker Boden* rarely interacted. As longtime resident Jacob Reifschneider recalled, it just "wasn't very good for a boy from the South to come down and court a girl from the North."[50]

Despite such sentiments, urban villagers were drawn together by necessity and by choice. Safe within their enclaves, first-generation immigrants invented exclusive and inclusive identities based on their heritages in the Volga colonies. As local populations swelled, families consciously segregated themselves into church congregations based on village of origin where they were free to speak their distinct dialects and practice their unique customs. Here they considered themselves *Balzerers* and *Kukkusers*. Simultaneously, performed cultural practices connected urban villagers in both Bottoms to a shared *Volger* identity. As a group, they stood out from the mainstream because they sang from the same German-language hymnal, built homes from similar mental blueprints, eschewed debt, favored home ownership, and valued large, extended families.

### Cosmopolitanism

The natural tendency toward particularism within the urban villages was not absolute, however, nor were the enclaves ever completely isolated. In fact, residents of the Bottoms were in near-constant contact with the mainstream; consequently, they necessarily grappled with the cosmopolitan worlds of work and regional, national, and international politics. Political discussions were generally filtered through a vibrant German-language newspaper that helped inform the immigrants about these and other issues. Through these worldly influences, *Volgers* confronted national German American and regional German Russian identities.

Work took urban villagers out of their communities, exposed them to mainstream culture, and revealed the dynamic tension that existed between economic patterns born in the old and new milieus. Formerly agrarian people, *Volgers* in Lincoln secured positions as laborers, small business people, and migrant workers in the sugar beet fields of the Great Plains. Most immigrants, including Anna Schwindt Giebelhaus and her family, accepted these unfamiliar occupations readily, as most had left the Volga colonies because they "couldn't make it there."[51] As a young woman of seventeen, Giebelhaus anticipated moving to a land where roasted pigs ran about the streets with forks and knives already stuck into their backs.[52] Once in the new community, the work ethic she imported from Norka helped keep food on the table for the family of fifteen children she started three years after her arrival.

Anna and Jacob Giebelhaus—both *Norkaers* from the North Bottoms—typified *Volgers* who opted to work as wage laborers in Lincoln. Their jobs introduced them to the English language and to relatively mobile life in America. After her birth family took up residence in a small structure on a subdivided lot on Charleston Street in 1902, Anna found a position as a maid at the Hotel Lincoln. There she learned English in six months from the other "girls" who worked with her. Unlike her mainstream coworkers, she relinquished most of her wages to her family until she married in 1905. Like most *Volger* women, she left the labor force after matrimony to work in the home. Fortunately, wages from Jacob's job with the Burlington Railroad—the largest employer of men in the Bottoms—were sufficient to support their rapidly growing family. His employment took them all to Wyoming and back, but the couple remained connected to the North Bottoms and the German Reformed Immanuel Church virtually their entire adult lives.[53] This connection was critical for Anna, who outlived her husband by forty years and was ultimately celebrated, along with eight of her peers, as one of the last known speakers of the *Norka* German dialect. In their time, they all probably shopped for groceries at Konrad Brehm's or Fred Reifschneider's stores on Tenth Street, the North Bottoms' main drag.[54]

Although they were entrenched in the German-speaking community, merchants in both enclaves also interacted with mainstream society on a regular basis. They certainly purchased their stock from English-speaking wholesalers and meatpackers. Henry and Rudy Amen made even larger concessions to the prevailing business climate by keeping their books in English from 1902 on. The customers they served, however, were universally immigrants, and dealings with this population had unique rhythms. In May 1915, for example, the Amens advanced groceries to forty-five South Bottoms families that were heading to the beet fields and then carried these debts until the farmhands returned in the fall.[55] This practice was commonplace in the grocery business throughout the *Volgers*' first fifty years in Lincoln.

For most urban villagers, seasonal work in the sugar beet fields was their introduction to life on the Great Plains. In fact, the majority of families in the North Bottoms reported working at least two seasons in beets.[56] Yearly migrations were especially attractive to newcomers, as it fit into a lifestyle imported from the Volga colonies. In the old country, a form of nomadic agriculture was practiced by the mid-nineteenth century as villages annexed distant plots to support their large populations. Bound by economic interests (each resident owned a portion of all public buildings) and tradition, families migrated to far-flung fields for the entire summer but returned to the village after harvest.[57] Similarly, the agrarian calendar allowed for periods of very hard work followed by winters of relative leisure. Finally, as everyone over three could work in the fields, large families were a boon in the beet industry, and many recruiters sought out Germans from Russia specifically.[58]

Beet-field labor was not only compatible with traditional patterns, it was also a contact point for mainstream economic elements. Organized recruitment, legal contracts, and modern transportation were all part of this industry. Serving the sugar beet companies as well as the itinerant labor force, agents—often merchants or pastors—established long-term relationships with field-workers whenever possible. They even visited families with good work histories each spring, seeking contract renewals. In order to avoid dissatisfaction from either party, transportation arrangements, work, and living conditions were all specified within the contracts; additionally, dispute mediation was handled by the sugar beet company representatives rather than farmers themselves. Before the work season began, train cars for the "beet-field specials" were left under the Tenth Street viaduct adjacent to the North Bottoms, and along the Fourth Street spur tracks in the South Bottoms. Families were allowed an entire week to load the necessary equipment for their sojourns.[59] To assure a steady supply of labor, advertisements—"*Achtung, Zuckerrüben-Arbeiter!*" (Attention, sugar beet-workers!)—were circulated as handbills and also appeared in newspapers typically from January to April.[60]

*Die Welt-Post*—a German-language weekly published in Lincoln beginning in April 1916—not only connected urban villagers to a world of work, it introduced them first to a German American identity and then to a more exclusive German Russian identity.[61] Civic-mindedness naturally led the newspaper's editors to report on the armed conflict in Europe. Subsequently, the politics of war introduced Lincoln's urban villagers to a nation that felt threatened by displays of Germanness. On the one hand, persecution and repression encouraged solidarity among all types of Germans and other ethnics across the Great Plains. On the other, war strengthened German Russian pride and particularism.

Perhaps attempting to overcome the perceived incompatibility between *Volks* Germans—ethnic Germans from outside the empire—and *Reichs* Germans, *Die Welt-Post* traced its journalistic roots back to the "Viennese Revolution" of 1848 and purported to be "the most widely circulated German Weekly in the West." Echoing the chauvinism common in the German-language press, the first issue's editorial salutation heralded Lincoln as the "approximate midpoint of Germanness in America." Celebrating a population of eight thousand served by thirteen congregations, the editors undoubtedly hoped to cross boundaries as they welcomed all with "German blood," whether from "Germany, Russia, Austria or Switzerland," and suggested that the "hearty German language" created "good public spirit."[62]

During its first year of publication, the newspaper optimistically expressed the shared German American hope that U.S. involvement in the conflagration was not imminent. As late as December 1916, headlines responded to President Woodrow Wilson's efforts to construct diplomatic "peace without victory" by announcing "Peace Moves Ever Nearer." The editors also attacked war boosters, such as Theodore Roosevelt, who was accused of "farting into the war horn" for talking about forming a volunteer army.[63] These proclamations were especially popular among urban villagers who, despite their Russian birthplaces and their forebears' oaths to the czars, accepted loyalty to the German empire rather than the Romanov domain. This development was especially telling of a powerful German identity, as none of the Volga colonies received immigrants from a united Germany. Still, as urban villagers applied for U.S. citizenship, many relinquished allegiance to the kaiser, not the czar.[64]

Not all *Volgers* shared this view of the war and the world. Many served in the Russian Army before emigrating, and many more had relatives doing so.[65] Aware of the pro-ally sentiments among a portion of their readership, the tone of the paper's reporting stressed a preference for peace, but it also expressed an ultimate loyalty to the United States. In February, headlines announced "War Stands in View! Wilson Breaks with Germany?" The text of this article respectfully focused on Wilson's speech to Congress as he described German violations of neutral nations' rights on the high seas. After the formal declaration of war on April 4, 1917, editors carefully translated Wilson's war message into German, an action that allowed readers to judge circumstances for themselves. Subsequent articles displayed the American flag and focused on Wilson's calls for all Americans to make common cause.[66]

Despite balanced reporting and a general loyalty to the United States, frequent and intense intellectual attacks on German speakers—ranging from renaming sauerkraut "liberty cabbage" to distributing propaganda demonizing Germans—were perpetrated across the country.[67] In the Bottoms, residents were treated to "burning crosses," "bodily abuse," and property vandalism as "mob spirit" was common in Lincoln and throughout the state.[68] In many respects the war reignited long-running American suspicions about German Americans, whose cultural chauvinism was expressed through opposition to any sort of prohibition, support of American neutrality, retention of the German language, and, in the case of Mennonites, pacifism. As a result, Wilson's insistence that America was fighting the German state not the German people often fell on deaf ears.[69]

Hysteria moved in official circles as well. As soon as war was declared, Nebraska's Committee for Public Information mandated that German-language presses begin disseminating propaganda supporting the U.S. war effort. For *Die Welt-Post*, this included displaying the motto "America 1st" on its masthead in English, and publishing "What Can I Do to Help My Country Win the War?"—a nine-point pledge authored by the Nebraska State Council of Defense. While the typical reader was becoming "a shining example in the service of this land," ever more restrictions were placed on German-language newspapers.[70] In October 1917 the U.S. Congress passed the Trading with the Enemy Act, which required German-language papers to file translations of stories relating to the war with the U.S. Post Office and to obtain licenses to continue publishing. Duplicating federal efforts, Nebraska mandated that "foreign language newspapers, magazines, periodicals and books" submit copies with translations to the Council of Defense beginning in the spring of 1918. This ultrapatriotic organization found a voice for its agenda in the *Lincoln Star*. The figurative war against German language and culture was also waged in Lincoln schools as the Nebraska Education Association supported an Americanization agenda. These efforts were in many ways unnecessary as few Lincoln schools—including Hayward School in the North Bottoms and Park School in the South Bottoms—instructed students in German.[71]

The generally moderate stance most urban villagers held regarding the war and the intangible "Russian factor" actually made conditions in the Bottoms better than in many German enclaves. *Die Welt-Post* was one of the few newspapers exempted from printing English translations of war news, and while many German-language churches were forced to close during the war, Friedens, whose minister had "influence," and First German (and perhaps the others) remained open.[72] In many cases, Volga heritage—but not Russian culture—was reclaimed, and a German Russian identity was advanced in the war's aftermath. By early 1919, *Die Welt-Post* had abandoned German Americanism and positioned itself as "biggest, best, and cheapest newspaper for the German Russian in America."[73] In reality, this statement reflected the paper's mission from its inception. While the *Die Welt-Post* provided international and national news, a great deal of space was reserved for church happenings in the Bottoms, letters and news from the Volga colonies, and information by and for residents who were temporarily out of their communities—most of whom were spread out along the Burlington trunk lines in the towns of Friend, Sutton, Harvard, Hastings, Bayard, and Scottsbluff.

The end of the war, however, did not end attacks on German Americans who were already saddled with a reputation for political "radicalism," or German Russians, especially after the rise of the Soviet Union and the failure of democracy in Europe. Rather than returning to normalcy, urban villagers were caught in the Red Scare that permeated America during the immediate postwar years. This event amplified the xenophobia that already existed before the war and heightened calls for Americanization of immigrants.[74]

In Nebraska, citizenship was equated with abandoning immigrant behaviors and languages, and prohibition of these tongues seemed quite desirable.[75] The Siman Act, passed in April 1919, was to be the vehicle for this transformation. It insisted, "No person, individually or as a teacher, shall in any private, denominational, parochial or public school, teach any subject to any person in any language other than the English Language," unless a student had successfully completed the eighth grade. Violation of the statute was a misdemeanor punishable by "not less than Twenty-five ($25) dollars, nor more than One Hundred ($100) dollars," or up to thirty days in the county jail. As an "emergency" existed, the act went into effect immediately.[76]

Not surprisingly, the state's actions were also treated as an emergency by most ethnic populations, who began a protracted fight against violations of their constitutional rights. The day after the bill was signed into law, *Die Welt-Post* labeled the action "un-American" and Nebraska as the most "intolerant state in the entire union" as they decried constraints on their "citizenship and religious rights." In defense of their community, merchants in the South Bottoms even joined together to place a full-page advertisement in *Die Welt-Post* praising urban villagers for buying war bonds and serving as soldiers. They proclaimed, "You want [nothing] but to be a patriot."[77]

Allying themselves with other European-born groups, residents of the Bottoms watched the four-year debate over language rights closely. *Die Welt-Post* subscribers, for instance, may have read Nebraska attorney general Clarence A. Davis's defense of this "Americanization Program" with skepticism. Although he assured them that the Siman Act did not affect foreign-language usage in Sunday, Saturday, or after-school church lessons, he also promised that any "attempt to evade" the program by "teaching other things under the guise of religious instruction, will be prosecuted without leniency."[78] Similarly, readers learned of attempts by the Missouri Synod Lutheran Church and various Catholic congregations to gain a temporary restraining order against the law on the grounds that many "German or Polish speaking" families would find it impossible to instruct their children in the basics of religion and culture "only in the English language." It was clear to all involved, however, that further court action would be forthcoming. Many ethnic citizens and many prominent legal scholars believed their efforts would eventually prove the Siman Act unconstitutional.[79]

The cause célèbre in this effort was Robert T. Meyer, a *Reichs* German immigrant and a teacher at Zion Parochial School in Hamilton County, Nebraska. Meyer, despite the concerns of his superiors, conducted a German Bible class during a designated recess period. A clear stretch of state law, on May 25, 1920, he was confronted by the Hamilton County attorney, admitted instructing fifth-graders in the German language, and was soon fined twenty-five dollars as prescribed by statute for his actions. Meyer appealed to the Nebraska Supreme Court on the grounds that his religious freedoms had been violated, but the conviction was upheld. The majority opined that the "baneful effects of permitting foreigners" to raise "and educate the children in the language of their native land" was "inimical to our own safety" as a society. Perhaps emboldened by the dissenting opinion that insisted the Siman Act was "the result of crowd psychology" caused by World War I, Meyer's lawyers immediately appealed the case to the U.S. Supreme Court.[80]

Anticipating difficulties in the judicial system, the Nebraska legislature acted to preempt decisions even before the Nebraska Supreme Court decision. Passed in April 1921 the Norval-Reed Act superseded and strengthened the Siman Act. Most importantly, English was "declared to be the official language of the state." Additionally, discriminating "against the use of the English language" for virtually any purpose became unlawful. Responding to concerns about religious freedom—Norval's original intention—the act allowed foreign-language religious instruction on the Sabbath and similar instruction at any time in the home. Finally, the authors included a clause that declared all sections of the act independent, and they averred that any court decision would affect only the sections specifically ruled unconstitutional.[81]

In *Meyer v. State of Nebraska* (1923), the U.S. Supreme Court coupled the Nebraska dispute with cases originating in Iowa and Ohio, and it left little of the Norval-Reed Act intact. After providing an eloquent but very general discussion of the nature of liberty as guaranteed by the Fourteenth Amendment, the Court determined that the "protection of the Constitution extends to all, to those who speak other languages as well as to those born with English on the tongue." Attempts to ban language instruction simply exceeded "the limitations upon the power of the state." In effect, this action ended an era of language restriction.[82] After the decision was announced, German-language instruction and worship in the Bottoms' eight congregations continued with renewed vigor.

Over the years, Lincoln's urban villagers—both in times of liberty and years of constraint—negotiated usable identities in response to a variety of economic and social possibilities. The German American label was briefly attractive, but the split among *Reichs* Germans and *Volks* Germans combined with mainstream xenophobia to make this designation generally unpalatable. While a German Russian specification was perhaps more comfortable and more accurate, intolerance and legal repression encouraged a pan-ethnic front as a means to retain religious and social freedoms. As internal crises passed, however, external forces redirected the attentions of most residents in the Bottoms.

### Transnationalism

A Volga German (*Wolga-Deutsch*) identity developed in Lincoln and parts of rural Nebraska as the result of post–World War I transnational contact with their former Russian homes. In fact, by their fiftieth anniversary in America, residents of Lincoln and Sutton, Nebraska, began to construct their ethnic communities as "Volga German colonies" in the United States.[83] Powerful transnational sentiment—always present in these enclaves—was responsible for this new designation. It was strengthened and promoted by the return of autonomous government in Saratov and Samara in the late 1910s and by famine in the region in the early 1920s.

Migration, whether supervised by Romanov or Soviet officials, was never a one-way affair. While the overwhelming movement during the early twentieth century was to the United States, a few birds of passage returned to the

Volga provinces. Armed with new capital from work in the beet fields of the Great Plains and American citizenship that exempted them from taxation and military service, this population often bought land, resumed farming, and rebuilt their lives in traditional, yet more affluent manners. World War I—which saw ethnic Germans living within the Russian Empire vilified—and the Russian Revolution largely ended this practice while reducing immigration into America to a trickle. Those who did arrive were generally fleeing Bolshevism. Still, wealthy travelers began to visit "Russia" as early as May 1920. These trips were expensive, and while this sort of tourism attracted hundreds of consumers, most Volga Germans on both continents remained close to their homes.[84]

Nevertheless, interest in the Volga colonies among Lincoln's urban villagers was at an all-time high, as it appeared that Catherine's promise of self-rule and ethnic preservation might be fulfilled through revolution. Fortuitously, Czar Nicholas II's abdication in March 1917 spared ethnic Germans throughout Russia from draconian orders to confiscate all German-owned livestock and agricultural surpluses in order to support the Russian war effort.[85] Unfortunately, the Volga colonies were soon embroiled in the Russian civil war. The Socialist Revolutionaries—revivals of the Bolsheviks and sometimes allies of the Mensheviks—established their base of power in the city of Samara in June 1918. Successive military campaigns plodded across the Volga provinces throughout the growing season before the "Greens" were dislodged in November.[86] Although Vladimir Lenin established the Autonomous Commune of Volga German Workers in October 1918, subsequent engagements of "White" and "Red" armies precluded any real stability in the colonies.[87] Peace and relative contentment did not return until 1924, when an eighteen-thousand-square-mile area became the Volga German Autonomous Soviet Socialist Republic (ASSR)—the first self-governing ethnic region within the Soviet Union. The seventeen years that this political entity existed were celebrated as a reprise of one hundred years of German "cultural superiority" in a Slavic region.[88] The population of eight hundred thousand who lived in the republic in 1931, however, owed a debt to Volga Germans in America.

The Volga colonists were emaciated by famine between 1921 and 1923 as man-made and natural forces converged to create true disaster. Life in a semiarid environment had taught Volga residents to store large food reserves, but these caches became impossible to maintain. Bolshevik forces were already fighting the Greens along the Volga when they began "compulsory grain requisitions" in May 1918.[89] Paying the toll that financed "war communism," German settlers were especially hard hit as grain stores and local livestock in the Autonomous commune were frequently commandeered by the Red Guard between 1918 and 1919.[90] Levies continued through 1920 as the Red Army's expansion from 2.5 million to 5 million men drained even more resources.[91] Even as the Bolsheviks consolidated power in 1921, severe, widespread drought already touched 25 million Soviet citizens and lingered relentlessly for three growing seasons. With no reserves left, an estimated 75 percent of the Meadow-Side population was on the verge of starvation by 1921 as the fields yielded less than the seeds planted.[92] The Mountain-Siders were only slightly better off.

Galvanized by the plight of their relatives, 120,000 Volga German Americans raised $1 million for relief during the three-year famine. In Lincoln, the money was funneled through churches, and individual contributions were proudly reported in *Die Welt-Post*. The American Volga Relief Society (AVRS) then worked in conjunction with Herbert Hoover's American Relief Association to help feed and clothe families in most of the Volga colonies.[93] Pride among the urban villagers for their ability to help was apparent throughout this process, and the developing Volga German identity was based on action and compassion.

The relief organization that evolved into "a brotherhood of Volga Germans" remained vital even after the crisis in the Soviet Union subsided. Boasting the motto "All for one," the fifth annual conference of the AVRS was held in Lincoln from June 23 to June 27, 1926. The event also marked the fiftieth anniversary of German Russian settlement in the United States. While hundreds of conventioneers traveled back and forth between Lincoln and Sutton for picnics, prayers, and general revelry, the organization promoted a Volga German agenda. Specifically, the organizers sought to reestablish a commitment to German language by inviting "famous speakers" to orate in "our mother tongue," promote the general prosperity of Volga Germans everywhere, find the ways and means to help them wherever possible, rekindle old friendships and make new acquaintances, and celebrate the Golden Jubilee in an "appropriate manner."[94]

The Lincoln celebration was both an immediate and a long-term success. In 1926 attendance was large, and spirits were high. In subsequent years a strong Volga German identity was promoted on numerous occasions. By the end of the decade, this ascription was so widespread that *Die Welt-Post* even declared itself "the organ of the Volga Germans" and proclaimed to be the "best newspaper" for this ethnic group in America.[95]

Whether they called themselves *Franker, Volger,* German American, German Russian, or Volga German, the identities that Lincoln's urban villagers constructed were complicated, convoluted, and rarely exclusive. Indeed, as the founding generation negotiated particular, cosmopolitan, and transnational influences, they often subscribed to more than one label at any given time. Particularism remained especially powerful as the original Russian village had long-standing emotional power. For example, relief pledges during the famine were generally made to help specific Volga colonies, and the organizations dispensing aid were bound to direct contributions to the appropriate places. The tendency toward insularity actually spawned separate relief groups in Portland, Oregon; Fresno, California; Greeley, Colorado; and Lincoln, Nebraska, as the four large enclaves of Volga German immigrants only worked well together when imminent starvation dictated cooperation.[96] Similarly, while largely a cosmopolitan influence, *Die Welt-Post* appealed directly to "readers from Norka, Huck, Frank, Beideck, Mohr, Grimm, Lawe, and etc." when they needed additional funding to survive a fivefold increase in the price of paper.[97]

The discussion surrounding language rights—which involved *Die Welt Post*—was both inconclusive and confusing to many of Lincoln's urban villagers. While this particular local newspaper remained a vital organ of communication, 244 of the nation's 522 German-language publications folded between 1917 and 1920.[98] German-speaking communities remained afraid of repression. Clearly, most celebrated the final *Meyer* decision, but they may not have been certain that harassment from the mainstream was over as they had seen legislated tolerance and intolerance come and go. Six years before the Siman Act, Nebraska passed the Mockett Law that allowed foreign-language instruction beginning in the fourth grade upon parental demand. While controversial, the Nebraska Supreme Court upheld the statute in 1916.[99] The legislature disregarded the judiciary in 1919 when it passed the Siman Law.

Even after the repeal of the Siman Law in 1923, the shift to English continued in churches, presses, and schools throughout the lives of the next generation. While *Volgers* had large enough populations to demand German instruction under Mockett, students even before the war "couldn't talk German in school" because parents and teachers both "insisted" that English was the language of secular learning.[100] Residents in the Bottoms, it appears, were already keenly aware that they and their children had one foot each in two different worlds.

Still, neither the keen awareness of national events nor the fascination for village of origin deterred residents of the Bottoms from maintaining a sense of transnationalism. Even as church congregations split along village lines, most members listed their place of birth as "Russia"; those listing a specific village were in the minority. (See Table 2-1.) The Volga German identity was also strong enough to connect Lincoln's urban villagers to three continents, not just two. In 1927, for instance, *Die Welt-Post* encouraged residents to celebrate the Fiftieth Jubilee of "Volga-German" settlement in Argentina.[101]

Despite fifty years of changes inside and outside the Russian Bottoms, residents in 1926 still belonged to their communities. As Jacob Reifschneider recalled, "It was all one nationality, one type of people, and you feel like you've got family all around."[102] From their ethnic enclaves some urban villagers—however they defined themselves—continued traveling to the beet fields each season, and others kept working hard as local laborers. In the process, Volga Germans began to take on many of the trappings of middle-class Nebraska, and mainstream businesses were anxious to provide them with a variety of goods and services. Empowered by economic advances, political and social changes soon followed. During the next fifty years, the identities of residents in the Russian Bottoms were further transformed by a new set of influences.

### "We Became Americanized": The Second Fifty Years

Lincoln's Volga German urban villages remained distinct and vibrant ethnic oases between 1920 and 1950 as continued neighborhood cohesion assured that denizens could avoid the "total alienation" they so often experienced in the American mainstream.[103] Ultimately, ethnic communities persisted during these decades as the combined population of the Bottoms increased dramatically. Despite growth in structures to match these numbers, the neighborhoods began to disperse after World War II; indeed, both enclaves faded to mere shadows of their former selves during the 1960s and 1970s.[104] Physical contraction was preceded by changes and abandonments of performed culture, and the once proud Volga German identity slipped into dormancy during the Russian Bottoms' second fifty years. The younger people even became "embarrassed by their Germanness."[105]

### Economic and Political Advancement

Identity shift and community contraction can both be attributed, in part, to markedly improved circumstances within the enclaves. Overt prejudice against the urban villagers largely subsided by the mid-1920s as memories of World War I, the Red Scare, and battles over language were obscured by an intoxicating era of prosperity. While still racialized by the mainstream, Lincoln's Volga Germans clearly realized an improved position within the greater community. They reinforced this trend by maintaining their niche as ready and reliable laborers. Ultimately, wage increases led to greater economic power, and remarkable demographic growth translated into expanding political influence, even during the Great Depression.

Initially, these gains were made largely without threatening the status quo. As most urban villagers made acceptable livings working as beet-field hands, domestics, railroad men, and construction workers, higher education was rare until the 1950s. Indeed, only a handful of German Russian students attended the University of Nebraska during this era, despite their enclaves' close proximity to this institution.[106] As they had done in the 1910s, the majority of urban villagers "went to the sugar beet fields" throughout the 1920s and 1930s. In fact, their increased numbers—the beet-field specials originating in Lincoln often pulled twenty-five coaches and twenty-five boxcars—aided this industry's expansion.[107]

Because physically demanding stoop labor was required to tend the fields, most mainstream workers spurned this form of employment. Volga Germans, on the other hand, had no qualms about accepting such toil and even used it to help establish their status as "white people." While they shared the beet fields with Mexican and Japanese immigrants, the ethnic Germans were the preferred hands in the business even though their contracts required each person to tend ten acres compared to the twelve to fifteen acres the other groups were expected to maintain. For many landowners and sugar beet companies, racial exclusion became more important than squeezing profits from their workers. These attitudes allowed Volga Germans to recast their identities in a favorable manner without taking on additional labor. Happy with their elite status, they were, as Marie Elizabeth Dittenber Schmidt re-called, not especially tolerant of their nonwhite coworkers. The itinerant ur-ban villagers distanced themselves from other workers and "just didn't let them interfere" with their daily business.[108]

In Lincoln, this workplace independence was less beneficial to the ur-ban villagers, as the national railroad Shopmen's Strike of 1922 separated Burlington employees into scab and unionist camps. The strike itself was the culmination of decades of wage and hour disputes. As both Lincoln and Havelock—the Capital City's railroad suburb—had extensive repair and maintenance facilities, many local families were affected. Agitation in these communities continued through 1923 and 1924, and the Burlington Rail-road ultimately appealed to the National Guard for assistance and blacklist-ed strikers. While the strike heightened tension between mainstream and urban village workers, it also divided Volga Germans among themselves as most unionists never returned to the shops. The resulting rifts within the Bottoms subsided slowly over the course of the next decade.[109] Fortunately, the strike occurred at the same time that work on the new state capitol be-gan, and many otherwise displaced workers started ten years of employment on this public works project.[110]

While even boom-time employment was tenuous, the mainstream com-munity increasingly praised Volga Germans for their resourcefulness and industry. Nebraska governor Adam McMullen in his address to a group of Golden Jubilee delegates, for instance, described Lincoln's urban villagers as "new citizens whose energy, frugality and industry helped to build up and maintain a magnificent country of peaceful homes and great enterprises."[111] Indeed, by 1926, his words accurately described the rapidly improving con-ditions in the Bottoms.

Necessitated by population growth and made possible by the habit of saving money, new housing was common in both urban villages in the 1920s. As a rule, the homes were notably larger, more substantial, and pat-terned after American structures. People electing to remain in their older dwellings often raised their foundations and dug basements. The added in-door space allowed residents to convert summer kitchens into storage and garage spaces. The expansion of neighborhood stores and a penchant for modern living encouraged the last vestiges of rural life to disappear from city neighborhoods, and fewer and fewer Volga Germans kept livestock on their properties.[112]

Similarly, church improvements continued throughout the 1920s. In the South Bottoms, First German constructed a new building on the west end of "main street" in 1920. Ebenezer, already on the edge of the enclave, razed its initial structure and started a brick building in July 1927. That same summer, Zion broke ground on Ninth and B, pushing the very limits of the community eastward. Across town, a dispute about ministers at St. John's Evangelical caused the congregation to split in two. The new church, also called St. John's Evangelical, erected its house of worship just four blocks away from the old. As of January 1928 the North Bottoms supported four thriving congregations.[113]

To aid this building boom, city improvements were finally extended into the enclaves. Water and sewage arrived in the early 1920s, and the fully plumbed bathroom—formally the sign of an Americanized family—became the new standard.[114] Additionally, the mud streets and wooden sidewalks were gradually replaced by cement and asphalt throughout the course of the decade.[115] Although the city dump—the bane of the North Bottoms—was not filled and sold until 1948, the substandard conditions of the first fifty years of settlement in both Bottoms were largely ameliorated by the joint efforts of citizens and government.[116]

Mainstream businesses—attracted by a "thrifty" population that earned "good wages"—also courted trade with Volga German consumers during the 1920s.[117] They offered urban villagers modern commercial goods. Advertisements for washing machines, gas water heaters, pianos, phonographs, telephones, and automobiles began appearing in the pages of *Die Welt-Post* in the early 1920s, and they soon became a regular feature. Over the next several decades, a symbiotic ethnic buyer and mainstream seller relationship developed. The newspaper encouraged this association by publishing an "Honor Roll of Lincoln business houses." The editorial staff then urged "the Volga German people of Lincoln" to patronize the honorees, who were also advertisers.[118]

Always anxious to curry favor in the community, *Die-Welt Post* began displaying "Lincoln's emblem of middlemen and manufacturers" as part of its contribution to the Chamber of Commerce's "Link Up with Lincoln" campaign.[119] The business community responded by inviting Volga Germans to the Second Annual Greater Lincoln Exhibition at the University

Coliseum in March 1928. While the invitation was printed in German in *Die Welt-Post*, "Progress"—the theme of the exhibition—was chiseled into a stone facade in English by a muscular workman. The advertisement also featured a locomotive and workers raising a skyscraper—two intimately familiar sights for many Volga Germans.[120] Although they remained laborers in an increasingly middle-class society, their contributions to the mainstream were readily recognized and their consumer dollars eagerly courted.

In the Bottoms and in the community at large, however, the Great Depression derailed economic progress. Available work contracted in the urban villages as the capitol was completed in 1932, mainstream households that formerly hired domestic help necessarily retrenched, and workers who remained with the railroad were often laid off for years on end. Consequently, everything in the Bottoms appeared "more or less rundown" during the 1930s. Still, while a few families lost money through risky investments, the habit of avoiding debt and paying cash allowed the resilient Volga Germans to hold their own economically.[121] Many families who had moved up the economic ladder in the 1920s returned to the beet fields to make ends meet. They often made "a pretty good livin' with it," as John Kapeller, Jr., recalled, and sometimes even earned enough to "buy a little better house."[122] While urban villagers certainly accepted relief and New Deal employment schemes, their close-knit families and communities still remembered the poverty of the early years in Lincoln and managed to survive with dignity and even grace.

Although times were hard financially, Volga Germans in Lincoln began flexing their collective political muscle during the 1930s. Always a cosmopolitan force, *Die Welt-Post* began encouraging its readers to vote for "German" candidates early in the decade. Through the pages of this organ, city council candidates, such as Paul Doerr, courted votes by promising to update water and light facilities in the Bottoms.[123] Admonishing urban villagers to "do your duty" by going to the polls, Henry Amen made an unsuccessful run for the council in 1933.[124] Always persistent, he was finally elected to the post in 1937 and served until 1943. Amen was so trusted by his constituents that they also elected him to the Board of Trustees of Sanitary District 1, where he served as chair for fifteen years in an era when storm drainage was still a vital issue for the urban villagers.[125] Attempting to form a coalition among ethnic and mainstream voters, Amen went on to run for mayor in 1943.

Campaigning in German and English, he stressed his city government and business experiences. Additionally, he reminded the city that three of his sons were serving in the armed forces. The city was not ready for an ethnic mayor, however; while Amen garnered almost three thousand votes, he lost in a landslide to Lloyd Marti, who drew eighty-five hundred.[126]

Amen's patriotism, although strengthened by his sons' actions, was never questioned during any of his campaigns, yet another indication of wide-scale acceptance of the Volga Germans. Even debates about war in the late 1930s and early 1940s raised little ire in the mainstream despite *Die Welt-Post*'s suggestion that Hitler's unification of the German peoples through *Anschluß* was a peaceful movement, and its position that America should never go to war again.[127] Even after World War II was under way, the urban villagers were largely spared the harassment they experienced in the 1910s, which was due, in part, to their insistence that they not "be out-done by other citizen groups" in their support of the war effort. Additionally, fol-lowing the attack on Pearl Harbor, all of Val Peter's newspapers averred that "time for political disagreement about international affairs has passed" and that "all American citizens of German blood" needed to "stand behind their government."[128]

Not surprisingly, Lincoln's urban villagers singled out the Japanese rather than the Germans as the archenemies of the United States.[129] This action was tempered by their experiences in the beet fields and by the general pre-disposition of mainstream America during the 1940s. While anyone with Japanese heritage was vilified, prejudice against German Americans rare-ly surfaced during this era, and when it did, cooler heads generally pre-vailed. The *Lincoln Star*, for example, ran a letter to the editor denouncing German-language choir music in Lincoln and suggested they turn "the pro-gram over to the Japs." The editors responded somewhat uncharacteristically, stating, "We have been through all that. . . . No good can possibly come out of a controversy over language."[130] Mainstream acceptance had come a long way in twenty years.

### Contractions of Performed Culture

Tolerance toward the Volga Germans slowly increased throughout their sec-ond fifty years in Lincoln. The urban villagers, however, were rapidly be-coming acculturated into the mainstream. In fact, between 1926 and 1976, most aspects of their performed culture—including family structure, music, language, and church organization—were either greatly transformed or lost entirely. With each new decade the focus of community and individual lives moved further away from the old churches and neighborhoods. Even the once proud Volga German press was on the brink of extinction.

Still, *Die Welt-Post* remained the "Organ of Volga Germans" until 1959, but its survival depended on Val Peter's practice of consolidating ailing Volga German papers into the Lincoln publication. The process began in 1927 when *Die California Post*—which served Fresno, Sanger, Dinuda, and Biola—was discontinued as an independent entity and assigned a page or two in each publication of *Die Welt-Post*.[131] By 1930 the scope of local reporting expanded from Lincoln, Omaha, and western Nebraska, and it began to focus also on Volga German enclaves in eastern Washington, Michigan, North Dakota, and Idaho—all sugar beet regions.[132] By World War II, news items from Kansas City and Denver were also receiving regular ink, presumably at the expense of formerly separate papers.[133]

While Peter launched *Deutsch-Amerika*, an illustrated Pan–German American newspaper, in 1935, the German-language press in the United States generally receded with the passing of the generation born around 1900.[134] Dialect distinctions among German speakers were rarely discussed by 1960, and even *Die Welt-Post* became simply "An American Newspaper printed in the German Language." For the next two decades, the paper focused on international and European news without mentioning the enclaves formerly so important to the readership.[135] Circulation steadily declined until only 527 subscriptions were active in 1976.[136] Peter's *Omaha Tribune* empire was down to its last eight newspapers in 1982 when a Winnipeg concern bought the vestiges of this formerly huge combine and consolidated it into a single paper.[137] The Volga German press in the United States had finally run its course.

Other cherished practices—all of them central to life in Saratov and Samara—were also on the brink of disappearing. One of the most telling signs of acculturation was a shift in family structure. In the Volga colonies as well as in the Bottoms for the first fifty years, the family hierarchy had "strong patriarchal overtones." Originally designed to strengthen the household economic unit, sons and daughters in Lincoln's most conservative families generally relinquished their wages to the family head until they were twenty-one. Additionally, they often married in accordance with their parents' wishes. Both practices were holdovers from the "mir" system.[138]

Arranged marriages had little meaning in Lincoln from the settlement's very beginning. Instead, patriarchs preferred that their children marry within the ethnic community. Consequently, weddings remained a joining of the bride and groom and a symbolic joining of their families as well. Paying homage to economic tradition, Anna Giebelhaus recalled that the groom bought the bride's dress, and that the bride bought the groom's shirt.[139] The families then split the costs of feeding and entertaining the reception party.

These costs were significant as wedding receptions were often three-day events that required food, music, and a large tent with a wooden dance floor.[140] The first day of the celebration was fairly subdued and focused on the church ceremony and a celebration for the immediate family. Subsequent events featured general revelry that reinforced the community hierarchy. Day two was set aside strictly for the older generation so if "they wanted to make fools of themselves they could do it without the younger people seeing them." Similarly, on the final day the young people could play without the watchful eyes of their elders. By the mid-1920s, however, the urban villagers, as Henry Reifschneider noted, "became Americanized and cut it down to one day."[141] The need to maintain age-based appearances had largely dwindled.

The demise of prolonged wedding celebrations was also the beginning of the end for vernacular music within Lincoln's urban villages. Indeed, by 1945, the command "*Spielen sie ein polka*" (Play us a polka) was rarely heard at wedding receptions or house parties; community dances also fell out of favor.[142] The formerly familiar sounds of fiddle and accordion that were used to drive the dancers' figures were replaced by commercial music from within the mainstream.[143]

The polkas and waltzes imported from the Volga colonies demonstrate that traditions, especially musical ones, are in a state of "constant reinvention and reinterpretation."[144] Rather than being a folk dance, the polka—named after a Polish woman—emerged in the metropolitan centers of Western Europe in 1844. Like the waltz, its use of eye contact and synchronized movement expressed gender relationships unknown in either courtly or peasant dances.[145] Its exact migration across Europe is not fully documented, but the polka and the waltz were the dominant dance and music forms in the Volga colonies by 1870. In order to suit the needs of the community, they were adapted to fit on the *Geige* (fiddle), *Hackbrett* (hammered dulcimer), and *Dudelsack* (bagpipes).[146] Musicians and dancers both preferred polkas with complicated melodies and unique endings that gave "people some time to stop" at the "big house weddings."[147] Rather than the familiar *oom-pah* sound, the use of the older instrumentation that favored a prominent melodic line must have produced an almost ethereal sound.[148]

In Lincoln, instrumentation for these rigorous dances initially reflected old-world patterns, as two violins, a hammered dulcimer, and a cello were the mainstays. The music soon experienced conflicts between individuals wishing to play and hear exact renditions of older sounds and those preferring to include modern American influences.[149] Although Saturday evening dances remained a popular diversion through the 1920s, couples were waltzing and "two-stepping" to music played on mandolin, violin, and piano.[150] To create more drive, accordions were soon added as additional rhythm instruments, and by the 1930s they captured the melody line as well. The airy and archaic *Hackbrett* had lost its place in the ensemble.[151]

During the World War II era, the Volga German polka was renamed the Dutch hop as musicians and dancers were anxious to appear patriotic.[152] Although musicians played established musical forms, this sound was new and vibrant because they used accordions backed by brass instruments. While Lincoln's urban villagers were certainly familiar with this modified musical form, the hotbed of Dutch hop was the Volga German colony in and around Greeley, Colorado, where young and old alike still enjoy polkas. Residents of the Bottoms, on the other hand, appear to have allowed vernacular music as an identity marker to lapse even prior to the war.[153] While the polka offered resistance to mainstream culture among Polish Americans, Tejanos, "Papago-Pima Indians," and some German Russians, this experience was by no means universal. Influenced by more modern trends, many urban villagers turned to Lincoln's public ballrooms and swing music as new forms of recreation.

Sacred music, on the other hand, lingered in a far more recognizable form as the old hymns were sung on a regular basis by first- and second-generation Volga Germans until the late 1960s. Because most individuals were not trained to read music, the Volga German hymnal printed just the words. Singers followed the piano or organ accompaniment and then memorized and repeated the familiar melodies throughout the courses of their lives. Stable musical forms, however, were threatened by a shift in language. As Jacob Volz—a lead organizer of the Volga Relief Society—observed, the "second generation speaks only partly the German language, but the third generation speaks only English."[154] Consequently, sacred music necessarily became Americanized.

The language change in sacred singing and in all other aspects of church life was gradually accepted throughout the congregations in the Bottoms as they were "faced with the choice of either losing the youth or introducing the English language."[155] For a while, the two tongues overlapped. Friedens, for instance, "had German completely until 1931." They switched the Sunday school over to English at that time. Luther League—an organization for teenagers—followed suit later in the decade, and finally by the mid-1950s the congregation was unable to find a German-speaking minister.[156] At Emmanuel, the confirmation class of 1934 comprised five youngsters tested in English and three in German, but even this latter group was already writing in the American script. At Zion, sermons were delivered in English by the late 1920s while hymns remained German.[157] Immanuel introduced separate English-language services in the 1930s but maintained worship in German at a different hour.[158] Dual-language congregations lingered into the post–World War II era in both the urban villages. When First German celebrated its sixtieth anniversary in 1948, the church marked the event with an English service at 2 p.m. and a German one at 7:30 p.m.[159] German-language services, although far less frequent, lived on in every church until the early 1960s.[160]

The language shift was not the only change in church life during this era of contraction. Secular self-help organizations—American Forward and the North Lincoln Welfare Society—emerged in the 1920s and became a new social focus for many urban villagers. Virtually unknown in the Volga colonies, these associations pulled interest and energy away from the churches. This shift was caused partly by religious fervor generated from within Volga German tradition and partly by external demands.

The Welfare Society was the secular offspring of Salem Congregational Church's Neighborhood House. Moving to its present location—1430 North Tenth Street—in 1927, the hall and organization hosted wedding receptions, dances, and Boy Scout meetings that were no longer welcomed in the churches.[161] Venue change was necessitated by the strict preferences of pietist revivalists who were called the "Brotherhood" or the "Brethren." Preferring a "priesthood of all believers" over trained clergy, this lay movement stressed emotion rather than ceremony within the church. Influencing the German-speaking world since the seventeenth century, pietism emerged in many of the Volga colonies around 1870; was transported to Sutton, Nebraska, in 1887 from Norka, Huck, and Balzer; and spread to Lincoln soon thereafter.[162] Its passion emboldened followers to intervene with established routines and social norms. The North Bottoms, it appears, was much more affected by the brethren than their sibling neighborhood.[163]

In the South Bottoms, secular organization was initially an expression of German Russian patriotism during World War I. The prototype of American Forward was founded in 1917, and it sponsored numerous parades and civic events through 1918. Revived in 1922 and incorporated in 1925, it promoted "the general welfare, friendliness, fellowship, social and moral improvements" of its members until 1974. This association boasted 600 men as well as a 350-member women's auxiliary, but it generally met in rented space and members' basements until 1951, when the organization bought the Emmanuel property at 745 D Street.[164]

The Emmanuel Lutheran congregation was happy to relinquish title to the building as they had already moved a mile south of the Bottoms. As if to sever the old ties, they joined the Missouri Synod—a typically *Reichs* German organization. Perhaps anticipating wide-scale change and an eventual exodus from the Bottoms when they moved in 1950, members of this parish were not the only ones who experienced significant sociological, theological, and demographic changes in the post–World War II era.

In the long run, reactions against cultural conservatism and denominational upheaval led to the reordering of all surviving churches in the urban villages. Others simply dissolved. Anachronistically, most churches in the Bottoms retained their old-world gender relationships well into the 1950s. This was most visibly demonstrated by seating arrangements where men and women sat on opposite sides of the aisle. In the original St. John's, for instance, adult males were on the right and adult females on the left. Children sat either in the front or in the balcony, depending on the practices of the specific congregation.[165]

Spatial separation reinforced the patriarchal family hierarchy. The greatest expression of this practice was demonstrated in brotherhood meetings, in which women were forbidden from speaking.[166] While such arrangements were acceptable to the oldest or most conservative community members, young, American-educated urban villagers preferred to focus on family unity rather than social segregation. Additionally, no longer tied to their neighborhoods through language and custom, many young people "just got away from" belonging to churches altogether.[167] With little interest in tradition, many established practices faded away. The old prayer meetings at Immanuel Reformed Church, for example, finally "died out" around 1972.[168]

These events were some of the last remnants of a performed culture that was already lapsing by 1940. Shifts in language use, family structure, and community entertainment were all readily apparent—especially among the younger urban villagers. Greater tolerance by the mainstream made ethnic cohesiveness more a choice than a necessity. Economic and demographic changes caused by U.S. involvement in World War II only accelerated the rapid integration already under way.

### Contractions of Community and the Volga German Identity

The Volga German enclaves, their institutions, and the unique identities they protected became markedly less distinct in postwar Lincoln. While church was always a central component of life in the Bottoms, the very denominations that residents chose to affiliate with were undergoing dramatic changes. As Rev. Edward O. Berreth recalled, by 1940, Congregational seminaries were engaged in a "big language fight" about "whether they should stay German or become English."[169] When English won out, Lincoln's churches were largely unable to find German-speaking ministers. German Congregationalism fell on hard times after this decision, and in 1957 the churches merged with the Evangelical and Reformed Churches—two other old German-language stalwarts—and the Christian Church to form the United Church of Christ (UCC).[170]

Although none of the Congregational churches in the urban villages abandoned the old label until the late 1960s, contraction was evident long before then. In the North Bottoms, Salem Congregational merged with the second St. John's—which adopted Lutheranism in 1956—to become Faith UCC in 1967. The new parish claimed the Salem building and sold the other to a Latvian church that housed some of Lincoln's Cold War immigrants.

The original St. John's Evangelical Church switched to Congregationalism in the late 1950s, and just before its building was razed, it also joined Faith. Surprisingly, Congregational churches in the South Bottoms experienced little turmoil during the denominational shift. Ebenezer and Zion quietly joined the UCC in 1970 and 1975, respectively.[171] Ignoring the tide of change, First German—apparently housing the scions of its original congregants—remained Congregational until the twenty-first century.

The retention of Volga German congregants was not universal for the other five surviving churches in the Bottoms. Immanuel Church—the North Bottoms oldest congregation—remains very connected to its past, although in 1980 it finally dropped "Reformed" from its name.[172] Conversely, Friedens Lutheran still stands as a landmark in the South Bottoms and still serves some of the "children and grandchildren" of its founders, but most of its current members do not live in the neighborhood and are not tied to the congregation through family tradition.[173] They simply prefer the intimacy of a small structure and spiritual community. Ebenezer and Zion experienced similar developments.

Demographic change in the Bottoms in the 1950s was not just a church-based issue. Physical and emotional movement away from the urban villages was predicated, in part, on an identity shift that favored, once again, German Americanism. The transition from Volga German to German American was encouraged by a change in transnational ties. The end of the Volga German ASSR in 1941 and the exile of its citizens into central Asia virtually erased links to the Volga colonies and their citizens. At that point, Lincoln's urban villagers transferred their need for connection to people in "*die Alten Heimat*" (the old homeland).[174] Echoing the generosity of the Volga Relief campaigns, aid in the forms of food, money, and supplies was funneled to Germany and Austria. While news from Russia was virtually absent, travel to the U.S.-controlled zones in Germany was available by fall 1946.[175] To many young urban villagers, the old world had shifted. As one *Reichs* German Lincolnite noted, "They don't put that Russian in there no more lately."[176]

The geographic change in homeland happened during an era of emotional and physical movement within Lincoln's urban villages. In an era of expanding possibilities, marital exogamy was a common way of realizing a more mainstream identity. Outmarriage in the Bottoms began on a large scale in the 1940s as local soldiers and sailors often came home with brides from around the United States and even from around the world.[177] Local women also found expanded options. Wilma Alles, for instance, wed Army Air Forces pilot Keith Reed, who was from outside the community.[178] He appeared unconcerned that his bride lived below Tenth Street—an area that many Lincolnites long considered undesirable.

Other young urban villagers chose education and relocation as paths to end this pattern of discrimination.[179] As Katherine Schmall recalled, "The kids get education, they move out, they moved out and our people passed away."[180] The Schmalls, with the exception of Katherine, who was retired and widowed in 1965, showed this propensity for movement. The family owned three adjacent lots on West F Street between 1920 and 1950, but only Katherine remained in the South Bottoms fifteen years later.[181] Similarly, the Lebsocks, a large merchant family who maintained businesses and residences in the Bottoms through 1950, closed their stores and moved several miles away from the old neighborhood. Henry and Barbara Amen remained in the home they built in 1918, and while three of their six surviving children remained in their neighborhood of birth in 1965, Rudy—who was still running the family business—moved farther out into south Lincoln and commuted to work.

Patterns in the North Bottoms were very similar. The Schwindts established nine households in the urban village by the 1920s. While still very connected to Lincoln in 1965, they maintained just two residences in the old neighborhood. The Reifschneiders moved east and south over time. Not always going far, many young families in the postwar era moved north into the Belmont neighborhood.[182] Here, they were able to find good housing—a scarce commodity in the immediate postwar era. Additionally, like many Americans in the automobile age, children raised in the Bottoms moved to the far-flung corners of the United States. Two of Emma Dinges's offspring, for instance, moved west to Arizona and Idaho, and those remaining in Lincoln did not live in the Bottoms.[183]

Developments among the neighborhood merchant houses also illustrated the growth and decline of German Russian ethnic communities in Lincoln. In the North Bottoms, the Reifschneider family—which maintained several businesses—and George Maser and Sons dominated the Tenth Street grocery trade. Hergenrader's garage was close by, as were a drugstore, barber shop, and beauty parlor—all owned by mainstream Lincolnites. Virtually all of these establishments were in place by the mid-1920s and remained vibrant until the early 1960s, when they declined and finally disappeared.[184]

Although these grocers all relied on urban villagers as their clientele, they necessarily modernized over the years. The small, behind-the-counter grocery stayed in the community until 1935, as evidenced by the longevity of Konrad Brehm's little store on Y Street. Ultimately, these were replaced by large establishments that displayed their goods on shelves.[185] Covering nearly an entire city block, the Cash and Carry was pioneered by Philip Reifschneider in 1925. At the time, this new enterprise on Tenth and Charleston was celebrated as a "Volga German" accomplishment by the entire community, and customers flocked to the store.[186] As this identity declined, however, so did loyalty to the local mercantile. Maser's closed its doors in 1966. The Reifschneider IGA remained in the family until about the same time, but was sold to a mainstream grocer who continued operations until 1980. By then, only one grocery, a filling station, and a drugstore remained in the vicinity.[187] These businesses were soon replaced by a national gas station, a minimart, and several restaurants that are more often closed than open.

Across town, the F Street merchants enjoyed a similar era of expansion that largely continued through the Depression before declining from 1950 to roughly 1970. The grocery trade was dominated by the Amens—who diversified throughout the 1920s—the Lebsacks, and the Lebsocks, who all shared the commercial strip with numerous coal dealers, fuel sellers, and a real estate office. As in the North Bottoms, this main street business district slowly contracted over the course of twenty years, and its original proprietors exited completely when the Amen family's store closed in 1971. As the German-speaking population that needed their services scattered, a plumbing business, an electrician, and a small food processor took over the storefronts, and the foot traffic and human vibrancy faded from the streets and sidewalks.

The decline of main street hustle and bustle and the ascension of modern residential rhythms in both the North and the South Bottoms represented an amazing paradox. Social, economic, and political gains achieved by urban villagers between 1920 and 1950 served to weaken the cohesiveness of their enclaves rather than strengthen them. Cosmopolitanism triumphed over particularism and transnationalism during this era; ultimately, the ethnic communities and the Volga German identity faded as a result.

As the twentieth century progressed, connection to the Volga colonies and their traditions became increasingly difficult to maintain. U.S. immigration policy and Soviet emigration policy combined to squelch outside movement into the Russian Bottoms. As a result, the German-speaking population slowly diminished. In Lincoln, there were approximately four thousand Russian-born residents in 1920, twenty-five hundred in 1940, and only a handful in 1965.[188] Aspects of performed culture waned as experience with the old villages was lost. The shift in language loyalty illustrates this point. The children and grandchildren of the founding generation first transferred loyalty away from village dialects toward standard German—the language of the church and the press. Large-scale acceptance of English gradually crept into the community as a matter of state and federal policy, but more importantly as a matter of convenience beginning in the 1920s. This move was finalized by the collapse of German Congregationalism in the 1950s and the decline of the German-language press. As early as World War II, any option but English was merely an artifact.

If they did not learn English at home, the younger generations—all products of natural increase—learned it in the public schools. These institutions also introduced urban villagers to the material benefits of mainstream society. Intent on achieving parity with their schoolmates, Volga Germans first modernized their own neighborhoods and then moved beyond their confines. Hard work had rewards but often came with a price: the loss of cultural uniqueness.

### Survivals, Revivals, and a New German-from-Russia Identity

By the mid-twentieth century, the scions of the Volga diaspora in Lincoln had largely abandoned the behaviors of their Russian villages and accepted mainstream cultural practices in their stead. It is a mistake, however, to assume that they were "assimilated" into the greater American society. In many respects, immigrants merely "adapt" to their new settings.[189] While adaptation is often quite thorough, pieces of the old performed culture often remain. The most prominent survival among Lincoln's former urban villagers was not the most salient identity factor among this population. Still, foodways were passed down from mother to daughter, even among families that married outside their ethnicity. Interest in these traditions was handed down quietly until the ethnic revival of the 1970s revitalized a sense of uniqueness among a population that began calling themselves "Germans from Russia."

### *The Ethnic Revival and the Invention of a German-from-Russia Identity*

Because so little remained of the immigrants' performed culture by 1970, the maintenance of an "official" community in Lincoln—one that retained the original language, rituals, and other cultural practices—was virtually impossible. Rather, the ethnic revival encouraged the creation of a "symbolic" community—one that shared a "biological connection to ancestors" as well as some level of cultural participation.[190] This new community of Germans from Russia included not only Volga colonists but also ethnic Germans who first settled in the Black Sea region, the Ukraine, and Volhynia at the request of the czars and then came to the Americas. Their substantially different experiences are described and celebrated by the American Historical Society for Germans from Russia (AHSGR), the revival's champion and most effective voice.

The AHSGR was organized in Greeley, Colorado, in 1968, "exclusively for educational scientific, religious, and charitable purposes."[191] Although it moved its international headquarters to Lincoln in 1973 to take advantage of available financial resources, its mission of fostering the "discovery, collection, preservation, and dissemination of information related to the history, cultural heritage and genealogy of Germanic Settlers in the Russian Empire and their descendants" remained constant.[192] Distinct cosmopolitan, particular, and international influences combined to produce a German-from-Russia identity that is celebrated in the North American West, the grasslands of South America, Germany, and several former Soviet republics.[193]

For Lincoln's Germans from Russia, international politics often hampered transnational ties. Because Soviet premier Joseph Stalin believed that ethnic Germans were a threat to national interests during Hitler's eastern expansion, the residents of the Volga German ASSR were exiled to central Asia beginning in 1941. Contact with their American relatives during this era was all but impossible. While Soviet policy toward ethnic Germans softened after Stalin's death in 1953, most Volga villagers remained in Kazakhstan and Siberia as their former holdings were reassigned to ethnic Russians. A handful of Volga Germans returned to Saratov and Samara beginning in 1957.[194] As of 2003, they numbered about 23,000—the approximate population of the region in 1767.[195]

Intent to reconnect with their roots, some AHSGR members visited their extended families in Asia during the late 1960s, despite difficulties caused by the Cold War. Emboldened by their growing organization and by a less oppressive Soviet regime, many joined the international lobby for the reestablishment of the Volga-German Republic. An estimated 2.1 million ethnic Germans whose ancestors settled in Russia during the eighteenth and nineteenth centuries were to be welcomed into this imagined entity. While optimism for the project abounded in the late 1980s, Russian president Boris Yelstin ended hopes of establishing a republic in 1992. Consequently, 600,000 ethnic Germans emigrated back to Germany between 1994 and 2004.[196]

This modern movement connected diverse populations—including the original 23,000 Volga Germans; 80,000 Black Sea Germans who settled in southern Russia between 1804 and 1845; 30,000 Germans who emigrated to the Ukraine between 1830 and 1865; and 150,000 Volhynia Germans who made their original journey between 1865 and 1875—to a homeland they left centuries earlier.[197] This amazing ethnic solidarity was already part of the German-from-Russia identity promoted by the AHSGR. Their mission includes connecting all ethnic Teutons who presently or formerly settled within Russian territory.

This cosmopolitan attitude is reinforced by the architectural design of its headquarters and museum. Located at 631 D Street on land donated by the Amen family, the building duplicates the shape of a Black Sea German Russian combined house and barn. Although a modern structure, its finish resembles puddled clay on a stone foundation typical of the region.[198] As no such buildings—either in form or materials—were imported from the Volga colonies, the building is architecturally out of place in Lincoln's South Bottoms. Still, this fine facility is in keeping both with the society's mission and with an identity that transcends the city and the Volga colonies. The museum's outbuildings—including a small chapel complete with Volga German hymnals, a summer kitchen, and an old general store and cobbler shop—would have been familiar to Lincoln's urban villagers in both form and function, especially because they include packed "beet boxes" that contain the tools and supplies for sugar beet workers.

The sculpture on the front lawn of the headquarters further reinforces the organization's themes of inclusiveness and tradition. Actually a replica of the sculpture *German from Russia Pioneer Family*, originally carved by Pete Felten, it represents all German émigrés.[199] It depicts a man, a woman, and two children dressed in clothing that was typical of settlers on the Russian steppes. Gathered around a plain cross (rather than the Catholic cross with a crucified Christ), it "personifies the moral, physical and religious strengths of those Germans who first left their homes to settle the far reaches of the Russian Empire."[200] Echoing the importance of family and gender separation of the old congregations, males are on the viewers' left and females on their right.

Despite the powerful imagery of the headquarters, cosmopolitan notions of inclusion often meet the particularism of village, region, and nation within the organizational structure of the AHSGR. Although it is an international organization, twelve of its thirteen districts are solely within the United States. All of Canada and "all countries outside the U.S.A." are relegated to a single entity. Most other districts are a series of states clustered into rather artificial regions—for example, the California district includes Hawaii. As settlement patterns favored prairies and plains, Nebraska, Colorado, and Kansas—states with the largest German Russian populations—constitute separate districts. Nebraska is further broken down into four chapters, one of them being Lincoln.[201]

The Lincoln chapter was already three hundred strong in 1971, just three years after its founding. Partly as a result of its success in organizing, the chapter hosted the AHSGR's second international convention.[202] Gerdi Stroh Walker was a typical member from this era. Born in 1946, she was among the younger generation—often the grandchildren of the community founders—who were interested in investigating their backgrounds and genealogies.[203] After hours of interviewing relatives and using the resources at the headquarters, she was able to trace her family back to 1748 when they still lived in Germany.

Reinforcing the particularism of the genealogist, the village remains an essential feature of the AHSGR. In fact, each German Russian colony is assigned a "village coordinator" who is charged with communicating "with all persons who share the same village heritage."[204] At the annual convention, an entire evening is set aside for "Village Night." This event helps coordinate the "sharing of family group records, maps, individual and family histories, video and audio tapes of memories, trip experiences, and other village information."[205] Some of the organizations have published books and articles about their ancestral homes, and many are in the process of gaining access to Genealogical Data Communications (GEDCOM)-format databases to aid in genealogical research.

Lincoln's six main contributing villages are well represented in this system. Norka currently boasts a newsletter as well as an extensive website. Frank, Balzer, and Huck all formerly had newsletters but have replaced them with websites. Beideck maintains a newsletter rather than an Internet source. Kukkus appears active and is the subject of a book published by the Fresno chapter, although information is not available online or via a newsletter.[206]

Particularism and internationalism have begun to fuse in the modern German-from-Russia mentality. Four of the organization's nine standing committees look back to either Russia or to Germany for inspiration. The Genealogical Research Committee facilitates family research, and the Archives Committee concentrates on materials from Russia and other former Soviet republics. In a similar vein, the Historical Research Committee encourages cooperation among "national and international archives," whether they are academic or governmental institutions. They are especially interested in the "Aussiedler program" and gathering information about recent immigration from Russia back to Germany. The Folklore/Linguistics Committee is charged with collecting and preserving "traditional customs, beliefs, tales, expressions, and teachings of Germans from Russia" as well as recording their dialects.[207]

### Survivals

In Lincoln, village dialects and folktales of the immigrants largely vanished in the early 1980s as the last members of the founding generation passed away. Germans from Russia and community organizations instead rely on portions of the local heritage that are still available, especially the built spaces in the North and South Bottoms. While still living neighborhoods with extant housing and graceful church steeples, the two communities are generally portrayed as part of the past. For example, the North Bottoms Historical Marker sits at the base of the Tenth Street viaduct that spans the Burlington yard. Located directly across the street from Immanuel Church, the monument explains that ethnic Germans settled in Russia in the eighteenth century and then moved to the Great Plains for jobs and land in the late nineteenth and early twentieth centuries. They settled in the Bottoms to take advantage of "diminished land values." Additionally, the third paragraph explains,

> The North Bottoms ethnic enclave developed its own businesses, social groups, churches, and schools. Small houses on long narrow lots followed either old world models or new American styles. In the

backyards, chicken coops, tiny barns, and summer kitchens recalled the old country agricultural community. Descendants have largely dispersed throughout Lincoln and the nation, but the North Bottoms reminds us of the old "urban villages" immigrants built in a new land.[208]

Similarly, because it was the "largest and probably most homogeneous ethnic neighborhood within the state" of Nebraska, the South Bottoms was designated a National Historic District in 1986.[209] This move allowed residents to take advantage of the Historic Preservation Act passed in 1966 and claim federal tax benefits.[210] As part of the process, the old ethnic enclaves became museum pieces in a complex, modern urban world.

Because revivalists often stress "conservation, preservation, [and] restoration," living traditions are often ignored.[211] Fortunately, the foodways of Germans from Russia have been retained in Lincoln and beyond. North Dakota State University and Prairie Public Television even produced a documentary celebrating part of the Black Sea German tradition, a kind of "soul food," in 2000. *Schmeckfest* celebrates noodle soup (*Knöphla*), schnitzel, schnapps, and Easter breads shaped like birds that have been prepared on the Dakota prairies since they were homesteaded. Church groups, in this case to the accompaniment of an accordion player, still feed entire communities during holidays.[212]

The passion for food is preserved in Lincoln as well. The annual AHSGR soup dinner, for instance, is held at the Welfare Society Hall in the North Bottoms at the end of February. The 2005 event featured chicken soup containing homemade noodles, dumplings, and broth. Accompanied by rye bread and a variety of desserts, long lines—complete with jokes about soup lines from individuals who lived through the Depression—and an overcrowded hall attest to the continued popularity of the old dishes, especially among elderly or middle-aged Germans from Russia.[213] These events remind Lincolnites such as George Kruse that when the urban villages were still vital communities, "Every Sunday was noodle soup."[214]

Recipes from this feast quite possibly came from *Küche Kochen* (*Kitchen Cooking*), a popular cookbook published by AHSGR. Initially released in 1973, it has gone through at least eleven printings and is still available from the AHSGR store.[215] The intriguing aspect of this particular publication is that most of the submissions list the colony of origin for each recipe. Perhaps because it was compiled in Lincoln, recipes from Frank predominate. Still, diversity in origin is noted in simple words. Dumplings, for instance, are referred to as *glöss*, *dampfnoodla*, *glace*, *glaze*, *klase*, *pirogen*, and *platshinta*—words that recall German and Russian dialects. The *runza*—a low-budget cabbage, onion, and ground beef pastry—is listed as cabbage burger, kraut-burger, *kraut baraks*, *bierochs*, *ranzen*, and *zweifel* and *kraut*.[216] Most of these names were eclipsed after the founding of Runza Restaurant in 1949.[217] The signature sandwich of this long-lived local chain often puzzles visitors to Lincoln, but to many area expatriates, the Runza is the essence of home. Despite such ubiquitousness, the wide variety of names used in the cookbook are intentional, as the project is dedicated "to the loving memories of our Great-Grandmothers, Grandmothers, and Mothers who diligently and faithfully preserved our heritage," or more aptly, heritages—as Germans from Russia, even those living only forty miles apart, were a remarkably diverse collection of peoples.[218]

Preservation is not only the watchword of the committee that edited this cookbook; it is the key concept to understanding the ethnic revival in Lincoln and the German-from-Russia identity that accompanies the movement. Food aside, actual survivals from the era of immigration are minimal in the twenty-first century. Consequently, revivalists congregate around a symbolic community that revolves around AHSGR, a tireless advocate for this new ethnic ascription. Locally, the organization's headquarters building serves as a gathering point for many volunteers and social groups that live in and around Lincoln. Internationally, its archive and library make it a center for historical and genealogical research.

While AHSGR membership includes scholars and students, it largely comprises elderly individuals and aging baby boomers who work on tracing their family trees.[219] Certainly noble pursuits and in keeping with the idea of preservation, the general lack of young people might indicate that the revival generation and its German-from-Russia identity is as temporal as the founding generation and their *Volger* ascription. Still, the revivalists have prepared a historical base should future generations wish to pursue their heritage.

At the center of the image they created is the idea that Germans from Russia were community builders.[220] The organization's location in the South Bottoms neighborhood—where four of the five old churches are still visible—serves to remind even the casual tourist of the contribution that the Volga German immigrants made to Lincoln. Perhaps as the children of the baby boomers age, they, too, will tire of mainstream consumer culture and search for roots in the North and South Russian Bottoms. On the other hand, perhaps they will become more detached from their heritage.

## Conclusion

The revival community in Lincoln would probably seem quite foreign to Anna and Jacob Giebelhaus and the other urban villagers who used the Norka dialect and maintained a performed culture nurtured in the Volga colonies. Additionally, the neighborhood they once knew remains extant, but instead of hosting home owners and families, 74 percent of its houses are rented—mostly to college students.[221] Demographic change in the North Bottoms happened slowly, but by the time Sam and Willard Giebelhaus left to serve in the U.S. armed forces in 1941, the multiple identities used by their parents already seemed dated, and many young urban villagers preferred ascriptions that cast them as part of Lincoln's mainstream.[222]

The acceptance of the Volga Germans as Americans was hastened by contributions to the war and the war economy during the 1940s. Their flow into the mainstream was first discussed by sociologist Hattie Plum Williams in the 1910s. Her work on the German Russians, which included both her M.A. thesis and her Ph.D. dissertation, never challenged the racialism of the Progressive Era. She contended that the urban villagers' designation as Russian displayed the "ignorance, prejudice and misunderstanding" of most Lincolnites. Rather than being the "lowest type of labor" or the "most hopeless political factor in the city," these people were indeed Germans, she argued, and worthy of respect. Ironically, they went from being Russian to German in popular sentiment just in time for continued harassment during World War I.[223]

Between the wars, the urban villagers remained in their two institutionally complete neighborhoods and provided the muscle and know-how to keep the city clean and connected to the outside world. In addition, community founders produced the next generation, whose adaptation into the mainstream was increasingly thorough. After World War II, many Volga Germans continued to frequent the Amens' store, which remained "a pivotal place" for the "hard-working, industrious ethnic community it served."[224] Others—especially younger people—moved out of the Bottoms and scattered throughout the Lincoln metropolitan area. The ways of the immigrant community were not lost altogether, however. Ralph Giebelhaus, for instance, remained active in America Forward, a South Bottoms patriots' organization, during the 1950s and 1960s. Still connected to his roots in the 1970s, he became an officer in AHSGR.[225]

He was joined in that organization by Ruth Amen—daughter of Barbara and Henry. Born in 1910 in the old family home on F Street, she saw her relatives define themselves alternately as *Frankers*, *Volgers*, and *Wolga Deutsch* before starting her education as a music teacher. While her career took her to the public school system in Monroe, Michigan; the Camp Fire Girls national headquarters in New York City; and the University of Northern Colorado in Greeley, she never lost touch with home. When Amen returned to Lincoln in 1968 to supervise teacher training at Nebraska Wesleyan University, however, she witnessed a marked decline in the old neighborhood. Many residents—including her parents—had even left Ebenezer Church and were attending services at First Plymouth Congregational Church, a mainstream congregation in the prestigious Mount Emerald neighborhood. While her father, who died in 1975, was never embarrassed by his heritage, the era of separation had passed, and urban villagers had largely integrated into life in greater Lincoln. Pride in their ancestry was merely dormant during this era, and the Amens soon championed the Germans-from-Russia identity. Although the effort extended beyond the family, the Amens helped make Lincoln the international headquarters of the AHSGR in 1971, served as its officers into the 1980s, and even donated the property where the present museum sits. When Ruth Amen died in January 2002, the new identity was strong enough among its members in Lincoln to include particular affiliations to regions and villages without challenging the Germans-from-Russia ascription.[226]

This organization championed a new and inclusive identity that celebrated the immigrant generation as community builders. Its local museum and headquarters—rather than locally owned businesses—serve as a community center for Lincoln's Germans from Russia. This new identity, while clearly a regeneration of ethnicity, never signified "a return to 'authentic' old world cultures."[227] Instead it is the current incarnation of a series of flexible identities that have served to define an ethnic population for 130 years.

## Chapter 3
# From the Big Village to the Urban Village
Omahas in Lincoln

Already in the prime of their lives, Charles D. and Elizabeth Saunsoci Stabler migrated from Omaha Nation—*Umóⁿhoⁿ móⁿzhoⁿ thóⁿ*—to Lincoln, Nebraska, in 1941. Accepting a recruiter's offer to work on the Burlington Railroad during World War II, they remained in the Capital City throughout the postwar era to take advantage of mainstream economic and educational opportunities. Never a glamorous proposition, the entire family labored seasonally in the sugar beet and potato fields of western Nebraska until 1954, and Charles took construction jobs the remainder of the year. Part of a very small founding generation of Omaha urban villagers in Lincoln—they knew only four other Indian families in the early years—the Stablers actively taught Omaha language and culture to a younger generation who lived in distinct, but dispersed enclaves. Parents of six, grandparents of twenty-nine, and great-grandparents of many more, they imported the "Omaha Way" into a new milieu and helped maintain it by hosting and participating in local dances, pow-wows, and various other Omaha "doings."[1]

Not strangers to close living quarters, the Stablers' relatives—all Omahas address each other as "relatives"—historically congregated with other Omahas in large villages of up to a thousand residents for large portions of the year. While this practice ended with American colonization, Omaha oral history recounts this form of urban living as well as visits to the salt basin that surrounds present-day Lincoln. Despite this familiarity, the Lincoln area became a foreign environment after Omahas negotiated the boundaries of their present reservation in 1854. The journey from Omaha Nation back into the salt basin took about one hundred years. Those who moved into Lincoln beginning in the mid-twentieth century necessarily entered "an alien culture of the white American mainstream." As former tribal chair Rudi Mitchell suggested, "In no way did the American urban life develop out of the aboriginal people of the midwestern plains tribes."[2]

Ironically, although "this country was their native home," their experiences learning to live in cities were comparable to immigrants from outside the United States. While they were U.S. citizens eventually entitled to free movement, Omahas arrived from a separate state—albeit a "domestic dependent nation"[3]—and they faced "racism, social discrimination, fear, cultural alienation," and the threat of the "loss of their native identity," just as Volga Germans had and Vietnamese would.[4] In many respects, identity issues superseded all other intellectual considerations among most urban Indian populations.[5] Although long familiar with American culture, citizens of Omaha Nation were in the majority on their reservation, and patterns of life proceeded in a distinctly Native fashion. Once in Lincoln, Omahas constructed ethnic enclaves and began adapting to a new and strange milieu where they were the minority. These urban villagers juggled particular, cosmopolitan, and transnational forces in the search for a stable identity within the city.

A very salient Omaha identity was supported by a particular cultural ideal called the "Omaha Way." This time-honored concept was central to community construction among Lincoln's indigenous urban villagers. Essentially a pattern of respectful behaviors handed down across generations, the Omaha Way was continually taught and reinforced by all members of the tribe long before migration into the Capital City. Never stagnant, it evolved from ancient woodlands origins, found a home on the Great Plains, and rambled through linearly organized mainstream society amazingly intact.[6]

Part of a shared indigenous circular philosophy, the Omaha Way sought "cultural balance"—balance between sky and earth elements of Omaha cosmology and balance between Native and mainstream worlds.[7] Intrinsically flexible, the Omaha identity was legally redefined by cosmopolitan forces throughout the twentieth century and appears to have been reconstructed to include urban dwellers. Additionally, the Omaha Way—despite encounters with racism—incorporated an "American" identity that was negotiated through contact with the U.S. military.

Omahas—urban villagers and nationals alike—were part of a transnational population that held dual citizenship in both sending and receiving cultures.[8] Because the hundred-mile distance between Macy and Lincoln was comparatively manageable, Omaha identity in the Capital City was constantly reinforced by contact with the Omaha Nation.[9] Part of a two-way exchange, mainstream influences exported by urban villagers also modified behaviors in the sending culture. While distinctions between the populations were often blurred, divisions still developed as nationals maintained that urban villagers modified the Omaha Way in accordance with mainstream preferences. Additionally, a "Pan-Indian" identity was a recognized part of urban Indian life beginning in the 1950s. While the urban villagers were sensitive to this identity, tribalism and the Omaha Way were never subsumed by this ascription.

Omaha Nation's status as a state within a state dictated a 150-year history of intense mainstream influence on the Omaha Way when emigration began. Consequently, particular and cosmopolitan forces often overlapped, but no influence was great enough to allow assimilation. Reflecting mainstream traditions, most Nebraskans throughout the nineteenth and twentieth centuries held the idea that Indian cultures would eventually be engulfed and replaced by "civilized" Euro-American ones.[10] Conversely, Nebraska's original inhabitants maintained that the Omaha Way was "far more sophisticated than any other culture" in defining "how a human being should live."[11] Still, the Omaha Way was never monolithic, and every Omaha in Lincoln on an individual basis experienced confrontations involving Indian and mainstream identities.[12]

## Community

The Omahas' presence in Lincoln was significant because it represented the majority of the Indian population in the city, and because it was a substantial portion of total Omaha enrollment. Although Native Americans made up 1 percent of the U.S. population and similar numbers within Lincoln, they constructed vibrant urban communities.[13] Not surprisingly, Omahas preferred to live among other tribal members, and reasonably distinct Omaha urban villages developed in the city as early as 1950.[14] Because populations were never large enough to allow neighborhood homogeneity, and inter-city movement was necessary as home ownership was uncommon, these "tribal communities" tended to be clusters of extended kinspeople.[15] Dispersed groupings reminded urban villagers of age-old, comfortable living patterns and served as the Omahas' day-to-day link to traditional cultures.[16]

Community-based organizations developed to facilitate interaction and provide social services to the urban villagers, and ultimately the Lincoln Indian Center emerged as the primary anchor of a growing community.

### Demography

Lincoln's urban villages formed and prospered in an era of general population recovery among Indians across the continent and among Omahas specifically. Never a large nation, historic numbers—probably about three thousand individuals—were decimated by disease and economic turmoil in the nineteenth century. Once confined to their modern political boundaries, populations grew slowly, increasing from approximately twelve hundred in 1886 to fourteen hundred by 1924.[17] By 1966, Omaha numbers approached twenty-six hundred and then grew to four thousand in 1992, fifty-six hundred in 2000, and approximately six thousand in 2005.[18]

Omahas were part of a postwar trend that saw rapid urbanization of indigenous populations. A mere 7 percent of Native Americans lived in mainstream cities in 1940. This percentage doubled by 1950, and redoubled by 1960. The growth recorded in 1960—and in subsequent years—was partly attributed to changes within the Census Department; race became self-reported rather than determined by the enumerator.[19] Still, between 1970 and 1990, the Native population teetered around 50 percent, and by 2005, 66 percent of "Indian people lived dispersed throughout cities."[20] Similar developments were seen in Nebraska. (See Table 3-1.)

In Lincoln, Indian population statistics showed consistent increases during the same time periods. Omahas always constituted the majority of Lincoln's Native population, although to mainstream residents they were likely not distinguishable from other Indian groups. The best available information placed them at 85 percent of the city's total Indian population in 1970.[21] Assuming the Omaha majority remained reasonably constant, the permanent Omaha population in Lincoln could easily have been over one thousand in 2000.

Despite the mobility necessitated by a renting population, urban Omaha communities were remarkably stable and their residences generally long-term. By 1956, 105 Omahas from thirty-three families clustered in the west end of the South Russian Bottoms. These early arrivals included Charles and

Table 3-1. Estimated American Indian Populations in Lincoln, Nebraska, and the United States, 1930–2000

|      | Lincoln | Nebraska | Nebraska Urban | United States |
|------|---------|----------|----------------|---------------|
| 1930 | 5       | 3,256    | NA             | 362,000       |
| 1940 | 2       | 3,401    | NA             | 370,000       |
| 1950 | 75      | 3,954    | 1,003          | 377,000       |
| 1960 | 360     | 5,545    | 1,971          | 523,000       |
| 1970 | 530     | 6,624    | 3,013          | 827,000       |
| 1980 | 920     | 9,145    | 4,718          | 1,418,000     |
| 1990 | 1,300   | 12,410   | 6,732          | 2,045,000     |
| 2000 | 1,600   | 14,896   | 9,700          | 2,476,000     |

Sources: U.S. Census; Onyema G. Nkwocha, *Health Status of Racial and Ethnic Minorities in Nebraska* (Lincoln: Nebraska Department of Health and Human Services, 2003); William N. Thompson, *Native American Issues: A Reference Book* (Santa Barbara, CA: ABC-CLIO, 1996), 162.

Elizabeth Stabler, Clyde and Lillian Sheridan, Frank and Evelyn Sheridan, Oliver Saunsoci, Sr., Shirley Cayou, and William and Alberta Canby. Although the housing vacated by Volga Germans was probably affordable, the urban villagers soon moved north and east, and by the early 1960s they reclustered in the Near South and Malone neighborhoods.[22] By the early 1970s the Clinton, Hartley, and Malone neighborhoods hosted growing Omaha populations whose enclaves were "composed of . . . small, stable" family groupings that had been in the community ten years or longer.[23] (See Map 3-1.) Many former South Russian Bottoms residents—including extended members of the Canby, Sheridan, and Stabler families—ended up in the Clinton-Malone-Hartley complex.[24]

Growth throughout the 1970s and 1980s favored town quadrants adjacent to the Lincoln Indian Center. By 1990 the largest Omaha concentrations remained in the three core neighborhoods, although "Indians" were identified in virtually every census tract in town. Over the next decade, Native populations generally increased in these same tracts, and in the Near South neighborhood.[25] A block-by-block city schematic demonstrates marked tenden-

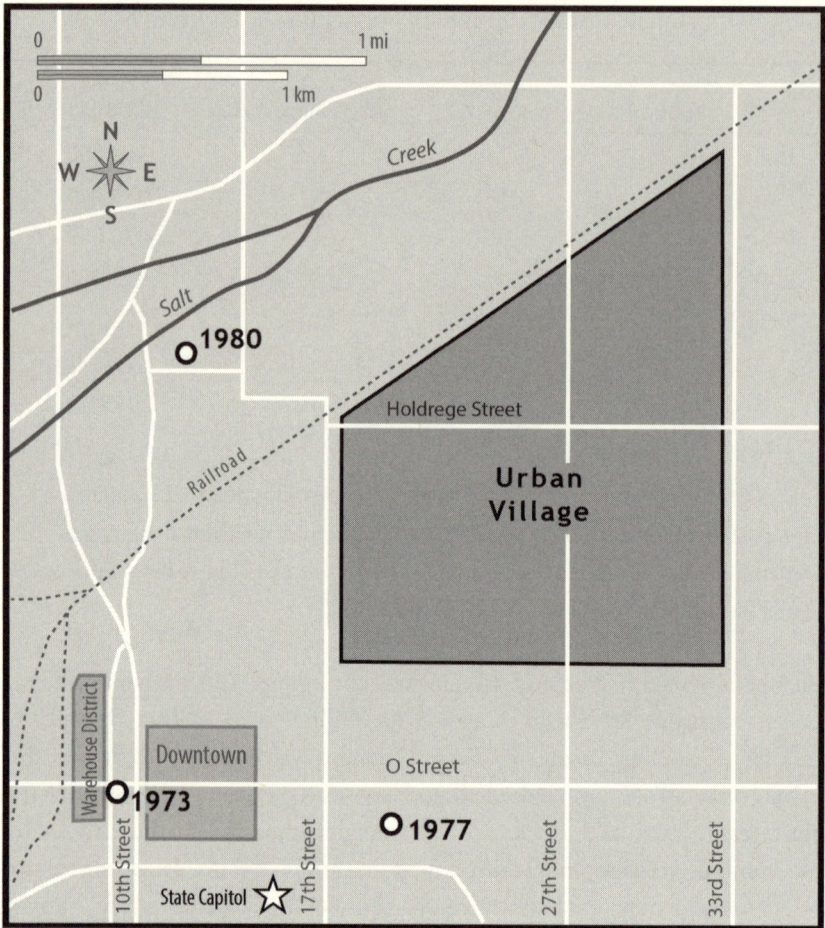

Map 3-1: Map of Core Omaha Urban Village in Lincoln, Nebraska. Permission granted by Ezra Zeitler.

cies for Omahas and other Indians to congregate in tight clusters within each referenced neighborhood.[26]

In general, long-term residency was hampered by low levels of home ownership among Omaha urban villagers. Of 246 core neighborhood units that housed 676 individuals in 2000, just twenty-nine structures—or about 12 percent—were owner-occupied.[27] These percentages were presumably much lower during the Omahas' early years in Lincoln. City directories suggest that residents who had been in town since the 1950s—including William and Alberta Canby, Shirley Cayou, Lorenzo and Eva Stabler, and Bernard and Loraine Vance—began buying homes in the early 1990s, but rarely before.

### Community Centers

In addition to congregating next to family and friends, Omaha urban villagers formed community-based social organizations that allowed them to stress Omaha identities. They partly duplicated patterns at Omaha Nation, which was home to fourteen community-based groups in the late 1950s.[28] The Roofers' Union and various veterans' organizations served as center points among Omaha men in the early years. More inclusively, the Lincoln Indian Club was established in 1952 by the few Indian families that lived in the Capital City as "an inter-tribal organization." They dedicated themselves to "sponsoring traditional gatherings including handgames, dances and meals."[29] The club boasted 250 mostly Omaha members by 1970. They remained active and largely Omaha in the twenty-first century and hosted six events—culminating with the Annual Indian Club Pow-Wow—in 2006.[30]

Organizations that focused on social activities did not meet all of the urban villagers' needs, however. The stress of relocation and the relative poverty of urban Omahas forced many to congregate in and around the City Mission and the Salvation Army—both located downtown—during the first three decades of residence in Lincoln.[31] While they were able to access social services from these institutions, they were necessarily confronting mainstream processes that may not have understood Indian worldviews.

Serving as an anchor for the Omaha community, the Lincoln Indian Center was incorporated in May 1969 and in full operation by 1971.[32] Its nine purposes were

1. To establish a continuing program which will help the American Indian help himself.

2. To help the American Indian adapt to urban life.

3. To make the American Indian aware of the available services in education, employment, housing, hospitalization, alcohol treatment and rehabilitation, credit union financing and membership.

4. To organize and create arts and crafts industries and develop job opportunities through the center.

5. To help in any way possible the American Indian both on and off the reservation.

6. To combat juvenile delinquency among American Indians.

7. To encourage sports programs among American Indians such as, but not limited to, baseball, football, track, and boxing.

8. To help eliminate prejudice and discrimination.

9. To defend human rights of the American Indian, guaranteed by law.[33]

Members of its board of directors were required to be Native, but the organization was open to all. Initially funded by mainstream religious organizations, full Indian control was assured by the passage of the Native American Programs Act in 1974. Consequently, the city of Lincoln added funding for other essential services, such as the Special Supplemental Nutrition Program for Women, Infants, and Children (WIC) and substance abuse programs, administered by Indians for Indians.[34]

Like individuals within the Omaha community, the Indian Center had several homes before it moved into its permanent facilities. Originally housed at Ninth and O Streets in a downtown storefront, the growing population required additional space. The search for a new home proved problematic. Forced into temporary quarters at 243 South Twentieth Street, the Lincoln City Council approved a nearby site at Twenty-Fourth and N made vacant by the destruction of an aging municipal swimming facility in 1977. There was great mainstream concern in the Antelope Park district that "Indians in the area have had a negative impact on the neighborhood and the center would increase this impact," and these plans were abandoned.[35] The present site for the center weathered similar criticisms, but as the North Russian Bottoms was already largely rental property, approval was imminent. Blessed by Charles Stabler—who was also a Road Man in the Native American Church—the new Lincoln Indian Center opened at 1100 Military Road in April 1980.[36]

In all of its locations, the center was always conceived as "a place that Indians could come to for their needs such as employment, food, health services or just to be around other Indians."[37] It soon hosted most of the community gatherings in the area, including handgames (described later in this chapter), pow-wows, various dances, and funerals. These events allowed Omahas to stay connected to the Omaha Way. Sometimes mired in inertia, other times dominated by vitality and hope, the Lincoln Indian Center was poised to continue championing Native issues in the twenty-first century. Wanting to get the center "on the front lines" of community development, Clyde Tyndall (Omaha) assumed the directorship in May 2005.[38] With a history in tribal government and economic development, he hoped to "expand the Indian Center's role as a viable human service agency" while refashioning its programs to become engines for economic development.[39]

Using the Indian Center as a base for most of their tenure in Lincoln, Omaha urban villagers built small but stable enclaves within mainstream neighborhoods. The success of early arrivals encouraged others to follow, and a burgeoning population gathered in the Capital City. While many enrolled Omahas moved to Lincoln, they maintained many of their traditional values in their urban villages.[40] Specifically, they constructed identities that focused on "cohesion in both the extended family and a strong emphasis on generosity and reciprocity."[41]

**Particularism: The Omaha Way**

Omaha identity was negotiated in Native space even before the nation migrated into Nebraska. *Umóⁿhoⁿ* literally means "upstream people" or "against the current," and the name was formed in response to separation from the Quapaws—"downstream people"—at the confluence of the Mississippi and Ohio Rivers. Together with their other cognate nations, the Osages, Kansas, and Poncas, they were part of the *Dhegíha* group of Siouan people who, according to stories of origins, were once a unified entity that lived either in the upper Ohio River valley or near the Great Lakes.[42] Their reasons for migrating have not survived, but it appears that Osages and Kansas went their own ways at the junction of the Missouri and the Mississippi Rivers, and Poncas were still with Omahas as they entered Nebraska sometime early in the eighteenth century.[43]

Deeply concerned with "relationships and community" that extended beyond human beings, Omaha identity was entrenched in the living Nebraska landscape long before the arrival of mainstream America.[44] Circular notions of time and space remain central in the Omaha cosmos. Although vexing to the colonial worldview, in "Indian time" the circumstances and essence of events matter far more than the chronology of happenings.[45] Augmenting this ever-expanding historical reservoir, adherence to distinctly Omaha social structures, connections to place, and the development of performed cultures—religion, music and dance, and language—had deep-seated and ancient meaning to modern Omahas. Always adaptable, Omahas learned to live on the Great Plains and then amid American culture. Cultural practices evolved continuously, and the mainstream was often used to "enrich" Native heritage.[46] Consequently, the majority of twentieth-century Omaha behaviors imported into Lincoln's urban villages were somewhere between traditional and mainstream ways.

### Social Structures

Omahas—urban villagers and nationals alike—survived historically "as communities of relations."[47] Kinship systems remained central to maintaining the Omaha Way in mainstream cities. Despite the disruption of ancient traditions, a working knowledge of clan and interpersonal relationships was imported into Lincoln by the urban village's founding generation, and much of this knowledge remained intact in the early twenty-first century.[48]

Family and clan status descended from an era of intense centripetal force that bound Omahas together when they established their nation in Nebraska. Complex relationships were established through blood, marriage, ceremony, ancient custom, and proximity in the tribal circle—the *húthuga*. Part of a gendered world, Omaha Nation consisted of five clans from the feminine earth moiety—*Wézhi$^n$shte* (elk), *I$^n$késabe* (black shoulder of the buffalo), *Hó$^n$ga* (leaders), *Thátada* (to the left of the leaders), and *Kó$^n$ze* (Kansa)—and five more from the masculine sky moiety—*Mó$^n$thi$^n$kagaxe* (earth maker), *Tesí$^n$de* (buffalo tail), *Tapá* (head of the deer), *I$^n$gthézhide* (red buffalo calf dung), and *I$^n$shtáthu$^n$da* (flashing eyes or lightning). Each clan had specific ceremonial responsibilities that produced such interdependence that permanent tribal division became increasingly unlikely.[49] Additionally, a mixed-blood clan—originally formed to accommodate the children of French men and Omaha women—emerged in the late eighteenth century.[50] Because the clans were elaborately interconnected, deep knowledge of their full traditions was fading by the 1970s as the last bilingual generation passed. Nonetheless, "public and private use of correct kin terms" kept clan status and knowledge of extended family relationships alive in the twenty-first century.[51]

Gender patterns common in urban villages were also imported from Omaha Nation and have deep roots in antiquity. Just as the *húthuga* had separate male and female halves, men and women were assigned separate tasks in the creation story.[52] Contributions to the community were based on gender division, but the value assigned the tasks was inherently equal. Women historically made the day-to-day decisions in their homes, prepared meals, protected traditions and religious items, gardened, and raised children. Men concentrated on hunting, raiding, and military protection. In the modern mainstream society, these tasks were replaced by earning livings as construction laborers, roofers, drivers, factory and warehouse workers, and mechanics. Women, when in the job market, were often employed as hairdressers and laundresses.[53]

Also based on values imported from Omaha Nation, Omaha urban villagers maintained great respect for their elders and for the overall health of their communities. The most able served their relatives by working at children's homes, as community organizers, and in positions at the Lincoln Indian Center. In these situations, however, younger urban villagers took on leadership roles formerly reserved for elders.[54] While situations sometimes changed, respect for the wisdom of age generally did not. Elders, especially women, continued to play important roles as "agents of cultural survival."[55] Additionally, the salience of Omaha identity often increased as individuals matured. Those experimenting with mainstream spirituality came back to the Native religious practices, for instance, and many who denied their heritage as youth began examining Omaha identity and celebrating the Omaha Way.[56]

### Place

Omahas were "deeply rooted in the soil of Nebraska" by the eighteenth century and remained so into the twenty-first.[57] Once on the Great Plains, they claimed a territory from the Platte to the Niobrara and from the Missouri to the headwaters of the Elkhorn. From this 35.6-million-acre area, they traveled for food and trade as far east as the Mississippi River, as far south as the Kansas River, and as far west as the Rocky Mountains. (See Map 3-3.) They established "Big Village," their most famous residence, around 1775 on a creek just north of modern Omaha Nation. Omaha Creek's floodplain was lined with cottonwoods and willows, a convenient source of fuel and mate-

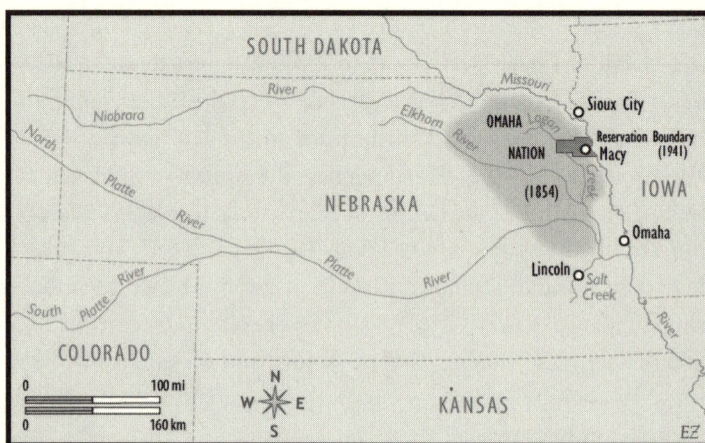

Map 3-3: Map of Omaha Nation and Surrounding Areas. Permission granted by Ezra Zeitler.

rials for construction of earth and timber lodges. The plain also contained fertile soil, and the Omahas boasted a 483-acre garden. Here, women cultivated "mother" corn, beans, melon, and squash in "grandmother" earth.[58]

Big Village was the center of an economic cycle known as the "Omaha Round" until the tribe moved one hundred miles down the Missouri River to escape epidemics and Sicangu Lakota raids. Corn was planted in May when the village was full. After tending the crop until June or July, the entire nation—save the infirm and a handful of guardians—swapped tipis for earth lodges and left for the summer buffalo hunt. The hunt was necessary for meat and social well-being, as the tribe's most important rituals were performed away from their "permanent" home. They returned to the village in time for a September harvest and rested through October. November and December were spent in small bands hunting deer and fowl in the river bottoms. The tribe reassembled in January and hunted buffalo again through March. In April they returned to Big Village to start the cycle anew.[59]

Intense bonds to their lands encouraged a tradition of skillful diplomacy that ultimately protected a small portion of their territory from an expanding United States. As celebrated on the modern Omaha Nation flag—a modern device with an ancient history—a "Heritage for Peace" with the United States began with a treaty of friendship in 1815.[60] To satiate U.S. demands for space, Omaha diplomats ceded claims to lands east of the Missouri River

in 1830 and 1836. Omaha diplomatic ability was employed in 1854 when
the creation of Nebraska Territory required further land cessions. Demanding the privilege of choosing a suitable site in a small corner of their old
domain, Omaha Nation removed to a 302,800-acre tract (an area approximately thirty miles by forty-five miles) in the Blackbird Hills of northeastern
Nebraska.[61] Situated just miles south of Big Village, they continued to live
in villages while successfully adapting American farming techniques to fit
into an economy that still favored communalism.[62] The Omaha Way, however, was disparaged by the federal government, which was determined to
deal with all "Indians from a position of dominance."[63] Consequently, land
loss was unavoidable, and Omahas were enticed into ceding the northern
portion of their reservation to displaced Winnebagos in 1865.[64] The same
treaty included provisions for allotment of communal land to individuals.
This process was implemented in 1871 and then again in 1883. Although
unpopular, allotment was seen as a method of maintaining residence in their
beloved territory.[65]

Prior to allotment, tribal particularism focused briefly on conflicts stem-
ming from adaptation to the new mainstream, and Omahas reorganized
themselves into three distinct villages. Living just north of Decatur, Nebraska, "woodeaters" were individuals who chose to enter the American economy by chopping and selling wood to steamboat companies. Residing next to
the Presbyterian mission, "Make-Believe-White Men" were a "progressive"
group wishing to advance their nation by including some American ways.
Finally, a traditionalist group—"those who dwell in earth lodges"—congregated just south of present-day Macy.[66] The underlying causes of these
divisions were largely resolved by 1883, and allotees generally chose lands
adjacent to people from their own clans. Ultimately, 1,194 individuals were
allotted 75,931 acres, and another 55,000 acres were reserved for the nation. About 25 percent of the personal parcels were located along Logan
Creek in the western portion of the Omaha Nation. Dominated by members
of *I<sup>n</sup>késabe*, *Thátada*, and *Tapá* clans, this sector appears to be the cultural
hearth of the generation that founded Lincoln's urban villages.[67]

Clan and family solidarity may have been rekindled by allotment, but village structure and self-sufficiency were interrupted by an American impulse
to assimilate Indians. The end result was dispossession and poverty, as "surplus" lands were sold to land-hungry Americans. Consequently, Thurston

County—initially comprising entirely Indian territory—was created by the Nebraska State Legislature on March 29, 1889. Arguing that Omahas used county services, they were illegally taxed by county officials. The need to pay these levies and a general unfamiliarity with commercial farming encouraged Omahas to lease land to mainstream farmers. When Omahas received clear title on their allotments under the Burke Act in 1906, the last vestiges of land protection were eliminated, and land-loss became endemic. By 1912, 90 percent of the land described in the earliest fee patents was in the hands of Euro-Americans. By the end of World War II, Omahas owned a mere 10 percent of their original reservation, and three-quarters were landless.[68]

While land holdings would begin to increase again in the 1950s, this nation of less than thirty thousand acres housed the sending culture for migration into urban America. Despite catastrophic losses, all Omahas remained tied to their land. Twentieth-century tribal leaders even suggested that "if every inch of their Omaha land was gone, these poor people would stay where it used to be and the ones who went to the cities would keep coming back to where it used to be."[69] Similarly, at the dawn of the twenty-first century, Tribal Council member Barry Webster still connected Omaha identity to a land base around the nation.[70] Alive with spiritual meaning and filled with ancestral graves, the land was indeed "precious" to Omahas.[71]

### Religion

In addition to an intense connection to the land, a shared sense of spirituality was central to Omaha identity. As Eunice Stabler noted, Omahas recognized no separation of church and state, and social structures, individual lives, and government "were founded upon religion."[72] Their doctrines proved remarkably adaptable as belief structures were fundamentally altered after 1854. Spirituality, however, remained central to community life, and religious forms stayed connected to Great Plains traditions. Ultimately, the Omaha Way survived in urban America as a series of ceremonies and prayers.[73]

The Omaha creation story records that in the "beginning all things were in the mind of *Wakóⁿda*." For a time, all creatures were "spirits," but people wanted a home. They tried living on the sun and then the moon but were dissatisfied. Descending from the sky, Omahas came to the earth to live in water before finally emerging onto land where they were given food, fire, and clothing. *Wakó"da*—the Omaha Creator—was seen as a "mysterious life power permeating all natural forms and forces and all phases of man's conscious life." All things owned and practiced by Omahas were gifts from this Creator.[74]

The gift most central to Omahas was *Umó"ho"xtí*—known in English as the "Real Omaha," the "Venerable Man," or simply the Sacred Pole. Considered a living being, this icon probably dates from the sixteenth century. It is a two-and-a-half-meter-long cottonwood branch cut from a tree that burned at night without being consumed by flames. Wrapped in hide and wearing a scalplock, the Sacred Pole was the center of the most significant religious ceremonies until the late nineteenth century. He represented "a common yet moveable center shared by all" Omahas whose cohesion depended on communal living patterns.[75]

Because religious practices were so intimately connected to a social and economic system that traveled across the Great Plains, life on the reservation strained maintenance of traditional beliefs. Finally, as buffalo hunting was discontinued after 1876, the annual renewal ceremony—which required that the Sacred Pole be anointed in bison blood—lapsed. Several generations later, mainstream observers described the Omaha Way as a "broken culture" because many rituals and behaviors had been abandoned or replaced.[76]

The underlying spirituality of the Omaha people, however, was already transferred to twentieth-century religions. Christianity, as Eunice Stabler averred, brought them "new doctrines of faith, and all its teachings" gave Omahas "hope for a future."[77] While contact with mainstream missionaries created practicing Mormons, Dutch Reformed Christians, Methodists, and Presbyterians, the most influential denomination was the Native American Church (NAC). Its rituals allowed Omahas to celebrate the creative power of *Wakó"da* in a modern adaptation.[78]

Cofounded in 1906 by Quannah Parker (Comanche), the NAC tailored Christian doctrine to fit the spiritual traditions of Plains peoples.[79] While the church employed familiar ceremonial items such as sage, cedar, and eagle feathers, its rituals centered around peyote, which was ingested as a sacrament. The "mild hallucinatory state" it produced allowed Indians to "reconnect to their spiritual traditions."[80] Worshippers attended meetings that began Saturday evening and ran until noon on Sunday. Sitting around a hearth in a specially arranged tipi, they drank peyote tea and sang and prayed to the rhythm of a handheld drum. While the rituals were often new in form, many prayers had deep traditions.[81] Depending on their religious leanings, participants reportedly saw the faces of "Jesus" or their "relatives."[82]

The "Peyote Road" was given to the Omaha Nation during the winter of 1906–7 by Otoes visiting from Oklahoma.[83] Immediately seen as "a good culture way," the remnant forms of older religions were replaced rapidly.[84] An estimated 50 percent of the tribe adopted the religion by 1911. By the 1930s the NAC was the most vital denomination among Omahas, and by the 1950s an estimated 90 percent of the nation's residents adhered to its doctrines. Observers reported that Omaha Tribal Council members were often active in the NAC in the 1950s and 1960s.[85] Surprisingly tolerant, the state of Nebraska never wholeheartedly prosecuted peyotism and in 1921 formally recognized the NAC.[86] Protected across the United States by the American Indian Religious Freedom Act (1978), NAC boasted two hundred thousand members nationally at the close of the twentieth century.[87] By 1975, about 45 percent of Lincoln's urban villagers reported they attended NAC meetings on a regular basis.[88]

NAC and Protestant denominations tended to have overlapping memberships, as exclusivity was not an inherent Omaha religious trait.[89] The Lincoln Indian Community Church—an "interdenominational and inter-tribal" organization—demonstrated the flexibility of Omaha spirituality. Sponsored by seven churches, its stated mission is to "respect, affirm and integrate the spiritual values of the American Indian people" with "the essentials of the Christian Faith." Omaha urban villagers and their families attended services weekly at the organization's offices in the Lincoln Indian Center.[90]

### "Doings": The Importance of Music and Dance

The most cogent events that reinforced the Omaha Way among Lincoln's urban villagers were community "doings." Participation in handgames, Gourd Dances, and pow-wows fostered "an inner world of continuity, where old clan ties, communal values, and traditional beliefs and meanings" were reaffirmed.[91] In addition to allowing the Indian minority a place and time to function as the majority, events also gave participants opportunities to practice the time-honored values of generosity and reciprocity.[92] These concepts were so central to the Omaha Way that there were many words for "thank you" in the Omaha language but no word for "please," as giving was an honor and a duty.[93] Besides redistributing wealth to those most needing it, gift reciprocity allowed urban villagers to "sacrifice" for the good of the community. Although designed for social enjoyment, doings were the vehicles of sacrifice and the prime methods of exposing children to proper Omaha behaviors.[94]

Handgame was an important form of recreation imported into the urban village.[95] More popular in Lincoln than at Omaha Nation, community members generally attended multiple events annually in the 1970s, and interest remained high over the next three decades.[96] Held in honor of specific occasions or individuals, those in attendance socialized, feasted, danced, and made monetary offerings to the event and their community.[97]

Rife with complicated meanings and ritualistic components, handgame was simple to play and designed for participants of all ages. Two players at a time hid stones in their hands. A feather carrier was assigned to guess which hands the stones were in. Score was kept according to the success of the stone hiders.[98] When the game was on, the singers sitting around the drum at the center of the arena warbled. The music stopped when the feather carrier correctly identified both stones and play changed sides. The competition to win four of seven sets was established by geography; those sitting on the east side of the circle played against those on the west. As the stones circulated clockwise around the room, all interested community members and other attendees were offered a chance to hide the stones.[99]

At the end of each set, two individuals on the losing side received rattles from the headman and led a dance clockwise around the drum. The rattle carriers' families and friends showed their affiliations by offering a sacrifice—usually a dollar or two by the twenty-first century—and falling into step behind them.[100] After the rattles were collected, round dances based on a simple but elegant sliding step ensued. Additionally, singers often performed proprietary songs as further reinforcement of kinship ties. These tunes were sung with the expectation that all family or clan members present would enter the dance arena.

As demonstrated by handgame, music, dance, and community were all intricately connected within the Omaha Way. In the nineteenth century, dances were divided into three categories: the sacred, those connected with bravery and war, and those for social pleasure.[101] While sacred dances were less common in the post–World War II era, the other two classes demonstrated cultural borrowing and changing traditions inherent in modern Omaha life.

Some "war dance" events and their hosting organizations had long connections to Omaha history. The *Hethúshka* society, for instance, was active from at least the time the tribe founded the Big Village to the late nineteenth century when it was in full decline.[102] The dance style it developed, however, remained well known, and the society was eventually revived by veterans of the U.S. Armed Forces in order to maintain memories of historic and heroic activities.[103] These warriors were honored by the American Folklife Center in 1985 and went to Washington, DC, to receive copies of an album of Omaha songs originally recorded on wax cylinders in the 1890s.[104]

However, Lincoln's urban villagers were more apt to participate in the Gourd Dance and be members of the accompanying Tiah Piah. Commonly performed by Omaha veterans, this war dance and its host society were gifts from the Kiowa Nation in 1970.[105] Dressed either in military fatigues or an ensemble consisting of a blue and red blanket, a feather fan, and a ceremonial belt, the men sounded "gourd" rattles and danced clockwise around the drum.[106] Modeling traditional gender behaviors, women, even those who served in the armed forces, danced in place on the outside edge of the arena.

The *Hethúshka* and Tiah Piah societies of the twentieth and twenty-first centuries recalled intricate patterns of behavior and social organization of bygone days. While the war dance formerly required giving away horses and goods, the urban villagers continued gifting blankets and other items and feeding all the guests. Similarly, pow-wows were a reassertion of an ancient ceremony known as *Hédewachi*—the festival of joy.[107] Noted by Lewis and Clark, modern organizers trace the event from 1804. Cherished by all Omahas, gifting and feasting behaviors remained vital in annual pow-wows held at the Lincoln Indian Center since 1976 and at Omaha Nation.

Pow-wows were actually "a contemporary form with a historical past."[108] Still driven by the "heartbeat of Mother Earth," participants dance to the drum as they have for millennia and still give thanks for the accomplishments and successes of the previous year. Pow-wow still meant "going home," as Omahas formerly returned from their summer buffalo hunt in August and presently regroup both in Lincoln and in Macy during that month as well.[109] The modern pow-wow, however, was largely a secular, Pan-Indian event that emerged when "religious dances" were suppressed or driven underground by BIA policies between 1889 and 1934. The few surviving dance forms revitalized during the 1950s were frequently performed out of context, as "fancy" contest dance styles became the norm. Athletic and beautiful, the *Hethúshka* set new standards for pow-wow dancing as it spread across the Northern Plains by World War I, and then across the Southern Plains after World War II.[110] By the mid-1950s, "Non-Indian concepts of competition and prize money had become increasingly important, ushering in the age of professional dancers who traveled a national circuit."[111]

Traveling from pow-wow to pow-wow, multiple dance categories were available for both men and women. Some dancers performed traditional figures, while others preferred modern styles that include powerful kinetic movement and juried competition. Significantly, women's roles at pow-wows have increased steadily since World War I. Active in planning and participating in modern events, they no longer danced around the edge of the arenas. In events like jingle dress dancing and the shawl dance, women took center stage.[112]

All dancers donned "regalia" to individualize their expressions while honoring family, personal, and tribal traditions. Regalia decoration included many traditional elements—eagle staffs, feather bustles, buckskin, and bear claws—as well as modern influences—American flags, military unit insignias, and snuff can lids. Part of a living culture, the symbolism portrayed in these adornments were powerful indications of the synthesis between Omaha past and Omaha present.[113]

To traditionalists, the pow-wow atmosphere changed from a celebration of thanksgiving to something akin to a carnival right around the time mass migration from Indian nations to urban areas began. These developments bewildered former Omaha chairman Alfred Gilpin, who was skeptical about the new ambience that permeated spectator behavior, dance styles, and characteristics of modern dance regalia.[114] Even as Omaha Nation marked the 201st anniversary of its fall pow-wow in 2005, urban villagers in Lincoln sought a more traditional and distinctly Omaha experience.

The Lincoln Indian Club pow-wow—held annually since 1976—was unique because it alternated between "traditional" and "contest" formats. Traditional pow-wows were "geared more toward teaching the younger generation to dance and drum."[115] In essence, they reinforced the Omaha Way and allowed participants, as Carrie Wolfe noted, to "go back to roots, back to our history."[116] Part of an age-old protocol, adults at such events asked their relatives in attendance to forgive their children for lack of decorum and urged them to instruct lovingly the novice dancers as they learned how to participate properly.[117] Omaha elder Alberta Canby confirmed this attitude in her role as cultural advisor to the Lincoln Indian Club, averring, "We're here to help the young members learn about powwow tradition."[118]

### Language

Alberta Canby was also active in preserving and teaching the Omaha language—a central component of the Omaha Way. Her efforts, however, merely augmented important cultural concepts that were "increasingly rendered in English language." A century of intense mainstream efforts to obliterate indigenous tongues left its mark on all Omahas. By the twenty-first century, urban villagers heard their language in occasional speeches by community elders and in the songs that permeated most secular and religious gatherings.[119] Many listeners did not understand the words, and despite prevailing attitudes that linked language with cultural retention, fluency in Omaha was increasingly uncommon both in Lincoln and in Omaha Nation.[120]

"Linguistic genocide" was institutionalized by nineteenth-century missionaries and boarding schools, and by the twentieth century, language loss was widespread among Native peoples. At least one-third of indigenous tongues in the United States had one hundred or fewer speakers in 1990. The Omaha language fell victim to gradual atrophy. By 1910 most Omahas had a good grasp of English. Although English as a first language was challenged by the architects of the Indian New Deal of the 1930s, it continued to be unofficial policy as long as the schools remained open, and by World War II the population was largely bilingual. Movement into cities, contact with the mainstream economy, and the influence of popular culture only decreased Omaha language usage.[121] While Omaha Community Council meetings were generally conducted in Omaha in the early 1960s, children of the era already spoke English at home.[122] Language loss was more severe among urban villagers than their national counterparts. Although self-reporting, one-third of nationals claimed Omaha as a first language in 1972, while all respondents in a similar survey in Lincoln reported English as a first language, though many claimed Omaha as a second tongue.[123] Despite language decline, young and old alike—including elder Susan Freemont—bemoaned that "young ones don't speak" Omaha anymore.[124]

Still, Omaha—a tongue that is both musical and "forceful and virile"—

has not been abandoned.[125] Part of the *Dhegíha* Siouan language family, it reflected Indian worldviews that were expressly concerned with the "minutiae of relationships."[126] Typically, Omahas center action rather than actor. Single verbs often stand as complete sentences as object and subject are often contextual. *Uné*, for instance, can mean "she is searching for it." Adding a syllable changes the relationship. *Uáne* can be glossed as "I am searching for it." Complexities in verb conjugation encouraged Omahas to train their children rigorously, allowing no slips "to pass uncorrected."[127] Instruction focused on concise pronunciation to impart a desired communication, as errors in syllable accents could dramatically alter meanings.[128]

By speaking Omaha, urban villagers and Omaha nationals "nurtured relationships with family, friends, and the natural world."[129] Consequently, a great deal of prestige was attached to the Omaha language, and few English words were added to its vocabularies. It remains one of the official languages of Omaha Nation in the early twenty-first century, despite a dearth of speakers.[130] In 1994 it was estimated that only 1 percent of all Omahas spoke their language fluently, and about one-half lived outside of Omaha Nation.[131] Fortunately, Lincoln in the twenty-first century was one locus for a movement to reclaim the language.

Because speaking Omaha "emotes strength," many tribal members "wished to see it carried forward."[132] A few remaining fluent speakers and a number of "hesitant speakers"—mostly who spoke as children—were enlisted to preserve the language.[133] These efforts were supported by most tribe, state, and federal policies, and three institutions of learning.[134] While these efforts may not ensure a return to fluency, some components of an important cultural marker will certainly survive. Elders were bemused by some of these developments; as Suzette Turner declared, "If the government left us alone maybe we could all talk Indian."[135]

Since 1995, strong efforts have been made to revitalize the language. The school system in Macy has been a key player in the movement. Its goals were explicit:

> The Mission of the Umonhon Nation Public School, through positive interaction with the Omaha tribal community, is to provide a student-centered education in a safe and respectful learning environment, allowing our students to strengthen Native American traditions yet flourish in other cultures.[136]

This philosophy was largely made possible by the Self-Determination and Education Assistance Act of 1975, which allowed local control of education and redirection of funds as deemed appropriate. In Macy, this included the acquisition of a full-time Omaha culture and language teacher—Vida Sue Stabler. She conducted her work at all grade levels in consultation with a group of fluent elders. Similarly, the Macy and Sioux City campuses of Nebraska Indian Community College (NICC) offered Omaha language courses under the tutelage of Elizabeth Saunsoci (Omaha) and linguist Ardis Eschenburg—an adopted member of the tribe.[137]

Language instruction also occurred in Lincoln. Elizabeth Stabler conducted language classes at the Lincoln Indian Center in the mid-1970s. Twenty-five years later, her adopted Omaha grandson, Mark Awakuni-Swetland—with the assistance of tribal elders—inaugurated an Omaha language program at the University of Nebraska. While the program has met with mixed approval in Omaha Nation, as many tribal members demanded "complete ownership of the Omaha language," a number of mainstream and Omaha students alike have completed the two-year sequence.[138] Additionally, Emmaline Walker Sanchez (Omaha), an instructor with the university's program, started a community education class in 2004 that proved popular with urban villagers.

The interest these courses generated in recent years has reinforced a traditional respect toward elders, especially those who maintained the old knowledge. The number of fluent speakers, however, continued to decline as virtually all students were learning Omaha as a second language. Many American Indians in Nebraska believe that efforts to restore Native languages will ultimately be successful, but will happen slowly. Organizations such as the NICC seem to be making giant strides, but as executive director of Nebraska Commission of Indian Affairs Judi M. Gaiashkibos noted, since "it took them [mainstream Americans] 100 year[s] to steal our culture one can't expect us to be fluent speakers in one generation."[139]

Unlike the Omaha language, the Omaha Way was retained and nurtured in Lincoln's urban village. Spiritually intense connections to the Nebraska landscape, native religious practices, ancient social structures, and the love of music and dance remained central to urban Omahas between 1940 and 2005. Intriguingly, aspects of performed culture imported into Lincoln were already influenced by mainstream forces, even during the founding generation's journeys back into the old salt basin. Modifications of the Omaha Way continued throughout their sojourn in the Capital City, but the Lincoln population often proved more culturally conservative than their Omaha national relatives.

## Cosmopolitanism

Because Omahas had "such wealth of tradition and culture," they were able to survive the onslaught of "the white man's civilization" for decades in both Omaha Nation and Lincoln's urban villages.[140] Mainstream influences that they confronted during the era of migration fundamentally changed Omaha identities, however. Never abandoning their primary ascription and tribal loyalty, what it meant to be "Omaha" was redefined by cosmopolitan forces that insisted on measuring Indianness through parentage rather than cultural constructions. Ultimately, Omahas internalized blood quantum dictates, although tribal membership criteria remained flexible and continued adapting to new circumstances. Urban villagers, many who moved for economic and educational opportunity, confronted the worlds of work and school in Lincoln with mixed success. In many instances they were reminded by the mainstream that they were Indians, and adaptation in the new milieu was not necessarily easy. Still, Omahas were proud "Americans," although they interpreted this ascription to fit into the Omaha Way.

### Omaha Blood

The very notion of what it meant to be Omaha was influenced by mainstream forces. In Native American culturescapes, identity depended on kinship ties, and individuals belonged first to a family, then to a clan, and then to a nation. Although blood descent may have been desirable, Omahas had mechanisms to adopt outsiders into their fold both as individuals and as groups.[141] The creation of the "half-breed" clan to accommodate children with French fathers demonstrated the flexible nature of the Omaha cosmos. Tribal membership depended largely on a willingness to practice the Omaha Way. This sort of self-definition began to dissipate by 1854 when Omahas reluctantly accepted their status as members of a "domestic dependent nation."[142]

Ultimately, annuity payments, land allotments, and land claims settlements all required proof of tribal identity. As a result, the legal definition of

"Omaha" was dictated by the BIA and revolved around lineage, place, and eventually blood quantum.[143] Between 1854 and 1934, enrollment in Omaha Nation generally required direct lineage to an individual who removed to the Blackbird Hills with the tribe. In many respects, being Omaha was place-based. This connection remained after the nation approved its constitution in 1936, but the Indian New Deal expanded tribal affiliations to include persons of "Indian descent" recognized by a tribe, descendants of an Indian living on a "reservation," or individuals with 50 percent or more Indian blood.[144]

Over the next twenty years Omaha tribal membership was defined as individuals appearing on the census roll as of April 1, 1934; children born in Omaha Nation; and children residing there who were approved by the tribal council. Anyone leaving Omaha country for a period of five years could have their membership terminated.[145] Blood quantum was not included in Omaha identity until 1954, when the constitution was amended to include children with one-half Omaha blood and individuals whose father would have been eligible for enrollment.[146] The "one quarter of Omaha blood" requirement first appeared in 1961 when an Indian Claims Commission settlement made $1.2 million available for disbursements to tribal members. Eventually, $750-per-capita payments went to individuals who met this standard with no regard to residence.[147] This led to a constitutional amendment that defined tribal membership as "all living persons whose names appear on the official roll of the tribe" as of September 14, 1961, and, for those born after that date, "aboriginal blood of the degree of one-fourth or more."[148]

In this manner, place was removed from the official description, and Omahas were free to migrate to cities without fear of losing their birthrights. Generations raised outside of Omaha Nation could also maintain tribal status. Conversely, while Omahas continued to adopt people into their culture, the Omaha Way no longer provided full recognition of these neophytes. Modern Omahas largely accepted imposed definitions of their ethnicity and were not considering a return to kin-based traditions.

Discussions of membership criteria remained in the twenty-first century. A recent survey on the Omaha Nation website provided four options for membership: one-eighth blood quantum, lineal descent, "consolidation of all Native blood," and the status quo—one-quarter blood quantum. Although only twenty-three individuals responded, the blood quantum options tied with seven votes each.[149] This discussion may be more than academic as gaming operations have produced per-capita payments since the 1990s, and reducing the blood quantum requirements would necessarily spread payments around.

### Work and School

Access to money—whether from work or entitlement schemes—remained a central concern among most Omahas wherever they chose to reside. In Lincoln, urban villagers often discovered that their skills translated poorly into the world of work, and many remained chronically underemployed. Cultural priorities often dictated greater comfort with seasonal or temporary employment patterns. Similarly, mainstream schools were rarely designed for Indian worldviews, and educational success was rare in the early years, although it became increasingly common as the twentieth century progressed. These internal factors were exacerbated by a persistent racism emanating from mainstream individuals and institutions.

New arrivals in Lincoln found that "survival was the first rule of order," and, as Oliver Saunsoci, Jr., explained, they "needed to find work."[150] His parents did just that. Oliver Saunsoci, Sr., "worked long hours" in construction, and Mae Blackbird Saunsoci did the same as a salad maker and dishwasher at the Capitol Hotel.[151] Just as the Volga Germans had done, most Omaha urban villagers in the 1940s and 1950s accepted work on the railroad and in migrant farm worker camps, performing tasks that most in the mainstream no longer wished to do. Remaining on the bottom rung of the economic ladder over the next several decades, Omahas worked primarily as unskilled or semiskilled laborers throughout their sojourns in Lincoln.[152]

Still, movement away from Omaha Nation was often a rational economic decision.[153] Assimilatory pressures and land allotment in the nineteenth and twentieth centuries created a spiral of poverty in the homeland. Land holdings were chiseled down to a total of only twenty-eight thousand acres. By the mid-1950s, only seven Omahas farmed. Heirship issues on remaining parcels made individual farming operations almost impossible. Additionally, casual labor in adjacent markets was squelched by postwar agricultural and demographic change. While farm employment remained the number-one source of jobs in the region, demand for workers dropped 42 percent between 1940 and 1960, and the entire population of Thurston County contracted. In 1959 the medium income in Nebraska was $6,203, but only $3,570 for residents in Thurston County. It was undoubtedly significantly less among Omahas. Unemployment in the homeland—even after wide-scale emigration—averaged 60 to 80 percent through the mid-1980s, and life expectancy was a mere forty-eight years as poverty and adult-onset diabetes were common conditions.[154]

One federal response to this dire situation was to recruit young Omahas into relocation schemes. Some were signed up at the Aberdeen, South Dakota–area BIA. Most were recruited from boarding schools at Flandreau, South Dakota; Haskell, Kansas; or Wahpeton, North Dakota. Omaha relocation was put in motion by Public Law 959 (1956). This act—first implemented in 1958 with a class of 397—provided vocational training and urban placement to individuals all across Indian Country. By 1972 a total of 35,500 Native Americans nationwide received some sort of mechanical education and job placement assistance.[155] Still others relocated to urban areas on their own without training. For Omahas this generally meant migration to Lincoln, Omaha, and Sioux City.[156]

Even with vocational training, economic problems remained acute among Lincoln's urban villagers. In 1971, for instance, only two-thirds of urban villagers were gainfully employed.[157] The other third faced the same jobs reality as urban Indians nationwide; they had over twice the unemployment rates of mainstream citizens, and nearly four times as many lived in poverty right into the twenty-first century.[158] Consequently, even during the affluent 1990s, many remained on public assistance to make ends meet.[159] They were, however, slightly better off than their relatives in and around Macy. In 1989, 41 percent of "Indians" in Lincoln lived below the poverty level, compared to 62 percent of the population in Omaha Nation.[160]

Living outside of Native space, however, urban villagers necessarily confronted racism on a regular basis. Omahas were constantly reminded they were different from the mainstream.[161] While many employers and individuals recognized them as "steady, reliable, and able people," age-old stereotypes persisted, and a significant portion of Lincoln's population saw all Indians as "shiftless, dirty, lazy, unreliable, and drunken."[162] These sentiments were well known among urban villagers, as discrimination was even more common in Thurston County than in Nebraska's cities.[163] As good race relationships were "indispensable to the success of the Omaha people's move toward self-sufficiency" and Omaha urban migrants' well-being, the We Shake Hands Program was inaugurated in 1957.[164] A combined effort of Omaha nationals, urban villagers, and mainstream volunteers from Lincoln and the city of Omaha, the program was promoted by the American Association of Indians in 1960 as one effort to "improve relations between Indians and their neighbors in the Great Plains."[165]

The explicit goal of all Omahas in the era of emigration was, according to elder Pauline Tyndall, "to find our place in America."[166] A spirit of official racial cooperation remained in Lincoln throughout the remainder of the twentieth century as mainstream individuals were generally welcomed at Omaha doings and encouraged to interact with their neighbors in the urban village. Despite these offerings, negative images of Omahas prevailed when locations for the Lincoln Indian Center were being debated in the 1970s. Similarly, few Indians were employed by mainstream governmental institutions, and law enforcement and social welfare organizations often seemed remote and hostile to Omahas.[167]

Consequently, Omahas committed to aiding their relatives found other channels for their goals. Frank Sheridan, for instance, moved to Lincoln in 1946 after getting out of the service. A graduate of Walthill High School, he served as a youth worker at the Salvation Army Community Center and as the Indian Center's student council and recreation director. In this capacity he worked closely with Lincoln Public Schools in educating and retaining Omaha students.[168]

Sheridan pursued these matters because he knew "there is some Indian students out there in them schools that's got the talent to do anything the white man's got."[169] Indeed, education was one of the motivations for urban migration, and by the late 1950s, Indians living in cities were already ahead of their rural counterparts in schooling.[170] Success was again relative, and although urban villagers on average completed tenth grade in 1971 compared to Omaha Nation's eighth-grade average, they remained undereducated.[171] Many Omaha students in the public school system found it difficult to go to classes "on a day-to-day basis amidst a lot of people who are not Indians." As Eleanor Baxter recalled, "Guidance teachers didn't know how to deal with Indians. Lots of people couldn't handle Indians because they didn't know what kind of people we were."[172] Additionally, children, at least in the 1970s, did not always have a positive Indian identity—making success in any endeavor less likely.[173]

It was clear to all Omahas that those who left school would find few jobs and no vocational training.[174] Fortunately, by the end of the twentieth century, urban villagers began to shed the "transient" label that perpetuated the reputation that they "can't keep up in classes."[175] Indeed, the number of Native Americans in Lincoln Public Schools remained fairly consistent in the 1990s, with between 350 and 400 students enrolled in almost equal numbers from kindergarten through twelfth grade—a total of about 1.3 percent of the school-age population. Many of them were active in Native American clubs and caucuses established by the school district within their particular schools.[176] In the early twenty-first century, Stablers, Sheridans, and other Indian children were frequently broadcast as honor roll students during the early-morning television news school-interest segments. Similarly, a small but vibrant cadre of Omahas enrolled at the University of Nebraska.

### American Identity

Despite discrimination and decades of assimilation efforts, Omahas, as tribal historian Dennis Hastings noted, sought an American identity as a means to "maintain a balance between tribal custom and society in general."[177] Partly based on ties to land and a history of peace with the United States, its most obvious manifestation was a proud tradition of military service. Young Omaha men—and eventually young women as well—enthusiastically enlisted in the armed forces as *wanó$^n$she* (soldiers) in order to reestablish their traditional roles as defenders of their nation.[178] The military also provided financial and educational opportunities generally not available in the urban villages or Omaha Nation.

American identities were celebrated as part of the Omaha Way at dance events as regalia was often rife with military components, and opening ceremonies always contained mainstream nationalistic references. By their very nature, Gourd Dances had distinct martial airs, and many dancers entered the arena in uniforms rather than regalia. At pow-wows, veterans often included unit insignias and flag references in their regalia rendered in bead work or embroidery. As women emerged as veterans, their jingle dresses were often adorned with shell casings rather than rolled snuff can lids.[179]

Ceremonial openings of Omaha Gourd Dances and pow-wows always included displays of patriotism and respect for veterans. Color guards—generally consisting of the American flag, the POW/MIA flag, and the Omaha

Nation flag—flag songs, and honor songs preceded most events.[180] As a general rule, dancers respectfully followed the flags into the arena and positioned themselves to hear the Omaha flag song. Flag songs were unique to each Indian nation and served the same purpose as the national anthem in mainstream culture.[181] Participants and spectators remained standing and at attention through an honor song dedicated to veterans at the event. After the honor song, the guard placed the colors next to the announcers' stage, saluted the flags, and exited the arena. At that point, all were at ease, and the event was under way.

The Omaha flag song was presented to World War I veterans for meritorious service in 1918. At that time, the colors of the American flag were reinterpreted to fit into an Omaha worldview. Red represented "Indians," white stood for the color of the "ghost of the NAC," and blue signified the "world of darkness."[182] These Omaha warriors were part of the force of twelve thousand soldiers to serve in the "Great War" and were among the first in a long line of *wanó^nshe* over the next eight decades.[183]

While military iconography and service to the United States had particular meaning to Omahas, they were also part of a Pan-Indian philosophy. The 190,000 Native Americans who donned uniforms during the twentieth century demonstrated "the highest record of service per capita" of any ethnic group in the United States.[184] The importance of this shared sacrifice cannot be underestimated. Service in World War I, for instance, was rewarded by full Indian citizenship in the United States. Indian nations mobilized 23,000 to 25,000 warriors during World War II—a full one-third of all able-bodied Indian men ages eighteen to fifty.[185] Their involvement helped bring mainstream attention to poverty among Indians and also increased intertribal contact. The 10,000 Indians who served in Korea and the 42,000 in Vietnam were almost universally volunteers. Their continued service through conflicts in Iraq and Afghanistan has earned Indians great praise. The Defense Department even recruited Native soldiers by suggesting the "requirements for successful military service—strength, bravery, pride, wisdom—match those of the Indian warrior."[186]

This American identity existed comfortably within the Omaha Way, and individuals took on military service intending to return to the dance arena with new adornments on their regalia. Similarly, mainstream education and urban employment—despite obstacles in obtaining them—have not altered fundamental Omaha behaviors or values. Those succeeding often work to benefit the general plight of their relatives. Still some cosmopolitan forces have made fundamental inroads on what being Omaha means. Historically, Omahas had methods to adopt outsiders into their society, and ironically, despite stated desires to assimilate Indians, the mainstream had no such procedures.[187] The modern use of blood quantum as a way to determine tribal membership originated in the mainstream but was stamped on Omaha consciousness out of economic necessity.

### Transnationalism

The movement to define Omaha ethnicity by blood rather than residence facilitated comfortable emigration from the homeland. Since World War II, movement between Omaha Nation and urban America has been fluid, and Omahas established a transnational community. Many individuals regularly traveled back and forth between Macy and Lincoln. In the process they established employment, support, and communication networks that kept those two places intimately connected. Additionally, many individuals in Lincoln remained enrolled in the tribe and were eligible for benefits as a result. These bonds and behaviors lasted for generations, and they are still vital in the twenty-first century. Indeed, the relationship between "host and home nations" proceeds without boundaries.[188]

Even tribal leaders traveled between sending and receiving cultures. Eleanor Saunsoci Baxter, the tribal chair in 2005, moved to Lincoln as a child in the mid-1950s with her family, who came in search of gainful employment. She grew up, was educated, and spent the first several decades of her working life among Lincoln's urban villagers. Baxter returned to Omaha Nation in 1993 with her own family and renewed a relationship with a place to which she was still deeply connected. In her words, "Today I am home."[189] Similarly, former council member Clyde Tyndall lived in Omaha Nation during his years of involvement in tribal government. He moved back to an urban village in Omaha, Nebraska—his original home—and served as that city's representative on the Nebraska Commission on Indian Affairs for eleven years. Migrating again, he was named executive director of the Lincoln Indian Center in May 2005.[190]

Omaha cultures in Omaha Nation, Lincoln's urban village, and population centers in Omaha and Sioux City were all remarkably similar, largely because the roads to and from Macy were so frequently traveled. While clearly some acculturation to mainstream ways was necessary among long-term urban dwellers, commitment to the Omaha Way was intense. The depth of these connections was not always acknowledged by Omaha nationals, however, and a rift between the populations became readily apparent. All Omahas were also influenced by a Pan-Indian identity, although for most, it never emerged as their main ethnic ascription.

Omaha migration to mainstream cities was not without precedent, as a few pioneers were already in motion after World War I. Eunice and George Stabler—both educated in boarding schools—were among a small population that moved their families around the Great Plains to keep them out of crippling poverty.[191] Actually proto-urban Indians, their presence in cities was advocated by Dr. Carlos Montezuma (Yavapai)—a founding member of the Society of American Indians—in the 1910s and 1920s.[192] While these early urban populations appeared statistically insignificant (see Table 3-1), they constructed a pattern for teaching their children the Omaha Way by making frequent summer pilgrimages to Macy so that their children could learn to dance. Their son, Hollis D. Stabler, brought his own children "home" each year from his residence in Wichita, Kansas. In this way, he allowed them to experience "the good part of being Indian in today's world," without being "scarred by the dependent poverty that affected so many of our people."[193]

Perhaps less adventurous than the Stablers, other Omahas took casual labor outside Omaha Nation for several weeks at a time during the 1920s and 1930s. While they made appearances in Lincoln, generally they returned home.[194] A few Omahas, although officially identified only as "Indians," resided and worked in Lincoln before World War II. Census returns listed twenty-five Indians in Lancaster County and five in the city in 1930, and twenty-three in the county and two in the city in 1940. Block data placed most in the Yankee Hill district, then a suburban area that hosted a brick factory and stockyards.[195] Early postwar arrivals who settled in the South Russian Bottoms also had access to employment in the brickyards and social contact with any remnants of the Yankee Hill enclave.

Sometimes described as "transient" and other times as "commuters," Omaha migrants could just as easily have been called "birds of passage" as their work in urban areas was intended to ease life after returning to the sending culture.[196] While transnational travels remained common, sojourns in cities during and after World War II tended to be longer. During the war when wages were especially good, Susan Freemont and her sister worked in Omaha at the Fontanelle Hotel laundry. They shared a "bi-i-ig" apartment with relatives and lived fairly comfortably. Like many in her generation, Freemont moved back to Omaha Nation permanently after she married.[197] Perhaps concerned about tribal enrollment or anxious to raise their off-spring in their own childhood homes, childrearing was often a life-changing event that brought individuals home. Others returned to be "better off."[198] Although work was more plentiful and better paying in mainstream cites, high rents, poor housing conditions, and lack of access to health care pushed many back to Omaha Nation.[199]

While a stable urban population emerged in the 1950s and expanded thereafter, the "Commuter Phenomenon" never dissipated. The dual pulls on the nation of employment in the city and family had Omahas driving back and forth.[200] Although probably an overstated population, former Indian Center director Marshall Prichard (Ponca) estimated that the city's stable Indian population of sixteen hundred was augmented by an additional sixteen hundred to two thousand seasonal workers in the early 1980s.[201]

A transnational Omaha Nation has not always been easy to envision. Former tribal chair Alfred Gilpin, for instance, observed, "Some of the people went away to the cities where uneducated men could find work and never came home again. But many go away and come home over and over again for it is hard to be Omahas anywhere except where the tribe is."[202] Gilpin's thoughts were accentuated by subsequent tribal chair Rudi Mitchell, who suggested that not only was Omaha Nation still "home," but that those entering "the dominant society with hopes of finding better employment, higher education goals, and a better way of life to raise their families" actually "attempted to be assimilated" by the mainstream.[203] Consciously or unconsciously, both leaders raised the issue of a pernicious rural-urban split among Omahas.

Divisions among urban villagers and Omaha nationals may have decreased over time as demographic shifts favored urban living, but there was still a sense that someone "was not a real Indian" unless they grew up in Indian territory.[204] In this vein, movement into cities was actively discouraged in the 1950s by tribal pressure aimed at keeping "members from 'going white.' "[205] Nationals still suggested that their urban relatives were somehow more "assimilated" in the twenty-first century.[206] On the other side of this cultural divide, some urban villagers began to see Omaha Nation as a vital center for ceremonial purposes—especially at pow-wow time—and a place to receive health care.[207] Because so many of their relatives also lived in Lincoln, most trips to Macy were more about business than visiting.[208]

The split was also apparent in economic benefits accrued from tribal membership. The issues surrounding the 1960s-era Indian Claims Commission (ICC) claims were relived with the advent of casino gambling. CasinOmaha—necessarily established on Blackbird Bend in Iowa—became the brightest star in Omaha Nation's economic picture when it opened in 1994.[209] While its profits have varied as competition from other outfits has increased, the casino and the legal fortitude necessary to open it have increased the tribe's collective self-esteem and encouraged many members to reexamine their heritage.[210] Additionally, revenues have brought infrastructure development to Omaha Nation and economic benefit to all enrolled Omahas. While tribal members receive per-annum payments, urban villager Darwin Philips maintained, "We're being neglected out there in that city world." From his viewpoint, money that should have been disbursed or held back for governmental functions was spent on council salaries and various forms of nepotism.[211]

Monetary woes exacerbated long-term political issues among urban dwellers, but as a population they have little say in tribal government. Indeed, enrolled members living outside of Omaha Nation were generally disenfranchised from tribal elections. According to the 1936 and 2003 constitutions, eligible voters needed to "have maintained continuous residence" in Omaha Nation for the six months immediately preceding the date of an election.[212] Similar requirements were necessary to serve on the council.

Despite such divisions, urban villagers remained distinctly Omaha even when presented with an appealing "Pan-Indian" identity that was prevalent in other urban areas. The marked shift away from tribal identities and toward an international one that "focused on a larger, more diverse group of Indians" was virtually a continent-wide development that emerged among urban Indians in the 1950s. In the process, "A particularly Indian form of identity politics emerged," one fueled by Native pride and insistent upon self-determination.[213]

This sort of Pan-Indianism was especially intense in the large urban communities that formed as the result of relocation-era policies. Before consolidation, tribal peoples in Los Angeles and Phoenix, for instance, were part of an "invisible minority" in their new milieus, and distances to their relatives in the old places were necessarily traveled infrequently.[214] Although disassociation with sending cultures was the norm, assimilation was an unacceptable option. Urban isolation was only a temporary condition as "prejudice and discrimination by non-Indian" neighbors served to unify Indians under a new nationalistic banner.[215] Additionally, intermarriage among various tribal groups invented a new people: "urban Indians."[216]

The maintenance of a unique Omaha identity among Lincoln's urban villagers appears in conflict with scholarship suggesting that urban Indians view themselves "more as 'Indians' and less as 'tribalists.'"[217] While probably true for some Omahas, the "conservative tendencies" of a people preserving parts of their heritage for their children pointed to the retention of a very specific Omaha identity.[218] Issues involving repatriation of Omaha burial remains in the late 1980s were a case in point. During the 1930s, the Work Projects Administration excavated 106 skeletons originally buried between 1780 and 1820 near the Big Village. Situated north of the modern boundaries of Omaha Nation, the project coordinators ignored ownership issues and sent the bones to Lincoln for preservation and storage in the osteology lab at the University of Nebraska.[219] The common practice of housing and displaying indigenous remains came to an end in Nebraska in 1989 when the state legislature passed the Unmarked Human Burial Sites and Skeletal Remains Act. Its provisions insisted on repatriation of existing remains and tribal notification when any indigenous burial sites were unearthed.[220] Using this statute, Pawnees—with representation from the Native American Rights Fund (NARF)—aggressively pursued legal actions to regain the possession of their people's remains. Preferring negotiation to confrontation, Omaha Nation ended its Pan-Indian involvement with the NARF and other Nebraska tribes and began their own negotiations with the university.[221] Ultimately, they established a repatriation schedule that included scientific analysis of their ancestors' remains. After a university research team presented their report that included a discussion of lead toxicity, the remains were reburied in October 1991.[222]

This tradition of cultural particularism had intense resonance among Lincoln's Omaha urban villagers as transnational connections remained so strong that second-generation Indians were rarely cut off from the traditions of the sending culture.[223] As seen in the Lincoln Indian Club's "traditional Omaha Pow-Wow," city enclaves often reinforced "tribal identity and resisted mainstream assimilation."[224] Pan-Indianism by the 1960s and 1970s stressed pride in ethnicity and Indianness and actually augmented a cultural, social, and political revitalization at Omaha Nation.[225] The revitalization of intense nationalism increased resolves among all members of the transnational community to remain Omaha through the tricentennial of the United States and beyond.[226]

As Lincoln and national Omaha populations have remained intimately connected, influences necessarily ran in both directions. Rifts between the populations were sometimes quite serious but rarely led to true disfranchisement. While Omaha Nation remained the ultimate keeper of the Omaha Way, Lincoln's urban village has become a worthy satellite of cultural maintenance. In many respects, those who stayed in Omaha Nation were "integrated" into mainstream life through the influences of their urban relatives.[227] The characteristic Omaha search for balance in the homeland included rising educational and economic aspirations for all children of the nation. The hope of many nationals was that the skills that their relatives gathered in the mainstream could be employed in and around Macy for all Omahas to enjoy.

## Conclusion

As Dennis Hastings suggested, the Omaha Way at the dawn of the twenty-first century still sought to "maintain a balance between tribal custom and society in general."[228] Consequently, interactions among particular forces and cosmopolitan influences allowed urban Omahas to continuously re-define cultural identity. Although never static, the modern cultural ideal retained basic traditional concepts.[229] A strong connection to the land, distinct religious preferences, intricate kinship networks, and an abiding love for Omaha music and dance have all survived in Lincoln's urban village. All things remained gifts, whether given by *Wakóⁿda*, Kiowas, or relatives at a feast. Mainstream values were used primarily to strengthen the Omaha Way.

For instance, urban villagers and Omaha nationals alike acknowledged the need for mainstream educations and the acquisition of job skills applicable to a modern economy.

Transnationalism allowed cultural preservation to occur in multiple population centers. The consistent movement between Lincoln's urban village, Macy, and ethnic enclaves in other nearby cities kept cultural content in all places relatively uniform. Still, claiming the greatest connection to place, Omaha nationals continued to argue that their identities were more salient than those of their urban relatives. Behaviors in Lincoln, however, indicated an unwavering commitment to the conservatism inherent in the Omaha Way. Remembered traditions in some instances—especially the "traditional" pow-wow—may best be preserved outside of the sending culture.

Lincoln's urban villagers understood that tribalism was not only necessary, but it was alive and well throughout the era of urban migration. Indeed, strong connections to the sending culture and a shared sense of tradition remained unbroken.[230] The survival of tribalism was a story of almost epic proportions. The Omaha Way was consistently assailed in the state of Nebraska since 1854. Encouraged to break communal ranks and farm owner-operated plots, cheated out of their allotments, threatened with termination, and relocated to cities as a matter of policy, Omahas and their culture have adapted in each case, and they "regularly stymied federal attempts at cultural re-engineering by staunchly defending tribalism."[231] Contact with international forces, such as Pan-Indianism, only served to strengthen this concept.[232]

Wielding cultural flexibility as a strength, Lincoln's urban villagers arrived with a knowledge of how not to "assimilate." Instead, they continually adapted and redefined the Omaha Way. These efforts were aided by developments within the sending culture. In the post–World War II era, Omaha Nation experienced dramatic legal, political, economic, and social revitalization movements. As awareness of problems and possible solutions increased, dire conditions at Omaha Nation improved somewhat. Still, a "diminishing viable land base," "insufficient housing," and "insecure revenues" required either mobility or drastic actions.[233] Not surprisingly, the resourceful Omahas employed both strategies.

The founding generation of urban villagers often faced "a choice between clinging to what remained of the homeland, or pursuing economic opportunity."[234] Pushed and pulled into a new milieu, they had no intention of changing social or cultural behaviors. Instead they worked to assure that relatives faced with the same options could come to a comfortable social climate. Omaha communities were built around families and community centers in age-old philosophical patterns. Spiritually, the circle remained unbroken in the minds of Lincoln's Omaha urban villagers.

Henry Amen, Sr., and family, 1915, RG3986-PH-2-3. Courtesy of Nebraska State Historical Society.

Exterior of the H. J. Amen Store, 201 F Street, Lincoln, Nebraska, August 28, 1947, RG2183-PH-1947-428-37. Courtesy of Nebraska State Historical Society.

A

Aerial view of Lincoln, including the North Bottoms neighborhood, ca. 1920, RG2158-PH-1-52. Courtesy of Nebraska State Historical Society.

German-Russian mothers and children, Lincoln, Nebraska, ca. 1910, RG2824-PH-0-180. Courtesy of Nebraska State Historical Society.

Citizenship class with Germans from Russia, Lincoln Night School, ca. 1916, RG2824-PH-0-193. Courtesy of Nebraska State Historical Society.

American Historical Society of Germans from Russia headquarters with "German from Russia pioneer family" in foreground. Photo by the author.

First German Congregational Church, South Bottoms. Courtesy of Gabrielle Elliott.

Friedens Lutheran Church, South Bottoms. Courtesy of Gabrielle Elliott.

Children at the Grand Entry of the 1983 Omaha Nation Pow-Wow in Macy, Nebraska, photograph by Dorothy Sara Lee, Omaha Indian Music, AFC 1986/038: FCP/0-DSL-214183-2/15. Courtesy of American Folklife Center, Library of Congress.

Adults at the Grand Entry of the 1983 Omaha Nation Pow-Wow in Macy, Nebraska, photograph by Dorothy Sara Lee, AFC 1986/038: FCP/0-CF-215338-1/7. Courtesy of American Folklife Center, Library of Congress.

Dancing to wax cylinder records at the 1983 Omaha Nation Pow-Wow in Macy, Nebraska, photograph by Carl Fleischhauer, AFC 1986/038: FCP/0-CF-214061-5/27/A. Courtesy of American Folklife Center, Library of Congress.

Lincoln Indian Center, third and present location. Courtesy of Gabrielle Elliott.

Lincoln Indian Center Pow-Wow Grounds. Courtesy of Gabrielle Elliott.

Interior of *Linh Quang* Buddhist temple. Courtesy of *Lincoln Journal Star.*

Performers practicing for the 2006 Vu Lan celebration at the *Linh Quang* Buddhist Temple. Courtesy of *Lincoln Journal Star.*

*Linh Quang* Buddhist temple, location since 2011. Courtesy of Gabrielle Elliott.

Vietnamese Roman Catholic Church in its third location. Photo by the author.

Sacred Heart Roman Catholic Church. Courtesy of Gabrielle Elliott.

Sacred Heart School. Courtesy of Gabrielle Elliott.

Immaculate Heart of Mary Roman Catholic Church, third and present location. Courtesy of Gabrielle Elliott.

Vietnamese Missionary and Alliance Church, second and present location. Courtesy of Gabrielle Elliott.

Vung-Tau Restaurant, Twenty-Seventh and Y Streets. Courtesy of Gabrielle Elliott.

Pho Nguyenn Restaurant, Twenty-Seventh and Vine Streets. Courtesy of Gabrielle Elliott.

Vina Market, Twenty-Seventh and Vine Streets. Courtesy of Gabrielle Elliott.

Saigon Plaza, Twenty-Seventh and Apple Streets. Courtesy of Gabrielle Elliott.

# Chapter 4
# Vietnamese Urban Villagers in Lincoln
## Clustered Communities and Flexible Identities

Maria Dan Vu fled Vung-Tau, Vietnam, as a boat person in 1979. Already married with two daughters, she took refuge in Malaysia and then in Indonesia before her harrowing journey ended in Boston in 1983, when she was reunited with her husband, Anton, a former South Vietnamese army officer. Six years later, the Vus moved to Crete, Nebraska, to live among Anton's relatives. Educational endeavors eventually brought them to Lincoln, where they obtained employment commensurate with their training and bought a house in a modest but desirable neighborhood. Maria Vu—a teacher and an accountant—served as community liaison with the Lincoln Police Department and as the director of the Asian Community and Cultural Center. In these capacities, she assisted in translating numerous public documents into Vietnamese in order to ease immigrant adaptation into mainstream Lincoln.[1]

The Vus' lives in Lincoln were somewhat atypical as they were both bilingual professionals. Nevertheless, their experiences contained elements shared by all Vietnamese who found new homes during the late-twentieth-century diaspora of Southeast Asians. Sent into motion by the disorders of war, the earliest arrivals came directly from the Republic of Vietnam (RVN)—South Vietnam—a nation that was founded in 1955 but fell to the Democratic Republic of Vietnam (DRV)—North Vietnam—in 1975. The united country was renamed the Socialist Republic of Vietnam (SRV). Geographic, political, and social divisions caused by the long conflict were so intense that people continued to flee the southern half of the new nation-state for decades after reunification.

Because the RVN was closely allied with the United States in a war against communism, America governmental and private humanitarian agencies worked in concert to resettle Vietnamese immigrants throughout all fifty states. Whether they were placed in Lincoln by refugee agencies or opted to come to the Capital City on their own, this new group of urban villagers sought physical and communal security and the opportunity to gain or regain middle-class status.[2] Confronted by a largely white mainstream at the end of an unpopular war, Vietnamese in Lincoln were called "gooks" and regularly told to "go back home." Additionally, there was a marked fear that the newcomers—especially those arriving in the late 1970s and early 1980s—would be burdens on an already strained public relief system.[3] Fortunately, these prejudices were tempered by increasingly compassionate attitudes toward immigrants and refugees. Consequently, although Southeast Asia and southeastern Nebraska share few environmental traits, the Capital City generally proved, as Hung Nguyen noted, to be "a friendly and safe place" for Vietnamese families.[4]

Community building in Lincoln began soon after the evacuation of Saigon in 1975 and continued unabated over the next three decades. Sharing Vietnamese identity and ideas about community, the immigrants formed cohesive neighborhoods first in affordable and centrally located neighborhoods.[5] They then moved outward to suit particular spatial and cultural needs as finances allowed. As the city was already built and populated, these urban villages were actually "small aggregates of Vietnamese living close to each other."[6] Their polynucleated living areas were connected by the development of Buddhist, Catholic, and Protestant houses of worship and an institutionally complete Vietnamese business district.

Within these spaces, these urban villagers experienced constantly evolving identity construction as particular, cosmopolitan, and transnational forces combined to produce multiple and overlapping ascriptions.[7] Intriguingly, Vietnamese throughout home and diaspora communities were described by cultural observers as a "factious, untrusting tribe" that was only unified when "besieged by larger forces."[8] As such, Vietnamese in Lincoln expressed both the imported frictions of a heterogeneous population separated by social class, geographic origin, and religious affiliation and the solidarity of an expatriate national group.[9]

The examination of particular forces—largely expressions of performed culture and shared beliefs—yielded a Vietnamese identity constructed from the experiences of several millennia. Within this overarching ascription, religious splits created clear divisions among urban villagers, but a distinct loyalty to the RVN helped ease such divides, at least among older residents. The urban villagers' interactions with cosmopolitan forces—forces dictated

by the mainstream—again reinforced Vietnamese solidarity, but also created generational friction. Uniquely, many young urban villagers developed
the ability to identify alternately with Vietnamese and American cultures.
Finally, transnational forces—intense contact with the sending culture—
produced a *Việt Kiều* identity in Vietnam and true "transnationalists" in the
United States.[10] Once again, the older generation's penchant for preserving
worldviews steeped in Cold War anticommunism tempered the unity of
international identities.

**Immigrant Communities**

Housing all these identities, Lincoln at the turn of the twenty-first century
hosted a vibrant Vietnamese community of about 5,000 individuals; about
3,700 were foreign born, with another 1,300 born in the United States.[11] (See
Table 4-1.) Unlike other Great Plains immigrant enclaves in Wichita and
Oklahoma City, Vietnamese urban villages in Lincoln were comparatively
small during the first years of the diaspora. The initial clustering of 114 families arrived as part of a humanitarian outreach effort in 1975, but the Capital
City did not seem destined to grow into a vibrant Vietnamese population
center. The founding families were only joined by a modest 60 to 175 Vietnamese immigrants annually for the next decade and a half. In the 1990s—
even before the United States and the SRV normalized relations—numbers
in Lincoln spiked as many more individuals were able to leave Vietnam or
Asian refugee camps.[12]

Table 4-1. Foreign-Born Vietnamese in Lincoln, Nebraska, 1970–2003.

|      | Lincoln | State |
|------|---------|-------|
| 1970 | NA      | NA    |
| 1980 | 532     | 1,428 |
| 1990 | 897     | 1,806 |
| 1995 | 2,197   | NA    |
| 2000 | 3,756   | 6,364[13] |
| 2003 | 3,774   | 6,755 |

Sources: U.S. Bureau of Census; Onyema G. Nkwocha, *Health Status of Racial and
Ethnic Minorities in Nebraska* (Lincoln: Nebraska Department of Health and Human Services, 2003); *Lincoln Journal-Star*, 24 December 1995, 1C.

Much like the Omahas' community, the survival of Lincoln's polynucleated Vietnamese urban villages—actually clusters of families within existing
mainstream neighborhoods—was assured once local populations reached
critical mass. Settled for over a decade, the earliest arrivals had already negotiated new lives and identities within the mainstream and willingly helped
successive waves of newcomers begin their adaptation. While federal officials classified most as refugees, a composite immigrant experience connected all Vietnamese who settled in the vicinity.[14]

### Waves

The human capital that established Vietnamese urban villages in Lincoln
arrived in the United States in three distinct "waves," and their experiences
in transit clearly impacted future developments in identity formation. Evacuees—the first wave—were transported under the auspices of the Indochinese Migration and Refugee Assistance Act. Those who arrived in Lincoln
were a small subset of the 130,000 Vietnamese soldiers and officials who
were airlifted out of the RVN in 1975.[15] The second wave comprised boat
people—often the families that evacuees left behind—who between 1978
and 1982 risked life and limb to get out of Vietnam by any means possible.
Often landing first in asylum countries in Asia, Vietnamese arrival into the
United States was eased by the Refugee Act of 1980, which allowed entry on
the basis that they were persecuted in their homeland. Once landed, they
were entitled to "effective resettlement" and assistance that encouraged rapid economic self-sufficiency.[16] The third wave arrived beginning in 1979 as
the result of Orderly Departure Programs (ODP) designed to prevent Vietnamese from becoming boat people. Part of an understanding negotiated
between the United Nations High Commissioner for Refugees and the SRV,
immigrants and refugees were allowed safe and predictable means to depart.
This wave continued arriving for two decades.[17] (See Table 4-2.) In addition
to welcoming the peoples of the "three waves," the Capital City gradually
became a point of secondary migration for individuals who were initially resettled elsewhere. In concert, these immigrants sired the second generation,
sometimes described as the "fourth wave."[18]

The arrival of evacuees in the Capital City was orchestrated, in part, by
the federal government, which dispersed resettlement to avoid straining an
ailing national economy.[19]At first blush, moving people from tropical South

Table 4-2. Vietnamese Refugee and Immigrant Arrivals into the United States, 1952–2000.

|  | Immigrant Arrivals | Refugee Arrivals | Arrivals for Period |
|---|---|---|---|
| 1952–1974 | 17,886 | NA | 17,886 |
| 1975 | 3,039 | 125,000 | 128,039 |
| 1976–1980 | 18,326 | 155,900 | 174,226 |
| 1981–1985 | 18,886 | 165,572 | 184,458 |
| 1986–1990 | 104,706 | 108,648 | 213,354 |
| 1991–1995 | 146,068 | 152,952 | 299,020 |
| 1996–2000 | 73,378 | 45,446 | 123,824 |
| Total | 387,289 | 753,518 | 1,140,807 |

Source: Max Niedzwiecki and T. C. Duong, *Southeast Asian American Statistical Profile* (Washington, DC: Southeast Asian Resource Action Center, 2004), 9–10.

east Asia onto the temperate grasslands of the Great Plains seemed unlikely, and Nebraska governor James J. Exon even bristled at proposed federal quotas that allotted 1,000 refugees to his state.[20] While not challenging Exon's suggestion that local placements be voluntary, U.S. senator Roman Hruska urged his fellow Nebraskans to welcome the Vietnamese, who, he argued, only "sought America's opportunity" and, like Cubans and Hungarians, a refuge from communism.[21] Accepting this humanitarian mission and setting a precedent for subsequent immigration, local chapters of Catholic Social Services, the Christian and Missionary Alliance, and Lutheran Immigration and Refugee Services agreed to sponsor 450 largely Christian Vietnamese—60 percent of whom were children—out of a resettlement center in Fort Chaffee, Arkansas. The federal government provided the agencies three hundred dollars per person to ease the transition into life in Lincoln.[22]

The influx of boat people had only modest effects on the overall population of Lincoln's newest urban villages. Their plight, however, increased local resolves to continue immigrant aid. Boat people fled repressive SRV policies using any available conveyance and risked their lives in the process.[23] Additionally, many Vietnamese government officials collected five thousand dollars per emigrant to guarantee safe departure from the country. This scheme contributed $4 billion to a stagnant economy but left émigrés penniless.

Multiple attempts to exit the graft-filled nation were often necessary, and success was never assured. An estimated 50 percent of boat people perished at sea, the victims of weather, unseaworthy vessels, or piracy. Survivors often spent years in refugee camps in Thailand, Malaysia, or Hong Kong before being admitted to safe havens in Australia, Canada, or the United States. Unlike evacuees, this second wave tended to be from outside Saigon, and their economic and social standings varied greatly.[24]

Under international humanitarian pressure to curtail the unregulated and perilous journeys of boat people, the SRV and twenty-six other nations implemented the Orderly Departure Program (ODP) in 1979. As a result, 523,000 Vietnamese were admitted to the United States over the next twenty years. Initially, individuals seeking family reunification and former U.S. or RVN employees were favored for entry.[25] While these individuals were not precluded before, the Amerasian Homecoming Act went into effect in 1989 and specifically mandated that "people of mixed Vietnamese and American parentage" and their families be allowed to immigrate.[26] Concurrently, the Humanitarian Operation Program was launched in order to offer asylum to internees of various "reeducation" projects. Individuals from this wave eventually impacted Lincoln, especially after the federal Office of Refugee Resettlement—citing low unemployment rates, job availability in many segments of the economy, and affordable housing—named it a preferred community for new arrivals in the early 1990s.[27]

The growth of the population of foreign-born Vietnamese in Nebraska was the second highest in the nation as numbers increased from eighteen hundred to nearly seven thousand between 1990 and 2000. While many arrived directly from Vietnam, others were part of an organic regrouping of people already in America wishing to reunite with friends and families.[28] This sort of "chain migration" was necessary because federal policies disrupted Vietnamese kinship systems. Recognizing only nuclear families, initial placements often deprived urban villagers of the comforts and support customarily generated by extended families.[29] When immigrants were able, they moved around the country in order to reestablish familiar social arrangements.[30]

Orange County, California, New Orleans, Houston, Dallas, New York, and Los Angeles were the largest centers of internal relocation. On the Great Plains, only the Denver-Boulder-Greeley metroplex, Oklahoma City,

Austin–San Marcos, Wichita, and Kansas City hosted larger Vietnamese urban villages than Lincoln.[31] The Capital City has a more modest demographic profile than the other host communities, but it continues to attract internal migration and external immigration. Entrepreneur Tim Nguyen, for instance, moved from Houston, Texas, to Lincoln because it offered a sense of community absent in the sprawl of East Texas.[32] Nguyen was especially attracted to Lincoln because it served as a "hub of refugee immigration" and had a reputation for encouraging ethnic businesses and neighborhoods to breathe "new life" into older inner-city areas.[33]

Part of this new life was a natural increase as immigrant parents produced 332,361 American-born children between 1975 and 2000, about 25 percent of the total "Vietnamese" population. Lincoln's 1,300 individuals in the second generation were typical of national developments.[34] Collectively a young population, this number is expected to swell rapidly in the twenty-first century. State agencies estimate that the Asian population in Nebraska will increase by 20 percent a year for the next several decades largely due to growing Vietnamese populations.[35]

### Polynucleated Urban Villages

Not surprisingly, Vietnamese residents of all ages intentionally settled in ethnic enclaves as "clustering" facilitated their "psychological adjustment" and eased their entry into a new economic climate.[36] The constantly expanding urban villages necessarily evolved in very fluid manners.[37] As populations across the Great Plains were increasingly suburban, initial Vietnamese clusters were established in core neighborhoods where home ownership and extended family unity was most possible.[38] As economic and social conditions changed, entire clusters sometimes regrouped in developing sections of the city. Rarely the majority population of any particular neighborhood, their "community" was in fact a series of urban villages that were connected by a business district on North Twenty-Seventh Street. (See Map 4-1.)

Vietnamese urban villages emerged and expanded between 1978 and 1990 as immigrants concentrated in the Hartley neighborhood—home of Sacred Heart Catholic Church and School—and in the Near South neighborhood. Hartley's housing stock was characterized by affordable single-family homes constructed in the 1920s, many of which were available for rental. Barely a mile away, the Near South neighborhood was formerly affluent, but

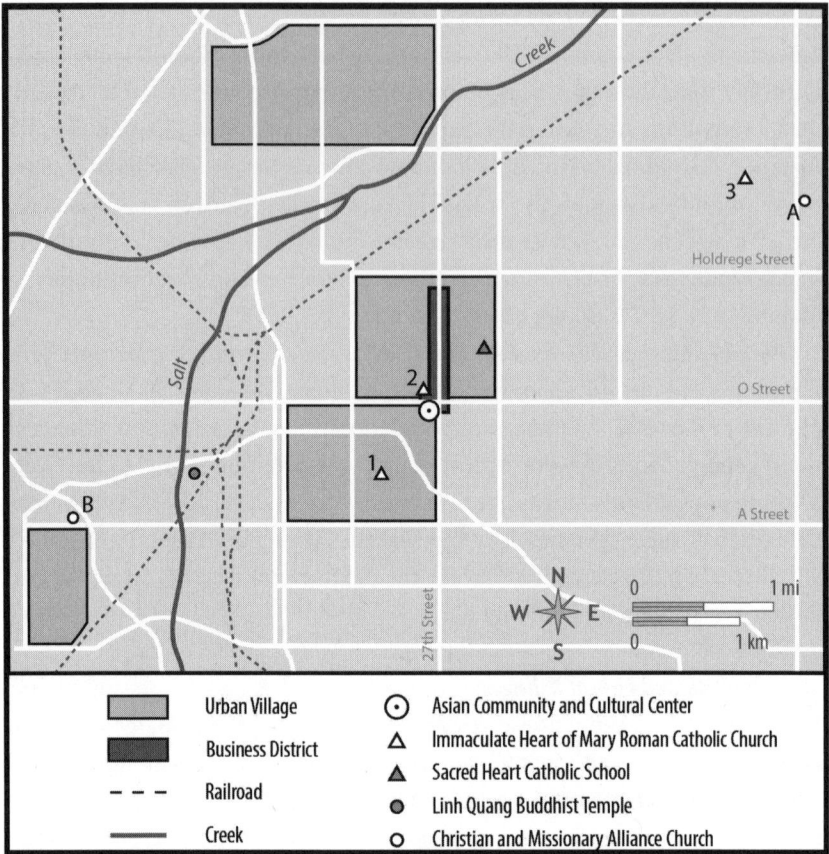

**Legend:**

| | |
|---|---|
| Urban Village | ⊙ Asian Community and Cultural Center |
| Business District | △ Immaculate Heart of Mary Roman Catholic Church |
| – – – Railroad | ▲ Sacred Heart Catholic School |
| —— Creek | ◉ Linh Quang Buddhist Temple |
| | ○ Christian and Missionary Alliance Church |

Map 4-1: Map of Vietnamese Urban Villages and Institutions. Permission granted by Ezra Zeitler.

its property values declined markedly in the 1960s and 1970s as multiunit apartment complexes replaced older structures and increased population densities. Additionally, smaller concentrations of Vietnamese settled in Northeast Lincoln, the Belmont neighborhood, greater Northwest Lincoln, and in the affluent area south of Highway 2 and west of Twenty-Seventh Street.[39]

Large-scale expansion was necessary to accommodate the growing Vietnamese population in the 1990s. Near South numbers increased slightly, but remained contained in the rental district between L and A Streets and between Ninth and Twenty-Seventh. The greatest activity among urban villagers focused on neighborhoods targeted by the city for residential re-development.[40] Mortgage rates were set below market rates in these tracts. Consequently, the numbers in the Hartley area were augmented by new arrivals in adjacent neighborhoods, and by 2000 the Hartley-Malone-Clinton urban village had the largest and densest population of Vietnamese in the greater community. Home owners also moved into newer housing in Northwest Lincoln and to developments around West A Street. Additionally, an increasingly affluent subset of the population—including Maria and Anton Vu—spread out across South Lincoln.[41]

Urban village formation and rearrangement was fueled, in part, by a cultural preference for property ownership, and 67.6 percent of Vietnamese in Nebraska owned their own homes by 2000.[42] The ratio of home owners to renters appeared somewhat lower in Lincoln's older, core urban villages. In the Hartley neighborhood, for instance, thirty-seven units were owner-occupied by "Asians" in 2000 compared to fifty-four rentals, a home-ownership rate of around 40 percent. Clinton and Malone—which have many rental units and high concentrations of students—had 30 percent and 13 percent owner-occupancy rates among "Asians," respectively.[43]

The Hartley-Clinton-Malone complex was likely home to new arrivals from Southeast Asia who worked hard to establish themselves. Consequently, poverty—as defined by the mainstream—was fairly common. In 1990 just over 30 percent of Asians in Lincoln were living below official poverty levels. In a statewide comparison, 10 percent of the general population and 20 percent of the Asian population lived below the poverty line.[44] Despite a continued influx of immigrants in the 1990s, poverty levels dropped during the decade, and by 1999 only 13 percent of Asians in Nebraska were living in poverty. Although Vietnamese in general made less than other Asians, they earned more than Hispanics, Native Americans, or African Americans.[45]

Vietnamese urban villagers, as they gained financial means, helped redefine Lincoln's housing market in the 1990s. Generally wishing to accommodate multigenerational families, they considered modest spaces to be between fourteen hundred and seventeen hundred square feet and preferred newer housing that was somewhat larger.[46] Attention to family hierarchy created special needs that often caused Vietnamese home owners to retrofit standing structures at an average cost of thirty-five hundred dollars. Master suites and master bathrooms, for instance, were eliminated because facilities for family elders could not be less than those of their grown children. Additionally, as real estate agent Chien Cao suggested, certain "tastes" and "requirements" encouraged urban villagers to recluster in newer neighborhoods where the housing industry willingly promoted and constructed residences with the front doors facing east and backdoors out of line with the entrances. Many builders clearly recognized that 40 percent of housing growth in the twenty-first century would likely come from immigrants.[47]

While structural requirements and population pressures led to residential reclustering, the Vietnamese business district remained in the heart of the Hartley-Clinton-Malone urban village. The North Twenty-Seventh Street strip by 2005 was host to many Vietnamese-owned restaurants, markets, auto repair centers, nail salons, fashion boutiques, coffeehouses, electronics supply stores, and insurance agencies. These cultural "focal points" were intimately connected to real estate, banking, and health-care services in other parts of town. Ultimately, although all types of customers were welcome in most of these businesses, they created zones of refuge for members of a community whose accommodation to mainstream patterns was ongoing.[48]

### Immigrants and Refugees

Like all new arrivals, the urban villagers' adaptation to life in Lincoln required large-scale identity transformation. Uniquely, until relations with the SRV were normalized in 1996, over two-thirds of foreign-born Vietnamese were classified as "refugees," and, in many instances, self-identified with that status.[49] In Lincoln, refugees continued arriving at least through 1994, the year that Xuan-Trang Ho and her family came seeking political sanctuary.[50] Refugees are defined as individuals who "*are forced to flee*" their home nations and are subsequently "unable or unwilling to return" because of "persecution or a well-founded fear of persecution" for reasons of religious, social, or political affiliation.[51] Empirical evidence suggests that these people were less likely to adapt American behaviors than immigrants.[52] Because many departed with little or no advanced planning, they were troubled they "did not have the protection of their dead ancestors."[53] Culturally fragile, they still faced the demands of adjusting to a new and foreign place.

To understand the complexity of the experiences of urban villagers, it is also useful to examine Vietnamese who "*choose to come* to a new life" and are classified as "immigrants."[54] By the broadest legal definition, immigrants are "persons lawfully admitted for permanent residence in the United States."[55] In some ways the concept encompasses all of Lincoln's urban villagers, but refugees were people accepted above and beyond the liberalized quotas of the Immigration and Nationality Act of 1965, and most were paroled into the country as a reward for resisting international communism.[56]

Politics aside, the experiences of Vietnamese "refugees" and émigrés were quite diverse. Early arrivals, for instance, were given preferential treatment and support by governmental agencies and social service organizations. Latecomers experienced more neutral treatment and relied on ethnic communities already in place.[57] All Vietnamese immigrants, however, were "born again" in new milieus.[58] Therefore, their old behaviors and beliefs were both challenged and strengthened by life in the United States.[59]

Whether Vietnamese in Lincoln started as refugees or not, they became immigrants when they started to build new lives in the United States.[60] The focuses of these lives were the decentralized urban villages that they organized and rearranged over the course of thirty years. Largely collections of neighbors who sought affordable spaces in reasonable vicinity to other Vietnamese, a distinct set of ethnic institutions cemented ethnic bonds. Despite the great physical and cultural dissimilarities of host and sending cultures, lasting communities of Vietnamese found ample room in Lincoln to lead the comfortable lives that eluded them in Southeast Asia.

## Particularism

These relatively stable ethnic enclaves allowed the new arrivals to concentrate on tradition and reestablish cherished behavioral patterns.[61] Steeped in particularism, most Vietnamese urban villagers maintained aspects of performed culture imported from Southeast Asia, especially language, family customs, religion, and traditional celebration practices. While the ethnic community in general was "marked by diversity in terms of region, immigration experience, religious outlook, ideology, and background," a shared sense of history served as a unifying agent.[62] Consequently, a "Vietnamese" identity was nurtured in Lincoln, but this overarching ascription was fragmented by Buddhist, Catholic, and Protestant loyalties. An intense attachment to the Republic of Vietnam, however, helped mitigate some of the strains of division.

### *Place*

A large and diverse nation of jungles and mountains, Vietnam is often compared to "a pole carrying two baskets of rice on its ends."[63] The country's narrow, mountainous hinterland—only thirty-five miles wide in places—connects the thousand-mile distance between the tropical Mekong River Delta in the south to the monsoonal Red River Delta in the north. (See Map 4-2.) Dominated by the dialects and worldviews of Saigon and Hanoi, respectively, these lowland regions constitute a mere 10 percent of the nation's two-hundred-thousand-square-mile area but host nearly 90 percent of its population.[64] South and North regional cultures are joined by a distinct Central identity that is epitomized by developments in and around the city of Hue.

Vietnamese urban villagers in Lincoln clearly recognized regional differences among themselves. As Lincoln resident Qui Nguyen suggested, "North pronunciation or something just harder to understanding."[65] The Vietnamese Student Association at the University of Nebraska was also keenly aware of sectional issues but chose to celebrate them by sponsoring an evening celebrating "*Việt Nam Ba Miền*," or the three regions in Vietnam, in 1998.[66] The

Map 4-2: Map of Vietnam, 1975. Permission granted by Ezra Zeitler.

association also acknowledged an ancient urban and rural split that further separated Vietnamese according to customs, dress, and marriage patterns.[67] These differences, however, were already largely obscured prior to immigration onto the Great Plains, and they have become arcane cultural artifacts within Lincoln's ethnic enclaves.

Among Vietnamese immigrant populations, "history and memory" often served as significant "political resources."[68] Indeed, an overarching Vietnamese identity was bolstered by a historical narrative that began in indigenous space, struggled through two thousand years of colonial encroachments, and celebrated several eras of full sovereignty that were marked by geographic expansion.[69] This uniform national history, however, was often shattered by regional divisions. Most significantly for Lincoln's urban villagers, the Geneva accords of 1954 attempted to end years of armed conflict by temporarily dividing Vietnam along the seventeenth parallel. This line was never intended to be an international boundary, and the decision to split Vietnam had long-lasting ramifications. Throughout the 1950s, both the North and the South claimed to represent the government of the entire nation.[70] While the South softened its stance, the North did not, and war to unify the nation forced many of Lincoln's urban villagers to flee Vietnam because they were and remain vehemently "anticommunist."[71] Indeed, such animosity was common among Vietnamese immigrants, as many held on to war-era memories as they re-created their identities in America.[72]

### History and the Politics of Separation

In some respects, political division is a modern device as the roots of Vietnamese identity stem from a shared creation story that was never forgotten even in eras of turmoil. Tradition dictates that the Dragon Lord, *Lạc Long Quân*, emerged from the sea to rid the Red River delta—the cradle of Vietnamese civilization—of evil demons. Before returning to the ocean's depths, he taught the people how to cultivate rice and how to wear clothing. A benevolent culture hero, Dragon later came back to expel an alien ruler who invaded from the north. In the process, *Lạc Long Quân* kidnapped *Âu Cơ*—the foreign king's wife—and hid with her in the mountains until the invaders' final retreat. The new princess of the mountains wed the old prince of the sea, and their progeny were the first Vietnamese.[73]

The creation story remains central to modern identity because it illustrates how multiple cultural influences combined to create Vietnamese civilization. Told and retold, it was introduced to the mainstream in the Capital City by a 2004 display at the Lincoln Children's Museum. "Dragons and Fairies: Exploring Vietnam through Folk Tales" recounted the adventures of *Lạc Long Quân* and *Âu Cơ* and entertained a new generation of young people half a world away from the Gulf of Tonkin and Phan Si Pang—the highest mountain in Vietnam.[74] It poetically explained how the Red River heartland of Vietnam was connected to the Tibetan Plateau and to the seagoing world of the Gulf of Tonkin.

While all diaspora and national Vietnamese share an identity built on several thousand years of history, many urban villagers in Lincoln constructed their identities in opposition to the communist regime that Ho Chi Minh and his followers established in Vietnam.[75] Indeed, most people in the diaspora fled their homeland because of political and religious constraints. They believed democracy and tolerance would have been preserved had Vietnam been unified under nationalist rule or had the RVN maintained its independence. Instead, years of war were followed by years of repression. The SRV's record on human rights became so abysmal that not only were former RVN soldiers and officials ruined or imprisoned, their children were routinely denied access to higher education and social advancement through the 1980s.[76]

From the SRV's perspective, the enemies of Vietnamese self-determination were first the French and then the combined forces of the United States, the RVN, and their allies. The liberation of Vietnam began on August 29, 1945, when Ho Chi Minh proclaimed the Democratic Republic of Vietnam's independence from Japanese and Vichy France forces. At this point, emperor Bao Dai abdicated and the Nguyen dynasty that was founded in 1802 officially ended.[77] Refusing to recognize the legitimacy of these events, France attempted to recolonize Indochina between 1946 and 1954. Fearing communist expansion in the region, the United States footed 78 percent of the cost.[78]

Despite superior weaponry and better funding, the French were defeated by DRV forces with finality at Dien Bien Phu in 1954, and the "First War of Independence" was settled. The Geneva agreement that separated Vietnam was signed shortly after the battle. The accord featured a plan to reunify the nation by popular vote in July 1956. These elections were never held, and domestic and international tension created a divisive atmosphere on both sides of the Demilitarized Zone.

Many of Lincoln's urban villagers were originally from the North but, like Hoa Tran's Roman Catholic family, moved to Saigon in 1954 to escape religious persecution.[79] Hoa's reputation as a leader who opposed political and cultural pluralism sent one million northern Catholics, Protestants, and Buddhists south of the seventeenth parallel during the two-year time frame allowed by the Geneva agreement.[80] Their movements were not in vain. After national partition in 1956 the DRV curtailed social and religious freedoms among all religious denominations.[81]

Ironically, developments in the South favored neither democracy nor religious freedom. President Ngo Dinh Diem abrogated responsibility to the Geneva Accords when he declared the southern government permanent and formed the Republic of Vietnam in 1955. Intimately connected to the Catholic Church, President Diem appointed family members and coreligionists to most posts in the new government and adopted harsh measures to keep the Buddhist majority in check. Consequently, he was never able to build a broad base of support and failed to promote meaningful economic or democratic reforms. Always in power at the pleasure of the United States, he was removed by coup in 1963. Six presidents followed Diem—although Nguyen Van Thieu served from 1965 to 1975. All required U.S. military support to remain in power.[82]

Governmental failure in the RVN was augmented by the DRV's efforts to forcibly reunify the country. The National Liberation Front (NLF) was formed in 1959, and a war of attrition began. For fourteen years, attacks directed by the DRV increased even as American military presence reached unprecedented levels. Facing internal pressures and little chance of final victory, the United States negotiated peace in January 1973 and withdrew, leaving the nation divided.[83] After regrouping for several years, the DRV began its final offensive in March 1975 and ended the war of reunification in April of that year.

Although formally dedicated to equality, life in the newly formed Socialist Republic of Vietnam proved untenable for millions of its residents. Continued warfare, economic deprivation, political repression, and religious persecution were commonplace. Lincoln resident Hien Dang was born in Saigon just after reunification and remembered that his uncle spent three years in a reeducation camp in the early 1980s. Despite familial involvement with the RVN, Dang fared relatively well prior to emigration in 1994, but he still felt fortunate to escape poverty and the rampant "corruption and bribery in the Vietnam government."[84]

In the midst of mass reeducation, foreign policy thwarted normalization efforts within Vietnam until about 1980. The SRV fought with neighboring Kampuchea (Cambodia) during the dry seasons of 1976, 1977, and 1978. Although glossed officially in ideological terms, unresolved border issues from the eighteenth and nineteenth centuries were largely the causes of these hostilities. Remembering ancient insults while protesting treatment of ethnic Chinese citizens—most in Saigon's Cholon district—China invaded Vietnam in February 1979. This seventeen-day campaign solved little, but smoldering resentments remained well into the next decade.[85]

SRV attitudes toward its newly incorporated southern citizens proved no more enlightened than its foreign policies, and revenge proved to be a common factor in its actions. After reunification, the new government eradicated private ownership, confiscated businesses, and became the central redistribution agent for all products in the South. These policies lasted well into the 1980s and helped create dire trade deficits with the few nations willing to do business with the SRV. Poor central planning and a period of drought only intensified these difficulties, and by 1980 food production was not even keeping up with population growth.[86]

Responding to these problems while attempting to overcome the effects of wartime urbanization and environmental degradation, the SRV created New Economic Zones (NEZs) in underdeveloped areas in both the North and South and then assigned "volunteers" to new communities in the hinterlands. Such projects were designed to stimulate agricultural production and repopulate the damaged "blank zones" scattered throughout the nation. They were the results of NLF activity and extensive American bombing— four million tons of American ordnance were dropped on the countryside. The ravages of war pushed many RVN citizens out of their villages and into cities. Saigon alone grew from two million residents in 1955 to seven million twenty years later. After a generation of such movements, few youth in South Vietnam had any knowledge of village life.

Consequently, between 1976 and 1980 the SRV planned to move four million people. The NEZs, however, were not habitable places, and rather than sending willing farmers, they were populated by former ARVN officers and government employees who struggled to rebuild the countryside under remarkable duress.[87] The government also sent individuals affiliated with the RVN to reeducation camps. Little more than prisons, the camps were places of hard labor—including clearing land mines—starvation, and summary execution. Confinements of up to fifteen years were not unusual, and perhaps one-third of all families in the South had at least one family member in prison.[88]

Uninspired and untalented leadership exacerbated the entire situation. After Ho Chi Minh's death in 1969, an aging politburo and tumultuous change in the Soviet world led to relatively inefficient central government as reformers who preferred economic liberalization fought conservatives through the 1980s.[89] These same leaders introduced a new ruling class in the South. Largely recruited from the "poor and landless peasantry," they were indoctrinated in party ideology, but they had little experience and often held grudges against those they governed.[90] Power abuses and outright graft were rampant in most sectors of the country, and bureaucrats and officials rarely heeded their own laws. Article 68 of the Constitution of 1980, for instance, guaranteed religious freedom. Both the Roman Catholic Church and the Unified Buddhist Association, however, were placed under immediate government supervision.[91]

Against this backdrop, many Vietnamese in the United States maintained anticommunist identities and—citing natural division within Vietnam—remained opponents of the SRV. They argued that "the north and the south have been divided between two states and two states of mind as early as 1600."[92] Indeed, the unification of 1802 was fleeting, as the French administration in essence created three Vietnams. From the southern perspective, their Buddhist heritage allowed for the construction of a region and a nation that was "liberal and flexible" and in many ways the land of opportunity. The North, on the other hand, was overcrowded, steeped in Confucian values, and overly concerned with the maintenance of hierarchy.[93]

Locally, this identity was embodied in an organization called the Vietnam Community of Lincoln. Founded in 2003, the organization maintains the belief that their country (RVN) was lost to an international insurgency. Politically active in its new milieu, the community rallied against John Kerry's presidential candidacy in 2004 because of his former stance as a veteran against the Vietnam War. Additionally, they argued that his U.S. Senate record failed to link the SRV to human rights violations.[94] Like many other organizations nationwide, the Vietnam Community of Lincoln maintained Cold War political sensibilities. For them, complete rejection of communism was vital to identity construction.[95] This attitude was passed down to the next generation, and as Thuyvi (Linda) Pham recognized, "My mom hate the North Vietnam."[96]

Still, in the newly formed urban villages in Lincoln, as in Vietnam, 90 percent of the population was ethnically Vietnamese, and despite some differences they were "both racially and culturally a remarkably unified people."[97] Thirty years of wars involving Vietnamese, Japanese, French, and American forces caused one of the biggest internal exoduses in the twentieth century, and regional place of origin as an identity marker was often subsumed by political sentiment.[98] Although families that fled from Hanoi to Saigon in 1954 and from Saigon to Lincoln in 1975 retained knowledge of their place of origin, most identify themselves as "Vietnamese."[99]

### Language

Communists and nationalists alike taught their philosophies to the Vietnamese people in a national language. Comprising distinct oral and written components, many urban villagers—along with people throughout the greater diaspora and residents of Vietnam—believe "that if the Vietnamese language survives, the Vietnamese people will survive."[100] A truly unique tongue, Vietnamese has served as a unifying factor guiding a shared identity from the Van Lang era through the present.[101] Because ancient Vietnam was at a human crossroads, the true origins of the language are sometimes debated. Most linguists, however, classify it as part of the Mon-Khmer division of the Austro-Asiatic Group. Consequently, Vietnamese is closely related to Khmer, Champa, Thai, and Hmong. As the language developed, the land and water split of the creation story became vital. Originating in the Red River Valley, the tongue of the masses was first spoken by seafaring peoples, but its proximity to southern China dictated Cantonese influences.[102]

At the dawn of the twenty-first century, survival seemed assured as an estimated eighty million people around the world spoke the language. In the United States, more than 80 percent of ethnic Vietnamese used their native tongue at home, even when English was a possibility. A small component of this total lived in Nebraska, as 1,075 families spoke Vietnamese regularly in 1990.[103] Lincoln resident Linda Tran was a fairly typical young urban villager. Although born in the United States, she was fluent in Vietnamese because it was the primary language within her multigenerational household.[104]

The city of Lincoln also offered many services—driver's license exams, for instance—in written Vietnamese. This romanized *quốc ngữ*—literally "national language"—script ascended slowly to become both an identity marker and a potent source of nationalist sentiment.[105] Introduced in the seventeenth century by the Jesuit Alexandre de Rhodes, *quốc ngữ* was a central component of a colonial educational policy called "transitional bilingualism." The French goal was to prepare a Vietnamese colonial elite to learn their masters' language by first familiarizing them with Roman characters and cutting out the Confucian mandarins who wrote Vietnamese in Chinese characters. Ten percent of the population was sent to school to participate in this program between 1861 and 1905.[106]

Instead of accepting permanent colonial rule, Vietnamese culture survived partly by incorporating sovereignty issues and language development into a single struggle.[107] Nationalists—including Ho Chi Minh—redefined the meaning of *quốc ngữ*. Initially used by collaborators, twentieth-century patriots turned the script into a symbol of solidarity.[108] Seen as a way of unifying the distinct regional dialects of northern, central, and southern Vietnam into one mode of written communication, the spread of *quốc ngữ* began in earnest in 1911. Six years later, *Nam Phong*—a national newspaper—emerged in the new script, and a revolution in modern literature began. By 1946 it was the language of instruction throughout Vietnam, and by 1968, both the DRV and RVN had achieved near universal literacy.[109]

### Family

Language also acknowledged proper family and social relationships and helped to maintain traditional Vietnamese identities. Even among Lincoln's Vietnamese urban villagers, Confucian norms dictated that individuals fulfill specific behavioral codes. Ultimately, "honor," "obligations," and "respect" were the watchwords of Vietnamese society, and these concepts were constantly reinforced in day-to-day interactions.[110] Employing few pronouns, the Vietnamese form of address, for instance, not only allowed people to greet each other, it also allowed them to assess each other. Salutations necessarily contain a series of words that express social rank, family relationships, and other positions in the Vietnamese hierarchy. Speakers often forgo "I" (*tôi*), for instance, in favor of a word that articulates an appropriate relationship.[111]

The most important relationships involve family, and elders suggest that "Without family you are no one."[112] Characterized by patrilineal descent and patriarchal authority, the traditional Vietnamese family was maintained by subsuming individual desires and promoting group order in economic, social, gender, marital, and religious matters.[113] Often the driving factor behind internal Vietnamese migrations, family designations contain both a nuclear unit—*nhà* (constructed along male lineage)—and an extended family unit—*họ* (generally made up of several nuclear units organized around a shared male ancestor). In combination, *nhà* and *họ* acted as the impetus for people sharing the same surname to live in close proximity. Additionally, they frequently served as an "economic safety net" and as sources of shared income for business ventures.[114]

Although these forms were necessarily far less developed in Lincoln than in Vietnam or Orange County, California, the ethos of family remained strong among urban villagers. The Tran Hung family of Lincoln, for instance, pooled money for the good of the unit. Tran's oldest son and his bride remained in the family home specifically to contribute to its economy. This arrangement was typical as local young men commonly remained in their elders' households until age thirty.[115]

This timeworn practice is comfortable in a culture where marriage not only joins a man and a woman but also joins two families perpetually in "space and time."[116] Such momentous events, then, required great consideration and planning. Traditionally, marriages were arranged by members of the extended family—although matchmaking was often a formality as children sought relationships on their own, even in Vietnam. Weddings were elaborate affairs that often required two ceremonies, one for family and close friends that tended to be fairly solemn as the groom's parents asked to bring the bride into the family. This occasion was followed by a more celebratory event, usually held at a restaurant or rented hall.[117]

After the celebrations, life settled down into routines where women tended to remain subservient to men. Although Vietnamese society contains a significant matrilineal component, especially compared to other Confucian cultures, it was a man's world in Vietnam and in Lincoln's ethnic enclaves.[118] Women necessarily showed respect, as Uyen Eileen Vu noted, "in the way you speak and the way you carry yourself." Issues of eye contact and demeanor continued to be extremely important in diaspora communities.[119] Additionally, women tended to remain in the family home prior to marriage, which generally occurred between the ages of eighteen and twenty-five.

While gender inequalities were prevalent among Lincoln's urban villagers, marriages tended to be stable and family order generally harmonious. Because Confucian norms remained in place, any undesirable behavior reflected poorly on an entire household.[120] Consequently, children were expected to "obey their parents in every way."[121] Still, because children are central to a culture that reveres its ancestors, family size tended to be large. In Vietnam, nuclear families often boasted eight or nine children. In Lincoln, however, mean family size was slightly over five people—still large by local mainstream standards.[122]

### Religion

The significance of family extended beyond life as Vietnamese traditionally honored their ancestors. Ritual appeals to dead relatives were designed to aid harvests and human fertility. Part of a multitheistic religious system,[123] ancestor worship remained vital into the twenty-first century among many Vietnamese Buddhists and Christians.[124] Similarly, altars to the Kitchen God and the God of the Hearth date into antiquity but remain common in Vietnamese psyches. A spiritual people, religious heterogeneity was the norm and exclusivity the exception.[125]

Despite tendencies for inclusion, the Vietnamese Missionary and Alliance Church, Immaculate Heart of Mary Church, and *Linh Quang* Temple protected unique Protestant, Catholic, and Buddhist identities in Lincoln. Each congregation was established by Vietnamese urban villagers to serve important but distinct roles in the retention of old-world culture.[126] Individually, they nurtured culturally specific practices that developed over the course of decades if not centuries.

Religious splits were not confined to diaspora communities. In Vietnam the cohesiveness of the village system was enhanced when all members of a community subscribed to the same doctrines. Consequently, hamlets and villages were generally Buddhist or Christian exclusively by the nineteenth century, and many remained that way even in the 1970s. The predilection for coreligionists to socialize among themselves remained common in urban Vietnam, and the practice was exported with emigration—an experience that favored Christians. While 90 percent of Vietnam was Buddhist, only 27 percent of first-wave refugees subscribed to these teachings.[127] Settlement patterns on the Great Plains also illustrated religious separation. In Lincoln, Christians—Catholics and Protestant alike—began arriving in 1975 and consistently outnumbered Buddhists, whose presence was not substantial until the 1990s. Vietnamese communities in Wichita and Oklahoma City, on the other hand, were numerically dominated by Buddhists during the same time period.[128]

Although they had the fewest practitioners and the shortest history in Southeast Asia, the Vietnamese Christian Missionary and Alliance Church was the first congregation that urban villagers founded in Lincoln. Established in 1975 by 50 members, the church has remained relatively small as membership in 2005 included approximately 125 adults.[129] Still, this modest congregation was part of the only sizable Protestant denomination in Vietnam. Its parent organization counted 37,222 adult members in 342 churches in 1964 and reported that proselytizing efforts were yielding 1,000 to 1,500 new baptisms annually. The church's growth, however, was uneven. Mission efforts began in Da Nang in 1911 and expanded into Hoi An, Haiphong, and Hanoi in 1915. Initial conversion successes were short-lived as the French banned Protestantism in 1928 because Vietnamese nationalists were using the church to cultivate connections in the United States—then viewed by Vietnamese as a beacon of liberty and self-determination. Silenced, but not eliminated, about two-thirds of North Vietnam's 2,500 Protestants fled south in 1954 to take refuge near the new denominational headquarters in Nha Trang. From this base of operations, the organization was soon administering one hundred church-affiliated schools throughout the South as well as an orphanage and other social services.[130] All furthered a doctrine averring that the Bible was the "inerrant" word of God given to humankind through divine intervention. While judgment was "imminent" and Christian belief exclusive, universal redemption was possible for those individuals who were willing to repent and "receive the gift of eternal life."[131]

In comparison, Vietnamese Catholicism merged universal Roman Catholic doctrine—which focused on "grace" and stressed community, interdependence, and responsibility—and Confucian tradition—which stressed the individual's place within family and social hierarchies. These two philosophies mixed flawlessly as both demanded individual spiritual and moral growth and the preservation of established social order.[132] While thousands and then millions of Vietnamese Catholics lived comfortably in Southeast Asia, the history of the church in Vietnam proved tumultuous. Initially operating at the pleasure of Vietnamese rulers, French and Portuguese missionaries spread the religion of their states at the behest of European merchants looking for the military and financial backing of their monarchs. The modest operations of the sixteenth and seventeenth centuries were discontinued in the eighteenth century, however, as foreign missionaries were habitually executed or exiled. France's role in displacing the Trinhs was rewarded by the Gia Long emperor's tolerance of Jesuits, who converted eight hundred thousand Vietnamese by 1800 and many more over the next twenty years. The remaining Nguyen monarchs returned to an earlier practice of repressing Christianity, but French colonization started a new era for the Catholic Church. Taking advantage of Confucian structures, missionaries concentrated on converting village headmen who held great sway among their relatives. When successful, conversion of entire villages was the norm. Using this practice, 10 percent of the Vietnamese population was Catholic by the twentieth century.[133]

Because of the efforts of Catholic Social Services, the Catholic minority has always been Lincoln's Vietnamese majority. In fact, most of the 450 arrivals in the 1970s were Roman Catholic. Their numbers allowed them to found Immaculate Heart of Mary Church in 1979, which was the "first canonical Vietnamese Church in America."[134] Membership steadily increased to between seventeen hundred and two thousand individuals by 2004.[135]

In juxtaposition, Vietnam's religious majority arrived late in Lincoln and did not found a congregation until 1992. In just a decade, however, six hundred practicing Buddhists were living among Lincoln's Christian Vietnamese urban villagers.[136] In true Vietnamese fashion, Buddhism was practiced in a manner that centered on living family as well as reverence to ancestors.[137] Vietnam hosts three denominations of Buddhism: the Theravada school—the predominant form imported from India; the Mahayana—a form imported from China and preferred by the Khmer minority; and an indigenous form of Vietnamese Buddhism that blends the two. All comfortably coexisted for over a millennium, and although Mahayana has the most practitioners, aspects from each tradition appear in the 160 Vietnamese Buddhist temples and centers in the United States.[138]

Traditionally, Vietnamese religious open-mindedness allowed Buddhists, Catholics, and Protestants to intermingle.[139] Still, fealty to specific doctrines and divergent historical developments within each often led to local divisions. Conversely, a shared history and language created solidarity among Lincoln's urban villagers, and adherence to familiar social arrangements helped solidify a Vietnamese identity. This ascription was modified slightly by loyalty to a now-defunct nation-state. Even though it was no longer an actual place, many urban villagers were united by their shared distaste for the policies and ideologies of the Socialist Republic of Vietnam. As a remembered place, however, the RVN remained a central component of identity among a people disconnected from smaller localities.

## Cosmopolitanism

The same religious practices that led to conflict in the SRV also exposed tensions that existed between Vietnamese urban villagers and greater Lincoln. Divisions were especially pronounced among Southeast Asian Christians who were influenced by mainstream governing bodies. Consequently, when seen as a cosmopolitan force, Vietnamese religious institutions reinforced a distinct Vietnamese identity. Similarly, secular organizations frequented by the urban villagers also tended to reinforce Vietnamese identity at the expense of an Asian ascription. The demands of work, school, and interaction with other mainstream organizations often created friction between adult immigrants and their children. For those acculturated in Vietnam, contact with mainstream structures strengthened Vietnamese identity. For younger individuals, it betrayed the difficulties of wanting to be Vietnamese and American at the same time and demonstrated the human ability to negotiate hybrid identities.

### Vietnamese Religious Institutions

While Vietnamese Buddhist, Catholic, and Protestant identities served to divide Lincoln's urban villagers, contact and tension with American coreligionists often served to reinforce a Vietnamese identity, especially among Christians who built their congregations in the shadows of mainstream institutions. Even after they established themselves in separate facilities—which were not necessarily in the same neighborhoods their practitioners inhabited—neither Protestants not Catholics were completely independent bodies.

*Hội Thánh Tin Lành Việt Nam* or "Society of Sacred Protestants of Vietnam"—the Vietnamese Christian and Missionary Alliance Church—ap-

pears to be the exception to the rule as its parishioners followed the phys-
ical church. Closely connected to the South Vietnamese war effort, many
Protestants were among the first wave of immigrants to arrive in Nebraska.
Always a small congregation, it shared quarters with the Rosemont Alliance
Church in northeast Lincoln for eighteen years. Initially led by Rev. Nguyen
Van Phan, the minister and many congregants lived in the neighborhood.
While physically and denominationally connected to the Rosemont Church,
Vietnamese parishioners remained separate by culture and preferred their
own services and institution. They relocated the church to a house in West
Lincoln in 1992 and began the process of growing their physical space. In
1999 construction of the present five-thousand-square-foot sanctuary at
1440 West A began, and its doors opened in April 2000. The reclustering of
Vietnamese from northeast Lincoln to West A Street happened rapidly at
this time.[140]

Conversely, *Giáo xứ Khiết-Tâm-Mẹ*—literally "Disciples of the
Pure-Hearted Mother"—or the Immaculate Heart of Mary Church was
located in Vietnamese neighborhoods for years before being relocated to
northeast Lincoln—a neighborhood showing a decrease in Asian residents.
Initially established at 2013 G Street, the original congregation of thirty families moved into larger quarters at 2601 P Street in 1991. The second building
included a chapel, a gymnasium, several classrooms, and a sanctuary that
held 380 people. While convenient to parishioners who lived in the Hartley-
Clinton-Malone urban village, the physical structure was derelict, and the
Vietnamese Catholic population was expanding rapidly. A larger facility at
6345 Madison Avenue in northeast Lincoln was obtained to house the parish's now four hundred families.[141]

Ministered to by the Vietnamese order of the Mother Co-Redemptrix,
but administered by the conservative Roman Catholic Diocese of Lincoln,
the congregation preferred Vietnamese ways but was often vexed by mainstream desires. On one hand, the diocese celebrated the Immaculate Heart
of Mary as part of a "national church" legacy that was "more than a century"
old.[142] Indeed, Catholic Social Services was touted for helping Vietnamese
to obtain a church "where they can worship in their own language, and preserve their culture and tradition."[143] On the other hand, this distinctive congregation is slated to vanish just as German and Czech national churches did
before them. Already described as the church for "Catholics of Vietnamese

descent," the diocese would welcome the eventual assimilation of the population, and Vietnamese Catholics were frequently encouraged to move closer to the mainstream in terms of language and practice.[144]

Encouragement to assimilate and move across town likely seemed subtle to Lincoln's Vietnamese Catholics, who were used to outright persecution and cross-country flight, and they had no intentions of leaving their own international order. The Congregation of the Mother Co-Redemptrix was established in 1941 in Phat Diem—a Catholic center just southeast of Hanoi. Many of its priests and brothers were among the one million refugees who fled south of the seventeenth parallel in 1954. In 1975, 185 members escaped Saigon and resurfaced in Fort Chafee, Arkansas. From there they moved on to the southwestern Missouri town of Carthage, where they rebuilt their order and became the spiritual home to Vietnamese Catholics in the United States.[145]

To give thanks for arriving in America safely and to celebrate Vietnamese culture, the congregation launched Marian Days in 1978. Each year in August, they gather in honor of "Mary Mother of God" who "rescued the children who came to this country by boat."[146] The event immediately became a homecoming for Vietnamese parishioners from around the country, including those in Nebraska, and ties that were stretched by geographic distance were reestablished. By 1981, six thousand attended; two years later, sixteen thousand; by 1987, over forty thousand; and by 2004, about seventy thousand. In this manner, the Vietnamese Catholic Church served to reinforce community among its practitioners. On a local level, both Immaculate Heart of Mary and Sacred Heart served as meeting places and centers of education for many in the community.[147]

Despite this particularism, the old Vietnamese tradition of inclusion remained alive and well in Lincoln. Marriage among Buddhists and Catholics was part of the culturescape. Yhanh Do and Tam Ngo, for instance, wed at the Immaculate Heart of Mary before reinforcing their vows in a Buddhist service at the bride's home in 1994.[148] The observance of *Tết*—the lunar new year—was an even greater cultural unifier. *Tết* functions both as the "grand birthday of all" Vietnamese and as a focal point of "self-identity and reverence for the past." Celebrations traditionally last an entire week, although mainstream pressures have pushed the most elaborate proceedings onto weekends. Activities range from lighting fireworks to chase away evil spirits, exchanging gifts, and attending religious services.[149] While Catholics and

Buddhists have separate ceremonies at their respective institutions, community-wide events have occurred at the Indian Center, the Malone Center, and the F Street Recreation Center in recent years.[150]

Outside of *Tết*, however, Buddhist contact with mainstream institutions did not occur regularly in Lincoln. *Linh Quang*—"Divine Light"—temple was founded in an old two-story house at 216 West F Street, just two blocks from the First German Congregational Church in the South Russian Bottoms. Making use of indoor and outdoor space, the property was both affordable—it was purchased for thirty-six thousand dollars but was constantly improved—and almost physically removed from the city. Significantly, construction of a grand new facility in West Lincoln began in 2007 and was completed in 2011.[151] This particular Vietnamese institution has not had to negotiate its legitimacy with an established Buddhist mainstream. In addition to *Linh Quang*, there are small Nichiren, Tibetan, and Zen Buddhist communities, but these largely comprise European American converts who may be interested in Vietnamese practices but are generally unable to access them due to language barriers.[152]

Operating in a culturally specific manner, *Linh Quang* demonstrated how the Vietnamese community employed public ceremony to connect immigrants to traditional culture.[153] Their observance of *Vu-Lan* Day, for example, was a celebration of a moment when "all Buddhists should pray together for their mothers and others, both alive and dead, who need salvation."[154] This event is now marked annually in Lincoln as in Vietnam on the full moon in the second month following the summer solstice. Responding to influences from the mainstream, *Linh Quang* also sponsors a Buddhist Youth Group that helps, as Minh Dao suggested, "younger kids, especially those who were born here, to learn about their traditions and customs."[155]

### Vietnamese Secular Institutions: Performed Culture in Negotiated Spaces

In addition to the long-familiar religious institutions, new organizations were created by urban villagers to help them interact with the host society.[156] The Asian Community and Cultural Center (ACCC) and an institutionally complete business district were prime examples of such establishments. Together they protect several aspects of performed culture, and they foster Vietnamese as well as Asian identities.

An independent ACCC was designed to maintain social services in immigrant communities as Church World Services, Catholic Social Services, and governmental organizations on all levels began to withdraw resettlement aid in Lincoln. Located at the south end of the Vietnamese business district, the center opened its doors in 1994 and immediately became a focal point of local Vietnamese populations. It took two years of effort by the Lincoln Interfaith Council (LIC)—a mainstream organization that coordinated grant moneys from charitable and federal sources—to found the center. Successful from the start, the ACCC shed LIC sponsorship in 1998 and emerged as a 501(c)3 nonprofit organization. The growth of Asian populations caused it to move to its second and larger home at 2615 O Street in October 2005.[157]

The center's stated mission is "To support and empower Asian people while sharing our cultures through our programs and services."[158] Services include conflict mediation, English lessons, credit counseling, youth leadership training, and citizenship classes. English language classes—while available to all—largely served local Vietnamese populations. The casual course was led by a center coordinator—an American citizen of Vietnamese ancestry—staffed by an AmeriCorps worker, and assisted by volunteers from the mainstream community. Largely a positive and friendly exchange, English conversation was punctuated with Vietnamese explanations that allowed advanced students to assist newcomers. While class size was small, solidarity of a larger Vietnamese community in Lincoln was reinforced as Christians and Buddhists intermingled and people from different regions of southern Vietnam interacted.[159]

Additionally, Asian culture was shared with mainstream Lincoln through the efforts of dance groups that perform the Lion Dance, the Dragon Dance, and the Lotus Dance in Vietnamese and mainstream civic celebrations. Sponsored by the center, all three styles have Vietnamese origins, but dancers from all backgrounds were welcome to participate. Originally a prayer to the Buddha for peace and prosperity, but popular among Christians as well, the Lotus Dance—*Múa Hoa Đăng*—is performed by young women and features vibrant and colorful choreography.[160] Its serene movements contrasted with the spectacular four-footed lion and six-footed dragon costumes whose dances are accompanied by a cacophony of cymbals and playful spectators chasing their tails. These "boisterous arts" were designed to ward off evil spirits during *Tết* and *Tết Trung Thu*—the harvest festival.[161] In Lincoln, both dances share similar stylings, and while movements can be performed by most young people, the best dancers are also martial arts practitioners. Part of flexible traditions, a focus on spectacle has replaced the esoteric aspects of martial arts even in Vietnam.[162]

By sheer population, Vietnamese often dominated events at the ACCC, although no real tension among other ethnicities seemed apparent. Vietnamese affiliation with an "Asian" organization raises interesting identity questions, however. As a general rule, Vietnamese was preferred over an Asian identity, as few found much meaning in the latter description. Uyen Eileen Vu, for instance, bristled at the mainstream assumption that all Asians were of the same heritage and needed to explain that she speaks Vietnamese rather than Chinese.[163] Part of this hostility was the rebellion against being seen as a part of an Asian "model minority" by the mainstream instead of being viewed as a discrete cultural group.[164]

Foodways and a distinct Vietnamese business district reinforced the desire to maintain a national identity. Food preparation in the home was vital to the maintenance of Vietnamese identity.[165] Studies in Oklahoma City noted that a mere 10 percent of immigrants reported dietary change even after two decades in the United States.[166] The pattern appears to have repeated itself in Lincoln as diets rich in grains—especially rice—vegetables, fish, meats, eggs, and herbs were common; in contrast, dairy products were largely absent. Catering to Southeast Asian preferences, four large food markets were located in the business district by 2005. Additionally, fresh fish was available at Mai Lea Seafood and at Midwest Seafood beginning in 2002. The latter operation was typical of Vietnamese business ventures connected to a greater diaspora community. Owned by Andrew and Tony Vuong, who arrived in America as teenagers in 1990, fresh produce from the Gulf Coast and from California was shipped in daily by relatives in the fish business in both locations.[167]

In diaspora culture, Vietnamese food functioned as a focal point for maintaining long-standing social and historical continuity.[168] The spring roll, for instance, even has its own creation story. According to legend, a grave tyrant enslaved a great chef and demanded that he prepare a new dish each new day or offer his life. The chef cooked valiantly for 999 days before coming to his last recipe. The kitchen goddess appeared to the chef and gave him directions for a feast that contained an herb that put the tyrant to sleep. Consequently, the chef escaped with his last recipe—the one for spring rolls—intact.[169] Essentially shredded vegetables and meats wrapped in rice paper and fried in oil, spring rolls dipped in fermented fish sauce are ubiquitous delights. They are available at a plethora of Vietnamese restaurants that have become part of Lincoln's culturescape.

Because cafe society provides important meeting places for Vietnamese men and boys, four Twenty-Seventh Street restaurants were open in 2005, and all maintained a healthy trade serving largely traditional cuisine. Many entrepreneurs kept a Vietnamese clientele but expanded their menus to reach a mainstream customer base as well. It appears this portion of the trade often blurs particularism as Chinese and Japanese dishes are readily available in many establishments.[170] Condiments such as fish sauce and garlic chili sauce make Vietnamese restaurants distinct.

### Mainstream Institutions

While Lincoln Vietnamese urban villagers were generally able to live, shop, and eat within Vietnamese spaces, they necessarily dealt with city government, work, and school—three institutions dominated by mainstream sensibilities—on a regular basis. In many respects, the city facilitated the maintenance of Vietnamese identity, and work reinforced separation from American society. School, on the other hand, forced younger individuals to confront language and cultural gaps that divided a Vietnamese identity from a mainstream one. Necessarily straddling two worldviews, a flexible hybrid identity developed that allowed individuals to switch ascriptions.

The older generations, however, were fully acculturated in Vietnam, and tended not to trust government officials because of inefficiency and graft in the sending culture. To its credit, the city of Lincoln took steps to assure a modicum of understanding between the mainstream and the urban villagers. In many cases, the Equal Opportunity section of the Lincoln City Charter was thoughtfully implemented, especially after the huge influx of immigrants in the 1990s.[171] To help ease concerns over bribes and fair treatment, the Lincoln Police Department hired cultural outreach workers to translate traffic citations and common directions into Vietnamese. Additionally, applications for marriage licenses, safety directions for public buildings, and other important documents were also published in *quốc ngữ*.[172] On a statewide level, voter registration and driver's license manuals and exams were also available in Vietnamese by the 1990s.

These efforts allowed some urban villagers to negotiate governmental procedures without translators. The need to confer in English in the workplace remained an issue, however. While an educated and bilingual minority commanded professional and entrepreneurial careers, the majority of adults born in Vietnam worked in factory settings that did not require good conversational English. This mirrors the national trend in which 80 percent of Vietnamese in the United States worked in blue-collar jobs.[173] In Lincoln, many became valued long-term employees as laborers in food processing, electrical manufacturing, and service and hospitality industries. Leading employers included Mapes Industries, Lincoln Plating, Yankee Hill Brick, Square D (an electrical manufacturer), Russell Stover Candies, Lester's Electric, Land and Sky (a furniture manufacturer), Farmland Foods, and ConAgra. Additionally, hotels and garment cleaners hired and retained many Vietnamese women.[174] These types of employment were reminiscent of early work patterns among Germans from Russia and Omahas.

Consequently, work often reinforced immigrant status and Vietnamese identity. Their jobs, while not necessarily fulfilling, were generally seen as an avenue to achieve middle-class financial status without relinquishing linguistic or cultural uniqueness.[175] Consequently, whether they were fishermen, farmers, or teachers in Vietnam, most urban villagers were "eager to work" in meatpacking even if it meant a reduction in social status. Most set out to contribute to the family economy in order to advance its communal status.[176]

Many first-generation urban villagers were content with their jobs, as their inadequate English skills often limited employment possibilities.[177] Hoa Tran suggested that even for educated people, a "for surviving job" was a necessity for many urban villagers.[178] Now a bilingual liaison with Lincoln Public Schools, his first job upon arrival in Lincoln in 1983 was in meatpacking, even though he had completed an American college degree. Similarly, Qui Nguyen gladly accepted work in meatpacking as it was one of the few jobs that allowed non-English speakers to earn ten dollars an hour in 1992. Ultimately, Nguyen left the business as it was "too hard" a job, where many of his coworkers injured themselves with knives. Having little formal education, he remained in manual labor but found a more comfortable niche as a chrome plater. Still, he often worked seven days a week, but he claimed this was his choice.[179]

Such rigorous placements, however, were often met with concern and consternation among observers from mainstream and immigrant communities alike. The jobs that urban villagers performed were often described as "difficult and dangerous," as they certainly took the types of work many other Americans no longer wanted. Additionally, younger members of the

Vietnamese community often acknowledged the positions their elders held with embarrassment.[180] While compassionate, both these inclinations belie individual goals and deny older notions of the dignity of honest labor. As home-ownership statistics indicate, many urban villagers achieved economic stability in the new milieu by accepting assembly-line jobs.

As most labor positions in Lincoln did not require much verbal communication, local employers welcomed Vietnamese because they had a reputation for industriousness. The workers themselves—often toiling alongside Mexican, other Asian, and European immigrants—attempted to learn on-the-job English to help them get along. There was also the perception that learning English would protect them from certain forms of unfair treatment, especially heavy workloads.[181]

While important to ease on-the-job interactions, English acquisition was imperative for younger urban villagers as their educations were in English only. In addition to language issues, mainstream schools served as "powerful cultural agents" for shaping attitudes, expectations, and behaviors.[182] Schools often compelled immigrant children and children of immigrants to examine Vietnamese, Asian, and American identities.

Demographically, the urban villagers remained a young population that fed schools near their residences. About 40 percent of the entire population of the earliest arrivals attended local schools in 1979—eighty-six students were in Lincoln public schools, seventy-five in parochial schools, and thirty-five at the University of Nebraska. By the turn of the twenty-first century, Vietnamese American students represented the largest group served by the public school system's bilingual liaisons.[183] While the percentage of Vietnamese individuals in the school-age population was only slightly higher than the mean, the proportion of young adults in the twenty-five- to thirty-four-year age range was almost twice that of the general population. As these particular urban villagers tend to enjoy high birthrates, a spike in enrollment is anticipated in the near future.[184]

Barriers manifested themselves as soon as Vietnamese youth entered schools in Lincoln. Such barriers included language difficulties, unfamiliarity with American culture, and racial prejudice toward immigrants from a region with a historically negative context. Even within the most ethnically diverse of these institutions, hurtful epithets were aimed at individuals laboring to grasp the language of their new home. Facility in English often separated those who adapted readily to the new milieu from those who did not. Fortunately, efforts were made to ease this sort of transition, and federal aid helped pay for English as a Second Language programs in schools with the largest immigrant populations.[185]

Students, however, still struggled with the language itself and the concept of being different from the mainstream. For most individuals, it took "one to three years to learn social English and five to seven years to learn academic English."[186] Even after years of study and observation, native Vietnamese speakers often grapple with tenses and plurality as these concepts in their language are contextual and denoted neither by vowel changes nor the use of suffixes. As a general rule, Vietnamese urban villagers wrote better English than they spoke, which eased learning, but other issues often influenced true success in schools.[187]

Educational achievement among young urban villagers varied dramatically, and connections to their enclaves helped some students and hindered others. Vietnamese elders in Lincoln often coached their children to gain education, become materially successful, and raise the status of the entire family. Thus encouraged, many students excelled in school and went on to succeed at the University of Nebraska and Nebraska Wesleyan University.[188] Indeed, as Hoa Tran asserted, the "dropout rate was very low comparing with other economic minority [*sic*]. Vietnamese students are very successful."[189]

For others, however, cultural loyalty was constructed to exclude some mainstream characteristics. Probably injured by racial prejudice, these urban villagers viewed success in school as a "white" endeavor. These were the individuals most at risk for gang activities.[190] Although the existence of such organizations created another stereotype, in many cities including Lincoln, gang activity was perpetrated by young men generally between the ages of fifteen and twenty-four.[191] The Lincoln Police Department was reluctant to provide information on such activities.

Fortunately, most urban villagers spent their time in school wisely as English competency and education were generally deemed to be vital components of future success. English acquisition and entry into the mainstream economy, however, changed many urban villagers' connections with the Vietnamese language. To accommodate American sensibilities, some individuals reworked their names. In the old milieu, family name preceded the familiar—Tran Phong, for instance, was actually Mr. Tran. In Lincoln, names were often juxtaposed—Phong Tran, for example. Many adopted American familiar names, placed them at the beginning of the sequence, and used them even more commonly than their Vietnamese names.

Similarly, because schools demanded English, students often lived in two linguistic worlds. Many necessarily spoke Vietnamese at home but used Vietnamese sprinkled with English words when talking to peers.[192] Still other young people in the twenty-first century "speak little if any Vietnamese."[193]

In addition to a new language, schools forced young urban villagers to deal with the concepts of independence and assertiveness. While these traits were valued in mainstream culture, they were often at odds with the traditional Vietnamese family hierarchy, which placed the group before the individual. Even university students, such as Duc Tran, struggled with the concept that "Authority [in the United States] is not based on age," but rather focused on accomplishment.[194]

### Generations

Examinations of the worlds of work and school demonstrated that identity formation for many Vietnamese urban villagers was a "complex negotiation of commitments and compromises."[195] Generational divisions further complicated the efforts of these immigrants in adapting to the mainstream culture. Familiarly, the construction of generations among Vietnamese in America includes the first generation—those born in Vietnam who generally emigrated as teenagers or adults—and the second generation—those born in the United States. Uniquely, there is also a "1.5 generation" that consists of individuals born in Vietnam who emigrated before they were eight years old. Consequently, they were acculturated in the United States, but they remained intimately familiar with the old milieu as well. The communities that provided first-generation immigrants with "a safety net of protection and support" often became a "burden to children."[196]

As a general rule, first-generation urban villagers remained deeply connected to the culturescapes of Vietnam. Preferring hierarchical and harmonious extended families, they often constructed support systems solely within the Vietnamese community and felt little pressure to abandon old-world patterns. Linda Pham even observed that older immigrants not only kept to Vietnamese circles, they generally did not trust outsiders.[197] As parents, they attempted to keep their children involved in affairs within the home and the urban village and dissuaded prolonged contact with new American peers.[198] Their greatest fear was that their children would become Americanized and, in the process, accept consumer culture and abandon traditional spirituality.[199] While the elders remained certain of their Vietnamese identities in the twenty-first century, they often described the next generations as "uncentered" and "uncertain of their identity." They called these individuals "*mất gốc*" (lost roots) because they appeared to be growing away from the values of their urban villages.[200]

The second generation—which in 2005 accounted for about a quarter of the population—was simultaneously scolded for moving away from traditional culture and praised for serving as cultural intermediaries for their older relatives. As Linda Pham observed, "I always have to translate for my mom."[201] Many demonstrated great facility moving back and forth between cultures, but the practice threatened the stability of the family hierarchy as youths were necessarily in charge during mainstream interactions. Consequently, they often were "caught between two cultures."[202] Some even suggested, "We don't really fit in." Indeed, Vietnamese saw them as Americans, and Americans saw them as Asians.[203]

Similarly, many in the 1.5 generation have challenged the authority of their elders by accepting mainstream preferences for gender and age equality.[204] Gender equality was a relative thing, however, and some young women suggested that men "assimilate" easier into the mainstream as their socialization patterns were less limited.[205] Conversely, women were still charged with taking care of younger siblings and expected to be mindful of family status. Still, the desire to be part of the new milieu was intense, and once again, younger urban villagers lived in "two different worlds." As Ngoc Dung Le averred, at home they had "to be Vietnamese," but outside of the house, they could "be American."[206]

As a result of such dichotomies, individuals in the 1.5 and second generations developed a hybrid identity that allowed them to move comfortably back and forth between the two cultures. Perhaps best described as "cultural switching," the new identity was more a dual entity than a synthesis. It encouraged young urban villagers to proudly proclaim, "I'm Vietnamese, but yet I also live in America."[207] Among community elders they *were* Vietnamese; in the mainstream public they *were* American.[208] Interestingly, as youths explored and incorporated the norms and values of the host culture, they frequently celebrated the religions, family structure, and language of the sending culture with renewed vigor.[209] While few urban villagers were truly bilingual, it appears many were bicultural.

Older and recently arrived urban villagers, on the other hand, especially those with limited English-language skills, remained distinctly Vietnamese. Their responses to cosmopolitan forces were generally utilitarian. They took what they needed in order to live comfortably, but socially they remained in the familiar spaces they constructed. Many jealously guarded being Vietnamese, because, as Son Tran—who arrived in 1991 as an eighteen-year-old—claimed, "You don't know what your identity is until you are at risk of losing it."[210]

### Transnationalism

While urban villagers in Lincoln remained fundamentally Vietnamese, they were already distinct from populations in Vietnam. Called *Việt Kiều*—overseas Vietnamese—in the sending culture, by 2000 they were part of a 2.7-million-person diaspora that was spread over one hundred nations. Not a self-imposed ascription, the term *Việt Kiều* was simultaneously undesirable but one that was associated with great material wealth.[211] Urban villagers who returned as tourists recognized these distinctions, but they also realized they had become part of a transnational "community." More a "social network" than a "place," this community fostered a new identity that allowed them to maintain social and economic ties to a symbolic homeland.[212] For some, behaviors were casual enough to be considered "translocal"—situations where immigrants' bonds to the sending society were not so intense.[213] For many others, consistent communication, remitting money, and regular trips home were the norm. These ties—whether translocal or transnational—were reinforced through popular culture and instantaneous technological contact.

#### *Politics of Separation*

Not all of Lincoln's Vietnamese urban villagers took part in their new transnational community. For immigrants who constructed their identities around the RVN and the Catholic Church in particular, interaction with the SRV seemed antithetical to their values.[214] Politically, fervent anticommunism remained a vital motivator well into the twenty-first century. For urban villagers in this camp, the 1975 decision to withdraw $3.25 billion in U.S. aid promised to the Hanoi government after the Paris Accords was justified by continued DRV aggression. As they gained citizenship in their new home, they often used foreign policy as a reference point for democratic participation. In the 1992 presidential election, for instance, many voted for Democrat Bill Clinton because they were concerned about Republican president George H. W. Bush's attempts to normalize economic relations with the SRV. Conversely, in 2004 many opted for Republican George W. Bush because of Democrat John Kerry's senatorial stance favoring normalization. Believing that living in Vietnam under communist rule was untenable, many lobbied for maintaining Vietnamese refugee status—even if classified as "economic refugees"—and continuing the practice of accepting high levels of immigration from Southeast Asia.[215]

Vietnamese Catholics in Lincoln were keenly aware of the repression of their coreligionists in the SRV and argued for continued separation. Indeed, many congregants of Immaculate Heart of Mary were descendants of refugees who fled south of the seventeenth parallel in 1954. Distrust of the Hanoi government was confirmed by reports from the eight hundred thousand Catholics who remained in their northern homes.[216] Saddening news continued to reach the urban villagers after their arrival in Lincoln. The organ of the Lincoln Diocese reported the dire situation for decades with stories that included, "Church in Chains in Vietnam," "Hanoi Churches Now Historical Monuments," "Vietnamese Bishops Harassed, Interrogated," and "Vietnamese Bishops Remain at Odds with Government."[217] While an estimated 1.5 million to 3 million individuals practiced Catholicism in twenty-five Vietnamese dioceses in the 1990s, conflict between the international church and the SRV government was common. SRV officials recently denounced the Vatican for granting sainthood to 117 Vietnamese martyrs who preserved their faith during purges in the eighteenth and nineteenth centuries. Lincoln's urban villagers undoubtedly joined the bishop of Hanoi in rejoicing over their canonization.[218]

### Political, Social, and Economic Ties

Issues of separation remained entrenched in older populations but began to dissipate among the 1.5- and second-generation urban villagers in the 1990s, even as the United States and the SRV were restoring political and economic relations. Contact with the sending society eased this transition. Vietnamese in Lincoln had great difficulty maintaining connections to home and family in the 1970s, and travel to Vietnam was not considered an option. SRV policies toward expatriates gradually softened beginning in the 1980s. Free-market reforms—*đổi mới*—were implemented in 1986, and overseas entrepreneurs were encouraged and increasingly likely to reconnect with their homeland. In addition to business involvement, elderly *Việt Kiều* were allowed to visit Vietnam by 1992. U.S. policies also eased the separation. In 1994 the economic embargo of 1975 was finally lifted. Normalization followed in 1995 as political diplomacy was formerly reestablished. In 2001, economic relations were normalized as well.[219]

The end result was that Lincoln's urban villagers and *Việt Kiều* across the United States were able to travel to Vietnam as tourists. Eight thousand American *Việt Kiều* made the journey in 1988, and the number of visitors increased each subsequent year. In 2000, 280,000 made the trip.[220] Lincoln's urban villagers were part of this new tourist industry. Xuan-Trang Ho, for example, returned to Vietnam twice since her arrival in the United States in 1994, once with her family and once with a group from Nebraska Wesleyan University.[221] Similarly, Loi Vo, a former ARVN pilot, has visited Vietnam six times since he flew out of Saigon and into exile in 1975.[222] Second-generation urban villagers also make the journey as many of their relatives remained in Vietnam.[223] A small travel industry even developed in Lincoln. Kim Son Video and Gifts, for instance, advertises "*Bán Vé Máy Bay, Chuyển Tiền Về VN*"—which means they sold airline tickets to locals and remitted money to people in Vietnam as well.

Even before visiting became commonplace, many overseas Vietnamese sent remittances home to aid their relatives. In the late 1970s, they were largely in the form of food and durable goods. By the mid-1980s they were almost universally monetary gifts sent through American-based merchants. By 1995 the money went through banks. In addition to aiding families, these gifts brought needed currency into the SRV and helped stabilize its economy. In all, over $2 billion has entered Vietnam over the last quarter century, most going to southern communities.[224]

People living in Vietnam have benefited from their *Việt Kiều* relatives in a number of ways. Linda Pham's mother, for instance, furnished the capital her grandfather needed to construct a new cement block home that was complete with a tile floor. This replaced a dwelling made of straw and wood with a dirt floor. In some respects, sending people abroad was part of family survival. As Pham noted, "My grandma want my mom to come here and like get a job and send her money. Like it would be an easier life over there in Vietnam. I think."[225]

Tourism, hard currency, and human capital have all influenced the nation. Originally from Phu Hoa Dong, Lincolnite Loi Vo noted that a vibrant tourism industry that catered largely to *Việt Kiều* grew up in and around the rice fields of his old hometown. Small investments by transnational entrepreneurs were increasingly common. In 2000 they committed 385 billion dong—slightly over $27 million—to various projects. Even many self-described anticommunists embraced the goal of bringing American companies into Vietnam to benefit the country of their birth.[226]

Transnational contact reinforced cultural ties and brought aid to an ailing economy. Many Lincoln Vietnamese urban villagers—especially members of the 1.5 and second generation—looked "to Vietnam as a source of identity validation."[227] Time was an important factor throughout the transnational community. Over one-third of Vietnam's population was born after the "American War" concluded. (See Table 4-3.) To this generation, the conflict was not a living memory; rather it was just one chapter in a prolonged struggle for nationhood.[228] Similarly, many young Vietnamese born in America were entrenched in the idea that RVN "fell to communism," but they do not remember the horrors of the war. Harboring few such memories, many urban villagers in the twenty-first century viewed Vietnam as a cultural cradle rather than a lost homeland.[229]

Table 4-3. Estimated Population of Vietnam, 1890–2005.

| 1890 | 10 million |
|------|------------|
| 1940 | 21 million |
| 1980 | 53 million |
| 1990 | 65 million |
| 2005 | 83 million |

Source: Ngo Vinh Long, "Vietnam," 9 in Douglas Allen and Ngo Vinh Long, ed. Coming to Terms: Indochina, the United States, and War (Boulder, CO: Westview Press 1991); Central Intelligence Agency: World Factbook, "Vietnam," https://www.cia.gov/library/publications/the-world-factbook/geos/vm.html#People.

### Popular Culture

For many Vietnamese in America, transnational identities formed because they enjoyed near-constant contact with the sending society. This allowed for frequent exchanges of information and material culture. These connections developed only gradually as trends in the SRV had little influence in the United States between 1975 and 1995. Still, as Vietnam emerged as the imagined center of a familiar and desirable culture, transnational communities were increasingly connected through cyberspace and a burgeoning music industry.[230] As a general rule, these developments were welcomed by younger urban villagers but questioned by their elders.

Before relations between America and the SRV were normalized, the *Việt Kiều* entertainment industry was centered in Orange County, California. One of perhaps thirty companies, Thuy Nga Productions was founded in 1989 and emerged as an industry leader by marketing a wide array of music, movie DVDs, and karaoke items. Packaged as part MTV and part Broadway musical, this truly American-based operation largely advertised in Vietnamese, but its copy was punctuated by English words and short English narratives.[231]

Typical of the entire "Little Saigon" industry, they produced and sold "a nostalgic blend of love tunes" sung by male or female soloists in Vietnamese. Enjoyed across the diaspora, the most popular works were sugary ballads that synthesized traditional elements with influences from global popular music. Musical accompaniment included modern instruments, such as keyboards, electric bass, and guitars, as well as distinctly Asian devices such as *Đàn Nhị*—a bowed Vietnamese stringed instrument renowned for its haunting melody lines. These recordings created a sense of wistfulness about precommunist South Vietnam. Because this music was aimed at a finite population, retail numbers were comparatively modest, and the sale of fifteen thousand copies was considered a hit.[232]

Popularity of the California-based industry reached its zenith in 1995, and while interest in music remained, a drastic shift occurred. Record sales in Little Saigon experienced a 70 percent drop over the next five years as a "musical invasion" from Vietnam was launched out of Ho Chi Minh City (Saigon) and Hanoi.[233] Made possible by trade policy shifts and plausible by young American transnationalists who wanted to "move on and open up and show these people what freedom is all about," a vibrant new source of music emerged in 1997.[234] Although not as smoothly presented and professionally staged as the Little Saigon product, the imported style focused on emotion and musical innovation. Paying homage to mainstream American popular culture, many Vietnamese bands employed hip-hop and rock and roll elements. These influences were largely absent in the domestic products, but they were welcomed by younger consumers who were tired of static nostalgia.[235]

While the Vietnamese recordings were available in stores in Orange County and in Lincoln, Nebraska, they failed to get air play on American radio stations. In fact, the music has become part of "a widening cultural divide" between the generations. In California, one concert by Vietnamese nationals was picketed by more protesters than the concert hall could seat. Most came waving RVN and U.S. flags, and despite the promoter's suggestion that lyrical content had changed less than musical style, they expressed concerns about the spread of "communist propaganda" within their communities.[236] Siding with the old guard, the only local radio station in Lincoln that carried Vietnamese-language programming preferred the established nostalgia of American artists.

Even those individuals most opposed to SRV popular culture have kept contact with relatives in the sending culture, and in the years since normalization they have enjoyed eased communications. Contact was initially slow and uncertain as urban villagers used letters, the telegraph, and the telephone to continue intercourse. Since the mid-1980s, many have gladly accepted the aid of new information technologies. The arrival of the Internet clearly improved transnational communication and eased community building among immigrants and Vietnamese nationals.[237] Additionally, it changed the nature of local and national news as members of the Vietnamese diaspora became increasingly connected.

Technology precluded the development of a Vietnamese-language press in Lincoln. Although some local news was broadcast in Vietnamese during the "South East Asian Youth Club"—a weekly show on community radio—information in print was confined largely to biweekly newspapers published in Southern California or in Canada. Toronto's *Thời Báo*, for instance, reportedly circulates over one hundred thousand copies, which were commonly found in restaurants around the Capital City. Additionally, a plethora of online "newspapers" were available from Australia; San Jose, California; and Hanoi in both Vietnamese and in English.[238]

Personal communication, however, has been facilitated by the Internet. Duyen Tu's parents, for instance, used Skype to speak frequently with relatives in Vietnam without incurring long-distance telephone charges.[239] Even in the tightly monitored SRV, "Virtual space allows for relative free expression" although many Internet groups employ self-censorship to placate authorities. Communication with the sending culture was not as easy as interactions among diaspora Vietnamese because personal computers in Vietnam remained unaffordable. Internet cafés, however, were ubiquitous by 2000, especially in large cities.[240] Consequently, messages were sent back and forth in cyberspace, and then passed along by more conventional methods. Ultimately, a sense of shared community was enhanced as *Việt Kiều* reconnected to the sending culture.

By the dawn of the twenty-first century, transnational Vietnamese were linked by technologies that often transcended the boundaries of nation-states.[241] In the United States alone, Lincoln was connected to Houston and Orange County by family and business operations decades ago.[242] Increasingly, these connections ran back to Vietnam as well. While rejected by many older urban villagers who still fear communism, transnationalism will certainly continue to influence the Vietnamese across the diaspora.

## Conclusion

While Lincoln's urban villagers must be readily identifiable as *Việt Kiều* in the cities and villages of Vietnam, they have become at once foreign and familiar. Their renewed contact may help maintain a Vietnamese identity in Nebraska as overseas travel has already altered language and social skills. Similarly, most particular and cosmopolitan influences support an overarching "Vietnamese" identity. While there were clearly divisions within this identity few appear to have abandoned it as their primary ascription.

The Vietnamese identity in Lincoln was founded on a shared sense of history that spanned three thousand years. It was maintained through the daily use of performed culture—especially language, traditional celebrations, and foodways—within polynucleated settlements. It was strengthened and zealously protected because of trying interactions with the mainstream. American Christian religious organizations, for instance, questioned some culturally specific practices, and the foundation of separate congregations diluted criticisms and protected the old practices through insulation. Similarly, while employment played a major role in Vietnamese adaptation to the mainstream, language and cultural barriers in the workplace often allowed retrenchment within the community. More defensively, Vietnamese actively avoided an imposed "Asian" identity by highlighting the distinctiveness of their own culture.

Formed by imported preferences and sustained to ease transitions into the new milieu, the Vietnamese identity in Lincoln was never absolute. Internally, it was divided by Vietnamese Buddhist, Vietnamese Catholic, and Vietnamese Protestant sensibilities. Traditionally tolerant of each other, interaction in Lincoln was common, but spiritual needs and loyalties among all three religions remained distinct.

The greater division was between generations. Immigrant loyalty to the RVN and their protection of Southeast Asian family hierarchies did not always make sense to 1.5- and second-generation Vietnamese. The younger urban villagers were in near-constant contact with the mainstream through their experiences at school and work and through their duties as cultural intermediaries. Consequently, new expectations were formed, new behaviors accepted, and ancient hierarchies questioned. Instead of moving toward an American identity en masse, a hybrid identity developed among younger urban villagers—an identity that appeared to strengthen the Vietnamese ascription. Still valuing Vietnamese ways, they maintained them alongside a new set of "American" behaviors. This often resulted in "cultural switching," the practice of alternating between Vietnamese and American identities. Still, despite great mainstream pressures and disuniting influences, the generations were more alike than they were different.

# Chapter 5
# Comparisons

Identities and Communities during the Long Twentieth Century

If food "is everyone's first language," then Lincoln in the twenty-first century hosts a lively dialogue.[1] Food is not a frivolous cultural artifact. By discussing dishes as commonplace as soup, 130 years of long-standing ethnic practices that celebrate divergent identities can be accessed by all residents of the Capital City. In addition to providing nourishment and interesting dining experiences, soups—while not the most salient indicators of ethnic identity—connect "past, present, and future" generations of distinct urban villagers.[2]

Although not popular restaurant fare, *Knöphla* or noodle soup remains available at American Historical Society of Germans from Russia (AHSGR) functions, and a variety of recipes undoubtedly warm countless local kitchens. There may have been one hundred names for *Knöphla* in the North and South Russian Bottoms prior to World War II, as the sending culture was actually a conglomeration of agrarian villages. Conversely, *watóⁿzi skíthe taní*—an Omaha corn soup graced with a hearty beef (or bison) broth and savory chunks of meat—has a single name reflecting the intense nationalism of its sending culture. Served with frybread rather than rye bread, it too is enjoyed primarily at community events and is often provided by the hosts of functions as acts of "sacrifice" for their relatives. Widely available in Vietnamese homes and restaurants, *phở gà* is a traditional yet transnational chicken noodle soup available in Hanoi and Saigon; Sydney, Australia; and Lincoln, Nebraska. Comprising a slow-cooked stock seasoned with ginger, shallots, and onions, this dish is served with blanched sprouts, basil or cilantro, green chilis, and limes on the side.[3] It is a favorite food from "a country of food," a place "of skinny people obsessed with eating."[4]

Soups can be sampled at the Welfare Society Hall in the North Bottoms, the Lincoln Indian Center, and at multiple locations in the Vietnamese business district. All three locations are specific to the enclaves that ethnic populations built in Lincoln. These places protected particular pieces of performed culture and housed ever-evolving, complex cultural identities. Cosmopolitan and transnational forces interacted with imported ideas to continually modify these ascriptions. Never finished products, numerous identities overlapped with each other, and still other designations were discarded or vanished over time. Still, German from Russia, Omaha, and Vietnamese identities remained long-term markers of distinction that are vital to living and evolving populations.

Viewed together, discussions about cultural identity among these three unique ethnic groups provide a long-range lens that focuses on a century of pluralism in Lincoln.[5] Within this emerging picture, the particular identities that matured in their urban villages were often framed by mainstream distrust and disapproval. Consequently, struggles over "ethnic, racial, and national" boundaries were inherent parts of the new arrivals' adaptations to life in the Capital City.[6] All three groups demonstrated that it was possible to take on a great number of American ideas and behaviors in order to survive in a new cultural milieu while maintaining distinct ethnic identities and cultural traditions.[7] Naturally, the ways each group accommodated to the mainstream depended on specific interactions at specific points in Lincoln's history.

## Pluralistic Communities

Lincoln's cityscape is necessarily a "historical-social-spatial" construction that included immigrant and migrant populations that were culturally different from the mainstream.[8] Establishing urban villages in significantly different eras, Volga Germans, Omahas, and Vietnamese were all subject to community discussions about their inclusion or exclusion. Over the course of the long twentieth century, fundamental shifts in the tone of the dialogues softened as mainstream objections to diversity decreased, but acceptance was never guaranteed. Never relinquishing agency, immigrant groups were aware of mainstream debates, but particular group interests were often the chief catalyst that urban villagers examined when they set out to build their enclaves. The oldest urban villages—now largely defunct—are officially celebrated in the twenty-first century, while the living enclaves are barely acknowledged.

Volga Germans encountered the full brunt of exclusionist philosophy in Lincoln for decades. Because many citizens maintained an amazingly re-silient assumption of mainstream superiority,[9] several generations of urban villagers remained "dumb Rooshians" to much of Lincoln. As a result, they abandoned their imported performed cultures very slowly.

Arriving after World War II, Omahas and Vietnamese formed their com-munities in an era when "cultural pluralism"—the idea that there was room for ethnic heterogeneity within the greater body politic—was emerging.[10] The desirability of pluralism, however, remains a hotly debated topic. The old assimilationist arguments remained, but other scholars averred that mainstream attempts at inclusion hide unexpected agendas. Multicultural-ism—an idea that emerged in the 1980s—supported shared access to space; while inclusive in some respects, it often "de-legitimizes" Native American territorial claims.[11] Mainstream citizens could claim as much right to oc-cupy lands on Omaha Nation, despite a long history of treaties, as Omahas themselves. Additionally, multiculturalism often stressed racial and eth-nic cooperation in the building of western American communities while downplaying inherent conflicts between ethnic groups. In reality, minority subcultures were necessarily excluded throughout the nineteenth and early twentieth centuries.[12]

Despite racial attitudes, cultural pluralism was "a fact in American so-ciety before it became a theory."[13] Indeed, many immigrant peoples made Lincoln their home. Favoring their own agendas, Volga Germans and Oma-has largely arrived through their own volition. The first wave of Vietnamese were resettled, but subsequent arrivals came by choice. All three groups built ethnic enclaves more as a matter of preference than out of fear of persecu-tion. Whatever mainstream inclinations prevailed, these particular urban villagers insisted on living among their own kinspeople whenever possible. New arrivals in the enclaves were connected by vertical social networks that linked generations of families and horizontal networks that joined neigh-bors and coreligionists.[14] Coherence to patterns of "family" and "cultural community" were challenged by the mainstream, but economic and politi-cal influences often reinforced separatism.[15]

Some middle-class immigrants—often leaders within their communi-ties—served as role models of modern economic development in Lincoln.[16] Most urban villagers, however, occupied the lower occupational rungs of an unfamiliar cityscape. Although they were agrarian peoples who often garnered wages from migratory farm labor, most *Volgers* who arrived around the turn of the twentieth century could not afford to own farmland and built distinctly urban lives. Due to their coming early into Lincoln, they constructed their enclaves from the ground up on the outskirts of downtown. Here they had access to the mainstream economy and little need of transportation services. Similarly, Omahas arrived as rural people and probably recognized some of their Teutonic neighbors from the beet fields. They came to escape poverty on their reservation during the post–World War II era. As migrant and casual agricultural work became more mechanized at this time, population and job growth across the Great Plains increasingly concentrated in communities of sixty thousand or more.[17] With nowhere left to build, Omahas and Vietnamese—who were already mostly urbanized— settled in Lincoln's affordable core neighborhoods, where they duplicated a common pattern of working as laborers and service personnel that *Volgers* had taken on decades earlier. All three urban villages hosted relatively fluid populations as affluent families moved into larger accommodations or out of enclaves altogether, usually to be replaced by newcomers.[18]

Despite these economic similarities, the physical forms of the various urban villages were variable and reflected distinct demographic and technological developments. Because they arrived into a relatively undeveloped walking city, the North and South Russian Bottoms grew up as classic urban villages. They housed large, homogeneous populations—at least as viewed from the outside—and they were institutionally complete as urban villagers did not need to leave their neighborhoods for most of their religious, social, and material needs. Their gradual, but nearly complete, adaptation to the mainstream coincided with marked "spatial decentralization"—often thought of as a benchmark of assimilation.[19] By the 1950s and 1960s, as Jacob Reifschneider recalled, Volga Germans were "pretty well spread out all over the city."[20]

Older *Volgers* that remained in the Bottoms recalled the in-migration of American Indian families along the western edges of their enclaves during these decades.[21] The larger mainstream community may have barely noticed this much smaller urban village until the 1970s when concern about placement of the Indian Center was at its height. While clustering was always apparent, decentralization was mandated by small numbers and low home-ownership levels. "Integrated pluralism"—small conglomerates surrounded by mainstream groupings—may best define Omaha spaces within Lincoln.[22] Advances in transportation, however, made congregating at community focal points relatively easy, and cultural preservation was carried on in ethnically heterogeneous residential environments.

Vietnamese numbers were initially too small to allow neighborhood homogeneity. Additionally immigrants arrived in core districts long after they had matured and then declined as individuals with substantial means moved to newer neighborhoods. In this changing world, the Vietnamese achieved "ethnic dominance"—they were the plurality rather than the majority—in certain neighborhoods by the mid-1990s.[23] A predilection for home ownership and the presence of a Vietnamese business district cemented settlement patterns. Enjoying the comfort of a relatively tolerant mainstream, all of Lincoln is invited to restaurants and shops on "North 27th Street" to "Try something Vietnamese"—whether it be *phở gà* or a dish ordered after asking the server to "recommend something fresh and different."[24]

Similarly, in the twenty-first century all Lincolnites were welcome to come into the urban villages to attend Germans-from-Russia soup suppers and Omaha doings.[25] By this time, the governmental mainstream acknowledged the historic Volga German neighborhoods while shying away from discussing modern ethnic enclaves.[26] There are, for instance, no historical markers celebrating the vitality of Omaha or Vietnamese citizens and their contributions to Lincoln. Perhaps their more recent arrivals preclude them from historical comment. Just as likely, contemporary concerns about racial profiling or other unseemly accusations may have caused this silence. Interested parties are able to access information about ethnicity primarily through the city planning department's publications compiled from census reports, but, with the exception of a recent oral history project, there has been little official acknowledgment of these ethnic places.[27]

Whatever forms urban villages manifested, all ethnic communities in Lincoln reinforced aspects of the urban villagers' imported identities by maintaining significant spatial and cultural insularity. In short, ethnic neighborhoods preserved cultures.[28] These enclaves continued to form even in an era of "growing tolerance" in the mainstream.[29] Over the years, there were significant differences in the way ethnic residents were treated. Volga Germans, for instance, necessarily provided for themselves and their communities without much sympathy from greater Lincoln. State and city governments as demanded by the Constitution and the city charter now provide interpretive services and other considerations for ethnic citizens.[30] The general population, however, may still harbor many age-old suspicions about immigrants and migrants.

### Ethnicity and Race

Throughout the twentieth century, some mainstream citizens responded negatively to urban villagers' behavioral differences and their appearances. Issues surrounding ethnicity, race, and racialism—all social constructions— highlighted continued tensions between particular and cosmopolitan forces. Culturally and behaviorally specific, "ethnic boundaries" and racial lines were issues with which the new arrivals contended in the course of their identity negotiations.[31]

Although race is no longer part of present-day scientific discourse, socially it remains significant even in the twenty-first century. It was an extremely important consideration when Volga Germans were colonizing the Bottoms. At that point in time, Americans "were white and immigrants were not."[32] In the fin de siècle world, whiteness was a marker of inclusion that went beyond skin color and involved cultural behaviors such as language usage. Performing stoop labor and other bottom-rung economic tasks were also indicators that even European immigrants were not quite white.

While physically indistinguishable from the 40 percent of Nebraska's population who claimed German heritage, *Volgers* were racialized the entire time they remained in their urban villages.[33] Culturally and linguistically distinct, their position within complex early-twentieth-century hierarchies—at least in the beet fields—was one step above Mexicans and Japanese laborers.[34] In Lincoln they helped build neighborhoods and infrastructure, but they remained part of the immigrant "problem" until World War II.[35] In the postwar era, race as a "symbol of cultural status" was extended to formerly excluded groups, including Jews and Germans who emigrated from beyond the pale of the *Reich*.[36] Intriguingly, Volga Germans became "white" and not ethnic almost simultaneously.

Although they took advantage of their Americanization—Amens, Giebelhauses, and Schwartzkopfs clearly participated at all levels of Lincoln society—their heritages were soon challenged as race and ethnicity became virtually interchangeable.[37] Immigrant numbers in Lincoln decreased dramatically after World War I, and in some respects, ethnic separation was legislated out of existence.[38] In the post–World War II world, mainstream Nebraska was commonly defined as a homogeneous collection of "immigrants" from the "United States or Europe."[39] Additionally, the ethnic revival of the 1960s and 1970s favored southern and eastern European Americans, especially Poles, Italians, Czechs, Slovaks, Slovenes, and Russians. Germans, who were formerly the "most separate and independent of immigrants," were allegedly "speedily absorbed into Anglo-American society."[40] Such constructions ignored the survival of the German-language press and the contributions of German speakers to litigation protecting diversity. Although Germans from Russia were often placed in a category by themselves, immigration historians aver that Teutons in Nebraska, despite their numbers, had "the weakest sense of peoplehood."[41]

As European ethnic identities became voluntary ascriptions, it appeared that cultural homogeneity and near-universal whiteness had been achieved.[42] As a result, ethnicity was racialized in postwar Lincoln as citizens were viewed as a collection of whites and a few exotic outsiders. As late as 1980 the nonwhite population constituted 4 percent of the city's population. The ethnoracial makeup of the Capital City began to change dramatically thereafter, and by 2004, ethnics increased their presence to 12 percent.[43] Lincoln, unlike many cities, has virtually no suburbs, so these statistics were not changed by the flight of whites out of town, although spatially, many middle-class residents of core neighborhoods fled to newer developments.

Used to being racialized if not confronted by overt racism, Omahas always accounted for less than 1 percent of the city's population, but clustering made them obvious in their urban village. Probably less harried in mainstream Lincoln than in the rural areas immediately adjacent to Omaha Nation, they still were forced to confront negative stereotypes that painted them as indolent drunkards. Unfortunately, the levels of Native American substance abuse and related chronic diseases were much higher than any other population's in the state.[44] The mainstream public rarely looks beyond these statistics to familiarize themselves with truly Omaha values.

Similarly, tribal ethnicity was frequently overlooked as "Indian" became a catchall racial designation. Omaha as an ethnicity exists primarily in an international Indian context. Fortunately, as mainstream tolerance increased during the era of urban migration, positive aspects of Omaha culture were revealed in the media. As early as 1962 the *Lincoln Star* ran a weeklong series on the Native American Church that highlighted its beliefs, rituals, and their promotion of "sobriety, industry, charity, and right living."[45] While press coverage about urban villagers was generally sparse, articles about "doings" were generally favorable.[46]

Human-interest stories also explored Vietnamese cultural traditions in Lincoln. The favorite topic is *Tết*—the Vietnamese Lunar New Year—which is always marked by colorful festivities and feasting.[47] Despite the favorable press, Vietnamese—who like Omahas remain both ethnically and racially separate from the mainstream—face two divergent stereotypes. A "Rambo" image formulated in Hollywood in the post–Vietnam War era continues to define Vietnamese as warlike and ruthless in the popular imagination.[48] They also faced the onus of being part of a "model minority," a racial designation assigned to all Asians, who are supposed to be better educated and make more money than other groups.[49]

The model-minority concept, however, has rarely defined the experiences of Lincoln's urban villagers. Vietnamese nationally in 1985 were the only Asian group whose income was below the national medium.[50] Over the years, Lincoln's populations were not the exception to this pattern. Vietnamese per-capita income in the Capital City in 2000 was $12,894, compared with $20,984 for the greater community. This gross inequity is partially mitigated by Vietnamese family structures. Median family income among urban villagers was $50,313, compared to $52,558 for the entire city.[51] Still, the model minority as far as economic clout was unrealized.

Language and education gaps continue to keep many of the new immigrants in positions at the bottom of the economic ladder. For instance, only 12 percent of first-generation Vietnamese in the United States hold college degrees. This statistic compares poorly to Koreans, who had college-graduation rates of 45 percent in the same demographic sample.[52] Consequently, the first generation of urban villagers necessarily pools its resources for continued family success while encouraging the next generation to raise family status by achieving what they had not. Facing pressure to excel in school not only at home but in public as well, many youths have difficulties adjusting to these great expectations.[53]

For their part, Vietnamese urban villagers face an unfamiliar cultural mix. From an Asian perspective, "America as a cultural identity is a hybrid of European civilizations."[54] To them, historical experiences of Volga German immigrants seem light years away. While immigrant experiences may not create bonds between people, sometimes they do create empathy. At the 1975 American Historical Society of Germans from Russia convention in Lincoln, Marie Fahrennruch Prichard said of the Vietnamese, "I love them. They need a country." In fact most of the seven hundred polled at the event shared this assessment. Francis Amen went on to encourage the newcomers to preserve their heritage as a mechanism to maintain pride in the face of inevitable discrimination from the mainstream.[55]

In this manner, German-from-Russia revivalists helped to educate mainstream Lincoln to the presence and needs of more recent arrivals.[56] This was a significant gesture, as "racial and ethnic discord," while not always overt in Nebraska, often lurks just beneath the surface.[57] Fortunately, discrimination often softens when divergent groups interact. Germans from Russia, Omahas, and Vietnamese all recognize this and frequently invite the mainstream public to events in order to stimulate positive exchange. Still, the latter two peoples remain racialized, and negative stereotypes are perpetuated. Continued ethnic pride, however, frequently eases these negative developments. Even those who have largely adapted to the mainstream take time to celebrate their distinctness. Consequently, retained and revived cultural identities still play a comforting role in the twenty-first century.

### Transnationalism, Internationalism, and Nationalism

While some argue that "identity is no longer based on territory" as communities and economies are increasingly globalized, place—whether remembered or revisited—remains vital in the long-term maintenance of ethnicity.[58] Germans from Russia, Omahas, and Vietnamese in Lincoln all built parts of their modern identities on transnational, translocal, or international ties to their sending cultures. Connections certainly varied from individual to individual, but considerations of homelands were part of "the struggle to determine how far to go in adapting to the new host society."[59] The related cosmopolitan influence of American nationalism also informed identities among all urban villagers.

True transnationalism required "simultaneity, persistence, and intensity" of contact and participation between individuals in host and sending communities. More casual contact is better defined as "translocalism," and internationalism in this context focuses on diaspora populations with mere memories of the sending culture.[60] Not surprisingly, access to points of origin became easier over time, and modern globalization and technology prolong transnational contacts. Omaha and Vietnamese urban-villager contact with their sending cultures is much more fluid for first- and second-generation populations then was ever plausible among *Volgers*. Ease does not guarantee transnational contact, but without the impediments of time and space, those wishing to remain connected can generally do so.

Indeed, transnationalism prior to World War II was accomplished only with great difficulty. Many Volga Germans communicated with the colonies in Russia via mail, but international service could take up to six months. Similarly, traveling back to the villages was arduous and expensive and most often occurred during emergencies. Before 1917, most available funds brought new *Volgers* to Lincoln, rather than returning urban villagers to the sending culture. After the Russian Revolution, diplomatic difficulties excluded continued emigration, and most contact was focused on humanitarian relief to relatives suffering from starvation caused by drought and Soviet callousness. By the time Germans from Russia could afford to travel and faster conveyances were in place, their cultural hearths had been displaced, and the urban villagers were largely acculturated to the mainstream.

Like *Volgers* of the 1910s and 1920s, Omaha urban villagers were often financially constrained, and travel was relatively expensive. Still, proximity to the Omaha Reservation assured near continuous economic and social contact with their kinsfolk in the sending culture. Despite the hundred-mile separation, the rapid transmission of information helped create a "prolonged reluctance" to acculturate. Additionally, because a return to Macy was always possible, a commitment to the receiving culture was never required.[61] This localized transnationalism often extended to Indian internationalism as numerous indigenous nations in Nebraska remained connected to each other but insulated from the mainstream for decades. Consequently, many Native Americans find comparisons between urban Indian migrants and other immigrants problematic as tribal identities are inherently more "resilient," "spiritual," and connected to place than identities of arrivals from far-flung continents.[62]

Clearly Vietnamese urban villagers in the early years of their diaspora experienced the same difficulties as Volga Germans in maintaining home-land ties. Uniquely, their financial capabilities expanded at precisely the time modern communication technologies matured. This was also an era when the political barriers that separated *Việt Kiều* from relatives in the Social-ist Republic of Vietnam were relaxed. Consequently, airplane travel to the sending culture became decidedly common by the early twenty-first centu-ry. Additionally, easy access to computer technology effected social connec-tions as thoroughly as transportation advances.[63] Today, the Internet links the 2.7 million *Việt Kiều* living in a hundred countries around the globe back to their cultural hearth and to each other.[64]

Although only Vietnamese use their native script in these communica-tions, computer access for all urban villagers currently plays the role the foreign language press did in the 1910s and 1920s. Localism is necessarily obscured by these developments. World and national news can be garnered from the variety of Vietnamese-language information sites scattered across the World Wide Web, but little of it applies to Lincoln. Local, but not par-ticular, the Asian Community and Cultural Center (ACCC) site is in many respects a Pan-Asian cosmopolitan influence. Although Vietnamese are nu-merically dominant in the Capital City, English is used as the lingua franca as people from China, Korea, South Asia, the Philippines, and beyond use the ACCC's resources and services.[65]

Native Americans in general and Omahas in particular are not adverse to new technologies, but Internet presence was not constant even in the twenty-first century. The Lincoln Indian Center launched its homepage in November 2008.[66] The site outlines the center's mission and history, and it lists officers, news, available social services, and events. As an organ for a Pan-Indian entity, it does not discuss Indian ethnicity. The Lincoln Indian Club, however, does not have a homepage. Its web presence is on social me-dia sites including MySpace and Facebook. It lists upcoming events, but pro-vides more information about individual members than the organization.[67]

Still, local news travels throughout the urban village and beyond in time-honored oral chains that connect community members. The Omaha sending culture, however, has embraced the Internet—a tool that began spreading across Indian Country in 1994. Many Native Americans suggest that the establishment of virtual communities aids in the maintenance of "coherent group identities."[68] Sometimes taking advantage of the versatility of electronic platforms, the Omaha Way was reinforced in the early 2000s by OmahaTribe.com—a website administered in Macy. Although not always accessible, the site is generally formatted like a daily newspaper, right down to its masthead, and its mission is to keep Omahas apprised of news and weather in and around Omaha Nation. The site also contained numerous interactive forums and is designed to serve as the homepage for all residents on the reservation.[69] Their relatives in Lincoln undoubtedly enjoyed staying abreast with developments through this site, even though no space was reserved for their events and concerns.

Because electronic capabilities eliminated the need for a foreign-language press, *Die Welt-Post* (1916–1982) had no counterparts in the communities of later arrivals. The newspaper itself emerged a generation after the North and South Bottoms were erected and stayed a generation after most residents had moved away. The former necessity of the printed word is recalled in the twenty-first century by a quarterly newsletter published at AHSGR headquarters, but the organization's website has a wider reach. No longer aimed just at urban villagers, both forums serve the broad revivalist community that studies the history of the Volga colonies and makes genealogical connections among ancestors scattered around the globe.[70]

Until they emigrated from Russia, Volga Germans were a people without a country. The merging of nation-state and ethnicity that defined political and social developments in the nineteenth and twentieth centuries actually happened after the colonists were in place in the eastern reaches of Romanov Europe.[71] As their cultural hearths were essentially independent, loyalty to the czars was always minimal. Although they had sentimental connections to the German Empire, the first modern country most *Volgers* affiliated with was the United States. They were anxious to demonstrate their loyalty to their adopted country through military service in World Wars I and II. Their scions continue this tradition.

Similarly, modern American nationalism helped inform the identities of Omaha and Vietnamese urban villagers. As dual citizens of Omaha Nation and the United States, Omahas' loyalty to flag and country has been unwavering since World War I. Tribal members, as Edward Cline suggested, are universally proud that "virtually all men" served even in the most unpopular wars.[72] As a people, they supported the Vietnam War even during the darkest days of mainstream protest, and they served without community dissent in Iraq and Afghanistan.

Equally anxious to prove their loyalty to their new nation, some Vietnamese urban villagers may not technically be citizens of any country. Most first-generation immigrants in Lincoln were connected to the now-defunct Republic of Vietnam (RVN), and, for many, citizenship in the sending culture was terminated with the fall of Saigon. Like *Volgers* before them, many Vietnamese may reside in the receiving society as landed aliens their entire lives. Language barriers and the cost of preparing for citizenship examinations are known to be discouraging.

By defining nation as "an imagined political community," many Vietnamese urban villagers maintain loyalty to the RVN and the United States.[73] At the 2006 ACCC Lincoln *Tết* celebration, for example, several elders were enlisted to explain traditions of giving, family hierarchy, and graceful reception of gifts to a largely mainstream audience. While not the topics of discussion, RVN and U.S. flags flanked these speakers as a matter of community protocol.[74] This unfailing loyalty to both nations allows older immigrants to construct identities as patriots and as comrades in arms to U.S. servicemen and -women. Honoring this tradition, many younger urban villagers served in the two Gulf wars.[75]

Because of these loyalties, Vietnamese immigrants often remain disconnected from the modern Vietnamese nation-state. An increasing number of 1.5- and second-generation urban villagers, however, see it as a cultural hearth. While youths have actively sought to rekindle contact to the sending culture, a generation gap has clearly developed over this issue.

Still, American nationalism has been remarkably constant among all three ethnic groups, despite continued discrimination. The maintenance of transnationalism, best defined as prolonged, intense, and persistent contact across international boundaries, was more variable. Proximity favored Omahas whose connections as a rule remained remarkably constant. Volga Germans commuted to Russian colonies with much greater difficulties and may generally have been perceived to be translocal. Since the revival, however, contact with other German Russians was international as the sending places only existed in memory. Vietnamese face an even greater physical distance, but modern technologies have truly made the world a smaller place. Additionally, their very recent arrival into the United States influenced desires to stay in contact, as many urban villagers have living relatives in the sending society. Transnationalism for them is a choice made with little inconvenience, at least for the time being.

**Performed Culture**

While proximity influenced the continued transmission of behaviors and ideas from the sending cultures, saliency of cultural identity in all of Lincoln's urban villages was intimately related to the maintenance of performed culture. These folk practices preserved alternative "source[s] of knowledge" that the new arrivals imported from their sending cultures. Additionally, they served as blueprints of sorts that aided immigrants in sorting out the conflicting old-world and new-world agendas.[76] Adaptations to mainstream practices and expectations replaced or eliminated the need for some of these behaviors, but Germans from Russia, Omahas, and Vietnamese all continue to celebrate certain aspects of their sending cultures in the twenty-first century.

As referenced in the Introduction to this volume, folkways are maintained in a variety of ways. Most significantly for this study, they exist like soup as "retentions"—long-term survivals that still demonstrate ethnicity; as "revivals"—cultural forms that have been returned to a community after a period of dormancy; and through "ethnic reintensification"—a process whereby residents born in urban villages learn folkways directly from the founding generation and continue performance without lapses.[77] While the lines between retention and reintensification may be thin, revivals are few and stand out clearly.

Lincoln's German from Russia population clearly demonstrates that ethnicity can be revived, but once "cultural artifacts are lost, succeeding generations do not typically revive them."[78] Their ethnicity exists historically, but—*Knöphla* and other foodways aside—few aspects of performed culture remain. Behaviors that formerly had great resonance within the North and South Bottoms slowly lost meaning. Over the course of several decades beginning in the 1950s, urban villagers dispersed from their enclaves, religious structures fizzled, and by the early 1980s, the last remnants of the Volga village dialects vanished. Ethnicity, however, outlasted performed culture.

Interest in a newly minted German-from-Russia heritage among third- and fourth-generation *Volgers* was part of a wider ethnic revival. Best seen as a grassroots cultural movement, the revival allowed "a selective return to roots." Groups chose certain aspects of their past as new identity markers and discarded much of the rest.[79] As the reservoir of behaviors that defined Volga Germans in early-twentieth-century Lincoln was no longer accessible, geographic and historical information emerged as the revivalists' preeminent focus.[80]

Place and history were deeply intertwined in this local revival. The AHSGR encouraged its members to research and reconnect with the original colonies of their ancestors. Most of the organization's intellectual energy is spent on examining these vanished cultural hearths or on pursuing family genealogy. While the old Russian Bottoms are not generally the subjects of revivalist efforts, research and socializing are done within their confines. AHSGR headquarters sits in the heart of the *Franker Boden*. Home to extensive archives and an ever expanding museum, it also serves as a social point for quilters and coffee drinkers. Across town in the *Norkaer Boden*, the annual Soup Supper is held in the old Welfare Society Hall. While still the original structure *Volgers* erected in 1927, the venue was purchased in 1994 for $4,000—a testament to its formerly dilapidated condition. Still under renovation, its taxable value increased from $103,000 to $174,000 between 2000 and 2005.[81] Clearly more of a community project than can be supported by the six-dollar fee to eat soup each spring, the revitalization of the hall allows the grandchildren of the North Bottoms founders to maintain particularism in a revival movement dominated by the historical district that now encompasses the South Bottoms.

Omaha urban villagers, on the other hand, are spatially connected to their neighborhoods only because of proximity to relatives. The stability of the Indian Center helps moderate endless mobility necessitated by low rates of property ownership. Additionally, proximity to Omaha Nation provides a spatial anchor for a people intimately connected to the Nebraska landscape. The urban migration began precisely in an era when Omaha Nation and the Omaha Way were experiencing revitalization. Although the sending culture was increasingly rich in tradition, its depressed economic state made out-migration a rational choice.

Omaha performed culture has largely been retained in Lincoln, and in many cases, been intensified. Indeed, "basic values remain strong" among most urban Indians.[82] Kinship relations and gift reciprocity, for example, are still central tenets of behavior within the urban village. While some local practices have necessarily been modified by the demands of mainstream materialism and competitive desires, others remain more "traditional" than those at Omaha Nation.[83] The Lincoln Indian Club Pow-Wow is perhaps the best example. Its emphasis on teaching Omaha children arena protocol and the meaning and method of Indian music recalls the original intent of Omaha fall celebrations far more than the modern contest-style pow-wow at Macy. While both preserve and transmit Omaha culture to future generations, the urban event places cultural tradition under a magnifying glass and attempts to reestablish protocols that have already vanished from the sending culture.

Omaha language, however, was not commonly retained in Lincoln. Only elders among the founding generation had a grasp of their native tongue—a pattern duplicated in the Omaha Nation. Subsequent generations appear not to have learned Omaha from relatives in either location. Sadly, Native Americans are barely a part of the Capital City's celebrated language diversity; at least forty-eight dialects were present in 2005. Fifty people reported speaking Navajo, 115 individuals claimed they spoke Dakota, but Omaha language was not reported on the list.[84]

Still, complete language loss is not a foregone conclusion, as tribal and mainstream efforts have been promoted to stem the tide. The U.S. Congress passed Native American Language Acts in 1990 and 1992, although federal efforts to implement programs to date have been halfhearted.[85] In 1999, however, the Nebraska legislature determined that teaching American Indian languages was "essential to the proper education of Indian children." To facilitate this goal, the legislature allowed tribes to certify their elders as "tribal language specialists" and eliminated the need to have state-licensed teachers present for classes to be accredited.[86] Even with these statutes in place, revitalization will require tribal initiative and control, and it may be another generation before language reintensification occurs.[87]

Conversely, Lincoln's 3,520 Vietnamese-speaking residents communicate in the third-most-common language of the city.[88] Some argue that continued immigration is the *"paramount reason for linguistic"* survival.[89] Vietnamese, however, entered a much different mainstream than Volga Germans. Those moving to Lincoln in the late twentieth century had the advantage of greater official facilitation of non-English languages. The Red Cross Language Bank, for instance, maintained a pool of bilingual volunteers working in thirteen different tongues—including Vietnamese—to aid residents in medical situations. Additionally, community liaison personnel for the Lincoln Police Department—Maria Vu and Jung Nguyen—received a two-hundred-thousand-dollar federal grant to translate the Nebraska Driver's Manual into Vietnamese. Marriage license applications and numerous other forms were also translated in 1996.[90] While particular village dialects prevailed in the Russian colonies, Vietnamese—even considering regional differences—speak and write a national language shared by eighty million people on all inhabitable continents. Mass communication ensured access to a large pool of colinguists that would remain available even if immigration stopped. Local use of Vietnamese is reinforced by the availability of recorded music and movie rentals at many Twenty-Seventh Street businesses.

Among Vietnamese, "language, ethnicity, culture, and in many respects religion" remain "bound together" in the newly formed urban villages.[91] These spaces remain dominated by the founding generation that anchors its status and identification nearly totally in family.[92] Most aspects of performed culture are retained among this portion of the population. The second generation—which currently comprises only a quarter of all urban villagers—is already negotiating a cultural identity that synthesizes old and new milieus.[93] Some behaviors will likely lapse, but other important cultural aspects will be intensified as Vietnamese and American patterns are frequently practiced in separate spheres.

Omahas and Germans from Russia have also negotiated interactions between imported culture and mainstream expectations. In many respects, they ended up on opposite ends of the behavioral adaptation spectrum. *Volger* particularism largely vanished while Omaha particularism appears to have increased. Although Vietnamese urban villagers are still in their first generation, both mainstream structures and internal predispositions suggest significant aspects of performed culture will be kept for decades to come.

## Conclusion

Foodways—as evidenced by the retention of *Knöphla, watónzi skíthe taní,* and *phở gà*—outlast many other markers of ethnic boundaries.[94] On rare occasions, culinary cultural traditions mix, and items such as the frybread runza—the cabbage, onion, and hamburger filling from the Russian Bottoms wrapped in Omaha deep-fried bread—emerge.[95] Other combinations of comfort foods are generally absent as most performed cultures remain deeply rooted in particular ethnic ways.

Whether behaviors and beliefs survived within the ethnic enclaves depended largely on how far the urban villagers were willing "to go in adapting to their host culture."[96] The Volga Germans' metamorphosis to Germans from Russia indicated that this ethnic group was willing to acculturate almost completely. Conversely, despite years of pressure to abandon traditional behaviors and beliefs, most Indian peoples remained distinct. While this was largely due to choice, the mainstream generally refused to accept the total assimilation it formerly demanded. Omahas were always reminded that they were Indians and frequently faced exclusion as a result.[97] Vietnamese were also racialized, and their ethnicity was blurred with other Asians. Increasing mainstream tolerance—at least at official levels—eliminated some of the negative cosmopolitan forces that Volga Germans and Omahas necessarily encountered.

Viewing ethnic enclaves in Lincoln as "extensions of homelands" is a valuable method for examining identity construction in immigrant and migrant groups.[98] Remarkably, Vietnamese transnational connections are nearly as strong as those of the Omahas. Distinct identities in both urban villages were regularly reinforced by contact with sending cultures. Germans from Russia, on the other hand, lost intimate connections with the Volga colonies generations ago. Their sending cultures survive as historical artifacts that inform a modern identity without reinforcing aspects of performed culture.

Despite significant variances among ethnic groups, Lincoln's urban villages housed and continue to house populations that preferred to remain distinct from the mainstream. Ironically, their strong family values and cultural conservatism are largely in step with twenty-first-century mainstream values; because diversity is often undervalued, however, many citizens in the Capital City are unaware of the cultural contributions urban villagers have made in the past and are poised to make in the future. Hopefully, the mainstream on the Great Plains will recall its past significant diversity and grow to embrace pluralism.

# Notes

## Introduction

1. Walter Nugent, *Into the West: The Story of Its People* (New York: Knopf, 1999), 4–6.
2. Anna Schwindt Giebelhaus, interview by Gertrude Schwindt, 16 July 1980, folder AV1.636.06, Neighborhood Oral History Project, Nebraska State Historical Society (hereafter NSHS), Lincoln, 1; Linda Ulrich, "Stablers Proudly Live Their Indian Heritage," *Sunday Journal-Star*, 20 April 1980, 1D; Mark J. Swetland, ed., *Umoⁿhon iye of Elizabeth Stabler: A Vocabulary of the Omaha Language* (Macy, NE: n.p., 1977), vi–vii; *Polk's Lincoln City Directory* (Kansas City, MO: Polk, 1985), 751.
3. Miguel Carranza, "The Search for Space and a Sense of Place: Mexicanos/Latinos Settle in the Heartland," oral presentation, Paul A. Olson Seminar in Great Plains Studies, University of Nebraska–Lincoln, 18 January 2006.
4. Gunther Peck, *Reinventing Free Labor: Padrones and Immigrant Workers in the North American West, 1880–1930* (New York: Cambridge University Press, 2000), 3.
5. Ibid., 4.
6. Ibid., 159–60.
7. Elliott Robert Barkan, "America in the Hand, Homeland in the Heart: Transnational and Translocal Immigrant Experiences in the American West," *Western Historical Quarterly* 35, no. 3 (Autumn 2004): 335, 345.
8. Addison Erwin Sheldon, *Nebraska: The Land and the People* (Chicago: Lewis Publishing, 1931), 287, 299.
9. Elliott Robert Barkan, "Proximity and Commuting Immigration: An Hypothesis Explored via the Bi-polar Ethnic Communities of French Canadian and Mexican Americans," in Jack Kinton, ed., *American Ethnic Revival: Group Pluralism Entering America's Third Century* (Aurora, IL: Social Science and Sociological Resources, 1977), 164–65.
10. Scott B. Vickers, *Native American Identities: From Stereotype to Archetype in Art and Literature* (Albuquerque: University of New Mexico Press, 1998), 27.
11. John M. Nieto-Phillips, *The Language of Blood: The Making of Spanish-American Identity in New Mexico, 1880s–1930s* (Albuquerque: University of New Mexico Press, 2004), 8.

12. David Bibas, *Immigrants and the Formation of Community: A Case Study of Moroccan Jewish Immigration to America* (New York: AMS Press, 1998), 2–3.

13. Nathan Glazer and Daniel J. Moynihan, *Beyond the Melting Pot* (Cambridge, MA: MIT Press, 1963), 15.

14. Kathleen Neils Conzen, David A. Gerber, Ewa Morawski, George Pozzetta, and Rudolph J. Vecoli, "The Invention of Ethnicity: A Perspective from the U.S.A," *Journal of American Ethnic History* 12, no. 3 (Fall 1992): 5.

15. Nancy C. Dorian, "Linguistic and Ethnographic Fieldwork," in Joshua A. Fishman, ed., *Handbook of Language and Identity* (New York: Oxford University Press, 1999), 25.

16. Milton M. Gordon, *Assimilation in American Life: The Role of Race, Religion, and National Origins* (New York: Oxford University Press, 1964), 30, 37; Sara E. Stoutland, *Neither Urban Jungle nor Urban Village: Women, Families, and Community Development* (New York: Garland Publishing, 1997), 30.

17. Peter Jackson and Jan Penrose, ed., *Constructions of "Race," Place, and Nation* (Minneapolis: University of Minnesota Press, 1994), 12.

18. Kathleen Neils Conzen, "Quantification and the New Urban History," *Urban History* 13, no. 2 (Spring 1983): 676.

19. Kathleen Neils Conzen, "Mainstreams and Side Channels: The Localization of Immigrant Cultures," *Journal of American Ethnic History* 11, no. 1 (Fall 1991): 7. See also Timothy R. Mahoney, "Urban History in a Regional Context: River Towns and the Upper Mississippi, 1840–60," *Journal of American History* 72, no. 2 (September 1985): 339.

20. Stephan Thernstrom, *The Other Bostonians: Poverty and Progress in the American Metropolis, 1880–1970* (Cambridge, MA: Harvard University Press, 1973), 30.

21. Conzen, "Mainstreams and Side Channels," 14.

22. Gordon, *Assimilation in American Life*, 38; Bibas, *Immigrants and the Formation of Community*, 3.

23. George E. Pozetta, ed., *Assimilation, Acculturation, and Social Mobility* (New York: Garland Publishing, 1991), vi.

24. Tony Waters, "Towards a Theory of Ethnic Identity and Migration: The Formation of Ethnic Enclaves by Migrant Germans from Russia and North America," *International Migration Review* 29, no. 2 (Summer 1995): 519.

25. Conzen, "Mainstream and Side Channels," 11.

26. R. B. Le Page and André Tabouret-Keller, *Acts of Identity: Creole-Based Approaches to Language and Ethnicity* (New York: Cambridge University Press, 1985), 2.

27. Peter G. Boag, *Environment and Experience: Settlement Culture in Nineteenth-Century Oregon* (Berkeley: University of California Press, 1992), 38, 80, 141; see also Gordon, *Assimilation in American Life*, 32–33, 79.

28. Waters, "Towards a Theory of Ethnic Identity and Migration," 521; Le Page and Tabouret-Keller, *Acts of Identity*, 180; Dorian, "Linguistic and Ethnographic Fieldwork," 31–32.

29. Mary Pipher, *The Middle of Everywhere: The World's Refugees Come to Our Town* (New York: Harcourt, 2002), 75.

30. Conzen et al., "Invention of Ethnicity," 22–23.
31. Waters, "Towards a Theory of Ethnic Identity and Migration," 520.
32. Meaghan Morris and Brett de Bary, *"Race" Panic and Memory of Migration* (Hong Kong: Hong Kong University Press, 2000), 3.
33. Vickers, *Native American Identities*, 10.
34. Waters, "Towards a Theory of Ethnic Identity and Migration," 521.
35. Stephen Stearn, "Ethnic Folklore and the Folklore of Ethnicity," *Western Folklore* 36, no. 1 (January 1977): 28.
36. Carole Hampton, "Native American Church," in Frederick E. Hoxie, ed., *Encyclopedia of North American Indians* (Boston: Houghton Mifflin, 1996), 418.
37. Peter N. Gregory, "Describing the Elephant: Buddhism in America," *Religion and American Culture* 11, no. 2 (Summer 2001): 236–39.
38. Gordon, *Assimilation in American Life*, 198.
39. Stearn, "Ethnic Folklore and the Folklore of Ethnicity," 14, 22; Joe Sawchuk, "Negotiating an Identity: Métis Political Organizations, the Canadian Government, and Competing Concepts of Aboriginality," *American Indian Quarterly* 25, no. 1 (Winter 2001): 73; Kathleen Neils Conzen, "Immigrants, Immigrant Neighborhoods, and Ethnic Identity: Historical Issues," *Journal of American History* 65, no. 3 (Fall 1979): 605.
40. Stearn, "Ethnic Folklore and the Folklore of Ethnicity," 18.
41. Pozetta, *Assimilation*, viii.
42. Pipher, *Middle of Everywhere*, 73.
43. Allen J. Williams, Jr., David R. Johnson, and Miguel Carranza, "Ethnic Assimilation and Pluralism in Nebraska," in Frederick C. Luebke, ed., *Ethnicity on the Great Plains,* (Lincoln: University of Nebraska Press, 1980), 220.
44. Richard D. Alba, *Ethnic Identity: The Transformation of White America* (New Haven, CT: Yale University Press, 1990), 164.
45. Stearn, "Ethnic Folklore and the Folklore of Ethnicity," 21; see also Alan M. Kraut, "Ethnic Foodways: The Significance of Food in the Designation of Cultural Boundaries Between Immigrant Groups in the U.S., 1840–1921," *Journal of American Culture* 2, no. 3 (Fall 1979): 417.
46. Kraut, "Ethnic Foodways," 413.
47. Ibid., 416.
48. Ibid., 414.
49. Benjamin P. Kracht, "Kiowa Powwows: Tribal Identity through the Continuity of the Gourd Dance," *Great Plains Research* 4, no. 2 (August 1994): 258.
50. Ibid., 257.
51. Lawrence McCullough, "The Role of Language, Music, and Dance in the Revival of Irish Culture in Chicago, Illinois," *Ethnicity* 7, no. 4 (December 1980): 438, 442.
52. Pipher, *Middle of Everywhere*, 71.
53. Oliver Zunz, "American History and the Changing Meaning of Assimilation," *Journal of Ethnic American History* 4, no. 2 (Spring 1985): 56.
54. Alba, *Ethnic Identity*, 38.
55. Zunz, "American History and the Changing Meaning of Assimilation," 55, 106; William A. Douglass, "Basque-American Identity: Past Perspectives and Future

Prospects," in Stephen Tchudi, ed., *Change in the American West: Exploring the Human Dimension* (Reno: University of Nevada Press, 1987), 191; Alba, *Ethnic Identity*, xiii, 1.

56. Waters, "Towards a Theory of Ethnic Identity and Migration," 518.
57. Ibid., 516.
58. Pozetta, *Assimilation*, viii.
59. Waters, "Towards a Theory of Ethnic Identity and Migration," 516.
60. Stoutland, *Neither Urban Jungle nor Urban Village*, 30.
61. Gordon, *Assimilation in American Life*, 40, 49–51.
62. Williams et al., "Ethnic Assimilation and Pluralism in Nebraska," 219.
63. Stoutland, *Neither Urban Jungle nor Urban Village*, 5.
64. Dorian, "Linguistic and Ethnographic Fieldwork," 27; Pipher, *Middle of Everywhere*, 78.
65. Gordon, *Assimilation in American Life*, 60.
66. Lynne B. Iglitzin, "The Seattle Commons: A Case Study in the Politics and Planning of an Urban Village," *Policy Studies Journal* 23, no. 4 (Winter 1995): 621.
67. Karel B. Bicha, "The Survival of the Village in Urban America: A Note on Czech Immigrants in Chicago in 1914," *International Migration Review* 5, no. 1 (Spring 1971): 73, 74.
68. Alba, *Ethnic Identity*, 19.
69. Richard D. Alba, "Social Assimilation among American Catholic National-Origin Groups," *American Sociological Review* 41, no. 6 (December 1976): 1030.
70. Thernstrom, *Other Bostonians*, 232.
71. Alba, *Ethnic Identity*, 253–54.
72. Pipher, *Middle of Everywhere*, 5.
73. Frederick Luebke, ed., *European Immigrants in the American West: Community Histories* (Albuquerque: University of New Mexico Press, 1998), vii.
74. Elliott Robert Barkan, *From All Points: America's Immigrant West, 1870s–1952* (Bloomington: Indiana University Press, 2007), xi.
75. Ibid., 7.
76. Ibid., 10, 457.
77. Peck, *Reinventing Free Labor*, 159.
78. Ibid., 3–7. While Peck examines transient workers—largely groups of men—many more family groups had both the stability of community and the ability to move for work. As the twentieth century progressed, fewer and fewer jobs required large-scale migration on the Great Plains, largely because agriculture was mechanized. While not discounting the endeavors of Hispanic farm laborers, this is not their story. Volga Germans and Omaha Indians abandoned migratory farming in the 1950s and 1960s. Vietnamese—already an urbanized or urbanizing population—largely avoided such labor schemes, as sufficient factory work was available.
79. Rudolph J. Vecoli, "The Significance of Immigration in the Formation of an American Identity," *History Teacher* 30, no. 1 (November 1996): 11.
80. Pipher, *Middle of Everywhere*, 71.

81. Donald L. Fixico, *The Urban Indian Experience in America* (Albuquerque: University of New Mexico Press, 2000), 59.
82. David A. Hollinger, "American Ethnoracial History and the Amalgamation Narrative," *Journal of American Ethnic History* 25, no. 4 (Summer 2006): 158.
83. Kevin Hannan, "Refashioning Ethnicity in Czech-Moravian Texas," *Journal of American Ethnic History* 25, no. 1 (Fall 2005): 32–33.
84. Nazli Kibria, *Family Tightrope: The Changing Lives of Vietnamese Americans* (Princeton: Princeton University Press, 1993), 19.
85. Giebelhaus, interview by Gertrude Schwindt, 1; Ulrich, "Stablers Proudly Live Their Indian Heritage," 1D; Swetland, *Umo$^n$ho$^n$ iye*, vi–vii; *Polk's Lincoln City Directory* (Kansas City, MO: Polk, 1990), 809; (2000), 593.

## Chapter 1

1. More precisely, Lincoln sits longitudinally at N 40°50', W 96°40'. See Andrew J. Sawyer, ed., *Lincoln: The Capital City and Lancaster County, Nebraska* (Chicago: S. J. Clark, 1916). For a discussion about the ninety-eighth parallel, see Walter Prescott Webb, *The Great Plains* (Boston: Ginn, 1931).
2. League of Women Voters, *A Handbook of Government: Lincoln and Lancaster County, Nebraska* (Lincoln, NE: League of Women Voters, 1968), 3.
3. Timothy R. Mahoney, "Urban History in a Regional Context: River Towns on the Upper Mississippi, 1840–1860," *Journal of American History* 72, no. 3 (September 1985): 339.
4. Kathleen Neils Conzen, "Mainstreams and Side Channels: The Localization of Immigrant Cultures," *Journal of American Ethnic History* 11, no. 1 (Fall 1991): 14.
5. Kathleen Neils Conzen, David A. Gerber, Ewa Morawski, George Pozzetta, and Rudolph J. Vecoli, "The Invention of Ethnicity: A Perspective from the U.S.A.," *Journal of American Ethnic History* 12, no. 1 (Fall 1992): 12; Milton M. Gordon, *Assimilation in American Life: The Role of Race, Region, and National Origins* (New York: Oxford University Press, 1964), 74.
6. Scott B. Vickers, *Native American Identities: From Stereotype to Archetype in Art and Literature* (Albuquerque: University of New Mexico Press, 1998), 31.
7. Edward W. Soja, *Postmetropolis: Critical Studies of Cities and Regions* (Malden, MA: Blackwell, 2000), 73.
8. Allen J. Williams, Jr., David R. Johnson, and Miguel Carranza, "Ethnic Assimilation and Pluralism in Nebraska," in Frederick C. Luebke, ed., *Ethnicity on the Great Plains*, (Lincoln: University of Nebraska Press, 1980), 218.
9. Nathan Glazer and Daniel J. Moynihan, *Beyond the Melting Pot* (Cambridge, MA: MIT Press, 1963), 13.
10. Daniel G. Blackburn, "Why Race Is Not a Biological Concept," in Berel Lang, ed., *Race and Racism in Theory and Practice* (New York: Rowman & Littlefield, 2000), 4.
11. Peter Jackson and Jan Penrose, eds., *Constructions of "Race," Place, and Nation* (Minneapolis: University of Minnesota Press, 1994), 4.

12. Ibid., 4–5; Blackburn, "Why Race Is Not a Biological Concept," 3, 6, 9, 14–16.

13. Linda Gordon, *The Great Arizona Orphan Abduction* (Cambridge: Harvard University Press, 1999), 198.

14. Patricia Nelson Limerick, *The Legacy of Conquest: The Unbroken Past of the American West* (New York: W.W. Norton, 1987), 290. See also Walter R. Allen, "The Dilemma Persists: Race, Class, and Inequality in American Life," in Peter Ratcliffe, ed., *"Race," Ethnicity and Nation: International Perspectives on Social Conflict* (London: University College Press, 1994), 60.

15. Peter Ratcliffe, ed., *"Race," Ethnicity, and Nation: International Perspectives on Social Conflict* (London: University College London Press, 1994), 6.

16. Akhil Gupta and James Ferguson, "Beyond 'Culture': Space, Identity, and the Politics of Difference," *Cultural Anthropology* 7, no. 1 (February 1992): 17; David E. Lopez, "Language Minorities in the United States," in James R. Dow, ed., *Language and Ethnicity: Focusshrift in Honor of Joshua A. Fishman* (Philadelphia: John Benjamin, 1991), 132.

17. Sara E. Stoutland, *Neither Urban Jungle nor Urban Village: Women, Families, and Community Development* (New York: Garland Publishing, 1997), 3.

18. Rudolph J. Vecoli, "The Significance of Immigration in the Formation of an American Identity," *History Teacher* 30, no. 1 (November 1996): 11.

19. Declaration of Independence; Diva Stasiulis and Nira Yuval-Davis, "Introduction: Beyond Dichotomies—Gender, Race, Ethnicity, and Class in Settler Societies," in *Unsettling Settler Societies: Articulations of Gender, Race, Ethnicity, and Class* (London: Sage Publication, 1995), 1.

20. Nancy C. Carnevale, "'No Italian Spoken for the Duration of the War': Language, Italian-American Identity, and Cultural Pluralism in the World War II Years," *Journal of American Ethnic History* 22, no. 3 (Spring 2003): 17; Benjamin R. Barber, "Blood Brothers, Consumers, or Citizens? Three Models of Identity—Ethnic, Commercial, and Civil," in Carol C. Gould and Pasquale Pasquino, ed., *Cultural Identity and the Nation-State* (New York: Rowman and Littlefield, 2001), 57; James A. Cohen, "Value Judgments and Political Assessments about National Models of Citizenship: The U.S. and French Cases," in Gould and Pasquino, *Cultural Identity and the Nation-State*, 123; Vine Deloria, Jr., *Custer Died for Your Sins* (London: Macmillan, 1969), 8.

21. William G. Robbins, *Landscapes and Promise: The Oregon Story, 1800–1940* (Seattle: University of Washington Press, 1997), 25.

22. Sawyer, ed., *Lincoln*, 65.

23. Alice Fletcher and Francis La Flesche, *The Omaha Tribe*, 2 vols. (1911; Lincoln: University of Nebraska Press, 1992), 2:342.

24. Robbins, *Landscapes and Promise*, 45.

25. Colin Calloway, *The American Revolution in Indian Country: Crisis and Diversity in Native American Community* (New York: Cambridge University Press, 1995), xv.

26. Indians—in Article I, section 2 of the U.S. Constitution—were omitted from population counts that determined congressional representation, an indication

they were to be barred from the polity; for purposes of commercial regulation, in Article I, section 8, they were denoted neither as "foreign Nations" nor as "States" but as a third entity whose status was undefined.

27. John R. Wunder, *"Retained by the People": A History of American Indians and the Bill of Rights* (New York: Oxford University Press, 1994), 213.

28. See *Johnson v. M'Intosh*, 21 U.S. 543 (1823).

29. *Cherokee Nation v. State of Georgia*, 30 U.S. (5 Peters) 1 (1831), 8, reprinted in Colin G. Calloway, ed., *First Peoples: A Documentary Survey of American Indian History* (Boston: Bedford/St. Martin's, 1999), 252–55.

30. "Treaty With the Oto, Etc., 1836," Charles J. Kappler, ed., *Indian Treaties, 1778–1883* (New York: Interland Publishing, 1972), 479–80.

31. *Worcester v. Georgia*, 31 U.S. 515 (1832). See also Caryn E. Neumann, "*Worcester v. Georgia*, 1832," in Donald J. Fixico, ed., *Treaties with American Indians: An Encyclopedia of Rights, Conflicts, and Sovereignty* (Santa Barbara, CA: ABC-CLIO, 2008), 655–56.

32. "Treaty with the Omaha, 1854," 16 March 1854, in Charles J. Kappler, ed., *Indian Treaties, 1778–1883* (New York: Interland Publishing, 1972), 139. Omahas first signed a treaty of friendship in 1815; see "Treaty with the Makah [*sic*]," 20 July 1815, in Kappler, *Indian Treaties*, 115–16.

33. Francis Paul Prucha, *The Great Father: The United States and American Indians* (Lincoln: University of Nebraska Press, 1986), 198.

34. Wunder, *"Retained by the People,"* 17. See also Bill Ong Hing, *To Be an American: Cultural Pluralism and the Rhetoric of Assimilation* (New York: New York University Press, 1997), 20.

35. *Elk v. Wilkins* 112 U.S. 94 (1884). See also Vine Deloria, Jr., ed., *Of Utmost Good Faith* (San Francisco: Straight Arrow Press, 1971), 84–85, 87–92.

36. *Elk v. Wilkins* (1884); Hing, *To Be an American*, 21. The racialism of the times was so intense Indians had to battle in the courts to be accepted as socially advanced enough to be considered humans rather than lesser beings.

37. Frank Van Nuys, "'The Stuff from Which Citizens Are Made': American Identity and Cultural Debate, 1880–1925" (Ph.D. diss., University of Wyoming, 1997), 2; John Higham, *Strangers in the Land: Patterns of American Nativism, 1860–1925* (New York: Atheneum, 1969), 108–9.

38. Vecoli, "Significance of Immigration," 18.

39. Robert A. Carlson, *The Quest for Conformity: Americanization through Education* (Toronto: John Wiley and Sons, 1975), 10.

40. "Indian Commissioner Thomas J. Morgan on the Need for Compulsory Education, 1892," in Albert L. Hurtado and Peter Iverson, ed., *Major Problems in American Indian History: Documents and Essays* (Lexington, MA: D. C. Heath, 1994), 377.

41. Raymond A. Mohl, "Cultural Assimilation *versus* Cultural Pluralism," *Educational Forum* 45, no. 1 (March 1981): 324–25.

42. See Eric Scott McCready, "The Nebraska State Capitol: Its Design, Background, and Influence," *Nebraska History* 54, no. 3 (Fall 1974): 327, 374.

43. See Richard K. Sutton, "Ernst H. Herminghaus: Landscape Architect," *Nebraska History* 66, no. 4 (Winter 1985): 372–91.

44. Federal Writers Project, *Lincoln City Guide* (Lincoln, NE: Woodruff, 1937), 68.

45. Hattie Plum Williams, *The Czar's Germans: With Particular Reference to the Volga Germans* (Lincoln, NE: American Historical Society of Germans from Russia, 1975), 3–4; Hattie Plum Williams, "A Social Study of the Russian German Population" (Ph.D. diss., University of Nebraska, 1915), 8; David J. Miller and Lydia A. Miller, account of visit to cousins in Alma-Ata, Kazakhstan, 21–23 July 1967, in William F. Urbach Papers, RG 1497.Am, box 1, folder 2, NSHS; Gerda Stroh Walker, *Die Welt-Post Index*, vol. 1, *1916–21* (Boulder, CO: Joshua Sky Walker, 1998), iv.

46. Lloyd Shaw, *Industries of Lincoln* (Lincoln, NE: State Journal Co., 1890), 7.

47. James R. Shortridge, *Cities on the Plains: The Evolution of Urban Kansas* (Lawrence: University of Kansas, 2004), 96.

48. As a conglomerate, the Burlington system has been known as the Chicago, Burlington and Quincy; the Burlington and Missouri River; and more recently the Burlington Santa Fe. See Shaw, *Industries of Lincoln*, 43–44.

49. Lincoln Chamber of Commerce, *Lincoln: Nebraska's Capital City, 1867–1923* (Lincoln: Woodruff Publishing, 1923), 8.

50. A. B. Hayes and Sam D. Cox, *History of the City of Lincoln, Nebraska: With Brief Historical Sketches of the State and Lancaster County* (Lincoln, NE: State Journal Company, 1889), 12.

51. U.S. Constitution, Article I, Section 8. Although scions of Africa were present throughout American history, the Constitution minimizes their presence and largely confines them to the status of property. This population is largely outside the scope of this investigation.

52. Vecoli, "Significance of Immigration," 10.

53. Edith Robbins, "German Immigration to Nebraska: The Role of State Immigration Agents," *Yearbook of German American Studies* 26 (1991): 94.

54. Jean Costanza Miller, "The Melting Pot Metaphor: Immigration and Identity in Early Twentieth-Century American Discourse" (Ph.D. diss., University of Maryland, 2000), 94; Van Nuys, "Stuff from Which Citizens are Made," 111.

55. Mary Pipher, *The Middle of Everywhere: The World's Refugees Come to Our Town* (New York: Harcourt, 2002), xvii.

56. Van Nuys, "Stuff from Which Citizens Are Made," 23; Higham, *Strangers in the Land*, 105; Mohl, "Cultural Assimilation *versus* Cultural Pluralism," 325; George E. Pozetta, ed., *Assimilation, Acculturation, and Social Mobility* (New York: Garland Publishing, 1991), ix.

57. Richard D. Alba, *Ethnic Identity: The Transformation of White America* (New Haven, CT: Yale University Press, 1990), 165; Pipher, *Middle of Everywhere*, 114.

58. Williams, "Social Study," 17; Hattie Plum Williams, "The History of the German-Russian Colony in Lincoln" (M.A. thesis, University of Nebraska, 1909), 84.

59. Frederick C. Luebke, *Immigrants and Politics: The Germans of Nebraska, 1880–1900* (Lincoln: University of Nebraska Press, 1969), 11, 25. Luebke defined

"German stock" as a category that included "all German born plus American-born persons who had one or more or both parents born in Europe."

60. Elliott Robert Barkan, *From All Points: America's Immigrant West, 1870s–1952* (Bloomington: Indiana University Press, 2007), 75.

61. Burlington Road Land Commissioner. *B. & M. R. R. Land in Nebraska* [German Language edition], trans. Kurt E. Kinbacher (Lincoln: *Nebraska Staats-Anzeigers*, 1882), "Views of Land Sales and Immigration," http://railroads. unl.edu. This pamphlet singles out an organ called *The Outsider in Wisconsin*. By the 1860s Wisconsin was codifying English-only educational policies. See Susan Jean Kuyper, "The Americanization of German Immigrants: Language, Religion and Schools in Nineteenth-Century Rural Wisconsin" (Ph.D. diss, University of Wisconsin, 1980), 117–22.

62. La Vern J. Rippley, *The German Americans* (Boston: Twayne Publishers, 1976), 174.

63. Walter Nugent, *Into the West: The Story of Its People* (New York: Knopf, 1999), 115–16.

64. For discussions of these populations, see Ophira Bahar, "The Lincoln Jewish Federation," *Memories of the Jewish Midwest* 6 (Winter 1990): 29; Rebecca Rosenbaum, "Interview with Rabbi Harry Jollt in Miami Beach, Florida, April 21, 1992," *Memories of the Jewish Midwest* 9 (Spring 1994): 25–26; Dennis N. Mihelich, "The Lincoln Urban League: The Travail of Depression and War," *Nebraska History* 70, no. 4 (Fall 1989): 313; Edward F. Zimmer and Abigail B. Davis, "Recovered Views: African American Portraits, 1912–1925," *Nebraska History* 84, no. 2 (Spring 2003): 62.

65. Federal Writers Project, *Lincoln*, 46.

66. Significant flooding occurred in 1881, 1885, 1900, 1902, 1908, 1909, 1910, 1914, 1923, 1942, 1947, and 1950. See *Lincoln Journal*, 24 May 1950, 1.

67. Hayes and Cox, *History of the City of Lincoln*, 175–76.

68. "Flood in the West Bottoms: Salt Creek Reaches from the Lake to the Viaduct," *Nebraska State Journal*, 8 June 1908, 2.

69. See *Nebraska State Journal*, 28 May 1914, 4.

70. "The People Make Meager Living from What Others Discard," *Lincoln Sunday Journal and Star*, 3 April 1938, 9B.

71. Higham, *Strangers in the Land*, 199.

72. Van Nuys, "Stuff from Which Citizens Are Made," 151.

73. Joshua A. Fishman, ed., *Language Loyalty in the United States: The Maintenance and Perpetuation of non-English Mother Tongues by American Ethnic and Religious Groups* (London: Mouton, 1966), 30.

74. Nebraska Constitution, Art. I, Sec. 27 (1920).

75. See *Meyer v. State of Nebraska*, 42 S. Ct. 625 (262 U.S. 390), (1923).

76. Calvin Veltman, "Theory and Method in the Study of Language Shift," in James R. Dow, ed., *Language and Ethnicity: Focusshrift in Honor of Joshua A. Fishman* (Philadelphia: John Benjamin, 1991), 147.

77. Barkan, *From All Points*, 216, 246–53, 468; U.S. Department of State, "The

Immigration Act of 1924 (The Johnson-Reed Act)," http://www.state.gov/r/pa/ho/time/id/87718.htm; Helen F. Eckerson, "Immigration and National Origins," *Annals of the American Academy of Political and Social Science* 367 (September 1966): 4.

78. Bradley H. Baltensperger, *Nebraska: A Geography* (Boulder, CO: Crestview Press, 1985), 76; Williams et al., "Ethnic Assimilation," 212–13.

79. Philip Gleason, *Speaking of Diversity: Language and Ethnicity in Twentieth-Century America* (Baltimore: Johns Hopkins University Press, 1992), 32; Vecoli, "Significance of Immigration," 22; Conzen et al., "Invention of Ethnicity," 29–30.

80. Charles Hirschman, "The Melting Pot Reconsidered," *Annual Review of Sociology* 9 (1983): 415.

81. John J. Bukowczyk, *And My Children Did Not Know Me: A History of the Polish-Americans* (Bloomington: Indiana University Press, 1987), ix, 88, 120.

82. Conzen et al., "Invention of Ethnicity," 25.

83. Gupta and Ferguson, 11. See also Gunther Peck, *Reinventing Free Labor: Padrones and Immigrant Workers in the North American West, 1880–1930* (New York: Cambridge University Press, 2000), 160.

84. Conzen, "Immigrants," 612.

85. Alan Mayne, "City as Artifact: Heritage Preservation in Comparative Perspective," *Journal of Policy History* 5, no. 1 (Winter 1993): 159, 161, 168.

86. Tom Holm, "Fighting a White Man's War: The Extent and Legacy of Indian Participation in World War II," in Peter Iverson, ed., *The Plains Indians of the Twentieth Century* (Norman: University of Oklahoma Press, 1985), 151–52.

87. Indian Citizenship Act, 2 June 1924, reprinted in Deloria, *Of Utmost Good Faith,* 94.

88. S. James Anaya, "International Law and U.S. Trust Responsibility toward Native Americans," in Richard A. Grounds, George E. Tinker, and David E. Wilkins, eds., *Native Voices: American Indian Identity and Resistance* (Lawrence: University Press of Kansas, 2003), 156–64.

89. Deloria, *Of Utmost Good Faith,* 94.

90. Wunder, *"Retained by the People,"* 44.

91. For the full text, see Deloria, *Of Utmost Good Faith,* 66–67.

92. Prucha, *Great Father,* 318.

93. Wunder, *"Retained by the People,"* 80.

94. Holm, "Fighting a White Man's War," 158.

95. Ibid., 153.

96. James B. LaGrand, *Indian Metropolis: Native Americans in Chicago, 1945–75* (Urbana: University of Illinois Press, 2002), 46–47, 55.

97. See Termination Resolution 1953 (67 US Statute b132) in William N. Thompson, *Native American Issues: A Reference Book* (Santa Barbara, CA: ABC-CLIO, 1996), 152–53; David R. M. Beck, "Developing a Voice: The Evolution of Self-Determination in an Indian Urban Community," *Wicazo Sa Review* 17, no. 2 (Autumn 2002): 120.

98. Public Law 280, 1953 (67 US Statute 588), in Thompson, *Native American Issues*, 152–53; Beck, "Developing a Voice," 120. While conditions in Indian Country generally improved under the Kennedy and Johnson administrations, termination and relocation officially ended in 1973 during the Nixon administration. Beginning an era of more enlightened Indian policy, numerous federal initiatives favored Native sovereignty and revitalization. Significant acts included the Indian Financing Act of 1974 (88 US Statute 77), The Indian Self-Determination and Educational Assistance Act of 1975 (88 US Statute 2203), the American Indian Religious Freedom Act of 1978 (92 US Statute 469), the Archaeological Resources Protection Act of 1979 (93 US Statute 721), the Indian Gaming Regulatory Act of 1988 (103 US Statute 1336), and the Native American Languages Act of 1990 (104 US Statute 1153). See Thompson, *Native American Issues*, 154–56.

99. Donald L. Fixico, *Termination and Relocation: Federal Indian Policy, 1945–1960* (Albuquerque: University of New Mexico Press 1986), 134–36.

100. Peter V. Snyder, "The Social Environment of the Urban Indian," in Jack O. Waddell and O. Michael Watson, eds., *The American Indian in Urban Society* (Boston: Little, Brown and Co., 1971), 207; Kenneth R. Philp, "Termination: A Legacy of the Indian New Deal," *Western Historical Quarterly* 14, no. 2 (April 1983): 188; Elaine M. Neils, *Reservation to City: Indian Migration and Federal Relocation* (Chicago: University of Chicago Department of Geography Paper no. 131, 1971), 76, 84; Donald L. Fixico, "The Relocation Program and Urbanization," in John R. Wunder, ed., *Native Americans and the Law: Constitutionalism and Native Americans, 1903–1968* (New York: Garland, 1996), 245–47. The relocation movement peaked in 1957.

101. Wunder, *"Retained by the People,"* 97–105.

102. Mihelich, "Lincoln Urban League," 64; Baltensperger, *Nebraska*, 70, 82.

103. U.S. Census Bureau, "Table 8: Race and Hispanic Origin," *Population and Housing Characteristics for Census Tracts and Block Numbering Areas, Lincoln, NE MSA* (Washington, DC: Government Printing Office, 1993), 18; U.S. Census Bureau, "Table 6: Population and Selected Categories of Race, 2000," *Nebraska: 2000: Summary Population and Housing Characteristics* (Washington, DC: Government Printing Office, 2002), 145.

104. See Wunder, *"Retained by The People,"* 135–40.

105. Calloway, *First Peoples*, 430.

106. Mark R. Scherer, *Imperfect Victories: The Legal Tenacity of the Omaha Tribe, 1945–1995* (Lincoln: University of Nebraska Press, 1999), 89, 94, 100.

107. Wunder, *"Retained by the People,"* 176.

108. Ibid., 213.

109. Miia Halme, "Indian Gaming, Sovereignty, and the Courts: The Case of the Miccosukee Tribe of Florida," in John R. Wunder and Kurt E. Kinbacher, eds., *Reconfigurations of Native North America: An Anthology of New Perspectives* (Lubbock: Texas Tech University Press, 2009), 160.

110. CasinOmaha generally provided some annual income for all enrolled tribal

members. It closed for fourteen months starting in June 2009, reopened, closed again after Missouri River floods of 2011, and reopened as the Blackbird Bend Casino in April 2013.

111. U.S. Department of Justice, Office of Tribal Justice, "Department of Justice Policy on Indian Sovereignty and Government-to-Government Relations with Indian Tribes," 30 January 2001, http://www.usdoj.gov/otj/sovtrbtxt.htm.

112. Zach Pluhacek, "Culture versus Economics: Natives Try to Keep Their Heritage Alive While Competing with Rising Gas Prices and Other Financial Issues," *Lincoln Journal Star*, 4 August 2008, 2A.

113. Edward W. Soja, *Postmodern Geographies: The Reassertion of Space in Critical Social Theory* (London: Verso, 1989), 188.

114. Pipher, *Middle of Everywhere*, 6.

115. Federation for American Immigration Reform, "City Fact Sheet: Lincoln, Nebraska," http://www.fairus.org/Research/Research.cfm?ID=1063&c=9.

116. John S. W. Park, *Elusive Citizenship: Immigration, Asian Americans, and the Paradox of Civil Rights* (New York: New York University Press, 2004), 130; Immigration Act of 1917, http://nths.newtrier.k12.il.us/academics/faculty/ Hilsabeck/SUMMER/han/immigration%20Act%20of%201917.htm. The small exception to exclusion was modern-day Iran.

117. See discussion of *Ozawa v. United States*, 260 U.S. 178 (1922), in Park, *Elusive Citizenship*, 122–24.

118. See discussion of *United States v. Thind*, 261 U.S. 204 (1923), in ibid., 124–27.

119. Roger Daniels, "Changes in Immigration Law and Nativism since 1924," in Franklin Ng, ed., *Asians in America: The Peoples of East, Southeast, and South Asia in American Life and Culture* (New York: Garland, 1998), 70.

120. William R. Tamayo, "Asian Americans and the McCarren-Walter Act," in Hyung-Chan Kim, ed., *Asian Americans and Congress* (Westport, CT: Greenwood Press, 1996), 340–45

121. Derek Leebaert, *The Fifty-Year Wound: The True Price of America's Cold War Victory* (Boston: Little, Brown, and Co., 2002), 106, 162, 167.

122. H. Brett Melendy, "Filipino, Korean, and Vietnamese Immigration to the United States," in Dennis Laurence Cuddy, ed., *Contemporary American Immigration: Interpretive Essays* (Boston: Twayne, 1982), 41.

123. Asian-Nation: The Landscape of Asian America, "The 1965 Immigration Act," http:// www.asian-nation.org/1965-immigration-act.shtml.

124. Paul Rutledge, *The Role of Religion in Ethnic Self-Identity* (New York: University Press of America, 1985), 6.

125. Hing, *To Be an American*, 28; Charles B. Keely, "The Immigration Act of 1965," in Kim, *Asian Americans and Congress*, 539.

126. Hing, *To Be an American*, 28.

127. Keely, "Immigration Act of 1965," 534, 539.

128. Kevin Allen Leonard, "Migrants, Immigrants, and Refugees: The Cold War and Population Growth in the American West," in *The Cold War and the American West, 1945–1989*, Kevin J. Fernlund, ed. (Albuquerque: University of New Mexico Press, 1998), 30.

129. Carl Abbott, *Metropolitan Frontier: Cities in the Modern American West* (Tucson: University of Arizona Press, 1993), 87; U.S. Census Bureau, "Table 4. Asian Population by Detailed Group: 2000," *Asian Population: 2000* (Washington, DC: Government Printing Office): February 2002, 9.

130. The 2000 U.S. Census Bureau listed 3,774 Vietnamese in Lincoln and a total of 6,364 in Nebraska. See U.S. Census Bureau, "Profile of Demographic Characteristics: Nebraska," http://factfinder.census.gov/servlet/QTTable?_ bm= y&-geo_id=04000US31&qr _name=DEC_2000_SF1; Vietnamese Studies Internet Resource Center, "Top 50 U.S. Metropolitan Areas by Vietnamese Population," http://vstudies.learnabouthm.ong.org/top50usmetar.html.

131. Leonard, "Migrants, Immigrants, and Refugees," 30.

132. Christopher W. Norris, "Peoples, Nations, and the Unity of Societies," in Carol C. Gould and Pasquale Pasquino, ed., *Cultural Identity and the Nation-State* (New York: Rowman and Littlefield, 2001), 21.

133. Alba, *Ethnic Identity*, 1.

134. George W. Bush, "State of the Union Address," 2 February 2005, http://www. gop.com/News/Read.aspx?ID=5118.

135. "Fair and Secure Immigration Reform," Fact Sheet, 7 January 2004, Republican National Committee, http://www.gop.com/News/Read.aspx?ID=3745.

136. Hing, *To Be an American*, 29; Nugent, *Into the West*, 353.

137. Vecoli, "Significance of Immigration," 15.

138. Monica Davey, "Nebraska Town Votes to Banish Illegal Immigrants," *New York Times*, 21 June 2010, http://www.nytimes.com/2010/06/22/us/22fremont. html?ref=nebraska.

139. Brent A. Nelson, *America Balkanized: Immigrations Challenge to Government* (Montgomery, VA: American Immigration Control Foundation, 1994), 17.

140. Ibid., viii.

141. Rob Toonkel, "U.S. English Supports Introduction of English Language Unity Act of 2003," U.S. English, Inc., 31 March 2003, http://www.us-english.org/inc/ news/preleases/viewRelease.asp?ID=14.

142. Carnevale, " 'No Italian Spoken,' " 5.

143. Lopez, "Language Minorities in the United States," 133.

144. Alexander Portes and Richard Schauffler, "Language and the Second Generation: Bilingualism Yesterday and Today," in Alejandro Portes, ed., *The New Second Generation* (New York: Russell Sage Foundation, 1996), 11.

145. Veltman, "Theory and Method in the Study of Language Shift," 145.

146. Nancy C. Dorian, "Linguistic and Ethnographic Fieldwork," in Joshua A. Fishman, ed., *Handbook of Language and Identity* (New York: Oxford University Press, 1999), 39.

147. William A. Douglass, "Basque-American Identity: Past Perspectives and Future Prospects," in Stephen Tchudi, ed., *Change in the American West: Exploring the Human Dimension* (Reno: University of Nevada Press, 1987), 195.

148. Glazer and Moynihan, *Beyond the Melting Pot*, 12.

149. Dorian, "Linguistic and Ethnographic Fieldwork," 31–32.

150. R. B. Le Page and Andrée Tabouret-Keller, *Acts of Identity: Creole-Based*

*Approaches to Language and Ethnicity* (New York: Cambridge University Press, 1985), 240.

151. Vacillations in federal policy regarding Indian rights and sovereignty weakened the ability and interest of Indian tribes to maintain and retain their languages. At the dawn of the twenty-first century, most American Indians speak English as their first language, and very few are monolingual in their original tongue. In general terms, the smaller a language group, the less the chance of linguistic survival. For many Indian nations, the local school system has been forced to take on language preservation as only a few elders are left to transmit this ancient knowledge. The generations between the elderly and the children were often unable or unwilling to learn the old tongue. See Lopez, "Language Minorities in the United States," 142; Joshua A. Fishman, ed., *Language Loyalty in the United States: The Maintenance and Perpetuation of Non-English Mother Tongues by American Ethnic and Religious Groups* (London: Mouton, 1966), 22; David Harding, "Native Self-Determination Building: The Crees of Northern Quebec and the Navajos of the American South West," in Wunder and Kinbacher, *Reconfigurations of Native North America*, 48–49.

152. Hoa Tran, interview by Haishu Zhu, 16 May 2006, Star City Treasures: Meet Your Neighbors, Lincoln City Libraries, Lincoln, Nebraska, http://www.lincoln-libraries.org/oral _history/Star_City_Treasures.htm, 13.

153. Doug Bereuter, "Lincoln Interfaith Council Observes 40th Anniversary in 1992," speech to U.S. House of Representatives, 26 November 1991, http:// thomas.loc.gov/cgi-bin/query/z?r102: E26NOI-A263. Bereuter was a longtime U.S. representative from Nebraska's First District, which includes Lincoln.

154. See Lincoln, Nebraska, "Lincoln City Charter, 2005," http://www.ci.lincoln. ne.us/city/attorney/charter.pdf.

155. Pipher, *Middle of Everywhere*, 55; U.S. Census Bureau, "Table 3.1: Country or Area of Birth of the Foreign-Born Population from Europe: 2000," and "Table 3.2: Country or Area of Birth of the Foreign-Born Population from Asia: 2000," http://www.census.gov.

156. U.S. Citizenship and Immigration Services, Fiscal Year 2003 Yearbook of Immigration Statistics, "Table 2: Immigration by Region and Selected Country of Last Residence, Fiscal Years 1820–2003," http://uscis.gov/graphics/aboutus/ statistics/IMM03yrbk/2003IMMtables.pdf; "Table B: Immigrants Admitted by Region and Top 20 Countries of Birth: Fiscal Years 2001–03," http:/uscis.gov.

157. See, generally, Neighborhoods, Inc., at http://www.neighborhoodsinc.org/ heart/neighborhoods.

158. Hartley History, Neighborhoods, Inc., http://www.neighborhoodsinc.org/ heart/neighborhoods/Hartley_history.htm.

## Chapter 2

1. Amen advertisement, *Die Welt-Post*, 29 May 1924, 7, translation by author.

2. "Ledgers, 1904–1948," Henry J. Amen Papers, series 1, volumes 1, 2, 3, Nebraska State Historical Society (NSHS), Lincoln; *Lincoln* [NE] *Evening Journal*, 10 July 1975, 1; 11 July 1975, 4.

3. Hattie Plum Williams, "The History of the German-Russian Colony in Lincoln" (M.A. thesis, University of Nebraska, 1909), 92; Mary Lynn Tuck, "*Sekundar-siedlung einer Ausseninsel (Norka-Wolgagebiet) im Lincoln, Nebraska: Bestim-mung der Sprachlichen Urheimat*" [Secondary settlement of an outside island (Norka-Volga region) in Lincoln, Nebraska: Regulation of the language of the homeland] (Ph.D. diss., University of Nebraska–Lincoln, 1983), 348; Aina Sirks, "A Study of a Nebraska German Dialect" (M.A. thesis, University of Nebraska, 1956), 13. Early censuses of Lincoln suggest the community was dominated by settlers from Ohio, New York, Pennsylvania, Illinois, Iowa, Indiana, and Missouri. For a brief synopsis, see *A Handbook of Government: Lincoln and Lancaster County, Nebraska* (Lincoln, NE: League of Women Voters, 1968), 3.

4. Hattie Plum Williams, "A Social Study of the Russian German Population" (Ph.D. diss., University of Nebraska, 1916), 8; George Schiller, "From Volga-German Heritage to Proud American," *American Historical Society of Germans from Russia Journal* 21, no. 1 (Spring 1998): 23; Esther Darauer, interview by Kathy Fimple, 16 February 1981, folder AV1.437.05, South Salt Creek Oral History Project, NSHS, Lincoln, 14. See also John Loos and Alex Loos, *The Migrant Beet Fielders: Germans from Russia* (Lincoln: n.p., 1975), 14; Roger L. Welsch, "Germans from Russia: A Place Called Home," in *Broken Hoops and Plains People: A Catalogue of Ethnic Resources in the Humanities: Nebraska and Thereabouts* (Lincoln, NE: Center for Great Plains Studies, Curriculum Development Center, 1976), 203.

5. Because immigrants rarely totally abandon their sending cultures, "adaptation" or "acculturation" are preferred terms in this essay rather than "assimilation," which often connotes merging completely into the mainstream. See Nazli Kibria, *Family Tightrope: The Changing Lives of Vietnamese Americans* (Princeton, NJ: Princeton University Press, 1993), 19.

6. Hattie Plum Williams, *The Czar's Germans: With Particular Reference to the Volga Germans*, ed. Emma S. Haynes, Philip B. Legler, and Gerda S. Walker (Lincoln, NE: American Historical Society of Germans from Russia [AHSGR], 1975), 218.

7. Gerda Stroh Walker, *Die Welt-Post Index, 1916–1921* (Boulder, CO: Joshua Sky Walker, 1998), iv; *Die Welt-Post*, 9 March 1925, 7.

8. Paul Rutledge, *The Role of Religion in Ethnic Self-Identity* (New York: University Press of America, 1985), 46; John Lauritz Larson, "Pigs in Space; or What Shapes America's Regional Cultures," in Andrew R. C. Cayton and Susan E. Gray, ed., *The American Midwest: Essays on Regional History* (Bloomington: Indiana University Press, 2001), 77.

9. Karen Leonard, "Changing South Asian Identities in the United States," in Maxine Seller and Lois Weis, eds., *Beyond Black and White: New Faces and Voices in the U.S. Schools* (Albany: State University of New York Press, 1997), 165; John M. Nieto-Phillips, *The Language of Blood: The Making of Spanish-American Identity in New Mexico, 1880s–1930s* (Albuquerque: University of New Mexico Press, 2004), 8; Philip Gleason, *Speaking of Diversity: Language and Ethnicity in Twentieth-Century America* (Baltimore: Johns Hopkins University Press, 1992), 124, 127, 139.

10. David Bibas, *Immigrants and the Formation of Community: A Case Study of Moroccan Jewish Immigration to America* (New York: AMS Press, 1998), 2–3; Richard D. Alba, *Ethnic Identity: The Transformation of White America* (New Haven, CT: Yale University Press, 1990), 38.

11. Glenda Norquay and Gerry Smyth, eds., *Across the Margins: Cultural Identity and Change in the Atlantic Archipelago* (New York: Manchester University Press, 2002), 3.

12. See Peter G. Boag, *Environment and Experience: Settlement Culture in Nineteenth-Century Oregon* (Berkeley: University of California Press, 1992), 38, 80, 141.

13. Walker, *Die Welt-Post Index,* iv.

14. James Long, *The German-Russians: A Bibliography of Russian Materials with Introductory Essay, Annotations, and Locations of Materials in Major American and Soviet Libraries* (Santa Barbara, CA: Clio Books, 1978), 3.

15. Among other things, the immigrants to Russia were guaranteed freedom of religion; long-term, no-interest loans to build homes and churches; a thirty-year tax exemption; and perpetual exemption from military conscription and troop quartering. See "Manifesto—Concerning Permission of All Foreigners Immigrating to Russia to Settle in Whichever Provinces They Desire and the Rights Granted to Them," trans. James W. Long, in Sidney Heitman, ed., *Germans from Russia in Colorado* (Fort Collins, CO: Western Social Science Association, 1978), 9–13. Estimates on immigrant populations vary slightly as the accuracy of census records is disputed. See Douglas Hale, *The Germans from Russia in Oklahoma* (Norman: University of Oklahoma Press, 1980), 3; Kenneth W. Rock, "Colorado's Germans from Russia," in Heitman, *Germans from Russia in Colorado,* 70; Williams, *Czar's Germans,* 98.

16. Long, *German-Russians,* 3; and Williams, *Czar's Germans,* 115–18.

17. Although Catherine's (1762–1796) use of social and economic incentives to encourage immigration was repeated in the Black Sea basin by Alexander I (1801–1825) in 1804, the perpetual privileges granted by royal manifestoes were easily rescinded. The first "systematic policy against the Germans in the empire" was unveiled in the 1855. Both Alexander II (1855–1881) and Nicholas II (1894–1917) found Germans' privileges a bane to the modernization of the empire, especially after emancipation of the serfs in 1861 created huge demands for land redistribution. In 1871, German colonists were placed on a par with all other subjects in the Romanov realm, and by 1874 universal conscription—a call that included ethnic Germans—was implemented. Aware of the historic agreement, the Russian Crown gave Volga Germans a ten-year window to emigrate unhindered. See Rock, "Colorado's Germans from Russia," 72; Williams, *Czar's Germans,* 162; Pauline Dudek, "The Germans from Russia," *Journal of Genealogy* 3 (April 1979): 26; Igor Pleve, trans. Richard Rye, "Beginning of Volga German Emigration to America," *American Historical Society of Germans from Russia Journal* 20, no 3 (Fall 1997): 25.

18. Williams, *Czar's Germans,* 218.

19. Sirks, "Study of a Nebraska German Dialect," 64. See also R. Heather Ropes-

Gale, "Immigration of Germans from Russia to Lincoln, Nebraska" (Honors thesis, University of Nebraska–Lincoln, 1989), 12; Williams, "Social Study," 8.

20. Rock, "Colorado's Germans from Russia," 71.

21. Karl Stumpp, *The Immigration from Germany to Russia in the Years 1763 to 1862*, trans. Joseph S. Height (Lincoln, NE: American Historical Society of Germans from Russia, 1978), 22.

22. Timothy J. Kloberdanz, "Plainsmen of Three Continents: Volga German Adaptation to Steppe, Prairie, and Pampa," in Frederick C. Luebke, ed., *Ethnicity on the Great Plains* (Lincoln: University of Nebraska Press, 1980), 59; Williams, *Czar's Germans*, 101.

23. Hale, *Germans from Russia in Oklahoma*, 1–6; and Williams, *Czar's Germans*, 100, 126, 194. This was a largely Protestant population. Hale suggests that 80 percent of the villages were Evangelical Christians, 13.5 percent were Catholic, and about 4 percent were Mennonites. Williams avers that 28 percent of the Volga population was Catholic in 1874.

24. Sergej Terjochin, *Deutsche Architektur an der Volga* [German Architecture on the Volga] (Berlin: Westkreuz Verlag, 1993), 44; Jacob Volz, *Commemorative Review of the Balzerer Reunion, August 1938*, trans. Hildegard Keller Schwabauer (Lincoln, NE: Boomer's Advertising, 1938), 4; Herb Femling, "Balzer History: 'Goloi-Karamisch' in Russian," http://www.femling.com/gen/balzer/balzlist.htm#History%20of%20the %20Balzer%20Colony; "Norka: A German Colony in Russia," http://www.volgagermans.net/norka/.

25. Geoffrey Hosking, *Russia: People and Empire, 1552–1917* (Cambridge, MA: Harvard University Press, 1997), 198–99; Isaac A. Hourwich, *The Economics of the Russian Village* (1892; New York: AMS Press, 1970), 19, 25; Volz, *Commemorative Review of the Balzerer Reunion*, 4; "Ende des Wolgadeutschen Staatswesens in Rußland" [The end of the Volga German state in Russia], *Die Welt-Post*, 23 October 1941, 7. The first land grants were more than sufficient to sustain the original population. By the late nineteenth century, intense cultivation, land overuse, and population growth made conditions tenuous. Balzer, for instance, grew from 479 people to 11,000 between 1772 and 1912. Their land allotment, however, remained 18,000 acres (about twenty-eight square miles).

26. Kloberdanz, "Plainsmen of Three Continents," 59; Williams, *Czar's Germans*, 101.

27. These dialects were remarkably productive and reflected many influences. By 1871 Turkish, Polish, Yiddish, French, Romanian, and Georgian words had been documented in the Volga colonies. See Karl Stumpp, *Fremdes Wortgut in der Umgangsprache der Russlanddeutschen* [Foreign words in the language of the German Russians] (Marsburg, Germany: N. G. Elwert Verlag, 1978), 295. In Lincoln, many English words—"das Basement," for example—crept into the dialect. See *Die Welt-Post*, 8 June 1916, 8.

28. Williams, "Social Study," 12; Tuck, "*Sekundarsiedlung einer Ausseninsel (Norka-Wolgagebiet) im Lincoln, Nebraska*," 17; Sirks, "Study of a Nebraska German Dialect," 11, 65.

29. Williams, "History," 59; Williams, "Social Study," 9; Sirks, "Study of a Nebraska German Dialect," 7. Fifty-nine of the original Volga colonies were in Saratov, and forty-five were in Samara.

30. Christine Kaiser, interview by Tuck, *"Sekundarsiedlung einer Ausseninsel (Norka-Wolgagebiet) im Lincoln, Nebraska,"* 309–11, translation by author.

31. Kloberdanz, "Plainsmen of Three Continents," 59. The railhead was in the city of Saratov.

32. Katherine Alles, interview by Stan Talley, 19 November 1981, folder AV1.437.04, South Salt Creek Oral History Project, NSHS, Lincoln, 9; Reinholdt [Rudy] D. Amen, interview by Stan Talley, 2 February 1981, folder AV1.437.03a-1, South Salt Creek Oral History Project, NSHS, Lincoln, 5; Leah Beideck, interview by Jo Miller, 4 August 1980, folder AV1.636.20, Neighborhood Oral History Project, NSHS, Lincoln, 10; Henry Reifschneider, interview by George S. Round, 20 July 1980, file 8/16/5, Love Library Special Collections, Lincoln, 13.

    Lincoln was the base for Protestant *Volgers* both as a settlement and as a stopping-off point. Topeka, Kansas, served the same purpose for Catholics. Mennonites tended to avoid cities.

33. Williams, "History," 64; Volz, *Commemorative Review of the Balzerer Reunion*, 8; Wolga Book Company advertisement, *Die Welt-Post*, 19 October 1916, 10.

34. Williams, "Social Study," 48. These statistics are for 1914.

35. Pastor R. C. Herholz, "Die neue Kirche der Salems-Gemeinde zu Lincoln, Nebr." [The new Church of the Salem Congregation in Lincoln, Nebr.], *Die Welt-Post*, 8 June 1916, 8, translation by author.

36. Reinholdt Amen, interview, 5.

37. Lucas Vischer, "The Reformed Tradition and Its Multiple Facets," in Jean-Jacques Bauswein and Lucas Vischer, eds., *The Reformed Family Worldwide: A Survey of Reformed Churches, Theological Schools, and International Organizations* (Grand Rapids, MI: William B. Eerdmans, 1999), 2.

38. National Park Service (NPS), "South Bottoms Historic District: Information Prepared by the Nebraska State Historical Society," Lincoln, NSHS, 1986, item 7, description 30; Williams, "History," 94. Emmanuel Evangelical Lutheran was sometimes listed under its German spelling—Immanuel—but appears here in a consistent form to differentiate it clearly from Immanuel Reformed Church in the North Bottoms.

39. William G. Crystal, "German Congregationalism on the American Frontier," http://www.ucc/aboutus/histories/chap_5.htm.

40. Vischer, "Reformed Tradition and Its Multiple Facets," 2, 15. See also Philip Benedict, *Christ's Church Purely Reformed: A Social History of Calvinism* (New Haven, CT: Yale University Press, 2002), 490–93.

41. Reinholdt Amen, interview, 5–6; Alles, interview, 9.

42. Terjochin, *Deutsche Architectur on der Volga*, 20.

43. Michael Koop, "German-Russians," in Dell Upton, ed., *America's Architectural Roots: Ethnic Groups That Built America* (Washington, DC: Preservation Press, 1986), 130; Madeleine F. Panarelli, "Influences on Early Twentieth-Century

Bungalow Housing in Lincoln, Nebraska" (M.A. thesis, University of Nebraska–Lincoln, 1981), 5; U.S. National Park Service, "Significance Sheet," *National Register of Historic Places—Nomination Form, History of the South Bottoms, 1986* (Lincoln: NSHS, 1986), 11, 15–16, 18. Summer kitchens were rectangular outbuildings used for food preparation during the warm months and storage during the winter. While many still stand in the Bottoms, they have been converted into workshops, tiny apartments, or oddly shaped garages.

44. Williams, "History," 58.

45. U.S. National Park Service, "Significance Sheet," 11; Pleve, "Beginning of Volga German Emigration to America," 25–26.

46. Conrad Kruse, interview by Molly Collins, 1 September 1980, North Bottoms Neighborhood History Project, folder AV1.636.10, NSHS, Lincoln, 3; Williams, "Social Study," 23–27.

47. Rock, "Colorado's Germans from Russia," 71; Ropes-Gale, "Immigration of Germans from Russia to Lincoln," 10.

48. Amen papers, "Ledgers 1914–1930," series 1, reel 1, NSHS.

49. Darauer, interview, 1.

50. Jacob Reifschneider, interview by Molly Collins, 2 September 1980, folder AV1.636.22, Neighborhood Oral History Project, NSHS, Lincoln, 22.

51. Giebelhaus, interview by Gertrude Schwindt, 16 July 1980, folder AV1.636.06, Neighborhood Oral History Project, NSHS, Lincoln, 1.

52. Anna Schwindt Giebelhaus, interview by Tuck, in "*Sekundarsiedlung einer Ausseninsel (Norka-Wolgabiet) im Lincoln*," 316, translation by author.

53. Giebelhaus, interview by Schwindt, 1; Giebelhaus, interview by Tuck, 316, translation by author.

54. Henry Reifschneider, interview, 23.

55. "Groceries—Beet Fields," Amen papers, series 1. Forty-three families repaid their tabs within a week of each other in November 1915. The remaining two paid down the debt over several months.

56. Giebelhaus, interview by Schwindt, 3–12; Sirks, "Study of a Nebraska German Dialect," 13; Tuck, "*Sekundarsiedlung einer Ausseninsel (Norka-Wolgagebiet) im Lincoln*," 20; Williams, *Czar's Germans*, 204; Ropes-Gale, "Immigration of Germans from Russia to Lincoln," 19. Most commonly, migration was to western Nebraska, eastern Colorado and Wyoming, northern Iowa, and the Red River Valley in North Dakota and Minnesota.

57. Henry Reifschneider, interview, 16; Williams, *Czar's Germans*, 159.

58. See, for example, the Great Western Sugar Companies advertisement ("*Rüben-Arbeiter gesucht!*" [Beet-workers sought], *Die Welt-Post*, 1 April 1920, 2.

59. See generally, Loos and Loos, *Migrant Beet Fielders*; Harold Stoll, "Beet-field Summer: Windsor, Colorado," *American Historical Society of Germans from Russia Journal* 15, no. 1 (Spring 1992): 6–10.

60. See Sheridan Sugar Company advertisement in *Die Welt-Post*, 8 April 1920, 8.

61. Published through 1982, *Die Welt-Post* was absorbed by the Omaha Tribune Company (Val and, later, William Peter's German-language newspaper combine) in April 1919. It continued to serve the greater Lincoln-Volga community.

62. *Die Welt-Post*, 22 February 1917, masthead; George Heinze, "Un das Publi-cum!" [About the public], *Die Welt-Post*, 13 April 1916, 1, translation by author. See also Williams, "History," 93; James M. Bergquist, "The German American Press," in Sally M. Miller, ed., *The Ethnic Press in the United States: A Historical Analysis and Handbook* (New York: Greenwood Press, 1987), 145–46.

63. "*Frieden Rückt immer Näher*" [Peace moves ever closer], *Die Welt-Post*, 28 December 1916, 1, translation by author; *Die Welt-Post*, 8 February 1917, 1, translation by author.

64. Williams, *Czar's Germans*, 179. A united Germany emerged in 1871, almost one hundred years after the Volga colonies were founded.

65. Alles, interview, 11.

66. *Die Welt-Post*, 8 February 1917, 1, translation by author; "*Kriegszustand ist mit Deutcshland erklärt!*" [State of war is declared with Germany], *Die Welt-Post*, 5 April 1917, 1; "*Der Präsident érläßt Aufruf an Volk*" [The president declares the cry of the people], *Die Welt-Post*, 19 April 1917, 2.

67. Paul Finkelman, "German Victims and American Oppressors: The Cultural Background and the Legacy of *Meyer v. Nebraska*," in John R. Wunder, ed., *Law and the Great Plains: Essays on the Legal History of the Heartlands* (Westport, CT: Greenwood Press, 1996), 38.

68. Letter from William Urbach to Mr. White, 6 April 1918, William F. Urbach Papers, MS3542, "Correspondence," box 1, series 1, folder 1, NSHS, Lincoln.

69. Welsch, "Germans from Russia," 210; Frederick C. Luebke, "Legal Restrictions on Foreign Language in the Great Plains States, 1917–1923," in Paul Schach, ed., *Languages of Conflict: Linguistic Acculturation on the Great Plains* (Lincoln, NE: Center for Great Plains Studies, 1980), 9.

70. *Die Welt-Post*, 13 September 1917, 1; 18 October 1917, 4. "America 1st" re-mained a standard until January 22, 1922.

71. Nebraska State Legislature, "Sedition Act," *Laws and Regulations Passed by the Legislature of the State of Nebraska*, 36th (Extraordinary) Session, March 26– April 8, 1918 (Lincoln: Secretary of State, 1918), Chapter 5, Section 6, 39; Bergquist, "German American Press," 148–49; Luebke, "Legal Restrictions," 5–7.

72. Darauer, interview, 14, Walker, *Die Welt-Post Index*, 242; Katherine Schmall, interview by Steve Larick, 16 September 1980, Folder AV1.437.18, South Salt Creek Neighborhood Oral History Project, NSHS, Lincoln, 8.

73. Motto on masthead. See, for example, *Die Welt-Post*, 2 January 1919, 1, transla-tion by author.

74. Legal language restrictions were not peculiar to this era. Illinois, Wisconsin, and Michigan had all passed mandatory English education laws in the late nineteenth century. Oklahoma and New Mexico even included English-language instruction clauses within their constitutions in the early twentieth century. By 1903, fourteen states required English instruction but also kept provisions for foreign-language instruction in the upper grades. This number increased only slightly over the next decade as seventeen states had such laws in 1917. In 1918, however, twenty-one states passed language laws. See Luebke,

"Legal Restrictions," 2, 11; Finkelman, "German Victims and American Oppressors," 34–35, 40–41.

75. Finkelman, "German Victims and American Oppressors," 37.

76. "An Act Relating to the Teaching of a Foreign Language in the State of Nebraska," *Laws, Resolutions, and Memorials Passed by the Legislature, 1919,* 37th Session (Lincoln: Secretary of State, 1919), chapter 249, 1019.

77. "*Das Unfreie Nebraska*" [Unfree Nebraska], *Die Welt-Post,* 10 April 1919, 4, translation by author; *Die Welt-Post,* 17 April 1919, 5.

78. See "Attorney General Davis Interprets School and Language Laws," *Die Welt-Post,* 8 May 1919, 5. The full text of his opinion was published in English.

79. "*Das Siman Shulgeseß gerichtlich angefochten*" [The Siman school law judicial appeal], *Die Welt-Post,* 18 May 1919, 5; Letter of Viggo Lyngby, attorney, to Edward P. Smith, mayor of the city of Omaha, on behalf of Danish Americans, *Die Welt-Post,* 29 January 1920, 3; "*Der Kampf Gegen das Simangeseß*" [The fight against the Siman Law], *Die Welt-Post,* 11 September 1919, 8.

80. *Meyer v. State* (1922), 107 Nebraska Reports 657; Donald Hickley, Susan A. Wunder, and John R. Wunder, "*Meyer v. Nebraska* (1923)," manuscript for *Nebraska Moments,* 2nd ed., unpaginated.

81. "An Act to Declare the English Language the Official Language of This State," *Nebraska, Session Laws Passed by the Legislature of the State of Nebraska, 1921,* 40th Session, (Lincoln: Secretary of State, 1921), Chapter 61, 244–45.

82. *Meyer v. State of Nebraska,* 42 S. Ct. 625 (262 U.S. 390) (1923); Luebke, "Legal Restrictions," 16.

83. "Jacob Bender in Sutton, Neb., *gestorben*" [Jacob Bender of Sutton, Neb., has died], *Die Welt-Post,* 22 November 1928, 3.

84. Pleve, "Beginning of Volga German Emigration to America," 26; John Dietz, interview by Reva Allen, 11 November 1980, folder AV1.437.06, South Salt Creek Oral History Project, NSHS, Lincoln, 8. For advertisements for Russian travel and an article about trips sponsored by Val Peter's travel agency, see *Die Welt-Post,* 13 May 1920, 3; *Die Welt-Post,* 25 March 1925, 3; *Die Welt-Post,* 27 February 1930, 7.

85. Marlette Schnell, "Volga Land," http://www.fp.calgary.ca/schnell/volga%20 Land.htm; W. Bruce Lincoln, *Red Victory: A History of the Russian Civil War* (New York: Simon and Schuster, 1989), 49.

86. Geoffrey Swain, *The Origins of the Russian Civil War* (New York: Longman, 1996), 8, 146, 168.

87. Conrad Brill, "Excerpt from *Memories of Norka,*" http://www.volgagermans.nt/ Volga%20 Revolution.htm, 1; Schnell, "Volga Land."

88. Brill, "Excerpt from *Memories of Norka,*" 1; "*Ende des Wolgadeutschen Staatswesens in Rußland*" [The end of the Volga German state in Russia], *Die Welt-Post,* 23 October 1941, 7.

89. Moshe Lewin, "The Civil War: Dynamics and Legacy," in Diane P. Koenker, William G. Rosenberg, and Ronald Grigor Suny, ed., *Party, State, and Society in Civil War Russia* (Bloomington: Indiana University Press, 1989), 414, 408; Lincoln, *Red Victory,* 61–65.

90. Emma Schwabenland Haynes, *The History of the Volga Relief Society* (Lincoln: American Historical Society of Germans from Russia), 28, 30, 54; Brill, "Excerpt from *Memories of Norka*," 1.

91. Lincoln, *Red Victory*, 362.

92. Haynes, *History of the Volga Relief Society*, 54; Lincoln, *Red Victory*, 465.

93. Haynes, *History of the Volga Relief Society*, 87–88; "American Volga Relief Society Letters and Documents," NSHS, http://www.nebraskahistory.org/lib-arch/research/treasures/ volga_relief.htm; Samuel Sinner, "Famine in the Volga Basin, 1920–1924, and the American Volga Relief Society Records," *Nebraska History* 78, no. 3 (Fall 1997): 134.

94. "*Einladung an alle Wolgadeutschen Amerikas zur fünften Konferenz und der Feier des Goldenen Jubilämus der Einwanderung der Wolgadeutschen in Lincoln und Sutton, Nebr.*" [An invitation for all Volga German Americans to the fifth conference and the golden anniversary of the migration of Volga Germans to Lincoln and Sutton, Nebr.], *Die Welt-Post*, 26 May 1926, 5.

95. *Die Welt-Post*, 12 April 1928, masthead. This motto remained until 1959.

96. Haynes, *History of the Volga Relief Society*, 11, 12, 84.

97. F. R. Lorenz, "*Ein Ernstes Wort an Unsere Leser!*" [An earnest word to our readers], *Die Welt-Post*, 22 July 1920, 8, translation by author.

98. Finkelman, "German Victims and American Oppressors," 48, 50; Bergquist, "German American Press," 150.

99. Luebke, "Legal Restrictions," 3, 11; Finkelman, "German Victims and American Oppressors," 40–41. See *State ex rel. Thayer v. School District* (1916), 99 Neb 338.

100. Conrad Kruse, interview, 7; John Schwindt, interview by Molly Collins, 19 July 1980, folder AV1.636.07 a and b, Neighborhood Oral History Project, NSHS, Lincoln, 16.

101. *Die Welt-Post*, 25 August 1927, 3.

102. Jacob Reifschneider, interview, 22.

103. The quote in the section head is from Henry Reifschneider, interview, 14–15.

104. Karel B. Bicha, "The Survival of the Village in Urban America: A Note on Czech Immigrants in Chicago in 1914," *International Migration Review* 5, no. 1 (Spring 1971): 73–74.

105. Welsch, "Germans from Russia," 203.

106. Adam Green, interview by Gertrude Schwindt, 22 July 1980, folder AV1.636.13, Neighborhood Oral History Project, NSHS, Lincoln, 3.

107. Conrad Kruse, interview, 5; J. G. (George) Dering, interview by Jo Miller, 7 July 1980, folder AV1.636.02 a and b, Neighborhood Oral History Project, NSHS, Lincoln, 18–19.

108. Marie Elizabeth Dittenber Schmidt, interview by Molly Collins, 11 August 1980, folder AV1.636.17, Neighborhood Oral History Project, NSHS, Lincoln, 6.

109. John Wertz, interview by Mark Beech, 26 September 1980, folder AV1.437.19 a and b, South Salt Creek Oral History Project, NSHS, Lincoln, 8; John Diet-

rich, interview by Lolly Wehrli, 10 November 1980, folder AV1.437.21, South Salt Creek Oral History Project, NSHS, Lincoln, 12–13; Alex Kahler, interview by Stanley Talley, 25 February 1981, folder AV1.437.12, South Salt Creek Oral History Project, NSHS, Lincoln, 10; Colin J. Davis, *Power at Odds: The 1922 National Railroad Shopmen's Strike* (Urbana: University of Illinois Press, 1997), 154–55.

110. Kahler, interview, 8.

111. *Die Welt-Post*, 24 June 1926, B1.

112. John Blum, interview by Stanley Talley, 13 October 1980, folder AV1.437.04, South Salt Creek Oral History Project, NSHS, Lincoln, 5; Marie Beltz, interview by Sandra Schmidt, 25 July 1980, folder AV1.636.19, North Bottoms Neighborhood Oral History Project, NSHS, Lincoln, 43; Darauer, interview, 7; John Schwindt, interview by Molly Collins, 19 July 1980, folder AV1.636.07 a and b, Neighborhood Oral History Project, NSHS, Lincoln, 5.

113. *Die Welt-Post*, 28 July 1927, 8; 19 January 1928, 8; 9 February 1928, 4; Andrew Beltz, interview by Sandra Schmidt, 25 July 1980, folder AV1.636.19 a and b, Neighborhood Oral History Project, NSHS, Lincoln, 3.

114. Williams, "Social Study," 31.

115. Andrew Beltz, interview, 33; Alles, interview, 10; Giebelhaus, interview by Gertrude Schwindt, 10; Molly Schlegel, interview by Gertrude Schwindt, 29 July 1980, folder AV1.636.03, Neighborhood Oral History Project, NSHS, Lincoln, 10; John Schwindt, interview, 5.

116. Marie Beltz, interview, 51.

117. *Die Welt-Post*, 29 March 1925, 7.

118. "German Buyers Guide," *Die Welt-Post*, 1 February 1934, 9.

119. *Die Welt-Post*, 1 January 1925, 1, translation by author.

120. Ibid., 8 March 1928, 6.

121. Lydia Schneider Robinson, interview by Kay Rapkin, 9 November 1980, folder AV1.437.20, South Salt Creek Oral History Project, NSHS, Lincoln, 7; Peter Krieger, Jr., interview by Eugene Wehrli, 25 November 1980, folder AV1.437.22, South Salt Creek Oral History Project, NSHS, Lincoln, 7; Conrad Kruse, interview, 16; John Beltz, interview by Sandra Schmidt, 25 July 1980, folder AV1.636.19, North Bottoms Neighborhood Oral History Project, NSHS, Lincoln, 26.

122. John Kapeller, Jr., interview by Anna Baker, 30 June 1980, folder AV1.636.05, Neighborhood Oral History Project, NSHS, Lincoln, 10.

123. *Die Welt-Post*, 27 April 1933, 5.

124. Ibid., 1.

125. *Lincoln Evening Journal*, 9 July 1975, 1.

126. *Die Welt-Post*, 29 April 1943, 8; 13 May 1943, 8.

127. See, for example, *Die Welt-Post*, 6 October 1938, 7; 10 November 1938, 7.

128. "We Are All Americans, Standing United in the Defense of Our Country," *Die Welt-Post*, 11 December 1941, 1.

129. See, for example, *Die Welt-Post*, 23 November 1944, 1; 30 November 1944; 5 June 1945, 2.

130. "As to Language," *Lincoln Star*, 10 March 1942, reprinted in *Die Welt-Post*, 26 May 1942, 7.

131. Haynes, *History of the Volga Relief Society*, 40; *Die Welt-Post*, 17 November 1927, 1.

132. See, for example, *Die Welt-Post*, 2 January 1928.

133. *Die Welt-Post*, 21 September 1944, 5.

134. See, for example, *Die Welt-Post*, 14 February 1935, 1.

135. *Die Welt-Post*, 13 July 1950, 1; 17 April 1959, 1; 5 May 1961, 1; 28 May 1982, 1.

136. Lubomyr R. Wynar and Anna Wynar, *Encyclopedic Directory of Ethnic Newspapers and Periodicals in the United States*, 2nd ed. (Littleton, CO: Littleton Unlimited, 1976), 85.

137. Bergquist, "The German American Press," 151.

138. Richard Sallet, *Russian German Settlements in the United States*, trans. LaVern J. Rippley and Armud Bauer (1930; Fargo: Institute for Regional Studies, 1974), 81.

139. Giebelhaus, interview by Gertrude Schwindt, 7.

140. Beideck, interview, 7.

141. Henry Reifschneider, interview, 14–15; Jacob Reifschneider, interview, 13–14.

142. Adolph Lesser, "Looking Back: A Lifetime of Memories and Music," *American Historical Society of Germans from Russia* 24, no. 2 (Summer 2001): 2; Brian A. Cherwick, "Polkas on the Prairies: Ukrainian Music and the Construction of Identity" (Ph.D. diss., University of Alberta, 1999), 50.

143. Giebelhaus, interview by Gertrude Schwindt, 7.

144. Cherwick, "Polkas on the Prairies," 10.

145. Charles Keil and Angeliki Keil, *Polka Happiness* (Philadelphia: Temple University Press, 1984), 9–11.

146. Sallet, *Russian German Settlements in the United States*, 84–85.

147. Elizabeth Feuerstein Wertz, interview by Jo Miller, 1 July 1980, folder AV1.636.01, Neighborhood Oral History Project, NSHS, Lincoln, 17.

148. A good example of hammered dulcimer, although in a religious context, can be found in Paulyne Langhofer and Robert Meter, *How Great Thou Art*, produced by the artists, date unknown. Available at AHSGR.

149. Cherwick, "Polkas on the Prairies," 2.

150. Elizabeth Feuerstein Wertz, interview, 17.

151. Lesser, "Looking Back," 2.

152. Ibid.

153. Cherwick, "Polkas on the Prairies," 22; Keil and Keil, *Polka Happiness*, 3.

154. Volz, *Commemorative Review of the Balzerer Reunion*, 15.

155. Sallet, *Russian German Settlements in the United States*, 109.

156. Darauer, interview, 7.

157. John Dietz, interview, 9.

158. Green, interview, 3, 10.

159. *Die Welt-Post*, 30 September 1948, 8.

160. Ibid., 19 May 1961, 2.

161. Henry Hugerader, interview by Jo Miller, 4 August 1980, folder AV1.636.15, Neighborhood Oral History Project, NSHS, Lincoln, 11, 15; Beideck, interview, 13; Welsch, "Germans from Russia," 213.

162. See generally, Paul Koehler, "The German Brotherhood: 272 Years of History from the Volga River in Russia, USA, Canada, South America, and Siberia," *Journal of the American Historical Society of Germans from Russia* 27, no. 4 (Winter 2004): 7–20; Ronald J. Gordon, "The Rise of Pietism in 17th-Century Germany," http://www.cob-net.org/pietism.htm.

163. Molly Schlegel, interview, 7.

164. Letter from William Urbach to Mr. White; Walker, *Die Welt-Post Index*, iv; Welsch, "Germans from Russia," 213; "American Forward Group Nearing 25th Anniversary," *Lincoln Sunday Journal & Star*, 20 May 1954, 2D. See also *Polk's Lincoln City Directory* for the years 1925 to 1975.

165. Henry Reifschneider, interview, 29; Mollie Lebsock Maul, interview by Molly Collins, 5 August 1980, folder AV1.636.14, North Bottoms Neighborhood Oral History Project, NSHS, Lincoln, 14.

166. Schlegel, interview, 7; Crystal, "German Congregationalism on the American Frontier."

167. George Kruse, interview by Molly Collins, 1 July 1980, folder AV1.636.18, Neighborhood Oral History Project, NSHS, Lincoln, 18.

168. Kapeller, interview, 14.

169. Rev. Edward O. Berreth, interview by Jo Miller, 7 July 1980, folder AV1.636.04, Neighborhood Oral History Project, NSHS, Lincoln, 4.

170. Sheryl D. Vanderstel, "United Church of Christ in Indiana," http://www.connerprairie.org/HistoryOnline/ucc.html.

171. Robinson, interview, 1. See *Polk's Lincoln City Directory*, 1969–1976.

172. Mollie Lebsock Maul, interview, 8; Andrew Beltz, interview, 5. See also *Polk's City Directory*, 1925–1980.

173. Melanie Feyerher, "Home Sweet Home: Settlers Found Sense of Community through Churches," *Daily Nebraskan*, 13 January 2005, 10.

174. *Die Welt-Post*, 28 August 1948, 14.

175. See, for example, ibid., 22 August 1945, 3; 12 September 1946, 2.

176. Alma Buettenback, interview by Mark Beach, 29 September 1981, folder AV1.437 a and b, South Salt Creek Oral History Project, NSHS, Lincoln, 5.

177. Clara Wertz, interview by Mark Beech, 26 September 1980, folder AV1.437.19, South Salt Creek Oral History Project, NSHS, Lincoln, 21.

178. *Die Welt-Post*, 18 January 1945, 4.

179. Darauer, interview, 14–15.

180. Schmall, interview, 5.

181. See *Polk's Lincoln City Directory*, 1920–1965.

182. George Kruse, interview, 15.

183. Emma Dinges, interview by Stanley Talley, 20 February 1981, folder AV1.437.07, South Salt Creek Oral History Project, NSHS, Lincoln, 5.

184. Jacob Reifschneider, interview, 7.

185. Ibid.

186. "Lincoln's *neueste Geschäfts-Ecke*" [Lincoln's newest business corner], *Die Welt-Post*, 1 March 1925, 5.

187. Henry Reifschneider, interview, 24; See also *Polk's Lincoln City Directory*, for business listings, 1925–1986.

188. Bicha, "Survival of the Village in Urban America," 73–74; Welsch, "Germans from Russia," 203; Walker, *Die Welt-Post Index*, iv; *Die Welt-Post*, 9 March 1925, 7; Samuel Sinner, "Famine in the Volga Basin," 134; H. K. Sawyers, *Five Volga-German American Houses: South Bottoms Historic District* (Lincoln, NE: Railroad Transportation and Safety Project, 1986), 8; Sallet, *Russian German Settlements in the United States*, 44.

189. Kibria, *Family Tightrope*, 19.

190. Cherwick, "Polkas on the Prairies," 5. See also John J. Bukowczyk, *And My Children Did Not Know Me: A History of the Polish-Americans* (Bloomington: Indiana University Press, 1987), ix, 88, 120.

191. American Historical Society of Germans from Russia (AHSGR) International, "Revised Bylaws, adopted July 8, 2004," Article II: Purposes, http://www.ahsgr/bylaws.htm.

192. Gary Seacrest, "German Russian Group Plans to Build New Headquarters," *Lincoln Journal*, 24 October 1979, 29; George G. Bruntz, *Children of the Volga* (Ardmore, PA: Dorrance & Co., 1981), 110–11; AHSGR, http://www.ahsgr.org. The Amen Family donated space for the original Lincoln headquarters and then deeded the necessary land for construction of the new headquarters building. While Lincoln residents and businesses donated money to construct the new museum, Germans from Russia throughout North America were equally generous. In their typical manner, the new museum was built without credit and debt.

193. Internationalism replaces transnationalism at this time as transnationalism requires persistent contact and involvement with the sending culture. The dispersal of the Volga colonies changed this relationship, and the sending culture evolved as a historical artifact. See, generally, Elliott R. Barkan, "America in the Hand, Homeland, and Heart: Transnational and Translocal Immigrant Experiences in the American West," *Western Historical Quarterly* 35, no. 3 (Autumn 2004): 331–54.

194. Lyudmila Koretnikova, "A Typical Volga-German Life Story," *Journal of the American Historical Society of Germans from Russia* 28, no. 2 (Summer 2005): 15.

195. Lyudmila Koretnikova, "The Migration of Germans from Russia," *Journal of the American Historical Society of Germans from Russia* 28, no. 2 (Summer 2005): 11.

196. Ibid.

197. Samuel D. Sinner, *The Open Wound: The Genocide of German Ethnic Minorities in Russia and the Soviet Union, 1915–1949—and Beyond* (Fargo, ND: Germans from Russia Heritage Collections, 2000), xi–xii, xxv, 1–9. The 2.1 million figure is the estimated German-Russian population as of 1989. Because the old

colonies were already assigned to ethnic Russians, the Soviet government was unable and unwilling to resettle them in the Volga basin.

198. Koop, "German-Russians," 130.

199. Felton was a contributor of many sculptures to the Kansas State Capitol.

200. AHSGR, http://www.ahsgr.org; "German from Russia Pioneer Family," http://www.ahsgr.org/statue.htm.

201. AHSGR, "Bylaws," Article VI, 3; and "ASHGR Chapters," http://www.ahsgr.org/chapters.htm.

202. *Lincoln Sunday Journal and Star*, 13 June 1971, 1F.

203. Patty Beurtler, "Walker Tracing Family Origin," *Lincoln Star*, 19 June 1975, 24.

204. AHSGR, "Villages," http://www.ahsgr.org/villages.htm.

205. Program, "36th Annual International Convention, Oklahoma City, Oklahoma, August 15–21, 2005," AHSGR, 13; and "Villages," http://www.ahsgr.org/villages.htm.

206. "Ancestral Village File Inventory," American Historical Society of Germans from Russia, http://ahsgr.org/Villages/inventory.htm; Kukkus Families home page, http://www.kukkus.com/; Betty Engel Muradian, *Kukkus: A German Village on the Volga* (Fresno: Central California AHSGR, n.d.).

207. AHSGR, "Bylaws," Standing Rule II, 11–15. The remaining five committees focus on the business of running an international organization.

208. The North Bottoms Historical Marker, Tenth Street viaduct, Lincoln, NE. Placed by the Nebraska State Historical Society, UCC Faith, and Immanuel Church, date unknown.

209. U.S. National Park Service, "South Bottoms Historic District," item 7; "South Bottoms Historic District National Registration of Historic Places Register Form;" "Significance Sheet," 1.

210. Alan Mayne, "City as Artifact: Heritage Preservation in Comparative Perspective," *Journal of Policy History* 5, no. 1 (Winter 1993): 168.

211. Cherwick, "Polkas on the Prairies," 11.

212. *Schmeckfest: Food Traditions of the Germans from Russia*, written and produced by Bob Dambach and Michael M. Miller, Prairie Public Television and North Dakota State University, 2000.

213. Author, field notes, AHSGR soup supper, Welfare Society Hall, 18 February 2005.

214. George Kruse, interview, 9.

215. *Küche Kochen* [Kitchen cookbook] (Lincoln, NE: American Historical Society of Germans from Russia, 1973). There are a plethora of cookbooks. See, for example, *Das Essen Unsrer Leute* [The food of our people] (n.p.: AHSGR, 1976); Nelly Däs, *Cookbook for Germans from Russia*, trans. Alex Herzog (Stuttgart, Germany: Landmanschaft der Deutschen aus Russland in Stuttgart, 1996; repr., Fargo: Germans from Russia Heritage Collection, 2003).

216. Loos and Loos, *Migrant Beet Fielders*, 88.

217. http://www.Runza.com/franchise.htm. Founded in Lincoln, there are presently seventy-five stores scattered across Nebraska, Iowa, Colorado, South Dakota, and Kansas.

218. *Küche Kochen*, i.

219. James Leiker, conversation with author, San Antonio, Texas, 8 June 2005.

220. Gwen Nobbe, "Determination, Pride Brought from Old Land," *Lincoln Sunday Journal-Star*, 13 June 1971, 6F.

221. Deena Winter, "Have 'The Bottoms' Hit Rock Bottom?" *Lincoln Journal-Star*, 16 October 2005.

222. "Veterans of World War II," Interlinc, City of Lincoln Parks and Recreation, http://ne.lincoln. gov/city/parks/parks/Parks/Veterans/bricks.htm.

223. Williams, "Social Study," 7–8; Dena Markoff, "Beet Hand Laborers of Sugar City, Colorado, 1900–1920," in Heitman, *Germans from Russia in Colorado*, 96.

224. *Lincoln Evening Journal*, 11 July 1975, 4; 9 July 1975, 1.

225. *Lincoln Evening Journal*, 9 July 1975, 1; 11 July 1975, 4; *Giebelhaus Family Chronicles, 1994* (Spruce, Alberta: Parkview Studios, 1994), 346–49.

226. *Lincoln Journal & Star*, 28 January 2002; 12 June 1983; *Lincoln Evening Journal*, 7 July 1973, 4; *Detroit* [MI] *News*, 19 January 2002; Ruth Amen folder, American Historical Society of Germans from Russia Archives, Lincoln, Nebraska.

227. Rudolph J. Vecoli, "The Significance of Immigration in the Formation of American Identity," *History Teacher* 30, no. 1 (November 1996): 22.

**Chapter 3**

1. Linda Ulrich, "Stablers Proudly Live Their Indian Heritage," *Sunday Journal-Star*, 20 April 1980, 1D; Mark J. Swetland, ed., *Umo$^n$ho$^n$ iye of Elizabeth Stabler: A Vocabulary of the Omaha Language* (Macy, NE: n.p., 1977), vi–vii. The Stablers were both born around the turn of the twentieth century.

2. Rudi L. Mitchell (Omaha), "A Comparative Study of Stressful Life Events among Native American Reservation and Urban Members of the Omaha Tribe of Nebraska" (Ed.D. diss., University of South Dakota, 1987), 20–21. Many Omahas denote their tribal allegiance by including their tribe's name in parenthesis following their names. This practice is common across Native America but not all Indigenous individuals opt to designate a tribal affiliation.

3. *Cherokee Nation v. State of Georgia* (1831), 30 U.S. (5 Peters) 1, 8, reprinted in Colin G. Calloway, ed., *First Peoples: A Documentary Survey of American Indian History* (Boston: Bedford/St. Martin's, 1999), 252–55.

4. Donald L. Fixico, *The Urban Indian Experience in America* (Albuquerque: University of New Mexico Press, 2000), x, 2–3. See also Mark Anthony Rolo (Bad River Ojibwe), dir., *Indian Country Diaries: A Seat at the Drum*, American Public Telecommunications and Adanvdo Vision, 2005.

5. Barry M. Pritzger, *Native America Today: A Guide to Community Politics and Culture* (Santa Barbara, CA: ABC-CLIO, 1999), 51.

6. Speech by Mitchell Parker (Omaha), Gourd Dance, Lincoln Indian Club Thirty-Fifth Annual Pow-Wow, Lincoln Indian Center, 5 August 2005; Mark Joseph Awakuni-Swetland, "Umo(n)ho(n) Ithae t(h)e—Umo(n)ho(n) Bthi(n): I Speak Omaha—I Am Omaha" (Ph.D. Diss., University of Oklahoma, 2003), 22.

7. Donald L. Fixico, *The American Indian Mind in a Linear World: American Indian Studies and Traditional Knowledge* (New York: Routledge, 2003), xii; Elaine M. Nelson, "Eunice Woodhull Stabler, Omaha Indian Writer, 1885–1963" (M.A. thesis, University of Nebraska–Lincoln, 2004), 5, 11, 22.

8. Omaha Nation sovereignty was increasingly recognized throughout the era of urban emigration. Recent developments have given Omaha Nation a police force—an organization only established in the 1970s, and an even more recent right to arrest lawbreakers on tribal lands "regardless of race." See, "Heineman Signs Cross-Deputization Agreements with Omaha, Winnebago," *Nebraska Commission on Indian Affairs Newsletter*, Summer 2005, 1.

9. Macy is an unincorporated village that is the administrative and population center of Omaha Nation. At the time of this writing it housed the Tribal Council, Omaha Nation Public School, Carl T. Curtis Health Center, tribal police and courts, a number of churches, and tribal housing projects. Macy is an abbreviation of Omaha Agency.

10. Robin Ridington, "Omaha Survival: A Vanishing Indian Tribe That Would Not Vanish," *American Indian Quarterly* 11, no. 1 (Winter 1987): 43.

11. Hollis Davies Stabler (Omaha), in Junior League of Lincoln Literary Project, "Transcript of Film Recordings of Omaha Indians," April 1976, Love Library Archives, University of Nebraska–Lincoln, 94.

12. Fixico, *Urban Indian Experience*, 7.

13. David R. M. Beck, "Developing a Voice: The Evolution of Self-Determination in an Indian Urban Community," *Wicazo Sa Review* 97, no 1 (Spring 2002): 117–18.

14. Fixico, *Urban Indian Experience*, 127.

15. Reportedly, one-half the Omaha population in Lincoln changed address annually. See Margot Pringle Liberty, "The Urban Reservation" (Ph.D. diss., University of Minnesota, 1973), 29.

16. Fixico, *Urban Indian Experience*, 5.

17. "Indian Census Rolls, 1885–1940," *National Archives Microfilm Publications* (Washington, DC: Government Printing Office, 1965), Roll 311, 62; Bureau of Indian Affairs, "Census: Omaha, 1915–1925" (Washington, DC: Government Printing Office, 1965), Roll 124, 732. Population statistics, whether census figures, enrollment numbers, or estimates from other sources, vary widely and are often different even within particular agencies. Self-reporting and inclusion of Indians mixed with "other" categories further complicate the issue. Population estimates are still useful as a point of reference, but accuracy cannot be ascribed to these statistics. Most probably, federal and local governments underestimate Omaha and Indian populations. Urban Indians probably overstate populations.

18. Margot Liberty, "Population Trends among the Present-Day Omaha Indians," *Plains Anthropologist* 20, no. 69 (August 1975): 225; Christiana E. Miewald, "The Nutritional Impacts of European Contact on the Omaha: A Continuing Legacy," *Great Plains Research* 5, no. 1 (February 1995): 76; Mni Sose Intertribal Water Rights Coalition, "Omaha Tribe of Nebraska, Community Environ-

mental Profile," http://www.mni.org; American Indian Relief Council, http://
www.airc.org.res_omaha.cfm?ep= 8+ec=5; Omaha Tribe of Nebraska, "Profile,"
http://www.omahatribeofnebraska.com/profile.html.

19. Carol Lujan, "As Simple as One, Two, Three: Census Underenumeration among
American Indians and Alaska Natives," EV90-19, 4, www.census.gov/srd
/papers/pdf/ev90-19.pdf.

20. Alan L. Sorkin, *The Urban American Indian* (Lexington, MA: D. C. Heath,
1978), 10; Brenda Norell, "Urban Indian Summit Mirrors Population Shift:
Families and Identity Are the Focus of New Coalition to Assist Urban Indians,"
*Indian Country Today*, 16 February 2005, 1A, 6A.

21. Margot P. Liberty, *Preliminary Report: A 1970 Census of the Indian Community
of Lincoln, NE* (Lincoln: University of Nebraska Anthropology Department,
1970), unpaginated.

22. Liberty, "Urban Reservation," 39; Allen Richard Longwell, "Lands of the Omaha Indians" (M.A. thesis, University of Nebraska, 1961), 33. The exact locations
of Indian households was not always clear, as census block analyses use the de-
scriptor "non-white" populations in the 1940, 1950, and 1960 Censuses. In 1970
the U.S. Census Bureau counted "Negroes" separately, but not Indians. See, for
example, *Polk's Lincoln City Directory* (Kansas City, MO: Polk, 1947). Successive
volumes yield a pattern.

23. Liberty, "Urban Reservation," 7, 39; Liberty, *Preliminary Report*.

24. The Saunsocis lived in Clinton in the 1970s but moved farther afield thereafter.
The Cayous generally moved northwest of central Lincoln. See *Polk's Lincoln
City Directory*.

25. See Lincoln-Lancaster County Planning Department, "Table 2: Comparison of
Race, Lancaster County, NE," July 2001, https://www.lincoln.ne.gov/city/plan
/reports/reports/2000rpt.pdf; Lincoln City Planning Department, "1990 Census
Tract Map: City of Lincoln and Vicinity," http://www.lincoln.ne.gov/city/plan
/reports/census2000/90ct.pdf; Lincoln City Planning Department, "2000 Census
Tract Map: City of Lincoln and Vicinity," https://lincoln.ne.gov/city/plan
/reports/census2010/00ct.pdf.

26. See U.S. Census Bureau: American FactFinder, "Race and Hispanic or Latino:
2000, Census 2000 Summary File," http://factfinder2.census.gov/faces
/tableservices/jsf/pages/productview.xhtml?src=CF.

27. City of Lincoln, Urban Development Department, www.lincoln.ne.gov. These
statistics were originally compiled by the U.S. Census Bureau and formatted in
information specific to the Everett, Hartley, Malone/Hawley, Clinton, North
Bottoms, South Salt Creek, Woods Park, Downtown, Near South, East Campus,
Havelock, and University Place neighborhoods. Lincoln's newer neighborhoods
were not considered in the scope of the Urban Development Department.

28. *Omaha Community Council News*, November 1958, 3. The organizations
included Minute Women, Friendly Club, War Mothers' Club, Big Crazy and
Group One, Group 2, Group 3, Old Original Native Church Group, Blackfeet
and Group 12, Group Eight, First Reformed Church, Junior Council W.S.H.,
and Reorganized Church of LDS.

29. "Lincoln Indian Club History," Program, Lincoln Indian Club Traditional Pow-Wow, 6–7 August 2005. Five of seven officers listed on the program were Omahas, as were many of the listed members.

30. Liberty, "Urban Reservation," 12, 117; Arthur M. Harkins, Mary L. Zeyman, and Richard G. Woods, *Indian Americans in Omaha and Lincoln* (Minneapolis: University of Minnesota Training Center for Community Programs, 1970), 34; "Lincoln Indian Club Events *Tentatively* Scheduled for 2006," flyer, January 2006.

31. Liberty, "Urban Reservation," 36.

32. "Tribal Member Recognized for His Role in the Development of the Lincoln Indian Center," OmahaTribe.com, 6 November 2005, http://www.omahatribe. com. There were forty urban Indian centers open in the United States by the end of the 1960s. In addition to social centers, they also actively promoted Native American economic and political advancement. See Fixico, *Urban Indian Experience*, 129; Sorkin, *Urban American Indian*, 107–10.

33. Sorkin, *Urban American Indian*, 110.

34. Ibid., 111; Gracie McAndrew, "Nutritional Hazards Corrected," *Lincoln Star*, 4 March 1977, 9; "Absorbing of Center Is Opposed," *Lincoln Star*, 25 February 1977, 3. Initial funders included the City Mission, the Reconciliation Task for the Disciples of Christ, and the Nebraska Conference of the United Methodist Church.

35. Gordon Winters, "Indian Center Park Site Approved," *Lincoln Star*, 16 August 1977, 18.

36. *Lincoln Journal*, 14 April 1980, 9. See also *Polk's Lincoln City Directory* for 1971, 1978, 1980.

37. Oliver Saunsoci, Jr., in "Tribal Member Recognized."

38. Jonnie Taté Finn, "Indian Center Taps Tyndall," *Lincoln Journal-Star*, 13 May 2005, 1B.

39. "Former NCIA Commissioner Clyde Tyndall Appointed Lincoln Indian Center Executive Director," *Nebraska Commission on Indian Affairs Newsletter*, Summer 2005, 3.

40. Fixico, *Urban Indian Experience*, 44.

41. Miewald, "Nutritional Impacts of European Contact on the Omaha," 95.

42. Alice C. Fletcher and Francis LaFlesche, *The Omaha Tribe*, 2 vols. (Lincoln: University of Nebraska Press, 1992), 1:70. Omahas recognized they once "lived near a large body of water in a wooded country where there was game."

43. John Ludwickson, "Historic Indian Tribes: Ethnohistory and Archaeology," *Nebraska History* 75, no. 1 (Spring 1994): 137; Donald David Ross, "The Omaha People," *Indian Historian* 3, no. 3 (Summer 1970): 19; Dale Rittenning, "Adaptive Patterning of Dhegiha," *Plains Anthropologist* 38, no. 146 (November 1993): 261. Material culture, including single-ply moccasin soles and bandoleer-style game bags, supports the idea of an eastern woodlands genesis.

44. Fixico, *American Indian Mind*, 7.

45. Ibid., xii.

46. Nelson, "Eunice Woodhull Stabler," 2.

47. Robin Ridington and Dennis Hastings, *Blessing for a Long Time: The Sacred Pole of the Omaha Tribe* (Lincoln: University of Nebraska Press, 1997), xx; see also Fixico, *Urban Indian Experience*, 41.

48. Liberty, "Urban Reservation," 142; Awakuni-Swetland, "Umo(n)ho(n) Ithae t(h)e—Umo(n)ho(n) Bthi(n)," 22. See also R. H. Barnes, *Two Crows Denies It: A History of Controversy in Omaha Sociology* (Lincoln: University of Nebraska Press, 1984), 124. Barnes includes an extended discussion about kinship terms (124–54).

49. James Owen Dorsey, *Omaha Sociology* (1884; New York: Johnson Reprint, 1970), 220, 252; Ridington and Hastings, *Blessing for a Long Time*, 112; Fletcher and LaFlesche, *Omaha Tribe*, 1:141, 142–95.

50. Liberty, "Urban Reservation, 97, 99. Clan membership was patrilineal, and while Omahas were an accepting nation, a new entity was needed to absorb a portion of the population.

51. Awakuni-Swetland, "Umo(n)ho(n) Ithae t(h)e—Umo(n)ho(n) Bthi(n)," 22. Family ties were so prevalent during the allotment years that clan members tended to congregate in grouped allotments. Migrants to Lincoln appear to have come largely from homesteads on the very western fringe of Omaha Nation where *I^nkésabe*, *Thátada*, and *Tapá* were common. See Mark J. Swetland, "'Make-Believe White-Men' and the Omaha Land Allotments of 1871–1900," *Great Plains Research* 4, no. 2 (August 1994): 210; Margaret Mead, *The Changing Culture of an Indian Tribe* (1932; New York: Capricorn, 1966), 33. Not surprisingly, mainstream family names were clan-specific as well.

52. Fletcher and LaFlesche, *Omaha Tribe*, 1:71–72. Men, for instance, were instructed in how to make tools, and women tended the hearths.

53. Nineteenth-century divisions are discussed in David J. Wishart, *An Unspeakable Sadness: The Dispossession of the Nebraska Indians* (Lincoln: University of Nebraska Press, 1994), 19–21; twentieth-century occupations were gleaned from the city directory. See, for example, *Polk's Lincoln City Directory* (Kansas City, MO: Polk, 1943).

54. Matthew Sheridan (Omaha), in Sylvia Lee, "The Indian Way: Keeping It Alive in Mid-America," in *As Long as the Grass Shall Grow* (Department Report no. 7, School of Journalism, University of Nebraska–Lincoln, 1971), 17.

55. Walter T. Kawamoto and Tamara C. Cheshire, "Contemporary Issues in the Urban American Indian Family," in Harriet Pipes McAdoo, ed., *Family Ethnicity: Strength in Diversity* (Thousand Oaks, CA: Sage, 1999), 97.

56. Author, field notes, conversation with Barry Webster, Omaha tribal council member, Omaha Council Chambers, 6 October 2005; see also Paula Porter Bennett, "Wisdom Great and Small: Omaha Indian Grandmothers Interpret Their Lives" (Ph.D. diss., University of Nebraska, 1996), 255–56.

57. Eunice W. Stabler (Omaha), *How Beautiful the Land of My Forefathers* (Wichita, KS: n.p., 1943), 7.

58. Fletcher and LaFlesche, *Omaha Tribe*, 1:36, plate 21; 2:605; John M. O'Shea and John Ludwickson, *Archaeology and Ethnohistory of the Omaha Indians: The Big Village Site* (Lincoln: University of Nebraska Press, 1992), 2, 5; Alice C. Fletcher, *Lands in Severalty to Indians: Illustrated by Experiences with the Omaha Tribe,*

*Proceedings of the American Association for the Advancement of Science,* vol. 33 (Salem, MA: Salem Press, 1885), 6–7; "History of the Omaha Tribe of Nebraska and Iowa," *Nebraska Indian Community College Catalogue, Academic Year 2005–2007,* 6.

59. O'Shea and Ludwickson, *Archaeology and Ethnohistory of the Omaha Indians,* 7.

60. Judith A. Boughter, *Betraying the Omaha Nation, 1790–1916* (Norman: University of Oklahoma Press, 1998), 30, 39; Wishart, *Unspeakable Sadness,* 45; Omaha Tribe of Nebraska, "Quarterly Stated Meeting, April 15, 2004" (Macy: NE: Tribal Administration, 2004), front cover. The flag—and many other Native Nation standards—can also be viewed online at the Indian Museum of North America, http://crazyhorsememorial.org/crazy-horse-museums-and-collections/the-indian-museum-of-north-america/. The modern Omaha flag contains a central circular element with the names of the seven clans—arranged roughly in their positions in the *húthuga*—that sent representatives to the traditional tribal council. A war bonnet in the center of the red circle is placed on a field of white. "Against the Current," "Umo$^{n}$ho$^{n}$," "The Omaha Tribe of Nebraska and Iowa," and "Heritage for Peace" are all in black. This flag's historic predecessor is not described in ethnographic reports, although clearly most Plains tribes carried national banners.

61. "Treaty with the Sauk and Foxes, etc., 1830," in Charles J. Kappler, ed., *Indian Treaties, 1778–1883* (New York: Interland Publishing, 1972), 305; "Treaty with the Oto, Etc., 1836," 479–80; "Treaty with the Omaha, 1854," 611–14.

62. Wishart, *Unspeakable Sadness,* 102, 117. Omaha Nation is situated geographically at N 42°6′, W 96°21′.

63. Francis Paul Prucha, *The Great Father: The United States Government and American Indians,* abridged ed. (Lincoln: University of Nebraska Press, 1986), x.

64. "Treaty with the Omaha, 1865," in Kappler, 872–73; Benjamin Hallowell, ed., "Quaker Report on Indian Agencies in Nebraska, 1869," *Nebraska History* 54 (Summer 1973): 181.

65. Wishart, *Unspeakable Sadness,* 161; Norma Kidd Green, "The Make-Believe White Man's Village," *Nebraska History* 56, no. 2 (Summer 1975): 245; Richmond L. Clow, "Taxing the Omaha and Winnebago Trust Lands, 1910–1971: An Infringement of the Tax-Immune Status of Indian Country," *American Indian Culture and Research Journal* 9, no. 4 (1985): 2; Boughter, *Betraying the Omaha Nation,* 104.

66. Swetland, "Make-Believe White-Men," 217–18; Awakuni-Swetland, "Umo(n) ho(n) Ithae t(h)e—Umo(n)ho(n) Bthi(n)," 16; Francis LaFlesche, *The Middle Five: Indian School-boys of the Omaha Tribe* (Madison: University of Wisconsin Press, 1963), xix; Wishart, *Unspeakable Sadness,* 120.

67. Swetland, "Make-Believe White-Men," 217–19; Liberty, "Urban Reservation," 97, 99.

68. Boughter, *Betraying the Omaha Nation,* 136, 139; Clow, "Taxing the Omaha and Winnebago Trust Lands," 7, 15; Janet McDonnell, "Land Policy on the Omaha Reservation and Forced Fee Patents," *Nebraska History* 63, no. 3 (Fall 1982): 399, 401, 406–7, 409; Miewald, "Nutritional Impacts of European Contact on

the Omaha," 94. The Burke Act was designed to limit abuses on Native American land. The original federal trust status of twenty-five years was lengthened unless an allottee was issued a certificate of competence by the local agent. Those deemed capable—most Omahas fell into this category—received fee patent to their land (clear title), and the trust period ended.

69. Alfred Wayne Gilpin (Omaha), "The Community Development Plan of the Omaha Tribe," *Omaha Community Council News*, August 1958, 2.

70. Author, field notes, conversation with Barry Webster.

71. Eunice Stabler, *How Beautiful the Land of My Forefathers*, 8.

72. Ibid., 43.

73. Ridington and Hastings, *Blessing for a Long Time*, xx.

74. Fletcher and LaFlesche, *Omaha Tribe*, 1:70; 2:570–71, 597; Eunice Stabler, *How Beautiful the Land of My Forefathers*, 44. The cosmic portion of the creation story was recorded by the Pebble Society. Emergence from water was recorded as part of the creation story shared by all Omahas. Some or all of the clans may have had their own creation stories as well.

75. Ridington and Hastings, *Blessing for a Long Time*, xvii, 54.

76. Ibid., 234, 243; Mead, *Changing Culture of an Indian Tribe*, xii.

77. Eunice Stabler, *How Beautiful the Land of My Forefathers*, 55.

78. Suzette Turner (Omaha), in "Transcript of Film Recordings of Omaha Indians," 4.

79. Weston La Barre, *The Peyote Cult*, 5th ed. (Norman: University of Oklahoma Press, 1989), 66, 113. See also Melvin R. Gilmore, "The Mescal Society among the Omaha Indian," *Publications of the Nebraska State Historical Society* 19 (1919): 163, 165.

80. Benson Tong, "Allotment, Alcohol, and the Omahas," *Great Plains Quarterly* 17, no. 1 (Winter 1997): 28. See also La Barre, *Peyote Cult*, 7, 58. Peyote was a component of pre-Columbian rites among some tribes on the Southern Plains.

81. Liberty, "Urban Reservation," 37.

82. Francis LaFlesche, "James Mooney and Francis La Fleschè (Omaha) Testify about Peyote, 1918," in Alfred L. Hurtado and Peter Iverson, ed., *Major Problems in American Indian History* (Lexington, MA: D. C. Heath, 1994), 359.

83. Malcolm J. Arth, "A Functional View of Peyotism in Omaha Culture," *Plains Anthropologist* 7, no. 7 (October 1956): 25.

84. Susan Freemont (Omaha), interview, April 1994, in Bennett, "Wisdom Great and Small," 147.

85. Arth, "Functional View of Peyotism in Omaha Culture," 25; Mead, *Changing Culture of an Indian Tribe*, 98; Sherry L. Smith, "Francis LaFlesche and the World of Letters," *American Indian Quarterly* 25, no. 4 (Fall 2001): 597; Wesley R. Hurt, "Factors in the Persistence of Peyote in the Northern Plains," *Plains Anthropologist* 5, no. 9 (May 1960): 26.

86. Tong, "Allotment," 29; Earl Dyer, "They Pray All Night: Indian Church Ideas Christian," *Lincoln Star*, 21 December 1962, 1. While fourteen states had laws making ritual peyote illegal by the early 1960s, Nebraska never enacted such prohibitions.

87. Pritzger, *Native America Today*, 279.

88. Liberty, "Population Trends," 226. The sample size was ninety-eight, and it polled nearly equivalent numbers of national and Lincoln residents.

89. Liberty, "Urban Reservation," 113.

90. Interchurch Ministries of Nebraska, "Lincoln Indian Community Church," http://www. interchurchministries.org/ministries/native/licc.htm. Reformed, Disciples of Christ, Episcopal, Evangelical Lutheran, Presbyterian, United Church of Christ and Methodist organizations comprised the seven.

91. Colin G. Calloway, ed., *Our Hearts Fell to the Ground: Plains Indian Views of How the West Was Lost* (Boston: Bedford/St. Martin's, 1996), 28.

92. Miewald, "Nutritional Impacts of European Contact on the Omaha," 113.

93. *Wíbthaho$^{n}$* is the root word for "thank you." It is conjugated to recognize relationships.

94. Speech by Dean Whitebreast, master of ceremonies, Lincoln Indian Club Traditional Pow-Wow, 6 August 2005, unpublished.

95. Mark Awakuni-Swetland, *Dance Lodges of the Omaha People: Building from Memory* (New York: Routledge, 2001), 45. Omaha handgame was an ancient gift from the Otoe Nation.

96. Liberty, "Population Trends," 226; Lee, "Indian Way," 17.

97. Awakuni-Swetland, "Umo(n)ho(n) Ithae t(h)e—Umo(n)ho(n) Bthi(n)," 200.

98. The number four was always significant, as it marks the number of cardinal directions and signifies completion in the Indian cosmos.

99. Author, field notes, Lincoln Indian Club Handgame and War Dance, 8 March 2003, Lincoln Indian Center; University of Nebraska–Lincoln Omaha language class handgame, 25 April 2003, Lincoln Indian Center; Awakuni-Swetland family handgame, 24 April 2004, Lincoln Indian Center.

100. Author, field notes, Lincoln Indian Club Handgame and War Dance, 8 March 2003, Lincoln Indian Center; University of Nebraska–Lincoln Omaha language class handgame, 25 April 2003, Lincoln Indian Center; Awakuni-Swetland family handgame, 24 April 2004, Lincoln Indian Center.

101. Awakuni-Swetland, *Dance Lodges*, 12; Dorsey, *Omaha Sociology*, 342.

102. Fletcher and LaFlesche, *Omaha Tribe*, 2:459–61.

103. Ridington, "Omaha Survival," 47.

104. "Omaha Indian Music," American Folklife Center, Library of Congress, http://memory.loc.gov/ammam/amhhtml/.

105. Benjamin R. Kracht, "Kiowa Powwows: Tribal Identity through the Continuity of the Gourd Dance," *Great Plains Research* 4, no. 2 (August 1994): 264; Tom Holm, "Fighting a White Man's War: The Extent and Legacy of American Indian Participation in World War II," in Peter Iverson, ed., *The Plains Indians of the Twentieth Century* (Norman: University of Oklahoma Press, 1985), 160.

106. Author, field notes, Veterans' Day Gourd Dance, 11 November 2002, Lincoln Indian Center.

107. John Turner (Omaha), in "'Transcript of Film Recordings of Omaha Indians," 78; Awakuni-Swetland, *Dance Lodges*, 52, 79.

108. Tara Browner, *The Heartbeat of the People: Music and Dance of the Northern Pow-Wow* (Urbana: University of Illinois Press, 2002), 145.

109. Nettie Grant Sikyta, placard at "Pow Wow Plains," exhibit, Great Plains Art

Collection, 15 December 2002, Lincoln, Nebraska; Hollis Davies Stabler (Omaha), in "Transcript of Film Recordings of Omaha Indians," 21; Whitebreast, speech.

110. Kracht, "Kiowa Powwows," 257–65; Browner, *Heartbeat of the People*, 29. Commissioner John Collier ended the ban during the Indian New Deal.

111. Browner, *Heartbeat of the People*, 31.

112. Ibid., 50, 53.

113. Tom Tidball, "Pow Wow Plains," photography exhibit, Great Plains Art Gallery, Lincoln, NE, 10 August–15 December 2002.

114. Ken Gray, "Indian 'Disheartened' by Changing Customs," *Lincoln Star*, 22 August 1973, 13.

115. Paraphrasing Barb Smith (Omaha), Lincoln Indian Club cultural adviser, in Jonnie Taté Finn, "Preparing for Powwow, With Eye toward Sky: Lincoln Indian Club Erects Four Tipis for This Weekend's Traditional Powwow," *Lincoln Journal Star*, 4 August 2005, 1B.

116. Carrie Wolfe (Omaha), president of Lincoln Indian Club, in Finn, "Preparing for Powwow," 1B.

117. Mitchell Parker (Omaha), speech, Gourd Dance at Lincoln Indian Club 35th Annual Pow-Wow, Lincoln Indian Center, August 5, 2005.

118. Alberta Canby (Omaha), in Finn, "Preparing for Powwow," 1B.

119. Awakuni-Swetland, "Umo(n)ho(n) Ithae t(h)e—Umo(n)ho(n) Bthi(n)," 22; Author, field notes, Veterans Day Gourd Dance; La Barre, *Peyote Cult*, 66. NAC meetings were conducted in English, the organization's lingua franca. Songs and prayers were specific to each nation and were reportedly rendered in Omaha.

120. Judi M. Gaiashkibos (Ponca/Santee), executive director, Nebraska Commission of Indian Affairs, interview by author, 31 October 2005, Nebraska Commission on Indian Affairs Offices, Lincoln, Nebraska.

121. James Crawford, *At War with Diversity: US Language Policy in an Age of Anxiety* (Clevedon, England: Multilingual Matters, 2000), 52–53, 57–58.

122. Rory M. Larson, "Acculturation Terms in Omaha" (M.A. thesis: University of Nebraska–Lincoln, 2005), 37, 75, 190; Bennett, "Wisdom Great and Small," 193–95; Earl Dyer, "Indians Determined to Solve Own Problems," *Lincoln Star*, 1 March 1960, 1. For narratives on nineteenth-century English acquisition, see Phillips G. Davies, "David Jones and Gwen Davies, Missionaries in Nebraska Territory, 1853–1860," *Nebraska History* 60, no. 1 (Spring 1979): 83; Valarie Sherer Mathes, "Susan LaFlesche Picotte: Nebraska's Indian Physician, 1865–1915," *Nebraska History* 63, no. 4 (Winter 1982): 502; Norma Kidd Green, "The Presbyterian Mission to the Omaha Nation Tribe," *Nebraska History* 48, no. 3 (Autumn 1967): 277; Wishart, *Unspeakable Sadness*, 122, 231.

123. Liberty, "Population Trends," 226; Liberty, "Urban Reservation," 44.

124. Freemont, in Bennett, "Wisdom Great and Small," 144; Hollis Davies Stabler, in "Transcript of Film Recordings of Omaha Indians," 97.

125. Fletcher and LaFlesche, *Omaha Tribe*, 2:606. See also James Owen Dorsey,

"Omaha and Ponka Letters, *Bureau of Ethnology Bulletin 11* (Washington, DC: Government Printing Office, 1891). Strictly an oral language, Omaha was assigned an orthography by ethnologist James Owen Dorsey in the late nineteenth century. He went on to teach some Omahas to read and write, and he published a number of their personal letters. It is unclear how widespread the practice of writing was. Fletcher and LaFlesche simplified Dorsey's system in the early twentieth century, and most Omaha remains recorded in some variation of this format.

126. Denny Gayton (Hunkpapa Lakota), "There Is No Alternative to Tribalism," paper presented at Native American Graduate Students Symposium, 11 November 2005, University of Nebraska–Lincoln.

127. LaFlesche, "James Mooney and Francis La Flesche," xvii.

128. Fletcher and LaFlesche, *Omaha Tribe*, 2:606.

129. Charles Wilkinson, *Blood Struggle: The Rise of Modern Indian Nations* (New York: Norton, 2005), 329–30.

130. Larson, "Acculturation Terms in Omaha," 7; Mni Sose Intertribal Water Rights Coalition, "Omaha Tribe of Nebraska."

131. Travis Cleman, "Keeping Alive in a Language and a Culture," *Lincoln Journal-Star*, 26 August 2004, 1A; Mark J. Awakuni-Swetland, ELF Omaha Language Curriculum Development Project, http://sapir.ling.yale.edu/~elf/Awakuni.html.

132. Awakuni-Swetland, "Umo(n)ho(n) Ithae t(h)e—Umo(n)ho(n) Bthi(n)," 88, 130.

133. Larson, "Acculturation Terms in Omaha," 76.

134. The U.S. Congress passed Native American Language Acts in 1990 and 1992; see Crawford, *At War with Diversity*, 61–62. The Nebraska legislature passed LB 475 in 1999, which proclaimed, "Teaching American Indian languages is essential to the proper education of Indian children." See Awakuni-Swetland, "Umo(n)ho(n) Ithae t(h)e—Umo(n)ho(n) Bthi(n)," 187.

135. Suzette Turner, in "Transcript," 62.

136. Umo[n]ho[n] Nation Public School welcome page, http://macyweb.esu1.org/about_school.htm.

137. Cleman, "Keeping Alive in a Language and a Culture," 2A; Nebraska Indian Community College, http://www.thenicc.edu.

138. Awakuni-Swetland, "Umo(n)ho(n) Ithae t(h)e—Umo(n)ho(n) Bthi(n)," 188.

139. Judi M. gaiashkibos, e-mail to author, 31 October 2005.

140. Eunice Stabler, *How Beautiful the Land of My Forefathers*, 8.

141. A. Irving Hallowell, "American Indians, White and Black: The Phenomenon of Transculturalization," *Current Anthropology* 4, no. 5 (December 1963): 523, 527–28.

142. See David R. Edmunds, "Native American Voices: American Indian History, 1895–1995," *American Historical Review* 100 (June 1995): 733–34; Gary Clayton Anderson, *Kinsman of Another Kind: Dakota-White Relations in the Upper Mississippi Valley, 1650–1862* (Lincoln: University of Nebraska Press, 1984),

ix–xi, 30.

143. The Supreme Court in *United States v. Rogers*, 4 How. 567 (1846) suggested "some Indian blood" was a necessity. Forty years later they allowed tribes to determine the criteria for citizenship; see *Eastern Band of Cherokee Indians v. United States and Cherokee Nation*, 117 U.S. 288 (1886).

144. William T. Hagen, "Full Blood, Mixed Blood, Generic, and Ersatz: The Problem of Indian Identity," *Arizona and the West* 27, no. 4 (Winter 1985): 317.

145. Omaha Tribe of Nebraska, "Constitution and Bylaws of the Omaha Indian Tribe of Nebraska, approved March 30, 1936" (Washington, DC: Government Printing Office, 1936), Article II, Section 1; and Article II, Section 5.

146. Liberty, "Urban Reservation," 26.

147. "Omahas Awarded Judgment," *Lincoln Star*, 7 September 1961, 17. The judgment was part of an Indian Claims Commission—an organization established in 1946—action originally filed as Case 225 in 1951. Omahas alleged that the conditions of the 1854 treaty were not carried out in good faith, and were eventually awarded money for five million acres of territory ceded to the United States in 1854 at $.20 an acre. Because the land was worth $1.50 an acre at that time, a settlement of $2.9 million was received. Much of this money was distributed in $750-per-capita disbursements. Six years later, each enrolled member received an additional $270 when Case 138—stemming from the 1830 treaty—was settled for $1.75 million. See Wishart, *Unspeakable Sadness*, 238–42; Mark R. Sherer, *Imperfect Victories: The Legal Tenacity of the Omaha Tribe, 1945–1995* (Lincoln: University of Nebraska Press, 1999), 48, 72.

148. Omaha Nation, "Constitution & Bylaws of the Omaha Tribe as amended November 18, 2003," Article II, Sections 1 and 2.

149. "Omaha Enrollment Survey," OmahaTribe.com, survey closed 5 January 2006.

150. Oliver Saunsoci, Jr., in "Tribal Member Recognized."

151. Eleanor Baxter (née Saunsoci), in Wynn L. Summers, *Women Elders' Stories of the Omaha Tribe: Macy, Nebraska, 2004–2005* (Lincoln: University of Nebraska Press, 2009), 38.

152. Listings of twentieth- and twenty-first-century occupations were available in the city directory. See, for example, *Polk's Lincoln City Directory* (Kansas City, MO: Polk, 1973).

153. Sorkin, *Urban American Indian*, 39.

154. Gilpin, "Community Development Plan," 1–2; "Initial Overall Redevelopment Plan," 11, 16, 20; *Omaha Community Council News*, June 1959, 4; Deborah Davis Jackson, *Our Elders Lived It: American Indian Identity in the City* (DeKalb: Northern Illinois University Press, 2002), 33; Longwell, "Lands of the Omaha Indians," 96; Miewald, "Nutritional Impacts of European Contact on the Omaha," 78, 93–95; Beck, "Developing a Voice," 119; Hollis D. Stabler, *No One Ever Asked Me: The World War II Memoirs of an Omaha Indian Soldier*, ed. Victoria Smith (Lincoln: University of Nebraska Press, 2005), 3–10.

155. James E. Officer, "The American Indian and Federal Policy," in Jack O. Waddell and O. Michael Watson, eds., *The American Indian in Urban Society* (Boston: Brown, Little and Company, 1971), 35; Suzan Shown Harjo, "The

American Indian Experience," in Harriet Pipes McAdoo, ed., *Family Ethnicity: Strength in Diversity* (Thousand Oaks, CA: Sage, 1999), 66; *Omaha Community Council News*, April 1959, 4; October 1959, 1; "School Students Home for Summer Months," *Omaha Community Council News*, April/May/June 1961, 2; "Omaha Tribal Agency Open House Is Friday," *Lincoln Journal*, 1 October 1971.

156. Donald L. Fixico, "The Relocation Program and Urbanization," in John R. Wunder, ed., *Native Americans and the Law: Constitutionalism and Native Americans, 1903–1968* (New York: Garland, 1996), 249, 253; Elaine M. Neils, *Reservation to City: Indian Migration and Federal Relocation* (Chicago: University of Chicago Department of Geography Paper no. 131, 1971), 168; Peter V. Snyder, "The Social Environment of the Urban Indian," in Waddell and Watson, *American Indian in Urban Society*, 219; Officer, "American Indian and Federal Policy," 53; U.S. Department of Commerce, Omaha Redevelopment Committee, Omaha Indian Reservation, Nebraska, "Initial Overall Economic Redevelopment Plan, Omaha Redevelopment Area" (Washington, DC: Area Redevelopment Administration, 1963), 25–26.

157. Nancy Sullivan, "The City: Land of Dim Promise," in *As Long as the Grass Shall Grow* (Lincoln: University of Nebraska School of Journalism, 1971), 26.

158. National Urban Indian Family Coalition, http://www.nuifc.org/facts.htm.

159. Bob Reeves, "Tribe Members, Reservations Benefit from Casinos," *Lincoln Star*, 31 December 1993.

160. U.S. Census Bureau, *1990 Census of Population: Social and Economic Characteristics: Nebraska, 1990 CP-2-29* (Washington, DC: Government Printing Office, 1993), 30, 37.

161. Author, field notes, conversation with Barry Webster.

162. Robert Agee, "Many Omahas Now Omahans: Indians Leave Reservation, but Their Problems Pile Up," *Omaha World-Herald Magazine*, 1 July 1956, 16G.

163. James B. LaGrand, *Indian Metropolis: Native Americans in Chicago, 1945–75* (Urbana: University of Illinois Press, 2002), 119.

164. Gilpin, "Community Development Plan," 2–3.

165. "Indians Determined to Solve Own Problems," *Omaha Community Council News*, January/February 1960, 3; "Mahas Make Great Strides in Development Program," *Omaha Community Council News*, August/September/October 1961, 7; "Omaha-Lincoln Groups Aid in Canning Project," *Omaha Community Council News*, July/August/September 1960, 8; Earl Dyer, "Colorful Indian Pow-Wow Shows Merging of Old and New," *Lincoln Star*, 19 August 1959, 1.

166. Pauline Tyndall (Omaha), in "Omaha Tribe 'Coming Closer' through Shake Hands Project," *Lincoln Star*, 26 January 1959, 3.

167. Harkins et al., *Indian Americans in Omaha and Lincoln*, 29–30.

168. Frank Sheridan (Omaha), in "Transcript of Film Recordings of Omaha Indians," 76, 91, 96.

169. Ibid., 96.

170. LaGrand, *Indian Metropolis*, 100; Peter Iverson, "Building Towards Self-Determination: Plains and Southwestern Indians in the 1940s and 1950s,"

*Western Historical Quarterly* 16, no. 1 (April 1985): 170.

171. Liberty, "Urban Reservation," 32, 40; Liberty, "Preliminary Report," unpaginated.

172. Summers, *Women Elders' Stories of the Omaha Tribe*, 40.

173. Reuben Snake, "Urbanization of the American Indian: One Man's View," in Gretchen M. Bateille, David Mayer Gradwohl, and Charles L. P. Silet, ed., *The World between Two Rivers: Perspectives on American Indians in Iowa* (1979; Iowa City: University of Iowa Press, 2000), 90.

174. U.S. Department of Commerce, "Initial Overall Economic Redevelopment Plan," 25–26.

175. Agee, "Many Omahas Now Omahans," 16G.

176. Charles D. Novak, *Lincoln Public Schools 2001–2002 Statistical Handbook* (Lincoln, NE: LPS District Office, 2001), 26–27; Lincoln Public Schools, http://www.lps.org.

177. Dennis Hastings (Omaha), in "New Morrill Hall Exhibit Traces Long History of the Omaha Tribe," *Sunday Journal Star*, 23 February 1992.

178. Awakuni-Swetland, *Dance Lodges*, 56, 64.

179. Author, field notes, Veterans Day Gourd Dance, 11 November 2002, Lincoln Indian Center.

180. Author, field notes, Gourd Dance; field notes, Lincoln Indian Club 35th Annual Pow-Wow.

181. Whitebreast, speech.

182. John Turner, in "Transcript," 1–2. In the mainstream cosmos, red represented hardiness and valor, white was indicative of purity, and blue stood for vigilance, perseverance, and justice. See "The Blazon of the Great Seal of the United States and Charles Thomson's Remarks and Explanation," http://www.greatseal.com/symbols/blazon.html.

183. U.S. Department of Defense, "20th Century Warriors: Native American Participation in the United States Military," http://www.defenselink.mil/specials/nativeamerican01/warrior.html.

184. Ibid.

185. Sorkin, *Urban American Indian*, 25; LaGrand, *Indian Metropolis*, 32.

186. U.S. Department of Defense, "20th Century Warriors."

187. Hallowell, "American Indians," 523, 527–28.

188. Elliott R. Barkan, "America in the Hand, Homeland in the Heart: Transnational and Translocal Immigrant Experiences in the American West," *Western Historical Quarterly* 35, no. 3 (Autumn 2004): 339.

189. Benjamin Tompson, "Historic Firsts in Tribal Election," 10 November 2005, http://www. OmahaTribe.com; *Polk's Lincoln City Directory* (Kansas City, MO: Polk, 1956). See consecutive years of directory. See also Summers, *Women Elders' Stories of the Omaha Tribe*, 6–40.

190. "Former NCIA Commissioner Clyde Tyndall Appointed Lincoln Indian Center Executive Director," *Nebraska Commission on Indian Affairs Newsletter*, Summer 2005, 3.

191. See Hollis D. Stabler, *No One Ever Asked Me*, 10–24.

192. Beck, "Developing a Voice," 135–36. For a discussion on Montezuma, see Peter Iverson, "Carlos Montezuma and the Fort McDowell Yavapai Community," *Journal of Arizona History* 22 (Winter 1981): 415–26.

193. Hollis D. Stabler, *No One Ever Asked Me*, 137.

194. Mead, *Changing Culture of an Indian Tribe*, 55.

195. U.S. Census Bureau, "Table 25: Indians, Chinese, Japanese, By Sex for Counties, and for Cities 10,000 to 100,000," *16th Census of the United States: Population*, vol. 2, *Characteristics of Population*, part 4, *MN to NM* (Washington, DC: Government Printing Office, 1943), 648; "Composition of Rural Nonfarm Populations, by Counties, 1940," 652.

196. Liberty, "Urban Reservation," 7.

197. Freemont, in Bennett, "Wisdom Great and Small," 166.

198. Norma (no last name given), in Bennett, "Wisdom Great and Small," 214–15.

199. Sorkin, *Urban American Indian*, 63, 83.

200. Liberty, "Urban Reservation," 7.

201. Ulrich, "Stablers," 1D.

202. Gilpin, "Community Development Plan," 2.

203. Mitchell, "Comparative Study of Stressful Life Events," 168.

204. gaiashkibos, interview.

205. Longwell, "Lands of the Omaha Indians," 28.

206. Author, field notes, conversation with Barry Webster.

207. Jackson, *Our Elders Lived It*, 155.

208. Author, field notes, conversation with Omaha elders, Horticulture Project Open House, 3 August 2005, Agronomy East Campus Experiment Station, University of Nebraska–Lincoln.

209. Mitchell, "Comparative Study of Stressful Life Events," 17–18. CasinOmaha, when open, was the largest employer on Omaha Nation, followed by the federal government. Casino gambling was made possible by the Indian Gaming Regulatory Act of 1988 (103 U.S. Statute 1336). Despite issues of sovereignty, Nebraska prohibited Las Vegas–style gambling. After legal wrangling, the facility was opened in Iowa on land Omaha Nation regained after lengthy political and legal maneuvering. A good account of efforts to regain Blackbird Bend is found in Scherer, *Imperfect Victories*, 89–114.

210. Awakuni-Swetland, "Umo(n)ho(n) Ithae t(h)e—Umo(n)ho(n) Bthi(n)," 38.

211. Darwin Phillips (Omaha), in Bob Reeves, "Tribal Government Hears Complaints," *Lincoln Journal Star*, 15 January 1994; see also "Off Reservation Indians Seeking In-Tribal Voice," *Sunday Journal and Star*, 22 October 1961, 1B.

212. Omaha Constitution, 2003, Article 5, Section 1; and Omaha Constitution, 1936, Article 5, Section 1.

213. LaGrand, *Indian Metropolis*, 2, 203.

214. Dale Kruzic, Conroy Chino (Acoma), and Beverly Morris (Aleut), producers, *Looking Towards Home*, Native American Public Telecommunications, 2003.

215. Harkins et al., *Indian Americans in Omaha and Lincoln*, 38.

216. LaGrand, *Indian Metropolis*, 162–64; Fixico, *Urban Indian Experience*, 6, 140.

217. Fixico, *Urban Indian Experience*, 3.

218. Liberty, "Population Trends," 225.

219. Karl J. Reinhard and A. Mohamad Ghazi, "Evaluation of Lead Concentrations in 18th-Century Omaha Indian Skeletons Using ICP-MS," *American Journal of Physical Anthropology* 89, no. 2 (June 1992): 183–85.

220. Unmarked Human Burial Sites and Skeletal Remains Act (1989), Neb. Rev. Stat., sections 12-1201 to 12-1212. The federal government passed a less comprehensive repatriation act in the following year. See Native Grave Protection and Repatriation Act (1990), 25 U.S. Code 3001, et. seq.

221. Tina F. Brown, "The Native American Grave Protection and Repatriation Act: A Necessary but Costly Act," *Nebraska Anthropologist* 12 (1995–1996): 92–94; Ridington and Hastings, *Blessing for a Long Time*, 201, 210–11.

222. Reinhard and Ghazi, "Evaluation of Lead Concentrations," 185.

223. Experiences in Lincoln were much different from Los Angeles and perhaps other relocation centers. See Rolo, *Indian Country Diaries*, for a discussion on long-distance contacts with sending cultures.

224. Gordon V. Krutz, "Transplanting and Revitalizing Indian Cultures in the City," in Jack O. Waddell and O. Michael Watson, eds., *American Indian Urbanization* (West Lafayette, IN: Purdue University, Purdue Research Foundation, 1973), 130.

225. In addition to ICC awards, avoiding termination, increased national sovereignty after retrocession, and land reclamation, Omahas negotiated the return of the Sacred Pole to Nebraska in 1989. Although this success required twenty years of work, many think that it has brought improved fortunes to the people—urban and national alike. Despite tribal division, many hope the Sacred Pole can reunite the Omahas and "take them back to the tribe's essential philosophical principles." See Ridington and Hastings, *Blessing for a Long Time*, 69, 151, 169.

226. Hollis Davies Stabler, in "Transcript," 97. See also Patti Jo King, "Urbanization's Effects on Tribalism," *Indian Country Today*, 20 July 2005, 1B. While Omahas were consistently the majority among Lincoln's Indians, local Poncas, Santees, Hochunks, and Lakotas—all Nebraska-based nations—maintained similar attachments to tribal identities, again largely due to transnationalism.

227. Raymond Breton and Gail Grant, *The Dynamics of Government Programs for Urban Indians in the Prairie Provinces* (Montreal: Institute for Research on Public Policy, 1984), 557.

228. Dennis Hastings (Omaha), in "Commemorating the Omahas," *Lincoln Journal*, 21 February 1992.

229. Fixico, *Urban Indian Experience*, 59.

230. gaiashkibos, interview.

231. Lisa E. Emmerich, "Marguritte LaFlesche Diddock: Office of Indian Affairs Matron," *Great Plains Quarterly* 13, no. 2 (Summer 1993): 163.

232. King, "Urbanization's Effects on Tribalism," 1B.

233. Awakuni-Swetland, "Umo(n)ho(n) Ithae t(h)e—Umo(n)ho(n) Bthi(n)," 36.

234. Victoria Smith, in Hollis D. Stabler, *No One Ever Asked Me*, 143.

## Chapter 4

1. Donna Biddle, "Asian Center Marks Grand Opening with Displays of Food and Performances," *Lincoln Star*, 28 April 1995; Marc Kransnowsky, "Former Boat People Ease Transition for Vietnamese," *Lincoln Star*, 2 March 1992; *Polk's Lincoln City Directory* (Kansas City, MO: Polk's, 2000).

2. Nazli Kibria, *Family Tightrope: The Changing Lives of Vietnamese Americans* (Princeton, NJ: Princeton University Press, 1993), 73.

3. Mary Pipher, *The Middle of Everywhere: Helping Refugees Enter the American Community* (New York: Harcourt, 2002), 332; "Germans from Russia Mostly Welcome Viets," *Lincoln Journal*, 18 June 1975, 11.

4. Hung Nguyen, quoted in "An American Success Story," *Southern Nebraska Register*, 2 December 1994, 7. See also Bob Reeves, "Vietnamese Find New Life," *Lincoln Star*, 1 December 1992, 4; Anh Quang Tran, "The Wichita Vietnamese" (Ph.D. diss., Kansas State University, 2002), 81.

5. Jesse Williams Nash, "Vietnamese Values: Confucian, Catholic, American" (Ph.D. diss., Tulane University, 1987), 12.

6. Richard C. Owens, "Vietnamese Homegardens in Lincoln, Nebraska: A Measure of Cultural Continuity" (M.A. thesis, University of Nebraska–Lincoln, 2003), 66.

7. Caroline Kieu Linh Valverde, "Making Transnational Viet Nam: Vietnamese American Community—Viet Nam through Money, Music, and Modems" (Ph.D. diss., University of California–Berkeley, 2002), 2.

8. Andrew X. Pham, *Catfish and Mandala: A Two-Wheeled Voyage through the Landscape and Memory of Vietnam* (New York: Farrar, Straus, and Giroux, 1999), 208.

9. Ngoc H. Bui and Joseph Stimpfl, "'Who Are These People Anyway?' Variations of Ethnic Identity within an Immigrant Population," in Esther Mikyung Ghymn, ed., *Asian American Studies: Identity, Images, Issues Past and Present* (New York: Peter Lang, 2000), 113–14; Paul Rutledge, *The Role of Religion in Ethnic Self-Identity* (New York: University Press of America, 1985), 53.

10. *Việt Kiều* means overseas Vietnamese. See Valverde, "Making Transnational Viet Nam," 2.

11. The 2000 U.S. Census Bureau listed 3,774 Vietnamese in Lincoln and a total of 6,364 in Nebraska. The 2010 Census listed 4,749 Vietnamese in Lincoln. See U.S. Census Bureau, "Profile of Demographic Characteristics: Nebraska," http://factfinder.census.gov/serlet/QTTable?_bm=y&-geo_id=04000US31&qr_name=DEC_2000_SF1; http://factfinder2.census.gov/faces/tableservices/jsf/pages/productview.xhtml?pid=DEC_10_DP_DPDP1. In addition to the foreign born, approximately 1,300 Americans of Vietnamese heritage lived in Lincoln in 2000. Teresa Trang Nguyen, Asian Community and Cultural Center community and youth coordinator, presentation, Asian Community and Cultural Center, 8 November 2005, Lincoln, Nebraska. Vietnamese numbers are quite probably underreported.

12. Vietnamese Studies Internet Resource Center, "Top 50 U.S. Metropolitan Areas by Vietnamese Population," http://vstudies.learnabouthmong.org/top50usmetar.html; Lloyd Shearer, "Vignettes of Vietnamese Refugees,"

*Parade*, 15 June 1975, 12; Nebraska Department of Social Services, quoted in Reeves, "Vietnamese Find New Life," 1; Bob Reeves, "State Renown for Its Refugee Aid," *Sunday Journal and Star*, 24 December 1995, 1C. See also Charles C. Munzy, *The Vietnamese in Oklahoma City: A Study in Ethnic Change* (New York: AMS Press, 1989). Lincoln in 2000 hosted the thirty-sixth-largest concentration of Vietnamese in the nation. On the Great Plains, only the larger communities of Dallas–Fort Worth, Denver-Boulder-Greeley, Oklahoma City, and Wichita had larger enclaves.

13. In total, Vietnamese foreign-born make up about a quarter of all "Asian Americans" in Nebraska. In 1990 there were 12,422 Nebraska Asian Americans, and in 2000, 22,767. See Onyema G. Nkwocha, *Health Status of Racial and Ethnic Minorities in Nebraska* (Lincoln: Nebraska Department of Health and Human Services, 2003), 22.

14. Valverde, "Making Transnational Viet Nam," 2.

15. Reed Ueda, *Postwar Immigrant America: A Social History* (Boston: Bedford Books, 1994), 39. More RVN employees were paroled into the United States by the attorney general in 1978. See Munzy, *Vietnamese in Oklahoma City*, 5.

16. Ricardo Inzunza, "The Refugee Act of 1980—Still the Way to Go," *International Journal of Refugee Law* 2 (1990): 413; U.S. Department of Health and Human Services, "The Refugee Act," http://www.acf.hhs.gov/programs/orr/policy/refact1.htm.

17. U.S. Department of State, Archive, "Refugee Admissions Program for East Asia," http://2001-2009.state.gov/g/prm/rls/fs/2004/28212.htm; Paul James Rutledge, *The Vietnamese Experience in America* (Bloomington: Indiana University Press, 1992), 65; Astri Suhrke, "Indochinese Refugees: The Law and Politics of First Asylum," in Franklin Ng, ed., *Asians in America: The Peoples of East, Southeast, and South Asia in American Life and Culture* (New York: Garland, 1998), 173; Ueda, *Postwar Immigrant America*, 50.

18. Teresa Trang Nguyen, presentation.

19. Darrell Montero, "Vietnamese Refugees in America: Toward a Theory of Spontaneous International Migration," *International Migration Review* 13, no. 4 (Winter 1979): 625, 641, 644.

20. Bob Guenther, "Exon Prefers Voluntary Basis for Dealing with Refugees," *Lincoln Star*, 29 August 1975, 1.

21. "Hruska Asks Open Arms for Refugees," *Lincoln Star*, 10 May 1975, 9.

22. Shearer, "Vignettes of Vietnamese Refugees," 12; "Nebraskans Plan for Viet Refugees," *Sunday Journal and Star*, 29 May 1975, 11C. See also Darrell Montero, *Vietnamese Americans: Patterns and Socioeconomic Adaptation in the United States* (Boulder, CO: Westview Press, 1979), 26. Resettlement throughout the United States was arranged by nine civilian organizations: U.S. Catholic Conference, Lutheran Immigration and Refugee Services, International Rescue Committee, United HIAS, Church World Service, Tolstoy Foundation, American Fund for Czechoslovakian Refugees, American Council for Nationalities Services, and Travelers Aid International Services. In addition to Fort Chaffee, resettlement centers were operating at Indian Gap, Pennsylvania; Eglin Air

Base, Florida; and Camp Pendleton, California.

Rural Nebraska recruited dozens of physicians from the first wave, and the state financed retraining in American medical methods at the University of Nebraska Medical Center and at Creighton University. As Lincoln did not have a shortage of doctors, the city was not included in these initiatives. See, for example, *Lincoln Star*, 13 May 1975, 1; 14 May 1975, 17; 22 May 1975, 7; *Lincoln Journal*, 25 June 1975, 27; 4 June 1975, 14; 3 June 1975, 15.

23. See, for example, Marc Krasnowsky, "Former Boat People Ease Transition for Vietnamese," *Lincoln Star*, 2 March 1992; Bob Reeves, "Family Who Overcame Bullets, Death at Sea to Be Honored," *Lincoln Journal Star*, 17 February 1996.

24. D. R. SarDesai, *Vietnam: Trials and Tribulations of a Nation* (Long Beach, CA: Long Beach Publications, 1988), 189; Hien Duc Do, *The Vietnamese Americans* (Westport, CT: Greenwood Press, 1999), 28; Valverde, "Making Transnational Viet Nam," 101; William J. Druiker, *Vietnam since the Fall of Saigon* (Athens: Ohio University Center for International Study, 1989), 67. The movement of boat people peaked in 1979.

25. U.S. Department of State, "Refugee Admissions Program for East Asia"; Rutledge, *Vietnamese Experience*, 65; Suhrke, "Indochinese Refugees," 173.

26. Reeves, "Vietnamese Find New Life," 1. See *Foreign Relations Authorization Act, Fiscal Years 1988 and 1989, Statutes at Large* 101, sec. 904, 1402 (1987). By 1993, eighty-eight thousand Amerasians—largely considered "half breeds" in Vietnam—were admitted. See Valverde, "Making Transnational Viet Nam," 103; Kiem Nguyen, *The Unwanted: A Memoir* (Boston: Little, Brown, and Company, 2001).

27. Valverde, "Making Transnational Viet Nam," 104; Reeves, "State Renown for Its Refugee Aid," 2C; Helen Mitrofanova, "Lincoln Is Gathering Place for Refugees from around the World," *Nebline*, October 2004, 10; Pipher, *Middle of Everywhere*, 6. See also *Foreign Relations Authorization Act, Fiscal Years 1988 and 1989 Act, Statutes at Large* 101, sec. 905, 1404 (1987). Resettlement was not unique to Southeast Asian populations. In the early twenty-first century, Lincoln ranked fifth in refugee settlement per capita nationally.

28. Elizabeth Grieco, "The Foreign Born from Vietnam in the United States," mpi: Migration Immigration Source, http://www.migrationiformation.org/USfocus /display.cfm?id=197; Montero, "Vietnamese Refugees, 625, 641, 644.

29. Hien Duc Do, *Vietnamese Americans*, 38, 41.

30. Karen J. Leong, Christopher A. Airriess, Wei Li, Angela Chia-Chen Chen, and Verna M. Keith, "Resilient History and the Rebuilding of a Community: The Vietnamese American Community in New Orleans East," *Journal of American History* 94, no. 3 (December 2007): 770.

31. Vietnamese Studies Internet Resource Center, "Top 50 U.S. Metropolitan Areas by Vietnamese Population."

32. Aaron Sanderford, "O Asian Garden Unites Cultures," *Lincoln Journal Star*, 17 October 2004.

33. Ibid.

34. Max Niedzwiecki and T. C. Duong, *Southeast Asian American Statistical Profile*

(Washington, DC: Southeast Asian Resource Action Center, 2004), 13.

35. K. Aguilar-San Juan, "Creating Ethnic Places: Vietnamese American Community Building in Orange County and Boston" (Ph.D. diss., Brown University, 2000), 60; Nkwocha, *Health Status of Racial and Ethnic Minorities*, 22.

36. Jacqueline Desbarats, "Indochinese Resettlement in the United States," in Franklin Ng, ed., *Asians in America: The Peoples of East, Southeast, and South Asia in American Life and Culture* (New York: Garland, 1998), 187; Aguilar-San Juan, "Creating Ethnic Places," 52.

37. Kibria, *Family Tightrope*, 21; Nash, "Vietnamese Values," 138–39.

38. For theoretical considerations, see Ric Dias, "The Great Cantonment: Cold War Cities in the American West," in Kevin J. Fernlund, ed., *The Cold War American West, 1945–1989* (Albuquerque: University of New Mexico Press, 1998), 71–72; Carl Abbott, *The Metropolitan Frontier: Cities in the Modern American West* (Tucson: University of Arizona Press, 1993), 155; Edward W. Soja, *Postmodern Geographies: The Reassertion of Space in Critical Social Theory* (London: Verso, 1989), 188.

39. *Polk's Lincoln City Directory* (Kansas City, MO: Polk, 1978, 1980, 1985).

40. The Near South and South Salt Creek Neighborhoods (South Russian Bottoms) were also targeted for residential redevelopment but have not attracted Vietnamese communities. Presumably, the housing stock does not suit their needs. See City of Lincoln, "Low-Moderate Income Area (LMI), Neighborhood Revitalization Strategy Area (NRSA), Lincoln, NE 2004" (Lincoln: Development Department, 2004, map).

41. U.S. Census Bureau, "TM-P004D, Percent of Persons Who Are Asian Alone: 2000, Lancaster County by Block Groups," http://fastfacts.census.gov/servlet/ CWSThematicMapFramsetServlet; *Polk's Lincoln City Directory* (Kansas City, MO: Polk, 1990, 1995, 2003). East Lincoln and Southeast Lincoln housed few immigrants of Vietnamese or any other origin.

42. Nebraska boasted a 71.2 percent home ownership rate for the general population in 2000 (Vietnamese Studies Internet Resource Center, "Vietnamese Household Tenure Data, Nebraska," http://site.yahoo.com/vstudies/viethoustend5.html). The main organizational site as of December 2005 moved to http:// www.vstudies.org, and in 2014 was at http://www.vietnamesestudies.org/.

43. City of Lincoln, Urban Development Department, "Statistics from 2000 U.S. Census," http://www.lincoln.ne.gov/city/urban/comdev/neighbor/maps&stats. htm. Statistics for more affluent neighborhoods were not readily available, but presumably were much higher. The city's statistics are not exclusive to Vietnamese, and student housing accounted for the especially low rates in the Malone neighborhood.

44. U.S. Census Bureau, "Table 11, Summary of Social and Economic Characteristics for Asian or Pacific Islander Persons and for Households and Families with an Asian or Pacific Islander Householder: 1990," *1990 Census of Population: Social and Economic Characteristics, Nebraska, 1990 CP-2-29* (Washington, DC: Government Printing Office, 1993), 34.

45. Nkwocha, *Health Status of Racial and Ethnic Minorities*, 31; Niedzwiecki and Duong, *Southeast Asian American Statistical Profile*, 21.

46. See Lancaster County Assessor/Register of Deeds, http://www.lincoln.ne/cnty/assess/property.htm.

47. Chien Cao, *"Chào Quí Vị và Các Bạn"* [Greetings to guests and friends], http://chiencao.woodsbros.com/AgentHome/Homepage.aspx; Bob Reeves, "Builder Customizes Homes to Fit All Cultures," *Lincoln Journal Star*, 2 October 2004.

48. Owens, "Vietnamese Homegardens in Lincoln," 62–63; Reeves, "Vietnamese Find New Life," 6; Aguilar-San Juan, "Creating Ethnic Places," 181, 157; Kibria, *Family Tightrope*, 19.

49. Craig Centrie, "Free Spaces Unbound: Families, Community, and Vietnamese High School Students' Identities," in Lois Weis and Michelle Fine, ed., *Construction Sites: Excavating Race, Class, and Gender among Urban Youth* (New York: Teachers College Press, 2000), 67; Todd B. Schneeberger, "Vietnamese Refugees: An Assessment of Their Loss of Identity and Trust" (M.A. thesis, University of Nebraska–Lincoln, 2000), x.

50. JoAnne Young, "Driven by Her Past: Wesleyan Student Earns Truman Scholarship," *Lincoln Journal Star*, 19 September 2005, 1C.

51. James M. Freeman, *Hearts of Sorrow: Vietnamese American Lives* (Stanford, CA: Stanford University Press, 1989), 11; U.S. Department of Justice, Immigration and Naturalization Service, *2000 Statistical Yearbook of the Immigration and Naturalization Service* (Washington, DC: Government Printing Office, 2002), 80. See also Rutledge, *Vietnamese Experience*, 6.

52. Melinda H. Le, "Behavioral Acculturation, Psychological Acculturation, and Psychological Well-Being across Generations of Vietnamese Immigrants and Refugees" (Ph.D. diss., University of Nebraska–Lincoln, 2004), 44; Freeman, *Hearts of Sorrow*, 11.

53. Andrew Pham, *Catfish and Mandala*, 21.

54. Melinda H. Le, "Behavioral Acculturation," 44; Steven J. Gold, *Refugee Communities: A Comparative Field Study* (Newbury Park, CA: Sage Publications, 1992), x–xi.

55. *Statistical Yearbook of the Immigration and Naturalization Service*, 13.

56. Jae-Hyup Lee, *Dynamics of Ethnic Identity: Three Asian American Communities in Philadelphia* (New York: Garland, 1998), 90.

57. Owens, "Vietnamese Homegardens in Lincoln," 31.

58. Rocky Pham, quoted in Ahrin Mishan and Mick Rothenberg, dirs., *But Dot: Life Like Dust* (San Francisco: National Asian American Telecommunications Association, 1994).

59. Kibria, *Family Tightrope*, 12, 14.

60. Montero, *Vietnamese Americans*, 7.

61. Ibid., 61.

62. Gold, *Refugee Communities*, 24.

63. Anh Quang Tran, "Wichita Vietnamese," 21.

64. Joseph Buttinger, *A Dragon Defiant: A Short History of Vietnam* (New York:

Praeger, 1972), 8; SarDesai, *Vietnam*, 1; Central Intelligence Agency, "Vietnam," *World Factbook*, http://www.cia.gov/cia/ publications/factbook/geos /vm.html; *National Geographic Atlas of the World*, 5th ed. (Washington, DC: National Geographic Society, 1981), 186–89. Vietnam is about equal in area to New Mexico. Longitudinally, it lies between E 102° and E 109°. Located entirely within the Tropic of Cancer, it sits between N 7° and N 22°. The northern climate has distinct wet and dry seasons, and the southern climate is generally wet year-round.

65. Qui Nguyen, interview by Kaitlyn Koenigsman, 25 May 2007, Star City Treasures: Meet Your Neighbors, Lincoln City Libraries, Lincoln, Nebraska, http://www.lincolnlibraries.org/oral_history/Star_City_Treasures.htm, 5.

66. "The Vietnamese Student Association Presents Its Sixth Annual Saigon Enchantment," *Scarlet*, 18 September 1998.

67. Freeman, *Hearts of Sorrow*, 60.

68. Leong et al., "Resilient History," 770.

69. A cogent Vietnamese identity emerged during the Van Lang feudal era in the seventh century BCE. *Nam Việt*—literally "South People" but most probably "people south of China"—emerged in 207 BCE when a Chinese general replaced the Van Lang rulers. This proto-nation remained an independent entity until 111 BCE, when it was incorporated into the Chinese empire.

Based on a Confucian order that mandated elite and foreign control, Chinese rule lasted through 939 CE. These colonial rulers divided the country into new administrative districts, created a system of government that required administrators to earn their positions through an elaborate civil service system, collected taxes, revolutionized agriculture, opened Chinese-language schools, and dramatically improved infrastructure. "Barbarism," however, remained the norm during the colonial era as the population of about one million refused to relinquish Vietnamese identities. Consequently, rebellion against the Chinese Han lords was commonplace and based on time-honored practices. Specifically, peasants maintained local village autonomy, and contact with the state was mediated by community councils composed of male elders. Confucian and village systems continued to coexist following the Chinese ouster as the examination system was adopted by Vietnamese emperors and became the basis of a pernicious split between the elite and the agrarian masses.

Still, the centralized, independent state proved more palatable than Chinese regimes as it consistently thwarted efforts to recolonize its territory, and it immediately launched the popular *nam tien*—"southern expansion"— movement. Claiming absolute power through a "mandate of heaven," this new political culture of expansion was enabled by the residue left by Chinese governmental and military frameworks. Over the course of eight hundred years, Vietnamese culture expanded from Ha Tinh to Ca Mau. Hue was incorporated by 1100. The Champa Kingdom that stretched from Da Nang to Nha Trang was conquered in 1471 and completely incorporated by 1720, and its Indianized population was marginalized or acculturated into the Vietnamese mainstream.

After the fall of Champa, the Khmer-dominated Mekong Delta was the next target of colonization, and military veterans were encouraged to forcibly take lands in this fertile area. By 1780 the cultural boundaries of the modern Vietnamese nation were in place, although political hegemony would prove more problematic. See Keith Weller Taylor, *The Birth of Vietnam* (Berkeley: University of California Press, 1983), 9, 13–14, 33, 42, 83; SarDesai, *Vietnam*, 2–3, 9, 26; Kibria, *Family Tightrope*, 41–42; Montero, *Vietnamese Americans*, 12; Buttinger, *Dragon Defiant*, 53; Sucheng Chan, ed., *The Vietnamese American 1.5 Generation: Stories of War, Revolution, Flight, and New Beginnings* (Philadelphia: Temple University Press, 2006), 4.

70. Patricia M. Pelley, *Postcolonial Vietnam: New Histories of the National Past* (Durham, NC: Duke University Press, 2002), 81.

71. Hoa Tran, interview by Haishu Zhu, 16 May 2006, Star City Treasures: Meet Your Neighbors, Lincoln City Libraries, Lincoln, Nebraska, http://www .lincolnlibraries.org/oral _history/Star_City_Treasures.htm, 2.

72. Jessica Meyers, "Phở and Apple Pie: Eden Center as a Representation of Vietnamese American Ethnic Identity in the Washington, D.C. Metropolitan Area, 1975–2005," *Journal of Asian American Studies* 9, no. 1 (February 2006): 76.

73. Taylor, *Birth of Vietnam*, 1; Buttinger, *Dragon Defiant*, 12.

74. Erin Andersen, "Fairies Explores Vietnam," *Lincoln Journal Star*, 22 October 2004.

75. Ho Chi Minh—a pseudo name meaning "he who is enlightened"—was born Nguyen Sinh Cuong, changed his name to Nguyen Aio Quoc (Nguyen the Patriot) while studying in Europe, and finally became Ho Chi Minh after a sojourn in the Soviet Union. He successfully tapped two thousand years of Vietnamese anticolonial sentiment and liberated the Red River heartland following World War II. His followers then reunited the entire nation in 1975. Widely popular because of his spare lifestyle and willingness to make sacrifices for his people, "*Bác* [Uncle] Ho" abandoned the democratic principles he learned at French and English universities and turned to communism after it became apparent that self-determination as described in the Treaty of Versailles would not be allowed in Asian colonies. Consequently, Ho became convinced that the efforts of one hundred thousand Vietnamese soldiers who served France in World War I were in vain. Hoping to rid his movement of racial overtones of the Enlightenment West, he moved on to the Soviet Union and a new field of political opportunity. See Gold, *Refugee Communities*, 50; SarDesai, *Vietnam*, 66, 71, 95; Andrew Pham, *Catfish and Mandala*, 228–29.

76. Jacqueline Desbarats, "Human Rights: Two Steps Forward, One Step Backward?" in Thai Quang Trung, ed., *Vietnam Today: Accessing the New Trends* (New York: Crane Russak, 1990), 48.

77. The first political unification of Vietnam occurred in the early nineteenth century, and it required civil war. Ultimately, *Dai Nam*—"the great south"—emerged after the Nguyen monarchy of central Vietnam defeated the Trinhs, who were based in Hanoi. Nguyen rulers completed unification in 1802 and used Hue as their capital. After the Trinhs' final defeat, Nguyen Anh—the

Gai Long emperor—claimed the "Mandate from Heaven" and assumed moral responsibility for his subjects during a reign that lasted until 1820. Under his direction, the Confucian examination system reached its apex, and the unified nation was effectively organized into twenty-six provinces that were administered through a well-regulated bureaucracy. See Benedict Anderson, *Imagined Communities: Reflections on the Origin and Spread of Nationalism* (London: Verso, 1983), 143; SarDesai, *Vietnam*, 3, 37, 40–45; Anh Quang Tran, "Wichita Vietnamese," 120; Chan, *Vietnamese American 1.5 Generation*, 10–11, 31; Oscar Chapius, *A History of Vietnam from Hong Bang to Tu Duc* (Westport, CT: Greenwood Press, 1995), 17; Neil L. Jamieson, *Understanding Vietnam* (Berkeley: University of California Press, 1993), 37.

78. Ironically, Gai Long's unification project opened the door for French encroachment. Initially, the European power was more than willing to provide military aid used in the struggle against the Trinhs in exchange for a monopoly on international trade and a tolerance of Catholicism. Between 1787 and 1820 the Nguyen and French alliance remained mutually advantageous and both sides respected the terms of their agreement.

Subsequent emperors—Minh Mang (1820–1840), Thie Tri (1841–1847), and Tu Duc (1848–1883)—were less tolerant of cultural and economic interference in their nation. Large-scale repression of Christianity became commonplace by the mid-1830s, and a decade later Tu Duc even offered rewards for killing Europeans. From 1840 on, missionaries and converts sought French military intervention to ease their plight, but internal revolution and wars in Europe made excursions to Asia impossible. By 1858, however, French emperor Napoleon III was ready to seek foreign empire and used the persecution of Catholics as a means to begin assaults on Vietnamese sovereignty.

Although early French campaigns were often poorly conceived, their superior military technology and fraudulent diplomacy allowed them to make rapid inroads into the nation. The Nguyen lords clearly misunderstood the ultimate French objective, and, once clear on the matter, their mandarins' attempts to block expansion using solutions written in Confucian classics proved futile. French rule was established over three provinces in the Mekong Delta in 1862—a territory they called Cochinchina. In 1883 Annam was established in Central Vietnam and Tonkin in the North. French conquest was complete, and Vietnam was no longer independent nor united. See Chapius, *History of Vietnam*, 188–95; Charles Kimball, "French Indochina," http://www.guideto-thailand-history/indochina.htm; Buttinger, *Dragon Defiant*, 56, 61; SarDesai, *Vietnam*, 51; Ngo Vinh Long, "Vietnam," in Douglas Allen and Ngo Vinh Long, ed., *Coming to Terms: Indochina, the United States, and War* (Boulder, CO: Westview Press, 1991), 11; Hoang Ngoc Thanh, "Quoc Ngu and the Development of Modern Vietnamese Literature," in Walter F. Vella, ed., *Aspects of Vietnamese History* (Honolulu: University Press of Hawaii, 1973), 192.

79. Hoa Tran, interview, 1.

80. Nationalists and RVN supporters feared both communism and Ho, who was a

ruthless adversary. Although he draped his movement in the garb of self-determination, Ho betrayed his rivals in *Việt Nam Quốc Dân Đảng*—a group of republican nationalists—by turning them over to French forces during the rebellions of the 1930s. He did so insisting that their era had passed and only a communist revolution could free Vietnam. See Anderson, *Imagined Communities*, 12; Kibria, *Family Tightrope*, 49; Chan, *Vietnamese American 1.5 Generation*, 42.

81. Freeman, *Hearts of Sorrow*, 271.

82. Montero, *Vietnamese Americans*, 17–19; Buttinger, *Dragon Defiant*, 93–95; Ngo Vinh Long, "Vietnam," 21–22, 33; SarDesai, *Vietnam*, 83, 88, 110.

83. Ngo Vinh Long, "Vietnam," 39, 44.

84. Hien Dang, interview by Katherine Lamie, 25 March 2006, Star City Treasures: Meet Your Neighbors, Lincoln City Libraries, Lincoln, Nebraska, http://www.lincolnlibraries.org/oral_history/Star_City_ Treasures.htm, 1, 2, 7.

85. Druiker, *Vietnam since the Fall of Saigon*, 167–68, 185.

86. Nghia M. Vo, *The Bamboo Gulag: Political Imprisonment in Communist Vietnam* (Jefferson, NC: McFarland, 2004), 37; Druiker, *Vietnam since the Fall of Saigon*, 57, 98, 106; SarDesai, *Vietnam*, 141–46.

87. Druiker, *Vietnam since the Fall of Saigon*, 14–15, 29; Chan, *Vietnamese American 1.5 Generation*, 50; Ngo Vinh Long, "Vietnam," 10; Buttinger, *Dragon Defiant*, 108; Trin Do, *Saigon to San Diego: Memoir of a Boy Who Escaped from Communist Vietnam* (Jefferson, NC: McFarland, 2004), 139–41. By 1975, ten million internal refugees crowded into South Vietnam's cities.

88. Nghia M. Vo, *Bamboo Gulag*, 154; Gold, *Refugee Communities*, 57; Druiker, *Vietnam since the Fall of Saigon*, 47.

89. Thai Quang Trung, "Factions and Power Struggle in Hanoi: Is Nguyen Van Linh in Command?" in Thai Quang Trung, ed., *Vietnam Today: Accessing the New Trends* (New York: Crane Russak, 1990), 9–10.

90. Nguyen Van Canh, "A Party in Decay: The New Class and Organized Crime," in Thai Quang Trung, *Vietnam Today*, 24–25.

91. Druiker, *Vietnam since the Fall of Saigon*, 13; Desbarats, "Human Rights," 49.

92. Nghia M. Vo, *Bamboo Gulag*, 9.

93. Ibid., 6–7; Nguyen Ngoc Phach, "Saigon and Cholon During the War," in Lesleyanne Hawthorne, ed., *Refugee: The Vietnamese Experience* (Melbourne: Oxford University Press, 1982), 76–77.

94. Margaret Reist, "Local Vietnamese Protest Kerry," *Lincoln Journal Star*, 2 May 2004.

95. Valverde, "Making Transnational Viet Nam," 109.

96. Linda Pham, interview, Park Teen Center, 5 April 2007, Star City Treasures: Meet Your Neighbors, Lincoln City Libraries, Lincoln, Nebraska, http://www.lincolnlibraries.org/oral_history /Star_City_Treasures.htm, 7.

97. Buttinger, *Dragon Defiant*, 12. Fourteen percent of Vietnam's population comprises indigenous peoples—most notably Hmongs, ethnic Chinese, Khmers, and Thais. See Pipher, *Middle of Everywhere*, 19; CIA, "Vietnam."

98. Kibria, *Family Tightrope*, 49, 52, 62; SarDesai, *Vietnam*, 111; Nghia M. Vo, *Bamboo Gulag*, 11, 14; Thuy Tien, "Tet 1968," in Hawthorne, *Refugee*, 36.
99. Author, field notes, Asian Community and Cultural Center (hereafter ACCC), 23 December 2005.
100. Anh Quang Tran, "Wichita Vietnamese," 222.
101. A complex and beautiful language, Vietnamese contains twenty-seven consonant sounds and thirty-eight vowel sounds. The plethora of vowel options emanates from the tonal nature of Vietnamese. Pronunciation is vital, as the difference between *ba*—"father"—and *bà*—"grandmother" or "m'am" is slight, at least to a nonnative ear. As Vietnamese is a monosyllabic language, the vowel sounds in "*Việt*," for instance, actually form a diphthong, a vowel combination where sounds bend in the speaker's mouth, rather than forming a two-syllable word. See *Langenscheidt's Pocket Vietnamese Dictionary: Vietnamese-English, English-Vietnamese* (New York: Langenscheidt, 2002), 13–15.
102. Taylor, *Birth of Vietnam*, 8; R. B. Smith, "The Cycle of Confucianism in Vietnam," in Walter F. Vella, ed., *Aspects of Vietnamese History* (Honolulu: University Press of Hawaii, 1973), 1; Buttinger, *Dragon Defiant*, 14.
103. Jae-Hyup Lee, *Dynamics of Ethnic Identity*, 114; Anh Quang Tran, "Wichita Vietnamese," 150; U.S. Census Bureau, "Table 18: Nativity, Citizenship, Year of Entry, Area of Birth, and Language Spoken at Home: 1990," *1990 Census of Housing: Population and Housing Characteristics for Census Tracts and Block Numbering Areas, Lincoln, NE MSA* (Washington DC: Government Printing Office, 1993). On the average, there were slightly more than four people per household.
104. Linda Tran, interview, January 2007, Park Teen Center, Star City Treasures: Meet Your Neighbors, Lincoln City Libraries, Lincoln, Nebraska, http://www lincolnlibraries.org/oral_history/ Star_City_Treasures.htm, 7.
105. Vietnamese remained an oral language until the tenth century when *nôm* was introduced by a bilingual mandarin class who wrote in Chinese. This writing system used Chinese characters to express spoken Vietnamese. While a body of poetry and literature developed in this script, only mandarins were able to read it. These two systems existed side-by-side until around 1918, when a literacy movement that was launched in the late nineteenth replaced them. See "Ch?-Nôm Script," *Omniglot: A Guide to Written Language*, http://omniglot.com /writing/chunom.htm; Conrad Schirokauer and Donald M. Clark, *Modern East Asia: A Brief History* (Belmont, CA: Wadsworth, 2004), 109.
106. John DeFrancis, *Colonialism and Language Policy in Vietnam* (New York: Mouton Publishers, 1977), 69, 229; Chapius, *History of Vietnam*, 170; Anh Quang Tran, "Wichita Vietnamese," 197. During the French colonial era the Confucian order was slowly phased out, and the examination system was ultimately abolished in the 1910s in all three districts. In its stead, a French-educated elite was recruited from the merchant class. These individuals were given Western educations and specifically trained to help the colonizers administer the empire. Ironically, the new elite proved not only capable as bureau-

crats, but they also sowed the seeds of modern Vietnamese independence. See Hien Duc Do, *Vietnamese Americans*, 11; Anh Quang Tran, "Wichita Vietnamese," 121; Anderson, *Imagined Communities*, 117; Nguyen Ngoc Phach, "Saigon and Cholon during the War," in Hawthorne, *Refugee*, 77; Chan, *Vietnamese American 1.5 Generation*, 15.

107. DeFrancis, *Colonialism and Language Policy in Vietnam*, 258.

108. Pelley, *Postcolonial Vietnam*, 39; Anderson, *Imagined Communities*, 117.

109. Hoang Ngoc Thanh, "Quoc Ngu and the Development of Modern Vietnamese Literature," 192, 214; Hien Duc Do, *Vietnamese Americans*, 3; Anh Quang Tran, "Wichita Vietnamese," 223; DeFrancis, *Colonialism and Language Policy in Vietnam*, 237, 240.

110. Andrew Pham, *Catfish and Mandala*, 107.

111. Ibid., 129–30; Anh Quang Tran, "Wichita Vietnamese," 223–25, 231; *Langenscheidt's Pocket Dictionary*, 14–15; Rosetta Stone Language Learning Success, *Vietnamese, Level 1: Tieng Viet* (Harrisonburg, VA: Fairfield Language Technologies, 2002).

112. Unidentified elder, in Bui and Stimpfl, "'Who Are These People Anyway?'" 115.

113. Schneeberger, "Vietnamese Refugees," 10.

114. Rutledge, *Vietnamese Experience*, 116; Kibria, *Family Tightrope*, 44, 55.

115. "Vietnam Cultural Values Serve Family Well in Lincoln," *Sunday Journal and Star*, 30 April 1995, 6J; Owens, "Vietnamese Homegardens in Lincoln," 26.

116. Nash, "Vietnamese Values," 281.

117. Rutledge, *Vietnamese Experience*, 118; Anh Quang Tran, "Wichita Vietnamese," 138.

118. Schneeberger, "Vietnamese Refugees," 18.

119. Uyen Eileen Vu, in Gwen Nugent, dir., *Between Two Worlds: Vietnamese Identity in America* (Lincoln: NETV/NETCHE, 1998).

120. Bui and Stimpfl, "'Who Are These People Anyway?'" 117.

121. Unidentified youth informant, in ibid., 116.

122. Nash, "Vietnamese Values," 282; Gold, *Refugee Communities*, 65; Owens, "Vietnamese Homegardens in Lincoln," 81, 26; Kibria, *Family Tightrope*, 44–46.

123. Never mutually exclusive practices, the three teachings coalesced to form a unique Vietnamese philosophical and religious framework that eventually permeated all other political and cultural institutions. Symbolized by the yin (the feminine earth) and yang (the masculine heaven), Daoism was a religious philosophy conceived by Lao Zi of China that sought to maintain balance within the universe. While philosophically important in the nation's development, only a minority of Vietnamese concentrated on Daoism. Buddhism, on the other hand, was the preferred religion of the agrarian masses, at least after the third century CE. Its four most sacred temples were dedicated to the Buddha of the Clouds, the Buddha of the Rain, the Buddha of Thunder, and the Buddha of Lightning and corresponded with natural forces that connected the Buddha to the monsoon season—the time of flooding fields. Additionally, Vietnamese

Buddhists stressed self-mastery and self-discipline as tools to build good karma as they sought enlightenment and the opportunity to be reincarnated in a better position in future lives. Finally, Confucianism—which emerged in China around the fifth century BCE—taught all Vietnamese to maintain a stable and peaceful society by obeying their obligations and responsibilities to family and social and hierarchy. See Rutledge, *Role of Religion*, 7, 23, 30, 31; "Taoism," http://www.religious tolerance.org/taoism.htm; Taylor, *Birth of Vietnam*, 81–83; Anh Quang Tran, "Wichita Vietnamese," 117–18.

124. Paul Kwan, Arnold Iger, and Paul Lundahl, producers, *Anatomy of a Springroll* (New York: Filmakers Library, 1992); "Animism," http://mcel.pacific.edu/as /students/vb/_animism.htm; "Vietnam," http://geographica.com/vietnam/; Hien Duc Do, *Vietnamese Americans*, 7.

125. Michael Barker, "Unintentional Yet Essential Political Ties: The Christian and Missionary Alliance in French Indochina," http://www.bucknell.edu/Beaucar-net/documents/Barker _Paper.pdf, 6; Andrew Pham, *Catfish and Mandala*, 121.

126. Rutledge, *Role of Religion*, 56, 65.

127. Son Ha, "The Village," in Hawthorne, *Refugee*, 10; Freeman, *Hearts of Sorrow*, 88; Montero, "Vietnamese Refugees," 627. The Republic of Vietnam was largely ruled by its Catholic minority, and religious tension detracted from the government's stability.

128. Rutledge, *Role of Religion*, 7. Oklahoma City boasted a population of four thousand Vietnamese in 1980, 60 percent of whom were Buddhist. In contrast, 30 percent were Roman Catholic.

129. Jeff Clinger, "Vietnamese Christian Missionary Alliance," http://www .nebraskaweslyan.edu/event/harvardel/vietnam/history.htm; Lincoln Interfaith Council; "Meet Set to Organize Vietnamese Congregation," *Lincoln Journal*, 23 June 1975, 16; "Rosemont Congregation in Midst of Great Refugee Experience," *Sunday Journal and Star*, 8 July 1975, 9C; Lincoln Interfaith Council, "Directory of Congregations and Faith Communities of Lincoln and Lancaster County," http://www.lincolninterfaith.org.fthfrm4ab.htm.

130. Christian and Missionary Alliance, *Missionary Atlas: A Manual of the Foreign Work of the Christian and Missionary Alliance* (Harrisburg, PA: Christian Publications, 1964), 61; Barker, "Unintentional Yet Essential Political Ties," 1, 3, 9, 11, 16; "What about the Church in North Vietnam," *Vietnam Today: News Magazine of the Vietnam Field*, Winter 1971, 2–3; Dave and Helen Douglas, Bob and Elaine Green, Royce and Betty Rexilius, Spence and Barbara Suther-land, "Nhatrang Is Truly a Center for Christian Service," *Vietnam Today: News Magazine of the Vietnam Field*, Fall 1973, 5.

131. Christian and Missionary Alliance, "The Alliance Doctrinal Statement," http:// www.calliance. org.

132. Nash, "Vietnamese Values," 81–85.

133. Chapius, *History of Vietnam*, 170; Monterro, *Vietnamese Americans*, 14; SarDesai, *Vietnam*, 46; Barker, "Unintentional Yet Essential Political Ties," 6; Buttinger, *Dragon Defiant*, 15.

134. Sister Loretta Gosen, *History of the Catholic Church in the Diocese of Lincoln, Nebraska, 1887–1987* (Lincoln, NE: Catholic Bishop of Lincoln, 1986), 301–2; "Vietnamese 'Tet' Happy New Year! Chuc Mung Nam Moi," *Southern Nebraska Register*, 23 February 1980, 8.

135. Lincoln Interfaith Council (hereafter LIC), "Directory"; church spokesperson Katie Tang, in Bob Reeves, "Vietnamese Church Celebrates 25 Years," *Lincoln Journal Star*, 19 June 2004.

136. LIC, "Directory."

137. Peter N. Gregory, "Describing the Elephant: Buddhism in America," *Religion in American Culture* 11, no. 2 (Summer 2001): 244.

138. "Vietnamese Buddhism," http://mcel.pacificu.edu/students/vb/summary.htm; Buddhist Studies Dharma Education Association and Buddhanet, "Buddhism in Vietnam," http://buddhanet.net-elearning/buddhistworld/vietnam-txt.htm; Gregory, "Describing the Elephant," 239. Figures were from 2001.

139. Freeman, *Hearts of Sorrow*, 117.

140. Clinger, "Vietnamese Christian Missionary Alliance"; LIC, "Directory;" "Meet Set to Organize Vietnamese Congregation," 16; "Rosemont Congregation in Midst of Great Refugee Experience," 9C. See also *Polk's Lincoln City Directory*, 1995, 2000.

141. "Vietnamese Catholics Purchase New Church," *Southeast Nebraska Register*, 14 December 1990, 1; LIC, "Directory." Membership figures supplied by church spokesperson Katie Tang. See Reeves, "Vietnamese Church Celebrates 25 Years."

142. "The Diocese of Lincoln Parishes, Institutions Diverse, Unique," *Southern Nebraska Register*, 11 May 1992, 19.

143. "Vietnamese 'Tet' Happy New Year!" 8.

144. *Southern Nebraska Register*, 14 May 1993, 1; "Vietnamese Bishops Ask for Catholic Commitment to Nation," *Southern Nebraska Register*, 20 October 1995, 1.

145. Gosen, *History of the Catholic Church in the Diocese of Lincoln*, 302; "Four Vietnamese Ordained during Marion Days," *Southern Nebraska Register*, 6 June 1981, 1.

146. Sister Maria Nguyen, quoted in Antonia Ryan, "Vietnamese Celebrate Faith and Culture at Marian Days," *National Catholic Reporter*, 24 September 2004.

147. "Vietnamese Celebrate," *Southern Nebraska Register*, 26 August 1983, 2; "Marian Day Attracts Thousands to Missouri Town," *Southern Nebraska Register*, 21 August 1987, 1; "Four Vietnamese Ordained during Marion Days," 1; Nash, "Vietnamese Values," 134.

148. Joanne Young, "Best of Both Worlds: Couple's Union Honors Both Eastern, Western Traditions," *Lincoln Journal Star*, 11 June 1994, 9.

149. Anh Quang Tran, "Wichita Vietnamese," 137; Rutledge, *Vietnamese Experience*, 146; Jae-Hyup Lee, *Dynamics of Ethnic Identity*, 119–20; Hien Duc Do, *Vietnamese Americans*, 92. Tet falls annually between January 19 and February 20.

150. "Vietnamese Celebrate Tet at Cathedral of Risen Christ," *Southern Nebraska Register*, 31 January 1976, 8; "Tet Celebration Reminds Vietnamese of Culture, Sacrifices," *Southern Nebraska Register*, 8 March 1996, 1; "Immaculate Heart of Mary Catholic Church," *Lincoln Journal Star*, 17 February 1996; Joanne Young, "Public Facilities Mark the Year of the Rat's Start," *Lincoln Journal Star*, 16 February 1996, 1D–2D; Margaret Reist, "Local Vietnamese Get Set to Ring in New Year," *Lincoln Journal Star*, 19 January 2004.

151. LIC, "Directory."

152. Ibid. While a small Asian population is involved in these three movements, most practitioners are European Americans. Nichiren is an evangelical Japanese form with many adherents nationally, but relatively few locally. Zen, although originating in China, is distinctly Japanese as well and is popular for its meditation strategies. Finally, Tibetan Buddhists follow the Dalai Lama in a practice culturally specific to inland Asia. All four organizations are nominally in contact, but practices and beliefs vary dramatically. Nationally, there are three to four million Buddhists in the United States—25 percent are European Americans—and adherents are growing rapidly, largely through increased Asian immigration. See Gregory, "Describing the Elephant," 236–37.

153. Centrie, "Free Spaces Unbound," 78.

154. Bob Reeves, "Buddhists Celebrate 'Mother's Day,'" *Lincoln Journal Star*, 14 August 1995.

155. Minh Dao, spokesperson for Linh Quay Buddhist Temple, in Bob Reeves, "Voices of Diversity," *Lincoln Journal Star*, 24 April 2004.

156. Munzy, *Vietnamese in Oklahoma City*, 185.

157. Mary Kay Roth, "New Asian Community Center to Open Its Doors Next Month," *Lincoln Star*, 24 October 1994; Reeves, "State Renown for Its Refugee Aid," 1C; Valverde, "Making Transnational Viet Nam," 102; Teresa Trang Nguyen, presentation; ACCC, "Making a Difference in Our Community," n.d., 5.

158. "Mission," Bulletin Board, Asian Community and Culture Center (ACCC), Lincoln.

159. Author, field notes, ACCC, November–December 2005.

160. Teresa Trang Nguyen, presentation; Vietnamese Cultural Society, Metropolitan Washington, "A Brief Introduction to Vietnamese Music and Dance," http://www.vcsm_w.org/activities/music_art_lit.html.

161. *Tet Trung Thu* is held on the fifteenth day of the eighth lunar month. Folklore dictates "that if the moon appeared yellow that night, that next year's crop would be plentiful and if the moon was bright orange that peace would reign in the country." See Hien Duc Do, *Vietnamese Americans*, 100.

162. Michelle Baran, "Celebration of Vietnamese New Year Features Taste of Southeast Asia," *Daily Bruin Online*, 2 February 2001, http://www.dailybruin.ucla.edu; "Lion and Dragon Dance," http://www.acjc.edu.sg/Spectra/VibrantCulture/Vietnam/toppage1.html; Hoang Huong, "Mid-Autumn: Dragons to the Streets," Vietnam.Net, 9 November 2005, http://www.vnn.vn.

163. See Nugent, *Between Two Worlds*.

164. Bui and Stimpfl, "'Who Are These People Anyway?'" 122.

165. Andrew Pham, *Catfish and Mandala*, 123.

166. Munzy, *Vietnamese in Oklahoma City*, 112.

167. Jeff Korbelik, "Midwest Seafood Keeps the Fresh Catches Coming," *Lincoln Journal Star*, 2 March 2005. The marquee on Vina Market states the market is "*Á Đông*," or Southeast Asian, rather than Vietnamese.

168. Owens, "Vietnamese Homegardens in Lincoln," 42.

169. Kwan et al., *Anatomy of a Springroll.*

170. Nash, "Vietnamese Values," 296–97. See also Jeff Korbelik, "Dat's Offers Oriental Fare for Down Town Dining," *Lincoln Journal Star*, 6 May 2005; Jeff Korbelik, "Wok Express Moves to Bigger, More Convenient Location," *Lincoln Journal Star*, 30 September 2004.

171. Title 11 of the charter states, "It is the policy of the City of Lincoln to foster equal opportunity" and to "protect, preserve, and perpetuate all constitutional rights." See Lincoln, Nebraska, "Lincoln City Charter, 2005," http://www.ci.lincoln.ne.us/city/attorney/charter.pdf.

172. Krasnowsky, "Former Boat People Ease Transition for Vietnamese," 2; "Marriage Info in Vietnamese," *Lincoln Journal Star*, 18 March 1996; City of Lincoln, Fire and Rescue Department, "*Tieng Viet*," http://www.lincoln.ne.gov/city/fire/pdf/translate/viet.htm.

173. Bill Ong Hing, *Making and Remaking Asian America through Immigration Policy, 1850–1990* (Stanford, CA: Stanford University Press, 1993), 138.

174. Teresa Trang Nguyen, presentation; Author, field notes, ACCC, 11 November 2005. For additional job placement information, see, for example, *Polk's Lincoln City Directory* (Kansas City, MO: Polk, 1995). Also see Owens, "Vietnamese Homegardens in Lincoln," 85–86, 105. In a survey of thirty individuals regarding gardening, Owens found that 44 percent of respondents worked in factories. Mean age of his sample was fifty-six and most had been in America eleven years. In Vietnam, 32 percent farmed, 18 percent were RVN employees, and 18 percent were self-employed. As a conglomerate, their mean income was $25,000. While a small sample, reported results seem to be supported by more general observations of the community.

175. Aguilar-San Juan, "Creating Ethnic Places," 27.

176. Linda Pham, interview; Teresa Trang Nguyen, presentation.

177. Owens, "Vietnamese Homegardens in Lincoln," 105. Many urban villagers' understandings of written English are well advanced. Generating conversational English, however, is a goal many are still achieving.

178. Hoa Tran, interview, 5.

179. Qui Nguyen, interview, 6–8.

180. Pipher, *Middle of Everywhere*, 98; Teresa Trang Nguyen, presentation; Young, "Driven by Her Past," 1C.

181. Reeves, "State Earns Renown for Its Refugee Aid," 1C–2C; author, field notes, ACCC, 18 November 2005.

182. Kibria, *Family Tightrope*, 146.

183. Hoa Tran, interview, 7.
184. Erin Andersen, "Students Get Cultural Education," *Lincoln Journal Star,*
    14 January 2005. See also City of Lincoln, Planning Department, "Table 4: Age
    and Race Comparison, Lancaster County, Nebraska," in *2000 Census Report:
    Lancaster County, Nebraska (MSA) Comparison of Demographic Characteristics,
    1990, 2000,* 8, 10. This dataset was specific to Asians; Vietnamese represented
    over 50 percent of all Asians in the county by 2000.

    Public schools record "Students of Color" as a single category—part of a
    growing Asian–Latin American–African immigration population. Elliot School
    serves the Malone and Near South populations and reported that 62 percent of
    its student body was in this category. It also remarked that twenty-six languages
    were spoken among the population. Clinton and Hartley reported about 50
    percent "students of color," while Sacred Heart—the nearby parochial elemen-
    tary school—reported that 60 percent of its students were Vietnamese. Schools
    in the Belmont, Northwest, and West A neighborhoods report 20 to 40 percent
    "students of color." Middle school and high school populations are necessarily
    more diffuse, but districting patterns were similar. See Lincoln, Nebraska, Lin-
    coln Public Schools, "LPS District Map," http://www.lps.org/about/districtmap
    /default.html; Lincoln, Nebraska, Lincoln Public Schools, "Elliot School:
    Student Profiles," http://www.lps.org; Erin Andersen, "Students Get Cultural
    Education," *Lincoln Journal Star,* 14 January 2005.
185. Bui and Stimpfl, "'Who Are These People Anyway?'" 121, 127; Reeves, "State
    Renown for Its Refugee Aid," 2C. See also Pipher, *Middle of Everywhere,* 114,
    332.
186. Pipher, *Middle of Everywhere,* 75.
187. Ibid., 64; author, field notes, ACCC, 18 November 2005.
188. Bui and Stimpfl, "'Who Are These People Anyway?'" 117; A survey of com-
    mon Vietnamese family names in the University of Nebraska–Lincoln campus
    directory yielded over 120 registered students. By 1990 the college graduation
    rate among "Vietnamese Americans" was already 17 percent, just 4 percent
    below the national average. See Niedzwiecki and Duong, *Southeast Asian Amer-
    ican Statistical Profile,* 16.
189. Hoa Tran, interview, 6.
190. Pipher, *Middle of Everywhere,* 171.
191. Hien Duc Do, *Vietnamese Americans,* 60.
192. Anh Quang Tran, "Wichita Vietnamese," 238; Duc Tran, in Nugent, *Between
    Two Worlds.* See also Bob Reeves, "Family Who Overcame Bullets," 1D.
193. "Tet Celebration Reminds Vietnamese of Culture, Sacrifices," *Southern Nebras-
    ka Register* 8 March 1996, 1.
194. Duc Tran, in Nugent, *Between Two Worlds.* See also Schneeberger, "Vietnam-
    ese Refugees," 10.
195. Bui and Stimpfl, "'Who Are These People Anyway?'" 120–21.
196. Ibid., 126. See also Jae-Hyup Lee, *Dynamics of Ethnic Identity,* 96.

197. Linda Pham, interview, 20.

198. Melinda H. Le, "Behavioral Acculturation," 1, 44, 117; Pipher, *Middle of Everywhere*, 225, 228.

199. Pipher, *Middle of Everywhere*, 221.

200. Andrew Pham, *Catfish and Mandala*, 63.

201. Linda Pham, interview, 16.

202. Bui and Stimpfl, "'Who Are These People Anyway?'" 12. See also Melinda H. Le, "Behavioral Acculturation," 12.

203. Teresa Trang Nguyen, presentation.

204. Kibria, *Family Tightrope*, 107.

205. Son Tran, in Nugent, *Between Two Worlds*.

206. Ngoc Dung Le, quoted in "Youths Occupy Different Worlds," *Lincoln Journal Star*, 30 July 1994, 1. Le was born in Vietnam but moved to the United States prior to age ten.

207. Bui and Stimpfl, "'Who Are These People Anyway?'" 123–24. See also Son Tran, in Nugent, *Between Two Worlds*.

208. Pipher, *Middle of Everywhere*, 162.

209. Melinda H. Le, "Behavioral Acculturation," 17, 42, 108–9.

210. Nugent, *Between Two Worlds*. See also Bui and Stimpfl, "'Who Are These People Anyway?'" 124.

211. Young, "Driven by Her Past," 5C. See also Valverde, "Making Transnational Viet Nam," 82.

212. Valverde, "Making Transnational Viet Nam," 15. See also Andrew Pham, *Catfish and Mandala*, 7.

213. Elliott Robert Barkan, "America in the Hand, Homeland in the Heart: Transnational and Translocal Immigrant Experiences in the American West," *Western Historical Quarterly* 35, no. 3 (Autumn 2004): 340.

214. Aguilar-San Juan, "Creating Ethnic Places," 154.

215. Druiker, *Vietnam since the Fall of Saigon*, 35; Aguilar-San Juan, "Creating Ethnic Places," 67; Reist, "Local Vietnamese Protest Kerry"; Don Watson, "Vietnamese to Bereuter: Let More In," *Lincoln Star*, 26 May 1995.

216. SarDesai, *Vietnam*, 109.

217. "Church in Chains in Vietnam," *Southern Nebraska Register*, 27 February 1976, 3; "Hanoi Churches Now Historical Monuments," *Southern Nebraska Register*, 22 August 1980, 8; "Vietnamese Bishops Harassed, Interrogated," *Southern Nebraska Register*, 11 December 1984, 3; "Vietnamese Bishops Remain at Odds with Government," *Southern Nebraska Register*, 28 January 1990, 1.

218. "Vatican-Vietnam Consensus Reported," *Southern Nebraska Register*, 13 March 1998, 9; "Vietnam Should Lift Restrictions on Religion," *Southern Nebraska Register*, 4 January 1991, 7; John Travis, "Vietnam Protests Sainthood Plans for Martyrs," *Southern Nebraska Register*, 18 March 1983, 2.

219. Aguilar-San Juan, "Creating Ethnic Places," 154; Valverde, "Making Transnational Viet Nam," 8, 108.

220. Valverde, "Making Transnational Viet Nam," 128.

221. Young, "Driven by Her Past," 5C.

222. Cindy Lange Kubik, "A Bumper Crop of Bumpers," *Lincoln Journal Star*, 14 July 2005.

223. See Linda Tran, interview, 2; Linda Pham, interview, 3.

224. Valverde, "Making Transnational Viet Nam," 122–30.

225. Linda Pham, interview, 2–5, 8.

226. Kubik, "Bumper Crop of Bumpers"; Valverde, "Making Transnational Viet Nam," 138; CIA, "Vietnam," 11; Trin Do, *Saigon to San Diego*, 225.

227. Valverde, "Making Transnational Viet Nam," 7–8. See also Aguilar-San Juan, "Creating Ethnic Places," 154.

228. Khuyen Vu Nguyen, "Memorializing Vietnam: Transfiguring the Living Pasts," in Marcia A. Eymann and Charles Wellenberg, eds., *What's Going On? California in the Vietnam Era* (Oakland: Oakland Museum of California, 2004), 154.

229. Valverde, "Making Transnational Viet Nam," 131; Khuyen Vu Nguyen, "Memorializing Vietnam," 155.

230. Valverde, "Making Transnational Viet Nam," 4–5, 207.

231. Thuy Nga Production, http://www.truyngaonline.com.

232. Richard Marosi, "Vietnam's Musical Invasion," *Los Angeles Times*, 8 August 2000, 1A. See also Valverde, "Making Transnational Viet Nam," 146–47; Vietnamese Cultural Society: Metropolitan Washington, "A Brief Introduction to Vietnamese Music and Dance," http://www.vcsm_w.org/activities/music_art _lit.html. Examples of American Vietnamese popular music in 2005 included "South East Asian Youth Club," KZUM Radio, Lincoln, Nebraska, FM 89.3. The show was hosted by Bich "Katie" Tang and aired Saturdays from 2:30 to 4:00 pm.

233. Valverde, "Making Transnational Viet Nam," 155–56; Marosi, "Vietnam's Musical Invasion," 1A, 5A.

234. John To, concert organizer, in Evan Harper, "Vietnamese Pop Concert in Anaheim Is Target of Protest," *Los Angeles Times*, 20 August 2001, 5B.

235. "From House to Hip-Hop, Beatz 3's Got It," *Viet Nam News*, 16 December 2005, http://wwww.vietnamnews.vnagency.com; "Hanoi Fans about to Rock at Festival," *Vietnam News*, 25 November 2005; Marosi, "Vietnam's Musical Invasion," 1A; Valverde, "Making Transnational Viet Nam," 169–71.

236. Marosi, "Vietnam's Musical Invasion," 1A; Harper, "Vietnamese Pop Concert in Anaheim," 5B.

237. Valverde, "Making Transnational Viet Nam," 220, 223.

238. See, for example, http://www.thoibao.com; http://vietbao.com.

239. Duyen Tu, interview, Park Teen Center, 5 April 2007, Star City Treasures: Meet Your Neighbors, Lincoln City Libraries, Lincoln, Nebraska, http://www.lincoln-libraries.org/oral_ history/Star_City_Treasures.htm, 18.

240. Valverde, "Making Transnational Viet Nam," 222, 225, 242, 259.

241. Ibid., 51.

242. See "Youths Occupy Different Worlds," *Lincoln Journal Star*, 30 July 1994, 5.

**Chapter 5**

1. Paul Kwan, Arnold Iger, and Paul Lundahl, producers, *Anatomy of a Springroll* (New York: Filmakers Library, 1992).
2. Richard C. Owens, "Vietnamese Homegardens in Lincoln, Nebraska: A Measure of Cultural Continuity" (M.A. thesis, University of Nebraska–Lincoln, 2003), 12, 131.
3. See Jefferey Alford and Naomi Duguid, "The Soup's Always On in Vietnam," *Eating Well: The Magazine of Food & Health*, January/February 1997, 40–41.
4. Andrew X. Pham, *Catfish and Mandala: A Two-Wheeled Voyage through the Landscape and Memory of Vietnam* (New York: Farrar, Straus, and Giroux, 1999), 123.
5. Brian A. Cherwick, "Polkas on the Prairies: Ukrainian Music and the Construction of Identity" (Ph.D. diss., University of Alberta, 1999), 13.
6. Gunther Peck, *Reinventing Free Labor: Padrones and Immigrant Workers in the North American West, 1880–1930* (New York: Cambridge University Press, 2000), 189.
7. Melinda H. Le, "Behavioral Acculturation, Psychological Acculturation, and Psychological Well-Being across Generations of Vietnamese Immigrants and Refugees" (Ph.D. diss., University of Nebraska–Lincoln, 2004), 17, 42, 108–9.
8. Edward W. Soja, *Postmetropolis: Critical Studies of Cities and Regions* (Malden, MA: Blackwell, 2000), 8.
9. Murray B. Binderman, "The State and Future of a Theory of Ethnicity," in Jack Kinton, ed., *American Ethnic Revival: Group Pluralism Entering America's Third Century* (Aurora, IL: Social Science and Sociological Resources, 1977), 16.
10. John J. Bukowczyk, *And My Children Did Not Know Me: A History of the Polish-Americans* (Bloomington: Indiana University Press, 1987), 106.
11. Diva Stasiulis and Nira Yuval-Davis, eds., "Introduction: Beyond Dichotomies—Gender, Race, Ethnicity and Class in Settler Societies," in *Unsettling Settler Societies: Articulations of Gender, Race, Ethnicity, and Class* (London: Sage Publication, 1995), 27.
12. Antonia I. Castañeda, "Women of Color and the Rewriting of Western History: The Discourse, Politics, and Decolonization of History," in Sandra K. Schackel, ed., *Western Women's Lives: Continuity and Change in the Twentieth Century* (Albuquerque: University of New Mexico Press, 2003), 47.
13. Milton M. Gordon, *Assimilation in American Life: The Role of Race, Religion, and National Origins* (New York: Oxford University Press, 1964), 135.
14. Kevin Hannan, "Refashioning Ethnicity in Czech-Moravian Texas," *Journal of American Ethnic History* 25, no. 1 (Fall 2005): 40.
15. Soja, *Postmetropolis*, 9.
16. John Bodnar, *The Transplanted: A History of Immigrants in Urban America* (Bloomington: Indiana University Press, 1985), 143.
17. Ric Dias, "The Great Cantonment: Cold War Cities in the American West," in Kevin J. Fernlund, ed., *The Cold War American West, 1945–1989* (Albuquerque: University of New Mexico Press, 1998), 71–72; Carl Abbott, *The Metropolitan*

*Frontier: Cities in the Modern American West* (Tucson: University of Arizona Press, 1993), 155.

18. Edward W. Soja, *Postmodern Geographies: The Reassertion of Space in Critical Social Theory* (London: Verso, 1989), 188; Bodnar, *Transplanted*, 187.

19. Jacqueline Desbarats, "Indochinese Resettlement in the United States," in Franklin Ng, ed., *Asians in America: The Peoples of East, Southeast, and South Asia in American Life and Culture* (New York: Garland, 1998), 187.

20. Jacob Reifschneider, interview by Molly Collins, 2 September 1980, folder AV1.636.22, Neighborhood Oral History Project, Nebraska State Historical Society, Lincoln, Nebraska, 11.

21. George Kruse, interview by Molly Collins, 1 July 1980, folder AV1.636.18, Neighborhood Oral History Project, Nebraska State Historical Society, Lincoln, Nebraska, 5–6.

22. Binderman, "State and Future of a Theory of Ethnicity," 17.

23. Bodnar, *Transplanted*, 177.

24. Bryan, the Asian Center Guy, "7 Simple Steps You Can Take to Discover Lincoln's Asian Culture," http://www.LincolnAsianCenter.org.

25. See, for instance, *Lincoln Chapter, The American Historical Society of Germans from Russia Newsletter*, January/February 2006, 6; Carrie Wolfe (Omaha), "Lincoln Indian Club Events *Tentatively* Scheduled for 2006." The Lincoln Indian Club schedules multicultural events on St. Patrick's Day and Cinco de Mayo and often invites Irish and Mexican dancers to perform demonstrations.

26. See, for example, the home page for Neighborhood Works Lincoln (formerly Neighborhoods Inc.), http://www.nwlincoln.org.

27. See, generally, Star City Treasures: Meet Your Neighbors, Lincoln City Libraries, Lincoln, Nebraska, http://www.lincolnlibraries.org/oral_history/Star_City_Treasures.htm.

28. Hannan, "Refashioning Ethnicity in Czech-Moravian Texas," 31.

29. Elliott R. Barkan, "America in the Hand, Homeland in the Heart: Transnational and Translocal Immigrant Experiences in the American West," *Western Historical Quarterly* 35, no. 3 (Autumn 2004): 339–40.

30. Leah Thorson, "Interpreters Fill Courtroom Niche," *Lincoln Journal-Star*, 31 May 2005.

31. Hannan, "Refashioning Ethnicity in Czech-Moravian Texas," 32.

32. Elliott Robert Barkan, *From All Points: America's Immigrant West, 1870s–1952* (Bloomington: Indiana University Press, 2007), 7.

33. Frederick C. Luebke, "Time, Place, and Culture in Nebraska History," *Nebraska History* 69, no. 4 (Winter 1988): 162.

34. See Peck, *Reinventing Free Labor*, 234.

35. Mary C. Waters, *Ethnic Options: Choosing Identities in America* (Berkeley: University of California Press, 1990), 1.

36. Janet Bauer, "Genealogies of Race and Culture in Anthropology: The Marginalized Ethnographers," in Berel Lang, ed., *Race and Racism in Theory and Practice* (New York: Rowman & Littlefield, 2000), 124.

37. Peter Jackson and Jan Penrose, ed., *Constructions of "Race," Place, and Nation* (Minneapolis: University of Minnesota Press, 1994), 5. For a discussion of "whiteness," see Barkan, *From All Points*, 6–13; Peck, *Reinventing Free Labor*, 166, 227–28.

38. Mary Pipher, *The Middle of Everywhere: The World's Refugees Come to Our Town* (New York: Harcourt, 2002), 5.

39. Luebke, "Time, Place, and Culture in Nebraska History," 154.

40. Michael Novak, *The Rise of the Unmeltable Ethnics: Politics and Culture in the Seventies* (New York: McMillan, 1972), 46–47.

41. Luebke, "Time, Place, and Culture in Nebraska History," 162.

42. Richard D. Alba, *Ethnic Identity: The Transformation of White America* (New Haven, CT: Yale University Press, 1990), xiv.

43. Bob Reeves, "Voices of Diversity," *Lincoln Journal Star*, 6 May 2005.

44. See Onyema G. Nkwocka, *Health Status of Racial and Ethnic Minorities in Nebraska* (Lincoln: Nebraska Department of Health and Human Services, 2003), 117–20. While not classified unduly as "heavy drinkers," "binge drinking" is a major issue, as are cirrhosis mortality (ten times more prevalent than in the general population) and diabetes mortality (six times the rates in the general public).

45. Earl Dreyer, "They Pray All Night: Indian Church Ideas Christian," *Lincoln Star*, 21 December 1962, 1. The series ran on page one through December 26.

46. See, for example, Jonnie Taté Finn, "Preparing for Powwow, with Eye toward Sky," *Lincoln Journal Star*, 4 August 2005, B1.

47. See, for example, Josh Swartzlander, "Asian Community Celebrates New Year," *Lincoln Journal Star*, 21 January 2006. Multiple articles report on Tet annually.

48. Son Tran, in Gwen Nugent, dir., *Between Two Worlds: Vietnamese Identity in America* (Lincoln: NETV/NETECH, 1998).

49. Anh Quang Tran, "The Wichita Vietnamese" (Ph.D. diss., Kansas State University, 2002), 175.

50. William Doerner, "To America with Skills," *Time*, 8 July 1985, 47.

51. U.S. Census Bureau, "Census 2000 Demographic Profile Highlights: Selected Population Groups: Vietnamese Alone or in Any Combination, Lincoln, Nebraska," http://factfinder.census.gov/.

52. Karen Pyke, "'The Normal American Family' as an Interpretative Structure of Family Life among Grown Children of Korean and Vietnamese Immigrants," *Journal of Marriage and Family* 62, no. 1 (February 2000): 242.

53. Ngoc H. Bui and Joseph Stimpfl, "'Who Are These People Anyway?' Variations of Ethnic Identity within an Immigrant Population," in Esther Mikyung Ghymn, ed., *Asian American Studies: Identity, Images, Issues Past and Present* (New York: Peter Lang, 2000), 122.

54. Jae-Hyup Lee, *Dynamics of Ethnic Identity: Three Asian American Communities in Philadelphia* (New York: Garland, 1998), 3.

55. "Germans from Russia Mostly Welcome Viets," *Lincoln Journal*, 18 June 1975, 11.

56. Rudolph J. Vecoli, "The Significance of Immigration in the Formation of an American Identity," *History Teacher* 30, no. 1 (November 1996): 23.

57. Luebke, "Time, Place, and Culture in Nebraska History," 163.

58. Pipher, *Middle of Everywhere*, xiii.

59. Barkan, "America in Hand," 341.

60. Ibid., 345.

61. Elliott Robert Barkan, "Proximity and Commuting Immigration: An Hypothesis Explored via the Bi-Polar Ethnic Communities of French Canadian and Mexican Americans," in Jack Kinton, ed., *American Ethnic Revival: Group Pluralism Entering America's Third Century* (Aurora, IL: Social Science and Sociological Resources, 1977), 165, 170, 178.

62. Judi M. gaiashkibos (Ponca/Santee), executive director, Nebraska Commission of Indian Affairs, interview by author, 31 October 2005, Nebraska Commission on Indian Affairs Offices, Lincoln, Nebraska.

63. David E. Nye, *Narratives and Spaces: Technology and the Construction of American Culture* (New York: Columbia University Press, 1997), 161.

64. Caroline Kieu Linh Valverde, "Making Transnational Viet Nam: Vietnamese American Community—Viet Nam through Money, Music and Modems" (Ph.D. diss., University of California–Berkeley, 2002), 82.

65. Asian Community and Cultural Center, http://www.lincolnasiancenter.org.

66. Lincoln Indian Center, http://www.indiancenterinc.org/.

67. See http://www.myspace.com/lincoln_indian_club; https://www.facebook.com/lincolnindianclub.

68. Ritva Levo-Henriksson, "Force and Possibility: Hopi Views about the Internet," in John R. Wunder and Kurt E. Kinbacher, eds., *Reconfigurations of Native North America* (Lubbock: Texas Tech University Press, 2009), 153.

69. OmahaTribe.com, http://www.omahatribe.com. As of 2014, the Omahas' web presence is at http://omaha-nsn.gov/.

70. The *American Historical Society of Germans from Russia Newsletter* has been issued quarterly for nearly thirty years. The http://www.ahsgr.org site was copyrighted in its current form in 2003.

71. See Jackson and Penrose, *Constructions of "Race," Place, and Nation*, 7–9.

72. Edward Cline (Omaha), in "Omaha Tribal Representatives Hit Moratorium," *Lincoln Journal*, 15 October 1969.

73. Benedict Anderson, *Imagined Communities: Reflections on the Origin and Spread of Nationalism* (London: Verso, 1983), 15.

74. Author, field notes, Tet presentation, ACCC, 27 January 2006.

75. See, for example, Tim Nguyen, quoted in Aaron Saunderford, "O Asian Garden Unites Cultures," *Lincoln Journal Star*, 17 October 2004.

76. Bodnar, *Transplanted*, 185.

77. Stephen Stearn, "Ethnic Folklore and the Folklore of Ethnicity," *Western Folklore* 36, no. 1 (January 1977): 18. A fourth category, "ethnic survivals," or practices retained with little concern for ethnic identity, may exist in Lincoln, but would be necessarily difficult to observe.

78. Hannan, "Refashioning Ethnicity in Czech-Moravian Texas," 32–33.

79. Bukowczyk, *And My Children Did Not Know Me*, 118–20.
80. Hannan, "Refashioning Ethnicity in Czech-Moravian Texas," 33.
81. Lancaster County, Nebraska, Assessor/Register of Deeds, http://www.lincoln.ne/cnty/ assess/ property.htm.
82. Donald L. Fixico, *The Urban Indian Experience in America* (Albuquerque: University of New Mexico Press, 2000), 60.
83. Ibid., 25.
84. Jonnie Taté Finn, "Study Lists Lincoln High in Linguistic Diversity," *Lincoln Journal Star*, 27 March 2005, 7B; Finn, "Lincoln Is a Land of Many Tongues," *Lincoln Journal-Star*, 27 March 2005.
85. James Crawford, *Hold Your Tongue: Bilingualism and the Politics of English Only* (Reading, MA: Addison Wesley, 1992), 60–61.
86. LB 475 (2005), in *Nebraska Commission on Indian Affairs Newsletter*, Winter 2005, 2; Mark Joseph Awakuni-Swetland, "Umo(n)ho(n) Ithae t(h)e—Umo(n) ho(n) Bthi(n): I Speak Omaha—I am Omaha" (Ph.D. diss., University of Oklahoma, 2003), 187.
87. Crawford, *Hold Your Tongue*, 60–61.
88. Finn, "Lincoln Is a Land of Many Tongues." English was the most common tongue; Spanish, the second.
89. Crawford, 128; see also Hannan, "Refashioning Ethnicity in Czech-Moravian Texas," 38.
90. Mary K. Wayman, "Red Cross Language Bank Aids Immigrants," *Lincoln Journal Star*, 26 December 1992; Bob Reeves, "Vietnamese Find New Life," *Lincoln Star*, 1 December 1992, 1, 4; "Marriage Info in Vietnamese," *Lincoln Journal and Star*, 18 March 1996.
91. Hannan, "Refashioning Ethnicity in Czech-Moravian Texas," 32.
92. Bui and Stimpfl, "'Who Are These People Anyway?'" 126.
93. See Bukowczyk, *And My Children Did Not Know Me*, 144.
94. Alan M. Kraut, "Ethnic Foodways: The Significance of Food in the Designation of Cultural Boundaries between Immigrant Groups in the U.S., 1840–1921," *Journal of American Culture* 2, no. 3 (Fall 1979): 417.
95. *Umóⁿhoⁿ Níkashiⁿga Ukéthiⁿ Uhóⁿ: Common Omaha Cooking* (Lincoln: Native Language Program, University of Nebraska Anthropology Department, 2002), 58–59, 80.
96. Barkan, "America in Hand," 341.
97. Fixico, *Urban Indian Experience in America*, 174; author, field notes, conversation with Barry Webster, council member, Omaha Council Chambers, 6 October 2005.
98. Barkan, "Proximity and Commuting Immigration," 163.

# Index

Page numbers in *italic* refer to illustrations.

1.5 generation Vietnamese, 163, 164, 166, 167, 171, 185

adaptation, 3, 4, 174, 186, 189, 205n5; Germans from Russia, 82, 89, 176; Omahas, 103, 113; Vietnamese, 129, 132, 138, 171, 186
Afghanistan, 119, 184
African Americans, xi, 14, 20, 38, 43, 137
Alexander II (Czar), 47, 206n17
Alles, Wilma, 80
allotment, 23–24, 33, 49, 103–4, 114–15, 126, 207n25, 222n51
Amen family, 84, 178, 216n192; Barbara, 44, 80, 90; Francis, 181; Henry J., 44, 47, 55, 57, 71, 72, 80, 90, *A*; Rudy, 51, 53, 57; Ruth, 90; store, 57, 81, 89, *A*
Amerasian Homecoming Act (1989), 134, 235n26
American citizenship, 25, 38, 61; Indians, 23, 24, 32–33, 119, 228n143; Germans from Russia, 59, 61, 64; Vietnamese, 165, 185
American Historical Society of Germans from Russia (AHSGR), 83, 84, 85, 87, 88, 90, 173, 181, 184, 187, *C*
American identity, 26, 92, 118, 120, 160, 171
American Volga Relief Society (AVRS), 65, 76
anticommunist, 131, 141, 145, 165, 167
Army of the Republic of Vietnam (ARVN), 129, 145, 166
Asian Community and Cultural Center (ACCC), 42, 129, *136*, 156, 157, 183, 185, 233n11
Asian identity, 157, 171
Asians, 20, 40, 137, 157, 163, 180, 190, 248n184
assimilation, xii, 16, 26, 30, 41, 175, 205n5; Germans from Russia; 82, 176, 190; Omahas, 93, 123–24, 125; Vietnamese, xii, 154
*Âu Cơ*, 142
Awakuni-Swetland, Mark, 112

Balzer, Russia, 47, 49, 50, 51, 52, 54, 77, 86, 207n25
*Balzerers*, 48, 52, 53, 55
Baxter, Eleanor Saunsoci, 118, 120
Beideck, Russia, 47, 49, 52, 54, 66, 86

*Beideckers*, 52
Belmont neighborhood, 80, 136, 248n184
Big Village, 91, 101, 102, 103, 108, 124, 191
bilingual(ism), 7, 41, 100, 110, 129, 147, 159, 161, 164, 188 birds of passage, 63, 122
Black Sea Germans, 31, 83, 84, 87, 206n17
Blackbird Bend, 36, 37, 123, 201–2n110, 231n209
Blackbird Hills, 103, 114
blood quantum, 113–15, 120
boarding school, 37, 110, 116, 121
boat people, 39, 132–33, 134, 235n24
Brehm, Konrad, 57, 81
Buddhism, 9, 152, 243–44n123
Buddhist(s), xii, 8, 42, 246n152; Vietnamese, 9, 130, 140, 143, 145, 149–51, 153, 155, 171; *Linh Quang* Temple, 155–56, *I, J*
Burke Act (1906), 104, 223–24n68, Burlington Northern Railroad, 3, 25, 45, 57, 61, 69, 86, 91, 198n48
Bush, George H. W., 165
Bush, George W., 37, 40, 165

Canby, Alberta, 95, 97, 110
Canby, William, 95
Cao, Chien, 138
Catherine the Great, 47, 49, 50, 64, 206–7n17
Catholic(s), xii, 26, 62, 84, 165, *K, L, M*; Germans from Russia, 49, 207n23, 208n32; in Lincoln, 130, 135, 140, 149, 150, 153, 154, 155, 165, 171; in Vietnam, 140, 143, 145, 151, 152, 154, 166, 240n78, 244n127; national parishes, 9, 154
Catholic Social Services, 133, 151, 154, 156
Cayou, Shirley, 95, 97
chain migration, 134

Charleston Street, 56, 81
*Cherokee Nation v. State of Georgia* (1831), 22
Chinese, 38, 39, 144, 238–39n69
Chinese Exclusion Act (1882), 38
Christian and Missionary Alliance Church, 133, *136*; Vietnamese, 153
Christianity, 9, 105, 151, 240n78
citizenship classes, 156, *C*
civilization, 22, 23, 24, 113, 141, 181
Cline, Edward, 184
Clinton, Bill, 37
Clinton neighborhood, 43, 95, 137, 138, 153, 220n24, 220n27, 248n184
Cold War, 78, 93, 131, 146
Collier, John, 33, 226n110
communism, 133, 139, 146, 169, 170; in Soviet Union 65; in Vietnam, 39, 129, 142, 146, 165, 167, 239n75, 240–41n80
Confirmation school, 50, 76
Confucian traditions, 145, 147, 149, 151, 238–39n69, 243–44n123
Congregation of the Mother of the Co-redemptrix, 154
Constitution and Bylaws of the Omaha Tribe of Nebraska, 33, 114, 123
Cosmopolitanism, 4, 56, 113, 152
creation stories, 8, 224n74
cultural pluralism, 21, 143, 174, 175, 190
cultural switching, 164, 171
Czechs, 9, 31, 154, 179, 234–35n22

Da Nang, Vietnam, 150, 238–39n69
Dao, Minh, 155
dance, 7, 9, 11; in German Russian community, 74–75, 76; in Omaha community, 91, 97, 99–100, 106–10, 113, 118–21, 125; in Vietnamese community, 156–57
Democratic Republic of Vietnam (DRV), 129, 142, 143, 147, 165
*Dhegíha*, 99, 111

diversity, 12, 14, 16, 23, 30, 179; among
 Vietnamese, 139; in Lincoln, xiii,
 xiv, 43, 174, 188, 190
Do, Yhanh, 155
Doerr, Paul, 71
doings, 91, 106, 107, 117, 177, 180
Depression of 1893, 27, 28
*Die Welt-Post*, 45, 58, 60–61, 65–66, 67,
 70–73, 184
Dinges, Emma, 80
Dragon Dance, 156
drum, 11, 106, 107, 108, 110

Ebenezer Congregational Church, 44,
 52, 53, 70, 79, 90
*Elk v. Wilkins* (1884), 23
Ellis Island, 26
Emergency Quota Act (1921), 30
émigrés, xii, 84, 134, 139
Emmanuel Evangelical Lutheran
 Church, 51, 76, 77, 208n38
English as a Second Language, xiii, 161
English language, 7, 24, 30, 41, 156,
 199n61, 210–11n74, 255n88; classes,
 156; Germans from Russian, 55–57,
 62–63, 66–67, 71, 76, 78, 82; Omahas, 110, 111, 204n151, 226n119;
 Vietnamese, 147, 156, 159, 160–62,
 164, 170, 183
ethnic revival, 9, 31, 42, 47, 82–83, 88,
 179, 186
ethnic saliency, 11
ethnicity, xii, xiv, 27, 29, 31, 39–40, 43,
 177, 181, 186; defined, 5, 6, 9–11,
 15–16, 19–20; German Russian,
 xi, 82, 90, 184; Indian, 125, 183;
 Omaha, 114, 120, 179; Vietnamese,
 189, 190
evacuees, xii, 132, 133, 134

F Street, 80, 81, 90, 155
Fifth Amendment, 36
First Amendment, 33
First German Congregational Church,
 52, 53, 60, 70, 76, 79, 155, *D*
floods, 29, 199n66, 201–2n110

folkways, 7, 9–10, 186
foodways, 82, 87, 157, 171, 186, 189
foreign language instruction, 30, 41,
 63, 66
Fourteenth Amendment, 23, 63
Frank, Russia, 44, 47, 49, 52, 66, 86, 87
*Franker Boden*, 48, 55, 187
*Frankers*, 51–52, 53, 54, 66, 90
Freemont, Susan, 111, 122
French among Omahas, 100, 113
French in Vietnam, 39, 142–43, 145,
 146–47, 150, 151, 240n78, 240–
 41n80, 242–43n106
Friedens Evangelical Lutheran Church,
 51–52, 53, 60, 76, 79, *E*

gang, xiv, 162
gender, 11, 74, 77, 85, 148; equality,
 163; inequality, 149; roles, 10, 108;
 structures, 9, 101
General Allotment (Dawes Severalty)
 Act (1887), 23
Geneva accords, 141, 143
German American 30, 59, 60, 61, 63,
 72, 73, 79
German American Identity, 30, 56, 58,
 66
German Congregationalism, 53, 78, 82
German language, 50, 59, 60, 62–63,
 65, 72, 76; church services, 76, 78;
 Norka dialect, 57, 89
German-language press, 45, 56, 58, 60,
 66, 73, 82, 179
Germans from Russia, xi–xii, 83, 86, 88,
 179, 182, 186, 189, *B*; beet workers,
 57; ethnicity, 6; identity, 5, 82, 90,
 190; immigration, 21, 31; language
 loss, 42; neighborhoods, 3, 13, 44,
 45
German Russian identity, 31, 56, 58, 60,
 61, 63, 66
giasshkibos, Judi M., 112, Giebelhaus
 family; Anna Schwindt, 16, 56, 74,
 89, 178; Jacob, 3, 56, 89, 178; Ralph,
 90; Sam, 89; Willard, 89
Gilpin, Albert, 109, 122

"gooks," 130
Gourd Dance, 106, 108, 118, 119
Great Depression, 29, 68, 71
Greeley, Colorado, 66, 75, 83, 90, 135,
    233–34n12
Gulf Wars, 185

half-breed clan, 113
handgame, 10, 97, 99, 106, 107, 225n95
Hanoi, Vietnam, 140, 146, 150, 154,
    165–66, 169–70, 173, 239–40n77
Hartley neighborhood, 43, 95, 135-136,
    137, 138, 153, 248n184
Hastings, Dennis, 118, 125
Havelock neighborhood, 69, 220n27
*Hethúshka*, 108, 109
Hispanic(s), 40, 137, 194n78
Historic Preservation Act (1966), 31,
    32, 87
Ho Chi Minh, 39, 142, 145, 147, 239n75
Ho, Xuan-Trang, 138, 166
home ownership, 43, 55–56, 93, 96, 135,
    137, 160, 176–77
Hue, Vietnam, 140, 238–39n69,
    239–40n77
Huck, Russia, 47, 49, 52, 54, 66, 77, 86
*Huckers*, 48, 52
hymns, 51, 75, 76

Immaculate Heart of Mary Roman
    Catholic Church, *136*, 149, 151, 153,
    154–55, 165, *M*
Immanuel Reformed Church, 51, 52,
    57, 76, 78–79, 86, 208n38, 217n208
immigrant(s), xiv, 7, 10–11, 12, 13, 45,
    178, 180, 182, 186; Americaniza-
    tion of, 61; Asian, 9, 39, 156, 160;
    communities, 16, 90, 131, 156;
    European, 14, 21, 30, 33, 45, 160,
    179; German, 53, 59, 62; German
    from Russia, 21, 25, 27, 48, 50, 66,
    82–83, 89, 181; Japanese, 38, 68;
    into Lincoln, xiii, 3–4, 5, 174–75;
    mainstream attitudes towards, 20,
    25–26, 32, 41, 55; naturalization of,

23, 25, 40; Vietnamese, 38, 129–37;
    138–41, 152–53, 155, 159, 160–63,
    170–71, 185
Immigration Act of 1917, 38
Immigration Act of 1924, 30
Immigration and Nationality Act
    (1965), 39, 139
Indian Citizenship Act (1924), 33
Indian Claims Commission, 114, 123,
    228n147
Indian Community Church, 106
Indian Gaming Regulatory Act (1988),
    37, 231n209
Indian New Deal, 33, 110, 114
Indian Religious Freedom Act (1978),
    106, 201n98
Indian Reorganization Act (1934), 33
Indian Self-Determination and Educa-
    tion Act (1975), 37
Indians, 10–11, 32, 34–37, 42, 94, 103,
    190; citizenship and, 21–24, 33, 35;
    demography, 94–96; Plains, 24, 30;
    *See also* urban Indians, individual
    tribes, Native Americans
Indochinese Parole Programs, 39
Iraq(is), 14, 42, 119, 183

Jews, 178

Kansas (tribe), 8, 99
Kapeller, John, Jr., 71
Kerry, John, 146, 166
Kim Son Video and Gifts, 166
Kiowas, 108, 126
*Knöphla*, 87, 173, 186, 189
Korea(ans), 119, 180, 183
Kruse, George, 87
Kukkus, Russia, 47, 49, 51, 52, 54, 86
*Kukkusers*, 55

*Lạc Long Quân*, 141, 142
language(s), xiii, xiv, 7, 42, 45, 158, 171,
    178, 180, 185; and identity, 42; loss,
    41, 76, 110, 111; prohibition, 61, 63
language retention, 7, 110

Latvians, 42, 78
Le, Ngoc Dung, 164
Lincoln Chamber of Commerce, 70
Lincoln Children's Museum, 142
Lincoln City Charter, 42, 178; Title 11, 42, 158
Lincoln City Mission, 97
Lincoln Council of Churches, 42
Lincoln Diocese, 154, 165
Lincoln Interfaith Council, 42, 156
Lincoln Indian Center, xii, 37, 42, 94, 95, 112, 117, 173, 183, *H*; nine purposes of, 97–98; pow-wows, 108
Lincoln Indian Club, 97, 109, 110, 125, 183, 188
Lincoln Police Department, 129, 159, 162, 189
Lincoln Public Schools, xiii, 117, 118, 159, 160
*Lincoln Star*, 60, 72, 180
*Linh Quang* Buddhist Temple, *136*, 149, 155, *I, J*
Lion Dance, 156
Little Saigon 168, 169
Lotus Dance, 156, 157

Macy, Nebraska, 93, 116, 120, 121, 123, 126, 182, 219n9, *F, G*; pow-wow, 108, 188
"Make-Believe-White-Men," 103
Malone neighborhood, 43, 95, 137, 138, 153, 155, 220n27, 236n43, 248n184, Marian Days, 154
marriage, 10, 74, 79, 100, 124, 141, 148–49, 155, 159, 189
Mekong River, 140, 238–39n69, 240n78
Mennonites, 49, 60, 207n23, 208n32
Mexicans, 14, 68, 160, 178
*Meyer v. State of Nebraska* (1923), 63, 66
Migration and Refugee Assistance Act (1975), 132
mir system, 49, 74
Missouri Synod (Lutheran), 62, 77
Mitchell, Rudi, 92, 122
Mockett Law, 66

model minority, 157, 180
multiculturalism, 40, 175

Native Americans, xi, 7, 14, 116, 137, 175, 179, 182–83; American policy towards, 20–24, 34–37; demography, 42, 93, 94, 118; in the military, 34, 119–20; languages, 24, 188
Native American Church (NAC), 8, 9, 98, 105, 106, 119, 180
Native American Language Acts, 188
Native American Rights Fund, 124
National Immigration Board, 26
National Liberation Front (NLF), 143, 144
nativist(s), 15, 26, 27
Naturalization, 25, 33, 38
Near South Neighborhood, xiii, 95, 96, 135, 136, 137, 220n27, 236n40, 248n184
Nebraska Commission of Indian Affairs, 112
Nebraska State capitol, 24, 25, 69, 71
Nebraska State Council of Defense, 60
Nebraska State Legislature, 62, 66, 104, 124, 188, 227n134
Nebraska Supreme Court, 62, 66
Nebraska Indian Community College, 112
Nebraska Territory, 22, 103
Nebraska Wesleyan University, 90, 161, 166
Neighborhoods, Inc., 43
New Economic Zones (NEZ), 144, 145
Ngo Dinh Diem, 143
Ngo, Tam, 155
Nguyen dynasty, 142, 151, 239–40n77, 240n78
Nguyen, Hung, 141, 130
Nguyen, Jung, 189
Nguyen, Rev. Van Phan, 153
Nguyen, Tim, 135
Nguyen, Teresa Trang, 233n11, 246n157, 247n174
Nguyen, Qui, 141, 160

Nguyen Van Thieu, 143
Nha Trang, Vietnam, 150, 238–39n69
noodle soup, 87, 173
Norka, Russia, 3, 47, 50, 52, 54, 56, 66,
    77, 85
*Norkaer Boden*, 48, 49, 55, 187
*Norkaers*, 51, 53, 56
North Lincoln Welfare Society, 76, 87,
    173, 187
North Russian Bottoms, 45, 98
North Vietnam, 129, 146, 150
Northeast Lincoln, 136, 153, 154
Norval Reed Act (1921), 62–63

Oklahoma City, 6, 131, 135, 150, 157,
    244n128
Omaha clans, 100, 103, 106, 107, 113,
    222nn50–51, 223n60, 224n74
Omaha Community Council, 110
Omaha elders, 101, 110, 111, 112, 188
Omaha identity, 92, 93, 99, 101, 104,
    114, 124
Omaha language, 91, 100, 107, 110–12,
    188
Omaha Nation, 3, 35, 37, 91, 102, 103,
    120–26, 187–88, *F*, *G*; enrollment,
    92, 114, 115, 175; Legal status, 93,
    219n8; poverty, 116, 118
Omaha Nation Flag, 102, 119
Omaha Nation Public School, 111–12
Omaha, Nebraska, 6, 23, 73, 122
Omaha Reservation, 3, 32, 35–37, 91,
    92, 103–5, 176, 182, 184
Omaha Tribal Council, 104, 106, 114,
    219n9, 223n60
OmahaTribe.com, 183–84
Omaha urban village, 93, 96
Omaha Way, 91–93, 99–113, 114, 118,
    120–21, 125–26, 183, 187
Orange County, California, 135, 148,
    168, 169, 170
Orderly Departure Program (ODP),
    132, 134
Osages, 8, 99
*Ozawa v. United States* (1922), 38

Pan-Indian, xii, 109, 119, 124, 125, 183;
    identity, 11, 93, 121, 123
Paris Accords, 165
Particularism, 4; German Russian, 47,
    51–52, 56, 58, 66, 81, 85–86, 187,
    189; Omaha 99, 103, 125, 189; Viet-
    namese 139, 154, 158
performed culture, xii–xiii, 5, 7, 11–12,
    16, 21, 41, 174; German Russian,
    45, 67, 72, 78, 82, 83, 89, 175, 186;
    Omaha, 100, 113, 187; Vietnamese,
    130, 139, 156, 171, 189
Peter, Val, 72, 73
peyote, 105, 106, 224n80, 224n86
Pham, Linda, 146, 163, 167
*phở gà*, 173, 177, 189
polka, 74, 75
Poncas, 8, 24, 99, 232n226
popular culture, 4, 110, 165, 168, 169
post-World War II era, 34, 42, 76, 77,
    108, 126, 176, 179
poverty, 12, 32, 35, 71, 97, 176; Omaha,
    104, 115, 116, 119, 121; Vietnamese,
    137, 144
pow-wow, 11, 91, 99, 106, 108–9,
    118–19, 126, *F*, *G*; Lincoln Indian
    Club, 96, 109, 125, 188; Omaha
    Nation, 108, 109, 123
Prichard, Marie Fahrennruch, 181
Protestant(s) xii, xiii, 9, 26; German
    Russian 8, 26, 50, 51–52, 207n23,
    208n32; Vietnamese 8, 130, 140,
    143, 149–50, 152–53, 171
Public Law 280 (1953), 35, 36
Public Law 959 (1956), 116

*quốc ngữ*, 147, 159
Quapaws, 8, 99

race, xi–xii, xiv, 4, 11, 20, 39, 94, 117,
    178
Red Cross Language Bank, 188
Red River (Vietnam), 140, 141, 142,
    146, 239n75

Red Scare, 29, 61, 68

Reformed Christians, 49, 51, 52, 53, 78, 105

refugee(s), xii, 38, 39, 130–35, 138–39, 150, 154, 165

Refugee Act (1980), 39, 132

regalia, 109, 118–19, 120

*Reichs (Deutch)* Germans, 27, 31, 53, 58, 62, 63, 77, 79

Reifschneider family, 80; Fred, 57; Henry, 74; Jacob, 55, 67, 176; Philip, 81

Republic of Vietnam (RVN), 3, 129–30, 132, 140–47, 169, 185, 244n127

"Rooshians," 44, 175

runza, 88, 189

Russian Revolution, 45, 64, 182

Sacred Heart Catholic Church and School, 135–36, *136*, 154, 248n184, *L, M*

Saigon, Vietnam, 39, 130, 134, 143–46, 154, 166, 173, 185

Salem Congregational Church, 51, 52, 76, 78

Salt Creek, 22, 29, 32, 44

Salvation Army, 97, 117

Samara Russia, 47, 50, 51, 63, 64, 73, 83, 208n29

Sanchez, Emmaline Walker, 112

Saunsoci family, 220n24; Elizabeth, 112; Mae Blackbird, 115; Oliver, Jr., 115; Oliver, Sr., 95, 115

Saratov, Russia, 47, 50, 63, 73, 83, 208n29

Schmall, Kateherine, 80

Schmidt, Marie Elizabeth Dittenber, 68

second-generation, 10, 41; Germans from Russia, 75, 76, 182; Omahas, 125; Vietnamese, 132, 135, 162–64, 166–67, 171, 185, 189

Self-Determination and Education Assistance Act (1975), 37, 112

seventeenth parallel, 39, 141, 143, 154, 165

Sheridan family, 95, 118; Evelyn, 95; Frank, 95, 117; Lillian, 95

Siman Act (1919), 61, 62, 66

Sioux City, Iowa, 6, 112, 116, 121

Slavs, 27, 48, 49, 64

South Russian Bottoms, 44, 46, 89, 94–95, 122, 173, 176, *E*

social Darwinism, 20, 23, 26

Socialist Republic of Vietnam, (SRV), 39, 131–34, 138, 144–46, 152, 165–66, 183

South East Asian Youth Club, 170, 250n232

South Vietnam, 129, 149, 169. *See also* RVN

Soviet Union, 31, 61, 64, 65, 239n75

St. John's Evangelical Church, 51, 52, 70, 77, 78

Stabler family, 91, 94–95, 118, 121; Charles, 3, 94, 98; Elizabeth, 16, 91, 95, 112; Eunice, 104, 105, 121; Eva, 97; George, 121; Hollis, 121; Lorenzo, 97; Vida Sue, 112

stereotypes, 34, 44, 116, 179, 180, 181

sugar beets, xi, 73; fields, 45, 56, 57, 64, 67, 68, 71, 72, 91, 176, 178; labor, 58

Summer Kitchens, 54, 69, 87, 208–9n43

Sunday school, 50, 76

Sutton, Nebraska, 61, 63, 65, 77

Tenth Street, 53, 57, 58, 76, 80, 81, 86

Termination Policy, 35, 36, 126, 201n98, 232n225

*Tết,* 155, 157, 180, 185, 245n149

*Tết Trung Thu,* 157, 246n161

third generation, 11, 31, 47, 76

"those who dwell in earth lodges," 103

Tiah Piah Society, 108

tourism, 64, 167

Trading with the Enemy Act, 60

Tran Bai Si, 3, 16–17

Tran, Duc, 162

Tran, Hoa, 42, 143, 159, 161

Tran Hung, 148

Tran, Linda, 147

Tran My Loc, 16

Tran, Phong, 162

Tran, Son, 164
translocal, 165, 181, 185, 216n193
transnationalism, 4, 174, 181–82, 185;
    German Russians, 45, 63, 66–67, 79,
    81, 83, 216n193; Omahas, 92, 120,
    122, 125–26, 232n226; Vietnamese,
    130–31, 164–65, 167–70, 173, 190
Trinh dynasty, 151, 239–40n77, 240n78
Turner, Suzette, 111
Twenty-seventh Street, xiii, 135, 136,
    137, 138, 158, 189
Tyndall, Clyde, 99, 120
Tyndall, Pauline, 117

U.S. Congress, 23, 25, 35, 39, 40, 59–60,
    188
U.S. Constitution, 22, 25, 33, 36, 63,
    178, 196–97n26, 198n51
U.S. Office of Refugee Resettlement, 38
U.S. military, 34–35, 39, 92, 108–9, 118,
    120, 143, 184
*Umónhonxtí* (Sacred Pole), 105
United Nations, 132
University of Nebraska, 37, 68, 112,
    118, 124, 141, 160, 161
Unmarked Human Burial Sites and
    Skeletal Remains Act, 124
Ukraine, 83, 84
United Church of Christ (UCC), 78, 79
*United States v. Thind* (1923), 38
urban Indians, 36, 94, 116, 121, 124,
    187, 219n17

veterans, 97, 108, 118–19
*Việt Kiều*, 131, 164, 166, 167, 168, 170,
    171, 183
Vietnam Community in Lincoln, 146
Vietnam War, xii, 146, 180, 184
Vietnamese diaspora, 129–31, 142,
    149–50, 157, 164, 170, 182
Vietnamese identity, 130, 139, 141,
    152–53, 157–59, 171, 238–39n69
Vietnamese language, xii, 139, 146–47,
    162, 169, 183

Vietnamese nationals, 169, 170
Vietnamese restaurants, 158
Vietnamese Student Organization, 141
Village Night, 85
Vo, Loi, 166, 167
Volga Colonies, 45, 47, *48*, 55–57, 89,
    184; during Russian Civil War 64–
    66; family hierarchy, 73; language,
    49, 50; religion, 53, 77
Volga German Autonomous Soviet
    Socialist Republic (ASSR), 64, 79, 83
Volga German identity, 63, 65, 66, 67,
    78, 79, 81, 190
Volga River, 31, 44, 47, 50, 54, 64
*Volger* identity, 48, 56
*Volgers*, 50–51, 53–54, 59, 66, 176, 178,
    182, 184–85, 186–87
Volhynia, Russia, 83, 84
*Volks (Deutsch)* Germans, 29, 58, 63
Voluntary Relocation Program, 35, 36
Volz, Jacob, 76
Vu, Anton, 129, 137
Vu, Maria Dan, 129, 137, 189
Vu, Uyen Eileen, 149, 157
Vung-Tau restaurant, *N*
Vung-Tau, Vietnam, 129
Vuong, Andrew and Tony, 157

*Wakónda*, 104, 105, 126
waltz, 74, 75
*wanónshe*, 118, 119
*watónzi skíthe taní*, 173, 189
We Shake Hands Program, 117
Webster, Barry, 104
wedding(s), 74, 75, 76, 148
white, xi, xii–xiv, 5, 14, 38, 68, 91, 130,
    162, 178–79
white Anglo-Saxon Protestant, xiii, 20,
    26
Wichita, Kansas, 6, 121, 131, 135, 150,
    233–34n12
Williams, Hattie Plum, 89, 207n23
Wilson, Woodrow, 29, 59, 60
Winnebagos, 24, 123

"woodeaters," 103
*Worcester v. Georgia* (1832), 22
World War I, 29–30, 32, 179; Germans
    from Russia, 45, 62, 64, 77, 89;
    Omahas, 109, 119
World War II, 3, 30–31, 38, 73, 78, 91,
    119, 179

Zion Congregational Church, 52, 53,
    62, 70, 76, 79